The Dynamic Interlanguage

Empirical Studies in
Second Language Variation

TOPICS IN LANGUAGE AND LINGUISTICS

Series Editors
Thomas A. Sebeok and Albert Valdman
Indiana University, Bloomington, Indiana

The Dynamic Interlanguage

Empirical Studies in Second Language Variation

Edited by
MIRIAM R. EISENSTEIN

New York University
New York, New York

Plenum Press • New York and London

Library of Congress Cataloging in Publication Data

The Dynamic interlanguage: empirical studies in second language variation / edited by
  Miriam R. Eisenstein.
      p.   cm. — (Topics in language and linguistics)
  Bibliography: p.
  Includes index.
  ISBN 0-306-43174-2
  1. Interlanguage (Language learning). 2. Language and languages — Variation. 3. Se-
cond language acquisition. 4. Language and languages — Study and teaching. 5. English
language — Study and teaching — Foreign speakers. I. Eisenstein, Miriam R. II. Series.
P53.D95   1989   89-16064
401'.93 — dc20   CIP

© 1989 Plenum Press, New York
A Division of Plenum Publishing Corporation
233 Spring Street, New York, N.Y. 10013

Printed in the United States of America

This book is dedicated to my children, Carla and Joshua

Contributors

H. D. Adamson, Department of English, University of Arizona, Tucson, Arizona 85721

Nathalie Bailey, Puerto Rican Studies Department and ESL Program, Lehman College, Bronx, New York 10468, and Ph.D. Program in Linguistics, Graduate Center of CUNY, New York, New York 10036

Leslie M. Beebe, Department of Languages and Literature, Teachers College, Columbia University, New York, New York 10027

Diana Berkowitz, English Language Program, Hofstra University, Hempstead, New York 11550

Miriam R. Eisenstein, Department of Communication Arts and Sciences, New York University, New York, New York 10003

Susan M. Gass, Department of English, Michigan State University, East Lansing, Michigan 48824

Jan H. Hulstijn, Department of Applied Linguistics, Faculty of Letters, Free University, Amsterdam, The Netherlands

Elsa Lattey, Seminar fuer Englische Philologie, University of Tübingen, Tübingen, Federal Republic of Germany

Chunok Lee, ESL/Linguistics, University of California, Irvine, California 92717

Helaine W. Marshall, Department of Communication Processes, University of Wisconsin–Green Bay, Green Bay, Wisconsin 54311

Ellen M. Rintell, Linguistic Minority Education Resource Center, Lawrence, Massachusetts 01843, and University of Lowell, Lowell, Massachusetts 01854

Robin Scarcella, ESL/Linguistics, University of California, Irvine, California 92717

Elaine E. Tarone, Department of Linguistics, University of Minnesota, Minneapolis, Minnesota 55455

Tomoko Takahashi, Department of Languages and Literature, Teachers College, Columbia University, New York, New York 10027

Albert Valdman, CREDLI, Indiana University, Bloomington, Indiana 47405

Evangeline Marlos Varonis, University of Akron, Akron, Ohio 44325

Jessica Williams, Department of Linguistics, University of Illinois at Chicago, Chicago, Illinois 60680

Lise Winer, Department of Linguistics, Southern Illinois University, Carbondale, Illinois 62901

Walt Wolfram, University of the District of Columbia, Washington, DC, and Center for Applied Linguistics, 1118 22nd Street NW, Washington, DC 20037

Nessa Wolfson, Graduate School of Education, University of Pennsylvania, Philadelphia, Pennsylvania 19104

Jane Zuengler, Department of English, University of Wisconsin–Madison, Madison, Wisconsin 53706

Preface

Recent work in applied linguistics has expanded our understanding of the rule-governed nature of language. The concept of an idealized speaker–hearer whose linguistic competence is abstract and separate from reality has been enriched by the notion of an actual interlocutor who possesses communicative competence, a knowledge of language which accounts for its use in real-world contexts. Areas of variation previously relegated to idiosyncratic differences in performance have been found to be dynamic yet consistent and lend themselves to study and systematic description.

Because language acquisition involves the development of communicative competence, by its very nature it incorporates variation and systematicity. Second-language acquisition is similarly variable, since interlanguage is subject to the same universal and language-specific conventions. In addition, aspects of the second language have been found to be unevenly acquired and are differentially reflected in particular contexts or settings. Yet, despite our expanding knowledge, this variability is only beginning to be treated in much of the second-language acquisition literature.

This volume presents the work of some researchers and methodologists who have taken on the challenge of including variation in their research designs and pedagogical recommendations. Variation is shown to be relevant to linguistic, social, and psychological aspects of language. It is apparent in the registers and dialects of the target language and in the interlanguage of learners. Variability is found to be influenced by context, relative social status, target-language variety, and language-mediated attitudes. The conclusions and insights contributed by this text are drawn in every case from the empirical data of the researcher. Each chapter begins with an orientation for the reader and includes a section on how data was collected and analyzed.

Part I addresses aspects of variation theory. Elaine Tarone points out that an understanding of the systematic variation evidenced by interlanguage requires a more complex model than has been advanced so far, a model which must rely on a thoughtful and more carefully planned research agenda. Jan

Hulstijn speaks to this point with his suggestion for combining the concept of vernacular as the least monitored style and a cognitive, information-processing view to provide a more fruitful basis for the study of variation. The possible relevance of Bickerton's bioprogram to second-language variation is examined in a careful study by H. Douglas Adamson, who compares English article acquisition by Korean children and adults and takes into account their relative cognitive development and use of first-language transfer as an interlanguage strategy. Another paradigm with potential to account for an aspect of second-language variation, speech accommodation theory, is assessed by Jane Zuengler through her empirical work on native–nonnative speaker interaction when relative status is systematically controlled. Her conclusion, like that of the other researchers in this section, is that the consideration of how multiple variables may interact must be built into our theoretical models.

 Adjustment in native and nonnative discourse is the organizing factor in Part II of this volume. Susan Gass and Evangeline Varonis treat the issue of corrective feedback to second-language speakers through an investigation of nonnative speaker dyads. They consider the factors that may allow nonnatives to incorporate accurate representations of other learners yet successfully avoid acquiring their errors. Elsa Lattey considers the nature of English and German foreigner-talk varieties and assesses the likelihood that observed differences stem from social factors such as differential treatment of specific national groups and/or the linguistic distinctions inherent in the two second-language targets. The effect of perceived cultural empathy displayed by a native interlocutor on interlanguage phonology is investigated by Diana Berkowitz, who, like Zuengler (Part I), addresses the extent to which accommodation theory can account for the learners' second-language performance.

Part III examines some of the roles played by alternative varieties in the acquisition process. An overview of the characteristics of nonnative institutionalized English is provided by Jessica Williams, who then focuses our attention on some grammatical aspects of Singaporean English present in her data. Written English as a second language is investigated by Robin Scarcella and Chunok Lee, who look to length of residence as a possible cue to different paths in the development of the second language in its written form. Lise Winer also studies written English, in this case accounting for transfer from Trinidadian Creole, the vernacular language of her subjects. Input from different English dialects is the theme of my research on the relative intelligibility of alternate varieties to which learners are exposed, a crucial issue in view of the importance attached to comprehensible input in second-language acquisition.

Additional factors which contribute to variation are addressed in Part IV. Walt Wolfram finds variability in tense marking due in part to surface-level constraints not commonly considered in interlanguage analyses. Leslie Beebe and Tomoko Takahashi find that relative social status affects the use of English by Japanese speakers in face-threatening speech acts. Another function, that of compliments, is described by Nessa Wolfson, who finds that natives and non-natives differ in their contributions to complimenting on the discourse level. The limited success with which emotion is conveyed by the narratives of non-natives is revealed by Ellen Rintell, who finds that native–nonnative differences in revealing emotion reflect different discourse features, including natives' greater stylistic variation in discourse.

Part V goes beyond questions of research and theory to address the pedagogical applications of what we have learned about second-language variation. Albert Valdman grapples with the difficult notion of how to choose a pedagogical norm for second-language teaching. Using data from French to illustrate his model, he considers psychological and social factors in light of geographical and sociolinguistic diversity. Variation in the use of the present perfect and preterit is investigated by Helaine Marshall, who offers concrete suggestions for how the native differences she has researched could be incorporated in the ESL curriculum. And finally, Nathalie Bailey analyzes an aspect of discourse-conditioned variation in the use of simple past and progressive tenses by English learners at different levels of development. Along with the other contributors to this part, she gives the reader specific suggestions for how the results of her investigation can be translated into more effective teaching.

Together, the chapters in this volume raise many questions about variation in second-language acquisition. It is clear that a considerable number of factors contribute to variation and that we are far from having investigated them all. Nevertheless, developing theories of acquisition, analyses of interlanguage data, and suggestions for second-language pedagogy must be informed by what we have learned about variation so far and constrained by what we have yet to learn.

I wish to express my thanks to C. William Schweers for his invaluable help in the preparation of the manuscript for this volume.

Contents

Chapter 7
The Effect of Cultural Empathy on Second-Language Phonological
Production
Diana Berkowitz

PART III.   Alternative Varieties and Second-Language Acquisition

Chapter 8
Variation and Convergence in Nonnative Institutionalized Englishes
Jessica Williams

Chapter 9
Different Paths to Writing Proficiency in a Second Language?
A Preliminary Investigation of ESL Writers of Short-Term and Long-Term
Residence in the United States
Robin Scarcella and Chunok Lee

Chapter 13

Sociolinguistic Variation in Face-Threatening Speech Acts:
Chastisement and Disagreement

Leslie M. Beebe and Tomoko Takahashi

Chapter 14

The Social Dynamics of Native and Nonnative Variation in
Complimenting Behavior

Nessa Wolfson

Chapter 15

That Reminds Me of a Story: The Use of Language to Express
Emotion by Second-Language Learners and Native Speakers

Ellen M. Rintell

PART V.   Suggestions for Pedagogy

Chapter 16

Classroom Foreign Language Learning and Language Variation:
The Notion of Pedagogical Norms

Albert Valdman

Chapter 17

Discourse Conditioned Tense Variation: Teacher Implications
Nathalie Bailey

Chapter 18

The Colloquial Preterit: Language Variation and the ESL Classroom
Helaine W. Marshall

PART I

Theoretical Issues in Interlanguage Variation

CHAPTER 1

On Chameleons and Monitors

ELAINE E. TARONE

1. INTRODUCTION

One of the most difficult problems faced by researchers in the field of second-language acquisition is the demonstration of the systematic nature of learner language, or interlanguage (Selinker, 1972). What does it mean to say that interlanguage (IL) is systematic when different research instruments, administered at the same time, provide different assessments of the status of the same form in the learner's IL? One measure may show a form occurring 75% of the time, and another measure may show it occurring only 20% of the time. Research on the nature of *system* in IL cannot be successful until the causes of systematic *variation* in IL have been isolated and identified. What causes this variation in IL form?

Several possible causes of variation in IL have been proposed. It is clear that different linguistic contexts may cause different degrees of grammatical accuracy of a form (cf. L. Dickerson, 1975; Wolfram, 1985). There is also evidence that variable IL performance may be caused by factors such as the identity and role of the interlocutor (Beebe, 1977a, 1977b), topic (Lantolf & Khanji, 1983), social norms (Schmidt, 1977), or the different functions that a given language form may play in the process of communication (Huebner, 1983, 1985). (For a detailed discussion of each of these proposals, see Tarone, 1988.)

An earlier version of this chapter was presented at the Second Language Research Forum at UCLA, February 1985. Research funds for the study reported in this chapter were provided by the Graduate School of the University of Minnesota, Grant #0350-4928-02. Results of this study are reported in more detail in Tarone (1985).

ELAINE E. TARONE • Department of Linguistics, University of Minnesota, Minneapolis, Minnesota 55455.

3

One of the most frequently suggested causes of IL variation is psycholinguistic in nature: attention to language form. It is suggested that when the learner attends to language form, accuracy in language form improves. There have been two different strands to this area of investigation—one following from the Monitor model (Krashen, 1976, 1977, 1981) and the other following from the Continuum (or Chameleon) model (Tarone, 1979, 1983, 1985).

It is interesting that each of these approaches has associated itself with a reptilian totem, the *chameleon* being a small lizard which changes its coloration in order to blend in with its surroundings, and the *monitor* being a rather large lizard which, according to legend, advises one of the presence or absence of crocodiles. The analogies being made here to the production of utterances in a second language are quite different, and the choice of reptiles seems to be singularly appropriate to the two approaches taken, as we shall see.

The accurate description of the phenomenon of variability in relation to elicitation task requires a resolution of the following questions:

1. Does the language production of second-language learners (SLL) reveal the existence of only two styles (as in Monitored and un-Monitored styles), or does it suggest that more than two styles exist (as the Chameleon approach would have it)?
2. When a task requires that the SLL pay more attention to language form, does grammatical accuracy improve?
3. Is the language production of SLLs variable only because different tasks require different degrees of attention to language form (as both the Monitor and Chameleon approaches have suggested), or are there other causes of variability (as some of the proposals mentioned earlier have suggested)?

In this chapter, I briefly outline the different predictions made by the Monitor and Chameleon models as to the sort of variability which will appear in the language productions of SLLs. I then describe recent research evidence which bears directly upon questions 1, 2, and 3 above and comment upon the adequacy of the two reptilian models with regard to their ability to predict the sort of variability which now seems to be related to elicitation task.

2. PREDICTIONS ON VARIABILITY

2.1. The Monitor Approach

The Monitor approach, proposed by Krashen (1981 and elsewhere), seems to make the following assumptions:

First, the approach assumes that the SLL possesses two completely independent systems of knowledge about the second language: an implicit knowledge system which consists of the unconscious knowledge of how to produce utterances and a metalinguistic knowledge system which consists of knowledge about the language being learned. Krashen terms this second body of knowledge the *Monitor;* the Monitor is accessible to conscious introspection and may be described by the learner in terms of consciously formulated grammatical rules. These two knowledge systems seem to be homogeneous; that is, each body of knowledge seems to be made up of a single set of invariant rules.

In using the second language, the SLL may make use of both knowledge systems. It is the implicit knowledge system which actually initiates utterances in performance, but the learner can modify the output of the implicit system by invoking rules from the metalinguistic knowledge system (the Monitor) under certain specific conditions (SLL having enough time, a focus on form, and a conscious knowledge of the relevant rule). Metalinguistic knowledge is thus available to the learner only as a Monitor; it cannot initiate utterances, it can only modify, or filter, the utterances generated by the implicit knowledge system. Language output which is Monitored tends to contain the most accurate (or targetlike) grammatical forms, and un-Monitored language output contains the most "errors" in terms of the target language (TL) and conforms to the so-called natural order of morpheme accuracy.

The primary focus of the Monitor approach is on the distinction between the implicit knowledge system and the metalinguistic knowledge system. Consequently, Krashen (1981) and others have done many studies eliciting two broad categories of data: data on the metalinguistic knowledge system, gathered by means of elicitation tasks where the specific conditions for Monitoring are met, and data on the implicit knowledge system, gathered by means of all other elicitation tasks. There does not seem to be any attempt to gather data relevant to variability *within* the implicit knowledge system itself; rather, this implicit knowledge system seems, in this approach, to be accessible by means of any data gathered in any situation, in any mode (oral/written), as long as the conditions for Monitor use are not present. These methods of data collection follow logically from what these researchers are interested in showing—that there is a dichotomy between language produced under conditions considered appropriate for Monitor use and other conditions.

Thus, in the Monitor approach, the only variability which is accounted for is the major dichotomy between the learner's behavior when "Monitoring" and when not "Monitoring." Monitoring, or the conscious application of grammatical rules, is conceived of as an either–or option, not as a continuum. As the analogy to the large lizard would suggest, the "crocodile" of error either is there or is not, so the Monitor either gives warning or doesn't.

While the Monitor approach does also allow for the idea of paying attention to language form as something distinct from the conscious application of grammatical rules, this idea is not developed to any great extent, nor does it result in any care taken to distinguish among various kinds of data gathered in un-Monitored learner language.

2.2. The Chameleon Model

The Chameleon model (Tarone, 1979, 1983, 1985) makes the following assumptions:[1]

The SLL's capability is best described by a single grammatical system rather than two; that system is not assumed to be homogeneous in nature but rather heterogeneous, made up of a continuous range of styles, just like any language system (Labov, 1969). All language systems, including that of the SLL, have a range of styles, from a careful style (defined as that style produced when the speaker pays most attention to language form) at one end of the continuum to a "vernacular" style at the other end (in which the speaker pays the least attention to language form). The capability of the SLL includes the careful and the vernacular styles of the system and the intermediate continuum of styles as well. The careful style of the SLL usually contains the most accurate grammatical forms, though it may also contain prestige native language (NL) variants (cf. Beene, 1980). The regularities evidenced in each style in the IL system may be described by sets of categorical and variable rules, and these descriptions may be systematically related to one another in the final complete description of the IL capability. In short, the language of the SLL, like the chameleon, changes aspects of its appearance *by degrees* to accord with subtle changes in the environment.

In accordance with this last assumption, the elicitation of IL calls for the use of tasks designed to ask subjects to pay varying degrees of attention to language form. Data elicited by each task are kept separate in order to provide accurate information about each style which makes up the continuous range of styles which constitute the IL system.

Both the Chameleon approach and the Monitor approach agree that attention to language form is the cause of task-related variation. But the two approaches differ with regard to the nature of that variation. The Chameleon model is concerned with accounting for variability in IL along the full range of language performance and conceives of IL capability as a continuum of styles. The Monitor approach, however, is primarily concerned with the difference

---

[1] Ellis (1985) proposes a model which is very similar to the Chameleon model described here, but it differs in that it proposes that the learner has both a variable competence *and* may variably apply different processes for accessing that competence. A critical evaluation of this model appears in Tarone (1988).

between SLL performance under very constrained circumstances (i.e., Monitored performance) and learner performance under *all other circumstances*. The Monitor approach does not attempt to account for variable occurrence of a form along a continuum just an either–or occurrence of the form. With regard to the study of inherent variability, then, the Monitor approach must be regarded as a partial model in that it only attempts to study a restricted sort of variation. The Chameleon model, on the other hand, urges us to elicit and study the full range of inherently variable IL data.

3. EMPIRICAL EVIDENCE

What research evidence exists which might support one or the other of these approaches? The empirical evidence on IL variation is described in detail in Tarone (1988). Here I simply describe a few representative studies.
a few representative studies.

Most research evidence is available on inherent variability in the phonology of IL. Researchers such as the Dickersons (1974, 1975, 1976, 1977) and Beebe (1980) have amassed quite a bit of data on inherently variable phonology. A typical finding of Dickerson and Dickerson (1977) shows that Japanese learners of English produced /r/ with varying degrees of correctness, depending on whether they were speaking freely, reading a dialogue, or reading a word list (tasks which are assumed to demand increasing attention to form). Correct production of the TL /r/ occurred most frequently in careful speech and least frequently in casual speech. Important for our discussion is the fact that more than two styles are evidenced here; this sort of finding accords more with the Chameleon than with the Monitor.

Beebe's (1980) research unfortunately did not attempt to elicit more than two styles of phonological production, so it cannot help us distinguish the Chameleon and Monitor approaches in that regard. Her study does, however, provide interesting information on the kinds of forms which occurred in the careful style of these SLLs. These Thai learners of English, in producing *final* /r/ in IL, followed the general pattern we have noted, with more TL forms (i.e., greater accuracy) in the careful style (listing words) than in the casual (conversing). But in producing *initial* /r/ in IL, the learners had *fewer* correct TL forms in their careful style and *more* in their casual style. Furthermore, their careful style seemed to be marked by more NL forms than the casual. Beebe (1980) explains this pattern by pointing out that the NL forms used in the careful style are prestige variants of the initial /r/ which are used more frequently in the careful style in Thai as well. Thus, it is not always the case that the careful style of phonology is more grammatically accurate than the casual style. While both the Chameleon and the Monitor approaches may allow for this possibility, neither one is able to predict at the present time those circumstances in which the SLLs will draw upon the NL rather than the TL in their careful style. (Beebe, 1982, reinterprets these results within a broad psychosociological theory.)

Less data are available on variability in the grammar and morphology of IL, since researchers generally have not attempted to systematically elicit such data. A review of research evidence on variation in the grammar and phonology of IL is provided in Tarone (1988).

Tarone (1985) and Tarone and Parrish (1988) report on a study which aimed to gather more data on the nature of task-related variability of grammatical forms in the language productions of SLLs. As details on these studies are reported elsewhere, I here summarize them only briefly.

4. PROCEDURE

Twenty subjects participated in this study, all of them adults learning English as a second language at the University of Minnesota at the advanced level. Chosen for study was the presence or absence in obligatory context of four TL forms: third-person singular present tense verb -s; the article; the noun plural -s; and third-person singular direct object pronouns. Three tasks were performed by the subjects: (1) a written sentence-level "grammaticality judgment" task; (2) an oral narration task, which required subjects to narrate a sequence of events depicted (nonverbally) on a video screen to a nonnative listener who was facing them and who had a related task to perform; and (3) an oral interview with a native speaker of English, focusing on the topic of the subject's field of study.

It was felt that most attention to language form would be required by the grammar test and the least by the narrative, with the interview requiring an intermediate degree of attention to form. Channel cues present in the tapes of the oral interview and the oral narrative seemed to validate the ordering of these two tasks relative to one another: the narratives contained fewer hesitations, were generally more fluent, and contained more laughter and joking comments—all these are channel cues which Labov (1969) uses to confirm a subject's use of the vernacular.

All the oral data were transcribed in standard orthography. Obligatory contexts for the four grammatical forms under investigation were then established in the transcripts for Tasks 2 and 3, and the presence or absence of the forms in these obligatory contexts was calculated.

5. RESULTS AND DISCUSSION

The results for these four grammatical forms as they were produced by the subjects on these three tasks are displayed in Figure 1.

The results of the study show that the inherent variability in relation to task evidenced by these subjects in their use of their second language was more complicated than predicted by either model. While more than two styles are evidenced on the three tasks, as predicted by the Chameleon model, the predicted regular relationship between attention and grammatical accuracy did not hold.

These results provide evidence that second-language users treated different sets of grammatical forms differently under identical style-shifting conditions. Some forms (like plural -s) did not seem to shift at all as tasks required greater or lesser degrees of attention to language form. Some (like third-person singular) seemed to improve with attention to form. And the accuracy rates of articles significantly decreased on tasks which were designed to require greater attention to form.[2]

This complex pattern of style-shifting was not predicted in its entirety by either the Monitor or the Chameleon models. As we see below, the failure of both models to accurately predict the complex pattern found may be due to the simplistic assumptions which both seem to share about attention to form as the *cause* of style-shifting.

Why is it that these SLLs produced articles and the direct object pronoun *least* accurately on the written test, while at the same time they produced third-person singular markers *most* accurately on that same test?

The Monitor approach has, I believe, the following explanation. Krashen (1982) has pointed out that not all morphemes are improved in accuracy in Monitored tasks. In fact, he has consistently argued that there are two sets of morphemes, some (the "learned" ones) produced more accurately when "Monitored," and some (the "acquired" ones) which he says *do not improve* with Monitoring. The third-person singular verb morpheme, Krashen argues, is one of those morphemes which improve in accuracy under conditions of Monitoring. Articles do not. Thus, in the Monitor framework, the third-person singular morpheme would be more accurate on the grammar test in this study because it is learned and can be Monitored under grammar test conditions. The article—and the direct object pronoun, presumably—are low in accuracy on the

---

[2] As reported in Tarone (1985), statistical measurement was possible only for the article. An ANOVA for repeated measures produced a $p < .0000$ for the article. The other forms studied were not elicited in sufficient numbers to permit a valid use of statistical measurement; for this reason, only descriptive statistics are used for the direct object pronoun, the third-person singular verb marker, and the noun plural marker.

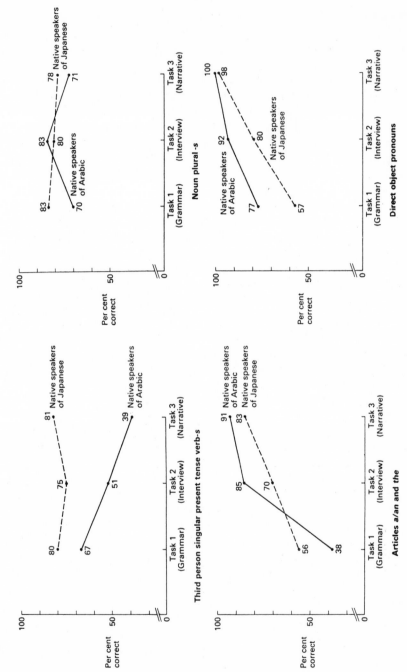

Figure 1. Learner accuracy on four English forms on three tasks: grammar test, oral interview, and oral narrative. (From Tarone & Yule, 1989; reprinted with permission.)

grammar test because they are acquired. Krashen's explanation for *why* some morphemes are learned and others are acquired is that the learned morphemes seem to be the ones which have fairly simple rules—rules which can be taught in the classroom and consciously remembered. Acquired forms on the other hand tend to be those which, like articles, have fairly complex rules which cannot easily be retained consciously in memory.

There are two problems with the explanation just outlined. First, the rule for the direct object pronoun does not seem to be a complicated rule; it seems to be fairly easy to retain consciously in memory, and so we might expect accuracy rates for this form to be more similar to those for third-person singular than to those for the article. Second, and more serious: the Monitor approach, as I understand it, predicts that accuracy rates for acquired forms *would not improve* on the grammar test—that is, that they would be the same on the test and in oral unattended performance—but *not* that accuracy rates would actually *improve* as attention to language form decreases. The Monitor approach cannot, it seems to me, explain in any non–ad hoc way why learner performance with articles and direct object pronouns actually *improved* as tasks required less and less attention to language form.

By the same token, the Chameleon approach cannot explain these results either, as it suggests that attention to language form should affect all IL forms in the same manner: changing them in the direction of greater proximity to the learner's formal norm. While the learner's formal norm may be composed of both TL elements *and* prestige NL elements, there is little evidence here that prestige NL elements are involved. In this study, the Chameleon approach cannot explain why attention to form should result in greater accuracy for some forms and less for others.

Perhaps, as mentioned above, a clue to the solution can be found in reexamining the notion of attention to form itself as *the* casual variable in styleshifting. Bell (1984) points out a number of difficulties involved in viewing attention to language form as the cause of task-related variability. Most seriously, attention to form can at best be only an intermediary, not an explanatory factor; we are still left with establishing what it is in the task that causes learners to pay attention to language form. We still need to identify those factors in the social situation which *cause* variability to occur in the language production of SLLs. When complex patterns of style-shifting such as those reported above occur, it seems particularly important to attempt to identify such factors and determine whether they may be able to account for these patterns.

At present, the best explanation for these results seems to be that, at the same time that we have ordered these tasks in terms of decreasing amount of attention to grammatical form (grammar test, oral interview, oral narrative), we have also ordered them according to at least two other criteria as well: (1) the connectedness of the discourse required by the task, and (2) the communicative pressure brought to bear upon the speaker to be clear in transmitting information to a listener.

In terms of connectedness of discourse, the grammar test, which we thought might require most attention to language form, consists of unconnected sentences. There is no cohesiveness at all beyond the sentence level. The narrative, which we thought would require least attention to language form, is a form of discourse which is very cohesive and which allows the speaker to be in total control of the discourse for an extended and predictable period of time. In the interview, while speakers may produce extended bits of discourse, their turns may be interrupted at unpredictable intervals by the interviewer and thus may be less cohesive. In short, there is a sort of inverse relationship in the study between the degree of attention to language form thought to be required by these tasks and the cohesiveness of the discourse elicited by them.

With regard to communicative pressure brought to bear upon the learner, the same sort of inverse relationship with "assumed attention to form" also holds. The grammar test involves no communication at all: there is no clear receiver of a message and, in fact, the learner is transmitting no transactional information at all. In the interview, while there is a listener, it is not clear to the speaker whether he or she is really interested in the content of the interview or, if so, why he or she needs this information. On the narrative, however, there is a listener who has a clear need for the information being transmitted: he or she needs to complete a task. The presence of this listener places the most communicative pressure upon the speaker to be clear in performing the narrative task. Thus, the tasks are also ordered in terms of amount of communicative pressure to be clear which is brought to bear upon the learner.

How can these observations account for the fact that the accuracy rates of different language forms shifted in different directions on the same sequence of tasks? It can be argued that both the article and the direct object pronoun "it" (which became more accurate as tasks required more cohesive discourse and as the speaker felt greater pressure to be clear) are forms which are more important in establishing cohesiveness and maintaining clarity in discourse than, for example, the third-person singular marker (which became less accurate as tasks required more cohesive discourse). In fact, in connected discourse, the third-person singular marker is completely redundant. In successfully narrating a story, however, the speaker must make sure that references to the various protagonists and objects which are crucial to the story line are clear; articles and pronouns are very important in maintaining this sort of clear reference. The same clarity of reference is also important in discussing topics in one's field of study, and so articles and pronouns are again important—but because the listener does not have as clear a need to keep track of entities in the interview as in the narrative, there may be less pressure on the speaker to use articles and pronouns to mark those entities as clearly. It may be that these forms were supplied least often in the grammar test because cohesiveness in discourse did not matter so much in the grammar test; as the oral tasks required the subjects to produce increasingly cohesive texts and as the subjects felt increasing pressure to be clear, they increasingly supplied these two forms in obligatory context.

If indeed this explanation can account for the differential pattern of style-shifting found between articles and the direct object pronoun, on the one hand, and third-person markers, on the other hand, we must then conclude that the style-shifting produced by these learners was governed not by a global attention to all language form but rather by the nature of the discourse which the tasks required and the degree of communicative pressure which the tasks brought to bear upon the learner. Such a conclusion indicates that style-shifting in IL is more complex than predicted by either of the reptilian models, which both rely on an oversimplistic view of global attention to language form as a cause of style-shifting. In particular, as tasks elicit increasingly cohesive discourse, and in circumstances which increasingly require that the speaker be clear in transacting information, some grammatical forms may improve in accuracy rate while others may decrease. Differential attention to these different grammatical forms may be an intermediary factor, but it is not productive, as Bell points out, to view attention as a monolithic causal factor; attention to form alone simply cannot predict these results.

6. CONCLUSION

What of the Monitor and the Chameleon? Clearly, task-related variability is more complicated than either the Chameleon or the Monitor could predict. A global causal constraint called "attention to form" simply cannot account for the data. While the chameleon approach seems to have been the more productive, both in generating accurate hypotheses about style-shifting and in leading to a methodology which could uncover complexities in the performance of SLLs it too seems unable to account for the complexities of task-related variability in IL.

What is needed is an evolution—a move away from simpler reptilian models and on to more complex (even mammalian?) models better able to adapt to this complex environment. In particular, it seems to be important to avoid viewing "attention to form" as a monolithic causal variable in style-shifting and, rather, to begin to tie observed patterns of style-shifting in IL to observable and well-controlled constraints in the elicitation situation.

Such constraints have already been mentioned at the beginning of this chapter, and evidence is beginning to accumulate on their nature. A detailed consideration of each of these constraints on task-related variation is provided in Tarone (1988). Clearly, the study just cited indicates that one cause of IL variability must be the *functions* of the forms being studied: forms important in maintaining cohesiveness of discourse may be expected to become more accurate as tasks require more and more cohesive discourse. In addition, forms which function to maintain clarity in transmitting information may be expected to increase as tasks place increasing communicative pressure upon speakers to be clear. A second cause of variation in IL is clearly the linguistic context of the forms being studied: tasks requiring the production of forms in minimal context may be expected to produce different accuracy rates than tasks which embed those forms in various linguistic contexts. A third cause of variation must be sociopsychological in nature, as Beebe and Giles (1984) argue: the identity and role of the interlocutor will clearly affect grammatical convergence or divergence processes; the topic of discourse will affect grammatical accuracy; the social norms prevalent in the elicitation situation will do so as well. Furthermore, all these causes of variation must interact in any particular elicitation situation. The identity of the interlocutor may activate certain social norms, causing, for example, phones in one linguistic context to improve in accuracy while phones in another linguistic context may decrease in accuracy; presence or absence of communicative pressure may interact with both of these factors; and so on. A more adequate model of IL variation must provide a role for all of these constraints and their interactions.

Clearly, such a model of IL variation will make far more complex predictions than either of the reptilian models and mandates a more careful research program than any we have been able to implement to date. In any research study in this area, this model suggests that we should hold all of these known constraints on variation constant, varying just one constraint at a time to establish the extent of its influence. Only by means of such a careful program of research will we ever be able to gain a complete understanding of the systematic variation inherent in interlanguage.

ACKNOWLEDGMENTS

I am grateful to Judy Fuller, the research assistant on this project, for her assistance in the collection and transcription of the data.

REFERENCES

Beebe, L. (1977a). The influence of the listener on code-switching. *Language Learning* 27 (2), 331–339.
Beebe, L. (1977b). Dialect code-switching of bilingual children in their second language. *CUNY Forum 3*, 141–158.
Beebe, L. (1980). Sociolinguistic variation and style shifting in second language acquisition. *Language Learning 30*(1), 433–447.

Beebe, L. (1982). The social psychological basis of style shifting. Plenary address, Second Language Research Forum, Los Angeles.

Beebe, L., & Giles, H. (1984). Speech accommodation theories: A discussion in terms of second language acquisition. *International Journal of the Sociology of Language 46*, 5–32.

Bell, A. (1984). Language style as audience design. *Language in Society 13*, 145–204.

Dickerson, L. (1974). *Internal and external patterning of phonological variability in the speech of Japanese learners of English: Toward a theory of second language acquisition.* Ph.D. dissertation, University of Illinois.

Dickerson, L. (1975). The learner's interlanguage as a system of variable rules. *TESOL Quarterly 9*, 401–407.

Dickerson, W. (1976). Language variation in applied linguistics. *ITL: Review of Applied Linguistics 35*, 43–66.

Dickerson, W., & Dickerson, L. (1977). Interlanguage phonology: Current research and future directions. In S. P. Corder & E. Roulet (Eds.), *The notions of simplification, interlanguages and pidgins* (pp. 18–30). Neufchatel: Faculté des Lettres.

Ellis, R. (1985). *Understanding second language acquisition.* Oxford: Oxford University Press.

Huebner, T. (1983). *A longitudinal analysis of the acquisition of English.* Ann Arbor, MI: Karoma.

Huebner, T. (1985). System and variability in interlanguage syntax. *Language Learning 35*(2), 141–163.

Krashen, S. (1976). Formal and informal linguistic environments in language learning and language acquisition. *TESOL Quarterly 10*, 157–168.

Krashen, S. (1977). The monitor model for adult second language performance. In M. Burt, H. Dulay, & M. Finocchiaro (Eds.), *Viewpoints on English as a second language* (pp. 152–161). New York: Regents.

Krashen, S. (1981). *Second language acquisition and learning.* Oxford: Pergamon Press.

Krashen, S. (1982). *Principles and practice in second language acquisition.* Oxford: Pergamon Press.

Labor, W. (1969). The study of language in its social context. *Studium Generale 23*, 30–87.

Lantolf, J. & Khanji, R. (1983). Nonlinguistic parameters of interlanguage performance. In J. Morreall (Ed.), *The Ninth LACUS forum, 1982* (pp. 457–472). Columbia, SC : Hornbeam Press.

Schmidt, R. W. (1977). Sociolinguistic variation and language transfer in phonology. *Working Papers in Bilingualism 12*, 79–95. Also in G. Ioup, and S. Weinberger (Eds.) (1987), *Interlanguage phonology: The acquisition of a second language sound system.* Cambridge, MA: Newbury House.

Selinker, L. (1972). Interlanguage. *IRAL 10*(3), 209–231.

Tarone, E. (1979). Interlanguage as chameleon. *Language Learning 29*(1), 181–191.

Tarone, E. (1983). On the variability of interlanguage systems. *Applied Linguistics 4*(2), 142–163.

Tarone, E. (1985). Variability in interlanguage use: A study of style-shifting in morphology and syntax. *Language Learning 35*, 373–403.

Tarone, E. (1988) *Variation in interlanguage.* Edward Arnold Publishers.

Tarone, E., and Parrish, B. (1988). Task-related variability in interlanguage: The case of articles. *Language Learning, 38*, 21–44.

Tarone, E., & Yule, G. (1989). *Focus on the language learner: Approaches to identifying and meeting the needs of second language learners.* Oxford: Oxford University Press.

Wolfram, W. (1985). Variability in tense marking: A case for the obvious. *Language Learning 35*(2), 229–253.

CHAPTER 2

A Cognitive View on Interlanguage Variability

JAN H. HULSTIJN

1. INTRODUCTION

In this chapter, I first examine Tarone's sociolinguistic approach to the study of interlanguage (IL) variability. I focus on Tarone's conception of the "vernacular style" as the speech style in which the speaker (L2 learner) pays least attention to language form. Tarone's approach is then contrasted with a cognitive, information-processing view on IL variability. I try to demonstrate how the two approaches can be combined so as to provide a more fruitful basis for research on second-language acquisition (SLA) processes. I then describe a study of my own, to illustrate two methodological points in the empirical study of IL variability concerning (1) the usefulness of pretest procedures to increase the chances that L2 learners will in fact exhibit variability in their IL performance, and (2) the importance of making a conceptual and empirical distinction between "task" and "task requirements."

2. AN INFORMATION-PROCESSING VIEW ON THE NOTION OF "VERNACULAR STYLE"

There is general agreement among authors of both sociolinguistic and psycholinguistic backgrounds that setting, task, and task requirements affect the degree of attention which language users pay to the formal correctness of lan-

JAN H. HULSTIJN • Department of Applied Linguistics, Faculty of Letters, Free University, Amsterdam, The Netherlands.

guage use. This attention to form is in turn thought to be responsible for the variability in their language production and comprehension (Dickerson, 1975; Ellis, 1985b; Gatbonton, 1978; Labov, 1970; Sato, 1985; Tarone, 1982). Some of these authors, most notably Tarone (1979, 1982, 1983, 1985, and Chapter 1, this volume), hold the view that this variability stems at least in part from a number of "styles." These styles can be located on a continuum, ranging from careful style to casual style, which Tarone refers to as vernacular. According to Tarone, this vernacular is the "basic," most "natural" style, occurring in informal communicative situations in which the language user pays least attention to form.

According to Tarone, the vernacular is primary in two senses. First, it is "primary in the sense of being most stable and consistent" (Tarone, 1983, p. 154). Second, it is primary in a developmental sense. This developmental primacy is a corollary of Tarone's assertion that her style continuum model allows for two means of IL internalization (1983, p. 155). In one, L2 learners spontaneously produce structures in their unattended speech (vernacular style). The other means of internalization manifests itself when learners adjust their production to the target norm. These adjustments appear first in careful style and spread from there to less formal styles until they show up in the vernacular. Thus, the primacy of the vernacular style in the developmental sense pertains to the claim that typical IL structures are acquired before correct target language structures. As a corollary, an L2 learner's vernacular style will first show typical IL forms and only later show adjustments to the target norm.

Tarone's approach to the notion of IL variability is essentially a sociolinguistic one, distinguishing a range of speech styles. In her 1982 paper (p. 81), she compares her sociolinguistic approach with the information-processing framework in cognitive psychology, which views language acquisition as the gradual transition from controlled to automatic processing (McLaughlin, 1980). She presumes that, in terms of the information-processing framework, vernacular style should be characterized as involving automatic processing.

In this section, I would like to pursue the line of reasoning in the information-processing framework, in order to ascertain the compatibility of Tarone's following two claims: (1) in the vernacular, typical IL forms appear before target forms, and (2) the vernacular style involves automatic processing.

The information-processing view holds that the acquisition of language skills starts with controlled processing. Controlled processing involves a focus of attention on individual language forms and their meanings and their integration into receptive and productive skills. Language learning consists of the taking in of linguistic information. For any linguistic information to be really taken in, that is, processed in such a way that it can later be retrieved from memory, a certain amount of attention is required (Hulstijn, 1986, 1987, 1989, 1990). The first few times that a certain word or structure is comprehended, more attention is needed than on later occasions. Similarly, in production tasks, all words and structures produced for the first few times will require a great deal of effort and attention, although this attention need not be conscious.[1]

Why is it then that the speech of L1 and L2 learners in the early stages of development contains so many nontarget forms? The most likely reason is that learners in these stages cannot yet process target utterances in their full complexity on all linguistic levels. These learners are restricted in their processing capacity by their limited knowledge. For the production of any form there are three possibilities. The required information can be (1) present and automatized (i.e., incorporated in an automatic procedure and therefore readily available), (2) present, but not yet automatized, or (3) absent. If, as in 2, there is little time to process the available but unautomatized information and, as in 3, when the required information is simply absent, then the learner has to resort to alternative means of expression, invoking various kinds of heuristics or strategies (Faerch & Kasper, 1980, 1984). The application of such heuristics may result in the production of various non-target-like forms. Thus, the information-processing framework views the production of non-target-like forms as stemming from the learner's attempt to convey information while lacking sufficient L2 skills. Some of these nontarget forms can become automatized in their turn (resulting in so-called fossilizations).

In the early stages of language acquisition, learners lack skill in the use of some forms, but not in the use of others. The former forms require attention; the latter do not. Thus, for L2 users, attention to form is always affected by their familiarity with individual forms, apart from and in addition to the influence exercised by their speech style. Hence, attention to form is likely to vary within just as well as between speech styles.[2] It is reasonable to assume that the productions of most second-language learners will remain for a long time the result of a mixture of some lexical and grammatical elements which are more automatized and other elements which are less automatized, the latter elements requiring more and the former elements requiring less attention.

We can now answer the question: To what extent is the information-processing view compatible with Tarone's claims concerning the dual primacy of the vernacular as the style (1) being most stable and consistent because the learner's attention is not focused on form, and (2) manifesting typical IL forms before correct target forms. The answer can be summarized with the following three statements.

---

[1] Paying attention to linguistic forms and their meanings does not imply consciousness on the part of the information processer nor a knowledge of explicit grammar rules, that is, a metalinguistic level of analysis (McLaughlin, Rossman, & McLeod, 1983; McLaughlin, 1987, chap. 6).

[2] This may explain the fact that some researchers have reported low amounts of systematicity in the vernacular style of nonadvanced L2 learners (Sato, 1985).

1. The definition of vernacular style as the style in which L2 users pay least attention to form is to be attenuated so as to allow for considerable differences in attention to individual forms. In other words, style itself does not determine the degree of attention to all produced forms alike. It is, consequently, impossible to make general predictions concerning the probability of occurrence of IL variability solely on the basis of style differences. Only forms not stemming from automatized information may vary with style.

2. Beginning language learners (due to their restricted language skills) are likely to pay more attention to individual elements than more advanced learners. This difference in attention between beginning and advanced learners may even exist when communicating in the vernacular style. To that extent, the vernacular speech of beginning learners may well exhibit more variability than that of advanced learners.

3. The production of nontarget forms does not necessarily originate in the vernacular. The first time that a nontarget form occurs, it may be the result of a heuristic device, invoked when the learner lacks knowledge or skill. This may happen in casual and careful styles alike. Automatized nontarget forms (fossilizations), however, are more likely to occur in casual than in careful style. If the learner knows what the corresponding target forms are, he or she is more likely to use the correct target form in careful style (due to heightened attention to correctness), while still using the fossilization in the vernacular style.

3. THE STUDY OF ATTENTION TO FORM IN INTERACTION WITH OTHER FACTORS

Tarone (1985, and Chapter 1, this volume) raises the question concerning the number of speech styles. She juxtaposes Krashen's Monitor Theory (1981 and elsewhere) with her own Chameleon model. According to Krashen, there are only two production modes: monitored and unmonitored production. The Chameleon model, on the other hand, claims the existence of more than two styles. The number of these styles, however, is not specified. Attention is not an on–off, or all-or-nothing matter, but a matter of degree (Tarone, 1979, p. 183).

It seems to me that, as Tarone now acknowledges, the question of whether there are two or more than two styles is inadequate. The style–number issue can become meaningful, however, if other theoretical concepts are brought into play. One could attempt to provide empirical evidence for the sole impact of focus on form. One study (Hulstijn, 1982, also reported in Hulstijn & Hulstijn, 1984) did in fact provide such evidence. However, what needs to be emphasized is that in itself the existence of attention's influence on production accuracy, and hence on IL variability, is fairly obvious. I would argue that whenever individuals perform a task requiring any skill, they will be *a priori* capable of improving the formal quality of their performance when focusing their attention on the standard for this skill, provided that they do have some knowledge of the (perceived) standard. This is such a basic assumption that it should only surprise us if empirical evidence for its support could *not* be provided.

What may make attention to form a worthwhile object of investigation, however, is the influence of other factors moderating its impact. For example, in our study (Hulstijn, 1982; Hulstijn & Hulstijn, 1984) we found that, contrary to what one might expect, successful monitoring of grammar rules does not necessarily require that learners be able to correctly verbalize them. In this study, we assessed learners' performance on three tasks: (1) a grammatical judgment task (on the basis of which potential subjects were selected for participation in the experiment proper); (2) an oral story-retelling task, which was administered under four experimentally manipulated conditions (with and without time pressure and with focus on form or on content); and (3) a conversation with the experimenter during which subjects were assessed on their ability to explicitly verbalize the two word-order rules under investigation (Inversion in main clauses, and Verb Final in subclauses; more details concerning these tasks and word-order rules are given in subsequent sections of this chapter). The results showed that learners who could not explicitly state the two word-order rules during the interview, and learners who could only state partly correct or even incorrect rules, had still been able to improve their performance in the experimental story-retelling task. When required to pay attention to form, they applied the two word-order rules correctly much more often than when required to pay attention to the content of their production. These learners had improved the accuracy of their production with the same percentage (although obviously not to the same level) as those learners who were able to explicitly state the correct rules. Thus, focus on form in the story-retelling experiment was shown to have equal impact on the production of learners both with and without correct rule knowledge.

We also assessed the relation between rule monitoring and cognitive style, that is, reflection versus impulsivity, but we did not find that reflective subjects made more use of the Monitor in the story-retelling experiment than impulsive subjects (cf. Krashen's distinction between underusers, optimal users, and overusers of the Monitor; Krashen, 1981, chap. 1).

Thus, more interesting than the study of the impact of attention to form (style-shifting, monitoring) on L2 production was the investigation into the possible relationships between monitoring and other factors: explicit rule knowledge and cognitive style.

It makes little sense to consider the effect of attention on learner language or to study the number of styles on the continuum as a research goal in its own right. Neither is it very meaningful to study variability (in learner language) for its own sake. We study variability in IL because we want to know how IL is caused to change diachronically and synchronically by various internal and external forces (a similar point of view to the study of variability is adopted by Ellis, 1985a, chap. 4). Hence, it is not so much the study of variability itself but rather the impact of internal and external forces upon it which may increase our theoretical understanding of SLA.[3]

In short, I would argue that the mere existence of attention to form and its general influence on language production is not particularly illuminating. The issue concerning the number of style differences in IL is worthwhile investigating only if the supposed styles can be hypothesized to be differentially associated with other relevant concepts in SLA theory in addition to the degree of attention paid to form.

4. SUBJECT SELECTION REQUIREMENTS FOR VARIABILITY RESEARCH

Investigations into IL variability within subjects (Ss), as caused by nonlinguistic factors (such as task and style differences), have to meet certain requirements. One crucial condition is that the IL feature under investigation can rightly be assumed to vary within Ss. If we cannot in advance expect Ss' performances to exhibit variability, it doesn't make sense to investigate if and how this variability is influenced by context factors. Consequently, one would generally select Ss on the basis of a pretest. For example, a researcher investigating the influence of style-shifting on the presence or absence of certain function words (e.g., copula, articles) or functional morphemes (e.g., verb endings) might first ascertain whether the potential Ss do indeed sometimes add these elements and leave them out at other times.

I demonstrate such a subject-selection procedure with my own study (Hulstijn, 1982). First however, I give a brief description of the two Dutch word-

---

[3] A similar point can be made in another SLA research area, pertaining to the hotly debated issue of whether L2 proficiency should be regarded holistically as one global proficiency or as consisting of various separate components (Oller, 1983; Vollmer, 1983). I have argued elsewhere (Hulstijn, 1985) that the existence of various proficiency components is in itself not very illuminating. What we are interested in, however, is whether and how various social, psychological, and educational factors differentially affect the supposed proficiency components. In a similar vein, I am arguing here that the influence of attention to form on language production by itself isn't illuminating. Instead, we must find out if and how social, psychological, and educational factors are differentially associated with speech styles and attention paid to form.

order rules under investigation: Inversion and Verb Final. Consider the following examples:

(1) *David heeft misschien een fiets.*
    (David has perhaps a bike.)

(2) *Misschien heeft David een fiets.*
    (Perhaps has David a bike.)

(3) **Misschien David heeft een fiets.*
    (Perhaps David has a bike.)

In sentence (1) the subject precedes the finite verb. In sentence (2), a constituent other than the subject has taken the first place, and the subject has moved to the third place. In traditional grammar this is called *inversion,* as it appears that the subject and finite verb in sentence (2) have been ''inverted,'' compared to that in sentence (1). Sentence (3) is incorrect; many foreigners make errors of type in sentence (3). Next, consider examples (4) and (5), representing subclauses:

(4) *Ik geloof dat David een fiets heeft.*
    (I believe that David a bike has.)

(5) **Ik geloof dat David heeft een fiets.*
    (I believe that David has a bike.)

From sentence (4), it can be seen that the finite verb takes the final position in a subclause. Many foreigners make errors as in sentence (5).

In our research on the influence of Time Pressure and Focus of Attention on the correct use of Inversion and Verb Final in the IL of Dutch learners, it was essential to select for participation in the experiment only learners who could be expected to exhibit variable use of both Inversion and Verb Final. Thus, we wanted to select Ss who would sometimes use Inversion correctly, as in (2), and sometimes incorrectly, as in (3). Such learners would also have to use Verb Final correctly on some occasions, as in (4), and incorrectly at other times, as in (5). Since the experiment itself dealt with variability in oral story retelling under four conditions, we reasoned that if learners were to exhibit variable performance even on a paper-and-pencil test requiring attention to form, they would be maximally likely to exhibit variable performance in an oral story-retelling task. We therefore chose a sentence correction task for the selection

of subjects. The Dutch learners who took this test had to judge the grammaticality of 40 stimulus sentences and had to correct observed errors. Twenty
sentences (10 correct and 10 incorrect) served as distractors. The remaining 20
sentences, containing 10 Inversion errors and 10 Verb Final errors, were scored.
In order to be selected as a subject in the experiment, a learner would have to
have an Inversion score as well as a Verb Final score of more than 10% but
less than 90% correct. The result of this test is in itself revealing: although
Inversion and Verb Final are extremely common errors in Dutch (and German)
IL, only one in four intermediate Dutch learners tested met *both* requirements.
Almost invariantly, performance on Inversion was better (more errors corrected) than on Verb Final (fewer errors corrected), suggesting that Inversion
is generally acquired (i.e., to the level of automaticity) before Verb Final (for
a discussion of the related literature see Hulstijn, 1984). The methodological
implication of this finding is that the more structures the researcher wants to
investigate, the more constraints are imposed on the subjects, if each subject
must exhibit variability in *all* these structures[4].

In addition to this grammar selection test, we administered a listening
comprehension test in order to ascertain whether potential Ss were able to comprehend samples of spoken Dutch similar to the samples used as stimuli in the
experiment. On the basis of these two selection instruments, 32 Dutch learners
were invited to participate in the experiment.

In the story-telling experiment, administered a few weeks after the pre-
tests, all Ss that had been selected with these procedures applied Inversion and
Verb Final in a variable manner, although their Inversion performance was
higher than their Verb Final performance (Table 1). Inversion performance varied from an average of 78% correct in Focus of Attention on Information with
no Time Pressure to 88% in Focus of Attention on Grammar with no Time
Pressure; Verb Final performance varied from 36% in Focus of Attention on
Information with Time Pressure to 59% in Focus of Attention on Grammar
with no Time Pressure.

The demonstration of IL variability required a great deal of attention and
effort in our study. But with these selection procedures, floor and ceiling effects in the use of Inversion and Verb Final could be avoided, allowing context
effects, if existent, to affect IL variability.

Inversion and Verb Final are relatively difficult word-order rules and may
therefore take longer to learn (Hulstijn, 1984). Hence the period of variable
performance may be relatively long, giving more room to the researcher to

---

[4] In her style-shifting study, Tarone (1985) analyzed four forms: third-person singular present tense
-*s*, noun plural, article, and direct object pronoun. However, it would be extremely unlikely that
all subjects were to exhibit variable performance on such widely differing forms. Tarone's findings (1985, appendix B) confirm this improbability.

Table 1. Mean Scores for Response Length, Speech Rate, Repeats, Self-Corrections, Information Units, Inversion, and Verb Final, across All 32 Subjects

Dependent variable		Focus of attention on:		
		Information	Grammar	Mean
1. Response duration				
(in seconds)	Time pressure			
	Present	21.2	25.4	23.3
	Absent	30.9	42.2	36.5
	Mean	26.0	33.8	
2. Speech rate				
(words/second)	Time pressure			
	Present	1.44	1.16	1.30
	Absent	1.08	0.77	0.93
	Mean	1.26	0.97	
3. Repeats				
(per 100 words)	Time pressure			
	Present	2.84	3.53	3.19
	Absent	2.48	3.83	3.16
	Mean	2.66	3.68	
4. Self-corrections				
(per 100 words)	Time pressure			
	Present	2.89	3.35	3.12
	Absent	2.83	2.91	2.87
	Mean	2.87	3.13	
5. Information units				
(correctly	Time pressure			
reproduced;	Present	3.07	2.65	2.86
maximum = 4)	Absent	3.11	2.66	2.89
	Mean	3.09	2.66	
6. Inversion				
(correct use in %)	Time pressure			
	Present	81.0	85.7	83.4
	Absent	77.6	87.9	82.7
	Mean	79.3	86.8	
7. Verb final				
(correct use in %)	Time pressure			
	Present	36.1	55.7	45.9
	Absent	37.6	59.1	48.4
	Mean	36.8	57.4	

investigate the influence of style shifting. However, in investigations of lin-guistically simpler features, such as, in English, the addition of third-person singular -s to the verb stem in present tense (Tarone, 1985), it may well be even more difficult to demonstrate the influence of style differences. The time period during which performance of an individual learner is variable may be as short as a couple of days, because this verb ending can be acquired relatively easily (and quickly) to the level of automaticity. Before this period, the learner may never supply this ending, and afterwards he or she may invariantly supply it, regardless of communicative situation. Hence, before or after this period, the learner is not of any use to an investigation of style-shifting on variable use of third-person -s. This underscores the importance of the inclusion of pretesting procedures in the study of IL variability.

5. THE DISTINCTION BETWEEN TASK AND TASK REQUIREMENTS

Following Labov, Tarone (1985) claims that variability in IL is related to task. As mentioned before, Tarone calls these task-related versions of IL "styles." Investigations into task-related variability, as conducted by sociolinguists as well as by IL researchers, are sometimes based on the assumption that tasks differentially cause learners to pay attention to language form. Tarone (1985, p. 375, note 3) explicitly states that the researcher cannot in advance be certain but can only assume that the tasks used in an investigation will indeed cause learners to focus on form in different degrees. It seems to me, however, that researchers can do better than assume (and hope) that this is so. They can try to actively manipulate the degree of attention to form. This can be done by varying the task instructions in such a way that the attention requirements will differ, while the task remains unchanged. The point is that "task" and "task requirements" are different notions. One can present subjects with the same task under different requirements, making different demands on their capabilities. This is illustrated with our study (Hulstijn, 1982; Hulstijn & Hulstijn, 1984).

In this study, we presented 32 adult learners of Dutch as a second language with the same task (story retelling) under four different conditions (repeated-measures design). Subjects, who were tested individually, listened to passages of L2 speech dealing with topics from everyday life. These passages were three or four sentences long (about 30 words). All passages contained approximately the same amount of information (four information units each, each unit being roughly equivalent to a proposition). Here are two sample stimulus texts, followed by their response frames (i.e., cues with which Ss had to begin their response) and their information units, all translated into English:

> *Stimulus text 19:* I was in hospital last month. The reason was that I'd broken my leg. I had to stay in hospital for five days. But the people there were all very kind to me.
> *Response frame:* Last month . . .
> *Information units:* (1) in hospital, (2) broken leg, (3) five days, (4) kind people.

Stimulus text 8: Recently, we had a radio stolen from our apartment. It was while we were on holiday. It's very easy for them to just open a window or something. But the whole thing cost us a good 800 guilders.

Response frame: This lady says that . . .

Information units: (1) radio stolen, (2) while on holiday, (3) it's easy to get in, (4) damages: 800 guilders.

After each passage had been presented, Ss were required to retell its content in L2. Ss were free to use their own words or the words from the stimulus passage. (The passages were too long for Ss to remember them word by word, but not too long to remember their content.) However, they had to begin their responses with a few words (the "response frame") projected on a screen by means of a slide projector. The response frames served as cues, forcing Ss to produce sentences of the types under investigation. For instance, in item 19 above, the frame "Last month . . ." elicites an obligatory Inversion context. Similarly, the frame "This lady says that . . ." (item 8) elicites an obligatory Verb Final context. The basic instructions for this experimental task read as follows (translated into English):

- First you'll hear a short text.
- Next you'll see a slide with a few words.
- Then you have to retell what you've heard.
  1. Start with the words from the slide.
  2. Continue in your own words.

Within this story-retelling task, two factors were manipulated: Time Pressure (present or absent) and Focus of Attention (on information or on grammatical correctness). This gave four conditions: Information/Fast, Information/Slow, Grammar/Fast, and Grammar/Slow. We were thus able to change the task requirements while holding the task constant. We created these differences in task requirements by explicitly *instructing* and *training* subjects. Subjects were instructed that they had to concentrate on information or on form and to perform their tasks as fast as possible or at their ease, depending on the experimental condition. Futhermore, Ss were trained in responding according to these instructions before the experimental stimuli were presented. During these practice sessions, Ss were given feedback on their responses and further encouraged to respond according to the specific demands of each condition. Thus, during the practice sessions of the two Information conditions (Information/Fast and Information/Slow), Ss were informed about information units missing in their responses; in the two Grammar conditions (Grammar/Fast and Grammar/Slow) they were informed about possible Inversion or Verb Final errors. (Note that at no point during the experiment did the experimentor inform Ss which grammar rules he was interested in, nor did he state any rules explicitly in his feedback during the practice session.)

During the training of the two Fast conditions (Information/Fast and Grammar/Fast), the experimenter timed Ss' responses with a stopwatch, informed them about their response times, and encouraged them to respond as fast as they could. During the two Slow conditions (Information/Slow and Grammar/Slow), he encouraged Ss to take as much time for their responses as they needed. Altogether, every S had to retell 68 stimulus passages. In each of the four conditions there were four practice items followed by twelve experimental items. The first condition to be administered was preceded by four items that served to make the S familiar with the story-retelling task, postponing the Time and Attention requirements until the practice session of each condition separately. Hence, of the 68 responses, only 48 (12 in each condition) were scored for analysis.

The dependent variables in these analyses were, for each condition (average of 12 responses) and subject:

1. Response Duration, measured in seconds.
2. Speech Rate (words/second).
3. Repeats (a Repeat is defined as a literal reiteration of a stretch of speech without change, the shortest Repeat consisting of one phoneme only).
4. Self-Corrections (Self-Corrections are similar to repeats in that they involve an interruption of the speech flow, the difference being that, in the case of Self-Corrections, the original utterance is being changed).
5. Information Units correctly reproduced (each stimulus text contained four Information Units; see items 19 and 8 above).
6. Inversion structures correctly used.
7. Verb Final structures correctly used.

The results of this experiment are shown in Tables 1 and 2. These results provided evidence that it is indeed only the Attention factor, and not the Time factor, that significantly and substantially influenced the grammatical correctness of Ss' L2 productions. Although the Time factor substantially and significantly affected the Response Duration and Speech Rate (variables 1 and 2), it did not affect their grammatical correctness (variables 6 and 7), their informational correctness (variable 5), nor their fluency (variables 3 and 4). It was Focus of Attention which was solely responsible for the difference in grammatical and informational correctness of the responses.

The separate manipulation of Time and Attention factors was motivated by the results of a previous study (Hulstijn, 1980). In that study we also used a story-retelling task, which had to be performed twice: first fast and later slowly, thus giving two conditions along the Time factor. In this previous study, the Time factor had caused a substantial and significant increase in the number of obligatory contexts from fast to slow condition, but the proportion of correct realizations in the slow condition had remained just the same. This indicated

Table 2. The Influence of Time Pressure and Focus of Attention

Dependent variable	Source	F ratio $(df = 1,30)$	$p<$
1. Response duration	Time pressure	66.28	.001
	Focus of attention	37.27	.001
	Interaction	19.33	.001
2. Speech rate	Time pressure	150.79	.0001
	Focus of attention	120.49	.0001
	Interaction	0.28	
3. Repeats	Time pressure	0.02	
	Focus of attention	11.18	.01
	Interaction	5.92	.05
4. Self-corrections	Time pressure	1.33	
	Focus of attention	1.96	
	Interaction	2.05	
5. Information units	Time pressure	0.44	
	Focus of attention	46.48	.001
	Interaction	0.08	
6. Inversion	Time pressure	0.10	
	Focus of attention	5.40	.05
	Interaction	2.33	
7. Verb final	Time pressure	0.46	
	Focus of attention	32.13	.001
	Interaction	0.09	

that the Time factor has only a quantitative, but not a qualitative, effect. That is why we decided to manipulate Attention independently from Time in our later study.

The conclusions from these experiments are the following: it is necessary to distinguish between task and task requirement (in terms of, e.g., attention paid to form) and it is possible to operationalize these notions independently from each other. This does not mean, however, that they should always be kept separate. Labov's (1970) method, which later was also successfully applied in L2 research (Dickerson, 1975), consisted of performance comparison on three different tasks (free speech, reading dialogues aloud, and reading word lists aloud). These elicitation procedures (in this order) created increasing proportions of standardlike pronunciations of certain phonemes. Although in this method the task was not held constant, it seems reasonable to conclude that this increase in targetlike production was due to an increase in attention paid to form. In general, however, for variability research it is preferable not to change tasks with task requirements but, rather, to manipulate task requirements while holding the task constant.

6. SUMMARY

In this chapter, I have tried to demonstrate how Tarone's sociolinguistic view on IL variability, based on the notion of the vernacular, can be enriched by a cognitive view, based on the notions of controlled and automatic information processing. I have argued that, even in the vernacular (most casual) style, attention to form is seldom altogether absent, and that the production of nontarget forms does not necessarily originate in the vernacular style, as claimed by Tarone. A nontarget form can occur as a result of a strategy compensating for the learner's lack of knowledge or skill to produce a certain form. This may happen in casual and careful style alike.

Furthermore, I have argued that, in order to increase our understanding of SLA processes, IL variability should not be studied in isolation, as caused by style-shifting (attention to form), but rather in interaction with moderating linguistic, social, and cognitive factors.

Finally, I described an IL variability study of my own, in order to illustrate two methodological points in the empirical study of IL variability. First, since L2 learners cannot generally be expected to exhibit variable IL performance on just any linguistic feature, it is important to include a pretest in the research design which will determine those learners who are in fact likely to exhibit variable performance on the linguistic features under investigation. Second, the distinction between "task" and "task requirements" enables the researcher to study the influence of style-shifting (attention to form) on IL variability by varying task requirements while holding the task constant.

REFERENCES

Dickerson, L. J. (1975). The learner's interlanguage as a system of variable rules. *TESOL Quarterly, 9,* 401–407.

Ellis, R. (1985a). *Understanding second language acquisition.* Oxford, Oxford University Press.

Ellis, R. (1985b). Sources of variability in interlanguage. *Applied Linguistics, 6,* 118–131.

Faerch, C., & Kasper, G. (1980). Processes and strategies in foreign language learning and communication. *Interlanguage Studies Bulletin, 5,* 47–118.

Faerch, C. & Kasper, G. (1984). Two ways of defining communication strategies. *Language Learning, 34,* 45–63.

Gatbonton, E. (1978). Patterned phonetic variability in second-language speech: A gradual diffusion model. *The Canadian Modern Language Review, 34,* 335–348.

Hulstijn, J. H. (1980). Variabiliteit in tussentaal [Variability in interlanguage]. *Toegepaste Taalwetenschap in Artikelen, 7,* 141–155.

Hulstijn, J. H. (1982). *Monitor use by adult second language learners.* (Doctoral dissertation, University of Amsterdam). University Microfilm International, RPD82-70028.

Hulstijn, J. H. (1984). Difficulties in the acquisition of two word order rules by adult learners of Dutch. In R. Andersen (Ed.), *Second languages: A cross-linguistic perspective* (pp. 61–73). Rowley, MA: Newbury House.

Hulstijn, J. H. (1985). Second language proficiency: An interactive approach. In K. Hyltenstam & M. Pienemann (Eds.), *Modelling and assessing second language acquisition* (pp. 373–380). Clevedon, Avon: Multilingual Matters.

Hulstijn, J. H. (1986). Kognitive Perspektiven in der Zweitsprachenerwerbsforschung. In H. Bolte (Hrsg.), Aspekten gesteuerten Zweitsprachenerwerbs. *Osnabrücker Beiträge zur Sprachtheorie, 34,* 24–35 (in German).

Hulstijn, J. H. (1987). Impliciete en incidentele verwerving van woordvormen en grammaticaregels in een tweede taal. In G. Extra, R. van Hout, & A. Vallen (Eds.). *Ethnische minderheden in Nederland: Taalverwerving, taalonderwijs en taalbeleid* (pp. 139–154). Dordrecht: Foris.

Hulstijn, J. H. (1989) Implicit and incidental second language learning: Experiments in the processing of natural and partly artificial input. In H. W. Dechert & M. Raupach (Eds.), *Interlingual processes*. Tübingen: Gunter Narr.

Hulstijn, J. H. (1990). A comparison between the information-processing and analysis/control approaches to language learning. *Applied Linguistics* (in press).

Hulstijn, J. H., & Hulstijn, W. (1984). Grammatical errors as a function of processing constraints and explicit knowledge. *Language Learning, 34*(1), 23–43.

Krashen, S. (1981). *Second language acquisition and second language learning*. Oxford: Pergamon Press.

Labov, W. (1970). The study of language in its social context. *Studium Generale, 23,* 30–87.

McLaughlin, B. (1980). Theory and research in second language learning: An emerging paradigm. *Language Learning, 30,* 331–350.

McLaughlin, B. (1987). *Theories of second-language learning*. London: Edward Arnold.

McLaughlin, B., Rossman, T., & McLeod, B. (1983). Second-language learning: An information processing perspective. *Language Learning, 33,* 135–158.

Oller, J. W. (1983). Response to Vollmer: "G", What is it? In A. Hughes & D. Porter (Eds.), *Current developments in language testing* (pp. 35–39). London: Academic Press.

Sato, C. J. (1985). Task variation in interlanguage phonology. In S. M. Gass & C. G. Madden (Eds.), *Input in second language acquisition* (pp. 181–196). Rowley, MA: Newbury House.

Tarone, E. (1979). Interlanguage as chameleon. *Language Learning, 29,* 181–191.

Tarone, E. (1982). Systematicity and attention in interlanguage. *Language Learning, 32,* 69–84.

Tarone, E. (1983). On the variability in interlanguage systems. *Applied Linguistics, 4,* 142–163.

Tarone, E. (1985). Variability in interlanguage: A study of style-shifting in morphology and syntax. *Language Learning, 35,* 373–403.

Vollmer, H. J. (1983). The structure of foreign language competence. In A. Hughes & D. Porter (Eds.), *Current developments in language testing* (pp. 3–29). London: Academic Press.

CHAPTER 3

Does the Bioprogram Affect Second-Language Acquisition?

H. D. ADAMSON

1. THE BIOPROGRAM

During the last 10 years, second-language scholars have looked to the field of pidgin and creole studies for insights into language acquisition. Among the important theories to emerge from this interdisciplinary effort are Schumman's (1978) Pidginization Hypothesis and Andersen's (1983) Nativization Hypothesis. The present study considers the implications for second-language acquisition of perhaps the most controversial hypothesis in pidgin–creole scholarship: Bickerton's Bioprogram Hypothesis.

 Bickerton (1981, 1984) suggests that creole languages can shed light on language acquisition because they exhibit natural or unmarked systems of negation, tense and aspect, articles, and so forth. To see why this is so, consider the traditional distinction between a pidgin language and a creole language. A pidgin is a second language that arises in a contact situation where speakers do not share a common language, as when speakers from many parts of the Pacific Basin immigrated to Hawaii at the beginning of the century to work as agricultural laborers. These speakers from diverse linguistic backgrounds did not learn the dominant language of the community—English—because they did not have adequate access to native English speakers. Instead, they created a lingua franca, Hawaiian Pidgin English (HPE). Pidgin languages are formed when a speaker of first language P attempts to learn second language T without adequate access to native speakers. In these circumstances the learner plugs lexical items from T into simplified syntactic patterns of P. Thus, the resulting pidgin language is

---

H. D. ADAMSON • Department of English, University of Arizona, Tucson, Arizona 85721.

both simplified and varied. The simplicity of HPE can be seen in examples (1) and (2).

> (1)   mi kape bai, 'mi chaek meik.
> me coffee buy, me check make.
> "He bought my coffee; he made me out a check."

> (2)   en den meri dis wan.
> and then marry this one.
> "And then he got married." (Bickerton, 1984, p. 74)

Bickerton (1984) observes that HPE is "extremely rudimentary in structure" (p. 174), since it has no consistent means of marking tense, aspect, or modality, no consistent system of anaphora, no articles, and no structure more complex than the single clause. The variation among speakers of HPE can also be seen in examples (1) and (2). This variation is caused by transfer from the speakers' different native languages. In (1), spoken by a Japanese speaker, the object precedes the verb, as in Japanese; but in (2), spoken by an Illocano speaker, the verb precedes the object, as in Illocano.

A creole language is more uniform and more complex than a pidgin. Not only do creoles show far less variation among speakers, but, according to Bickerton, creoles which could not have had a common ancestor exhibit remarkable similarities. Creoles arise when children grow up in a pidgin-speaking community and attempt to learn the pidgin as a first language. Since the rudimentary pidgin does not fulfill all the requirements of a native language, the children expand it, adding the features that the pidgin lacks: a tense–aspect system, a system of anaphora, and ways of embedding. To do this, the children tap linguistic information that is encoded in the human genes. This information is the language bioprogram.

An example of bioprogram information is the specific–nonspecific distinction (SNSD) of noun phrases (NPs), which in English is marked by articles. Bickerton (1981) divides NPs into four types along two dimensions. All NPs are + specific or − specific and + known to hearer or − known to hearer. An NP is + specific if it refers to an existing entity, − specific if it refers to a general or hypothetical entity. An NP is + known if it has been mentioned previously in the discourse, is part of the speaking situation, or is part of general knowledge. Table 1 contains examples of the four kinds of NPs and shows the various ways they are marked by English articles. Notice that the English article system is not consistent. Generic NPs can be marked with *a, the,* or zero; + specific NPs are marked with *a* when first mentioned, and thereafter with *the,* and so on. On the other hand, according to Bickerton (1981, pp. 56–58, 247–248) the creole article system is very consistent. In creoles, NPs are divided into two types: + specific and − specific. Minus specific NPs take the zero article; + specific NPs take *the* when + known and *a* when − known.

Table 1. The Four Types of Noun Phrases and How They Are Marked
by English Articles[a]

Type of noun phrase	Example
Type 1	
+ specific	1. He saw a lion. *The* lion came running out.
+ known	
"Definite"	
Article: *the*	
Type 2	
− specific	1. *The* camel is a useful animal.
+ known	2. *A* camel is a useful animal.
"Generic"	3. _____ Camels are useful animals.
Articles: *the*, *a*, zero	
Type 3	
− specific	1. He didn't see *a* lion.
− known	2. He didn't see _____ zebras.
"Other"	
Articles: *a*, zero	
Type 4	
+ specific	1. He saw *a* lion.
− known	2. He saw lions.
"Indefinite"	
Articles: *a*, zero	

[a] Adapted from Bickerton, 1981, p. 249.

Bickerton claims that the creole system of clearly dividing NPs into + specific and − specific reflects a basic semantic distinction which arises from two different kinds of cognitive structures: percepts and concepts. A percept is a mental image of a particular entity on a particular occasion, such as my memory of the van that just drove past my window; a percept is + specific. A concept is a mental image of a class of entities, such as my mental image of vans in general; concepts are − specific. From an evolutionary standpoint, percepts are more primitive than concepts. The ability to perceive goes pretty far down the phylogenetic ladder—at least as far as frogs, who, we know, can perceive flies. The ability to abstract a concept from many percepts is rarer, and it obviously has great survival value. Bickerton (1984) explains that this abstracting ability enables an organism to generalize about its environment—to reason in terms of generics rather than in terms of particulars. He invites us to imagine human ancestors saving their skins by reasoning that, "Wounded boars do such and such, so I can anticipate what will happen and be ready to act appropriately" (p. 227). The concept "wounded boars" is, of course, generic.

Thus, according to Bickerton, the ability to make the SNSD is innate in human beings. Children are born with the "wired in" ability to perceive the world in terms of entities and classes of entities, because percepts and concepts are stored in memory in different parts of the brain. Naturally, this innate knowledge affects first-language acquisition, in both the creole situation and the normal situation. Bickerton (1981) claims:

> Those semantic distinctions whose neural infrastructure was laid down first in the course of mammalian development will be the first to be lexicalized and/or grammaticized in the course of human language development. (p. 242)

This claim leads Bickerton to propose the SNSD Hypothesis:

> When a substantial body of early child language is properly examined, there will be found to be a significant skewing in article placement, such that a significantly higher percentage of articles will be assigned to specific reference NP, while zero forms will persist in nonspecific environments longer than elsewhere. (Bickerton, 1981, p. 154)

Thus, according to the SNSD Hypothesis, in normal first-language acquisition, the child's first hypothesis about how to use articles will resemble the creole article system.

2. CZIKO'S REVIEW OF ARTICLE ACQUISITION IN CHILDREN

Cziko (1986) tested the SNSD Hypothesis by reviewing seven studies of children's acquisition of English and French articles. Cziko elaborated Bickerton's prediction in one way. Brown (1973) had found that a significant error in young children's use of articles was using *the* with +specific, −known NPs, as when Sarah said, "I want to open the door," and her mother said, "What door?" (Brown, 1973, p. 353). Brown noted that Sarah failed to mark *door* as −known because she assumed that her mother shared her own point of view, an assumption expected in young children because they are "egocentric" in Piaget's sense. Thus, Brown's subjects were able to mark the SNSD before they were able to mark the known–unknown distinction. Taking the factor of egocentricity into account, Cziko (1986) predicted that children would acquire articles in the four stages shown in Table 2. Stage 1 is the SNSD Hypothesis, stages 2 and 3 involve sorting out the fact that in English and French *a* and *the* can occur with both +specific *and* −specific NPs. Stage 4, the adult system, is finally reached when the child becomes sensitive to the known–unknown distinction. Cziko notes that stage 3 is so at variance with normal usage that it may last for only a short time or be absent. Thus, the main difference between Bickerton's theory and Cziko's expanded theory occurs in stage 2, where Cziko predicts that children will make the "egocentric error" of using *the* with +specific, −known NPs.

Table 2. The Four Stages of Article Acquisition Predicted by Cziko

---

Stage 1 (the SNSD Hypothesis):
   The creole system. The child tends to use *a* and *the* with +specific NPs and zero with −specific NPs. Characteristic errors are *the* used with +specific, −known NPs; *a* used with +specific, +known NPs; and zero used with all −specific NPs.
Stage 2:
   The child uses *a* with −specific NPs, retaining *the* with +specific NPs. The characteristic error would be *the* used with +specific, −known NPs.
Stage 3:
   The child begins to use *a* with +specific NPs, but because of egocentricity does not yet know that *a* is restricted to +specific NPs that are also −known. This stage predicts an increase in the correct use of *a* for +specific, −known NPs, and an overgeneralization of *a* so that it is incorrectly used with +specific, +known NPs.
Stage 4:
   Losing egocentricity, the child marks the known–unknown distinction and achieves the adult system, described in Table 1.

Cziko (1986) concludes that the seven studies of children's article acquisition generally support the SNSD Hypothesis and mainly support his own four-stage hypothesis. He comments:

> Strong evidence for the core SNSD Hypothesis is provided by Brown . . . and by Maratsos. Also consistent with the SNSD Hypothesis are other results. . . . No studies indicated that children failed to attend to SNSD either in production or comprehension. (p. 896)

Evidence for Cziko's four-stage model is present but less strong. Cziko notes:

> With respect to the Four-stage Hypothesis of article acquisition, the studies reviewed here collectively offer quite impressive support. . . . However, four of the experiments reviewed did not produce the pattern of errors predicted by stage 2. [They] showed that children as young as two to four years of age correctly used the indefinite article for +specific, −known referents. . . . An explanation . . . is that [these] experiments simply did not include children at stage 2. (p. 896)

Cziko's analysis of the seven studies of children's article acquisition is summarized in Table 3, which shows that in three of the seven studies it was possible to test the SNSD Hypothesis and that all three studies supported the hypothesis. This evidence suggests that despite the inconsistent way adult English and French mark the SNSD, children can make this distinction at a very early age, as Bickerton predicted. As shown in Table 3, the evidence supporting Cziko's four-stage hypothesis is less strong. Nevertheless, four of the seven studies in which it was possible to test Cziko's hypothesis, including the one longitudinal study, supported the four-stage hypothesis and its claim that be-

Table 3. Summary of Cziko's Literature Review

Study	Eng. or French[a]	Long. or exper.[b]	Compatible with Bickerton[c]	Compatible with 4-stage model[d]	Comments
Brown (1973)	Eng.	Long.	Yes	Yes	Did not report zero article use.
Bresson (1974)	French	Exper.	Not applicable	Yes	All referents were + specific.
Maratsos (1976)	Eng.	Exper.	Yes	Unclear	On a minority of the tasks subjects showed early sensitivity to known–unknown distinction.
Warden (1976)	Eng.	Exper.	Not applicable	Yes	All referents were + specific.
Karmiloff-Smith (1979)	French	Exper.	Yes	Yes (see comment)	Some evidence of early sensitivity to known–unknown distinction.
Emslie & Stevenson (1981)	Eng.	Exper.	Not applicable	No	All referents were + specific. Strong evidence of early sensitivity to known–unknown distinction.
Garton (1983)	Eng.	Exper.	Not applicable	No	Possible flaw in research design.

[a]Were the children acquiring English or French?
[b]Was the study longitudinal or experimental?
[c]Is the study compatible with the SNSD Hypothesis?
[d]Is the study compatible with the four-stage hypothesis?

cause of egocentricity children will use *the* with + specific, − known NPs in stage 2 and *a* with + specific, + known NPs in stage 3.

3. A STUDY OF ARTICLE ACQUISITION IN KOREAN-SPEAKING ADULTS

There is considerable controversy over the question of whether adults learning a second language use some of the same cognitive mechanisms that children use learning a first language. Several studies (reviewed below) suggest that they do. An intriguing question, then, is whether the bioprogram principles can influence second-language acquisition. Do beginning second-language learners, like young children, tend to use articles with + specific NPs? In adapting the bioprogram hypothesis to second-language acquisition, two points must be kept in mind. First, transfer from L1 can affect L2, so a bioprogram influence in article acquisition might show up only in the interlanguage of subjects whose L1 has no article system, such as Korean. Second, since adults have passed the egocentric stage, they should not go through the four stages suggested by Cziko for children. With these points in mind, a modified SNSD Hypothesis can be proposed:

> In the early stages of English acquisition, Korean-speaking adults will tend to use articles with + specific NPs and to omit articles with − specific NPs.

To test this hypothesis, the interlanguage of 14 adult Korean speakers was examined. The subjects had been living in northern Virginia for various lengths of time and spoke English at various levels of proficiency, as measured by a cloze test (see Table 4). None of the subjects was currently enrolled in an ESL program, although all had taken ESL classes, either in Korea or as adult school students in the United States. The subjects were interviewed using an open-ended instrument designed to elicit informal English. They were asked to tell how long they had been in the United States, to describe the physical location of the interview, to talk about their families, to describe a typical day, and so on. Each interview lasted about one hour. The interviews were recorded and transcribed, and the transcriptions were coded for article usage. All NPs were marked either + specific or − specific. Repeated NPs and NPs that were in set phrases, such as "in the morning," were not counted, nor were proper names or NPs that were marked with other determiners. Then, the article (if any) used with each NP was noted. In addition, all NPs that were sentence subjects were marked in order to test for a phenomenon reported by Huebner (1983), who found that a Hmong speaker did not at first use articles with sentence subject NPs. Huebner attributed this strategy to the fact that Hmong is a topic-prominent language which does not attach any marker to sentence topics. He believed

Table 4. The Subjects of the Study

Subject	Cloze score	Sex	Time in U.S. (yrs.)
1	32	M	5½
2	57	F	2½
3	61	F	2½
4	59	M	12
5	42	M	1
6	55	F	2
7	69	M	9[a]
8	58	F	9
9	18	F	7
10	15	F	1
11	33	F	9
12	31	F	9
13	52	F	5[a]
14	6	F	5

[a] Months.

that his subject first interpreted *the* as a marker of the sentence topic and so did not use it before NPs that were subjects. Despite the fact that Korean is a topic-prominent language, no evidence was found that the Korean speakers used this strategy. The final step in the data tabulation was to count the number of articles used before +specific and before −specific NPs.

The data analysis showed that the subjects' most common strategy by far was to omit articles. The following examples give some of the flavor of their interlanguage:

Q: Can you tell me about your first day in the U. S.?
A: Well, it's hard to remember about it. Change of time a little bit different. [Subject 3]

My husband is pastor. [Subject 9]

I want more English speak and grammar, and I went there everyday. But everyday: "Is this pencil?" "Is this a hamburg?" [Subject 5]

It was found that when the subjects did use articles, they used them correctly. In all the data there were only six cases of using an incorrect article—*a* for *the*, or vice versa, or either article for zero. Thus, the frequency of article use was equivalent to the accuracy of article use. This fact made it possible to rank the subjects in order of frequency and accuracy of article use and then to divide them into a high-proficiency group and a low-proficiency group. The dividing line fell between subjects 8 and 9, as shown in Table 5. The groups were divided at this point because it was the lowest point at which the high-proficiency subjects and the low-proficiency subjects had significantly different scores.

Table 5. How the Subjects Used Articles

Subject	Overall percentage articles supplied	Use/contexts + specific	Percentage articles supplied	Use/contexts − specific	Percentage articles supplied	Difference between percentage + specific and − specific
High-proficiency group:						
1	82	24/28	86	4/6	67	19
2	80	20/28	71	35/41	85	−16
3	71	2/27	74	7/11	64	10
4	66	29/41	70	13/22	59	11
5	64	33/53	62	10/14	71	−11
6	63	16/25	64	10/16	63	1
7	57	6/8	75	2/6	33	42
8	45	10/24	42	7/14	50	−12
Low-proficiency group:						
9	31	18/54	33	2/11	18	15
10	21	5/16	31	0/8	0	31
11	17	4/16	25	0/8	0	25
12	16	4/24	17	0/1	0	17
13	6	0/32	0	3/17	18	−18
14	5	3/48	6	0/16	0	6

Table 6. Research Design

Test	Independent variable	Dependent variable	Dependent variable
1	Correlation of difference in rank	Rank by accuracy of article use	Rank by cloze score
2	Low proficiency in English	Frequency of article use before + spec. NPs	Frequency of article use before − spec. NPs
3	High proficiency in English	Frequency of article use before + spec. NPs	Frequency of article use before − spec. NPs
4	Comparison of difference	Difference between articles before + spec. NPs and − spec. NPs in high-proficiency group	Difference between articles before + spec. NPs and − spec. NPs in low-proficiency group

After the high-proficiency and low-proficiency groups were formed and all of the data listed, four statistical tests were run, as outlined in Table 6.

Test 1, a Spearman's rho test, was run to determine the correlation between the subjects' rank in article accuracy and their overall English proficiency as measured by the cloze test. The results showed a significant correlation at the .05 level between the subjects' accuracy of article use and their cloze score ranks (rho = .79, df = 12). This correlation is expected. It means that as overall English proficiency improves, accuracy with articles also improves. That there is not a perfect correlation demonstrates that a second-language learner can have a high overall proficiency in English without the same level of proficiency for each individual morpheme.

In test 2, a t test, the difference between the frequency of article use before + specific and − specific NPs for the low proficiency group proved to be slightly less than significant at the .05 level (t = 1.8, df = 5). This result was somewhat disappointing, since the modified SNSD Hypothesis predicts that low-proficiency subjects will use articles more often before + specific than before − specific NPs. Nevertheless, although statistical significance was not reached, the low-proficiency group did use articles twice as often before + specific NPs than before − specific NPs (18% versus 9%). The lack of significance is probably due to the small number of articles used by this group.

In test 3, also a t test, the difference between the frequency of article use in + specific and − specific environments for the high-proficiency group proved to be not significant at the .05 level ($t = 1.0$, $df = 7$), as expected. We can be confident of these results since the high-proficiency group used many more articles than did the low-proficiency group.

Test 4, an analysis of variance, measured the difference between article use before + specific and − specific NPs in the high-proficiency group and the low-proficiency group. In other words, it answered the question: Compared to the high-proficiency group, did the low-proficiency group use articles more often before + specific NPs than before − specific NPs? This was the crucial test of the modified SNSD Hypothesis. Let us examine more closely what it measured. We know that the high-proficiency group used articles with about equal frequency before + specific and − specific NPs. We know that the low-proficiency group used articles with greater frequency before + specific NPs than before − specific NPs (although due to the small number of tokens this difference was not quite significant). Test 4, then, measured the difference between these two frequencies. The difference proved to be significant at the .05 level ($f = 19.6$, $df = 1$ and 12). These results support the modified SNSD Hypothesis and suggest that, lacking information about how to use articles from their native language, the Korean speakers fell back on the SNSD Hypothesis supplied by the bioprogram. As they became more proficient in English, they revised this hypothesis and adopted hypotheses more like the actual English rules.

4. DISCUSSION: SIMILARITIES AND DIFFERENCES IN FIRST- AND SECOND-LANGUAGE ACQUISITION

The comparison of article acquisition by children and by Korean adults points up both similarities and differences. The main similarity is that in the beginning stage, both groups tended to use articles before + specific NPs. This finding suggests that both groups can use similar—and possibly innate—cognitive mechanisms in language acquisition. This possibility is suggested by Bickerton, even though in general he does not see similarities in adult and child language acquisition. Bickerton claims:

> There are clear areas (such as basic word order) where the innate mechanism seems to make no hypotheses and where in consequence only the L1 model can be followed, others (such as the [SNSD]) where innate hypotheses can override L1 influences. (quoted in Meisel, 1983, pp. 128–129)

Andersen (1983) finds even more similarities in adult and child language acquisition. His Nativization Hypothesis claims that these similarities appear in pidgin and creole situations as well as in normal first- and second-language acquisition situations. According to the Nativization Hypothesis, language acquisition in all four circumstances can be divided into an initial stage and a later stage. In the initial stage, the learner constructs a simple or unmarked grammar, in part by relying on universal cognitive mechanisms. This movement toward an internal norm is called "nativization." In the later stage, the initial simple grammar is gradually replaced by structures from the target-language grammar. This movement toward an external norm is called "depidginization" in the case of pidgins and "decreolization" in the case of creoles. Andersen introduces the term *denativization* to cover movement toward an external norm in all four circumstances.

The Nativization Hypothesis, at least as far as it applies to first-language acquisition and creolization, receives support from Slobin (1985), who suggests that children possess a Language Making Capacity (which appears to be similar to the bioprogram) that "constructs similar early grammars from all input languages" (p. 1,160). Slobin states: "I suspect that many of the principles of Basic Child Grammar will also appear in the development of creoles and in processes of historical language change, along lines suggested . . . by Bickerton (1981)" (p. 1,162). According to Slobin, the Language Making Capacity constructs this simple system by using universal cognitive "operating principles."

There is evidence that adult as well as child language learners use Slobin's operating principles. Meisel (1983) studied how Spanish and Italian immigrants to Germany acquired German as a second language. He found that these subjects acquired German word-order rules in an invariant sequence. In the first stage, sentences had the order subject–verb–object–adverb, with optional deletion of any element. In the next stage, adverbs could be placed sentence initially. In a later stage, subject and verb could be inverted, as in questions.[1] All of Meisel's subjects learned to front adverbs before they learned to invert subject and verb. Meisel explained this fact by Slobin's (1973) operating principle D, "avoid interruption or rearrangement of linguistic units" (p. 199). According to Slobin, the verb and its direct object constitute such a unit. Inversion moves the verb away from its direct object, interrupting a basic linguistic unit, but fronting an adverb does not. Thus, Meisel's (1983) study supports the Nativization Hypothesis by showing that in the initial stages of language acquisition adults can use the same operating principles as children to construct a simple linguistic system. In sum, Bickerton, Andersen, Meisel, and Slobin agree that, at least in some circumstances, similar cognitive mechanisms are involved in first-language acquisition and adult second-language acquisition. This conclusion is supported by the data on article acquisition.

There are, of course, differences in first- and second-language acquisition. The most often noticed difference is the phenomenon of transfer in second-

[1] In German questions, the subject and main verb can be inverted. This used to be the case in English, as in Shakespeare's question to Time, "Why work'st thou mischief in thy pilgrimage/ Unless thou couldst returne to make amendes?"

language acquisition. The study of Korean speakers' article acquisition was designed to minimize transfer effects, but one effect could not be eliminated: the tendency of Korean speakers to omit articles. This tendency among speakers of languages without article systems was noted by Gilbert (1983), who studied the acquisition of German articles by two groups of speakers. The first group contained speakers of Greek and Romance languages, whose native languages have article systems similar to German. The second group contained Turkish and Yugoslav speakers whose native languages do not have article systems. Gilbert (1983) found "a much more frequent use of the German article by speakers of the three Romance languages and Greek" (p. 173). Did the Korean speakers use articles less frequently than the children? It is difficult to compare the two groups since there is no independent measure of language proficiency, such as Brown's (1973) Mean Length of Utterance; nevertheless, it appears that the Korean speakers did use articles less frequently. For example, in one of the studies reviewed by Cziko, Karmiloff-Smith (1979) found that older children (ages 6;0 to 11;7) used the zero article (incorrectly) with + specific NPs (the only type of NP in the experiment) for only 2% of their responses. The younger children (ages 3;4 to 3;11) used the zero article with + specific NPs for only 20% of their responses. But even the high-proficiency Korean speakers used the zero article with + specific NPs for 40% of their responses, and the low-proficiency group used the zero article before + specific NPs for 82%. Thus, it appears that, as with the Turkish and Yugoslav speakers, the absence of an article system in the Korean speakers' first language affected their article acquisition.

A second difference between first- and second-language acquisition that emerged from this study was that the children's "egocentric" use of *the* with + specific, − known NPs was not observed in the adults. As we have seen, according to Cziko, two different kinds of cognitive principles affected the children's article acquisition: the SNSD Hypothesis and the egocentricity principle. What is the nature and the relationship of these two kinds of principles? One possibility is that they reflect Slobin's (1985) distinction between "language-specific categories" and "emerging conceptual categories." The former are the linguistic manifestations of Basic Notions, which arise from the way human beings perceive and interact with the world. For example, the Basic Notion of figure and ground may arise from the way the human eye perceives the edges of objects against a background and may underlie the various grammaticizations of topic and comment. The SNSD is a strong candidate for a Basic Notion, since (according to Bickerton, 1981, p. 248) it is based on a neurological structure and underlies the grammatical categories + specific NP and − specific NP.

The known–unknown distinction, on the other hand, seems to involve emerging conceptual categories. These categories, which include gender distinctions and the Turkish distinction between witnessed and nonwitnessed events, emerge later than language-specific categories because they require a further development of cognitive capacity as well as input from the target language. A difference between child and adult language acquisition, then, may be that children are able to work on language-specific categories, such as those implied by the SNSD, before working on emerging conceptual categories, but adults can work on both from the beginning. Nevertheless, even for adults the bioprogram may suggest language-specific categories, such as + specific and − specific NPs, as initial hypotheses about how the target language is structured.

In conclusion, the comparison of children's and Korean-speaking adults' acquisition of articles suggests both differences and similarities in first- and second-language acquisition. Children, but not adults, must wait for adequate cognitive capacity to develop before acquiring emerging conceptual categories. Adults, but not children, are affected by transfer from the first language. Both groups may have access to language-specific categories, such as those suggested by the bioprogram.

Clearly, more research on the relationship between the bioprogram and second-language acquisition is called for. A needed improvement on the present study would be to examine adult Koreans' article acquisition longitudinally. In addition, it would be very interesting to look at the acquisition of the three other distinctions that Bickerton claims are motivated by the bioprogram. These distinctions, all of which affect the verbal system, are the state–process distinction, the causative–noncausative distinction, and the punctual–nonpunctual distinction. If, as Bickerton claims, these distinctions arise because of the basic architecture of human cognition, it seems reasonable that they should affect the early stages of second-language acquisition. Such studies would add to the rapidly growing literature on the connection between second-language acquisition and language universals, which demonstrates that the study of second-language acquisition can contribute to an understanding of the mind.

ACKNOWLEDGMENTS

My thanks to Dr. Mary Ciske for coding the data and doing the statistical tests and to the Mellon Foundation for a postdoctoral fellowship to the University of Pennsylvania, during which I completed this research.

REFERENCES

Andersen, R. (1983). Introduction:A language acquisition interpretation of pidginization and creolization. In R. Andersen (Ed.), *Pidginization and creolization as language acquisition* (pp. 1–56). Rowley, MA: Newbury House.
Bickerton, D. (1981). *Roots of language.* Ann Arbor, MI: Karoma Publishers.

Bickerton, D. (1984). The language bioprogram hypothesis. *Behavioral and Brain Sciences, 7,* 173–221.

Bresson, F. (1974). Remarks on genetic psycholinguistics: The acquisition of the article system in French. *Problemes actuels en psycholinguistique* (pp. 67–72). Paris: Centre Nationale de la Recherche Scientifique.

Brown, R. (1973). *A first language: The early stages.* Cambridge, MA: Harvard University Press.

Cziko, G. (1986). Testing the language bioprogram hypothesis. *Language, 62* (4), 878–898.

Emslie, H. C., & Stevenson, R. J. (1981). Preschool children's use of the articles in definite and indefinite referring expressions. *Journal of Child Language, 8,* 313–328.

Garton, A. F. (1983). An approach to the study of determiners in early language development. *Journal of Psycholinguistic Research 12,* 513–25.

Gilbert, G. (1983). Transfer in second language acquisition. In R. Andersen (Ed.), *Pidginization and creolization as language acquisition* (pp. 168–180). Rowley, MA: Newbury House.

Huebner, T. (1983). *A longitudinal analysis of the acquisition of English.* Ann Arbor, MI: Karoma Publishers.

Karmiloff-Smith, A. (1979) *A functional approach to child language: A study of determiners and reference.* Cambridge: Cambridge University Press.

Maratsos, M. (1976). *The use of definite and indefinite reference in young children.* Cambridge: Cambridge University Press.

Meisel, J. (1983). Strategies of second language acquisition: More than one type of simplification. In R. Andersen (Ed.), *Pidginization and creolization as language acquisition* (pp. 120–157). Rowley, MA: Newbury House.

Schumann, J. (1978). *The pidginization process.* Rowley, MA: Newbury House.

Slobin, D. I. (1973). Cognitive prerequisites for the development of grammar. In C. A. Ferguson & D. I. Slobin (Eds.), *Studies in child language development* (pp. 175–208). New York: Holt, Rinehart and Winston.

Slobin, D. I. (1985). Cross-linguistic evidence for the language-making capacity. In D. I. Slobin (Ed.), *The cross-linguistic study of language acquisition* (pp. 1159–1249). Hillsdale, NJ: Lawrence Erlbaum.

Warden, D. A. (1976). The influence of context on children's use of identifying expressions and references. *British Journal of Psychology, 67,* 101–112.

CHAPTER 4

Assessing an Interaction-Based Paradigm
How Accommodative Should We Be?

JANE ZUENGLER

1. INTRODUCTION

In the last several years, Giles' Speech Accommodation Theory (SAT) (Bourhis & Giles, 1977; Giles, 1973; Giles & Smith, 1979) has received attention in the second-language acquisition (SLA) literature as a paradigm for explaining second-language (L2) performance variation. A number of data-based studies (e.g., Beebe & Zuengler, 1983; Zuengler, 1982) have illustrated the need to draw on SAT for an understanding of speech shifts observed in L2 speakers, and Beebe and Giles (1984) agree, arguing that SAT subsumes both first language (L1) and L2 variation.

No one, however, is suggesting that SAT is the only explanation for L2, or L1, sociolinguistic variation. For that reason, it is important to assess its extent of application to performance variation and, for our interests, to L2 performance in particular. This chapter has that as its purpose. Focusing on data collected in a study of native speaker (NS)–nonnative speaker (NNS) interactions, I critically assess the viability of SAT for explaining the performance of NNSs in interactions with NSs. As the findings are presented, it is argued that they reveal limitations in the applicability of SAT (1) because NS–NNS interactions are in some respects different from NS–NS interactions and (2) because NS–NNS interactions are in some respects *the same as* NS–NS interactions.

JANE ZUENGLER • Department of English, University of Wisconsin–Madison, Madison, Wisconsin 53706.

2. BACKGROUND

First presented in the 1970s by Howard Giles, SAT combines several already developed social psychological theories to explain why speakers vary their speech (i.e., make accommodations) in interactions with others. According to SAT, speech shifts occur as speakers express their values and intentions to their interlocutors. Shifts are described as "convergence" or "divergence," which can be actual or intended. Convergence involves speakers modifying their speech to become more similar to their interlocutors, while divergence occurs when speakers maintain or emphasize their linguistic differences. It is beyond the scope of this chapter to present a detailed discussion of the theory; the reader is referred instead to Giles (1973), Giles and Smith (1979), and Beebe and Giles (1984).

Within the field of SLA, several studies exist which have been conducted within an SAT framework (Berkowitz, Chapter 7, this volume; Zuengler, 1982, 1985, 1987), have drawn, in part, on SAT (Young, 1987), or have reinterpreted data from an SAT perspective (Beebe & Zuengler, 1983). Two studies have shown that SAT can explain L2 performance variation as a function of the salience of ethnicity in an interaction. Zuengler (1982) asked native Greek and Spanish-speaking subjects to respond, in English, to an Anglo speaker who made remarks threatening to their ethnic identity. Subjects' responses were analyzed with respect to their production of three phonological variables. Results indicated that there was variation according to the nature of response. That is, the subjects who provided a very personal response, and/or made clear reference to their ethnic group in their answer, produced fewer correct sounds. The other subjects, those who responded to the Anglo's threats by objectifying their answer (i.e., by speaking in the third person), and who made no clear reference to their particular ethnic group, produced more correct sounds. The conclusion was that some of the subjects may have identified strongly as ethnic group members, and they defended their ethnic solidarity through making their L2 phonologically distinctive from that of the Anglo interlocutor. The other subjects, who increased in correctness, thereby making their speech more similar to the Anglo, might have been psychologically converging toward the target-language (TL) speaker.

In Beebe and Zuengler (1983), it was argued that data from Puerto Rican and Chinese–Thai children could be reinterpreted from an SAT perspective. Both groups of children varied their L2 production according to whether they were speaking to someone of their own ethnic group or to someone who was an "outsider." Phonological variation among the Chinese–Thai children was reported on. Beebe and Zuengler (1983) concluded that the children were accommodating to an interlocutor who shared their Chinese ethnicity, and they did so by making their L2 Thai pronunciation sound more Chinese. In reporting on the Puerto Rican children, the authors focused on the relative amount of talk between the children and their interviewers. The Puerto Rican children, it was argued, showed signs of accommodation; the more the interviewer talked, the more the child talked. When the interviewer spoke less, the child also spoke less. This, it was explained, illustrates convergence. Though the children converged toward all three of their interviewers, two of whom were also Hispanic and one who was Anglo, there was one interviewer with whom they showed somewhat less convergence. That interviewer was Hispanic, like the children. However, the children might have viewed her as possibly separate from their ethnic group, since she was English, and not Spanish dominant. It was felt that such a perception may have dampened their otherwise strong inclination to converge toward the interviewer.

As we have seen, both Zuengler (1982) and Beebe and Zuengler (1983) conclude that ethnicity may become salient in an interaction and, if so, can have an effect on the speaker's L2 performance. SAT, it is claimed, enables us to explain the adjustments that occur. In a 1987 study, Young basically supports SAT as an explanation for some of his subjects' performance variation, but he argues for a refinement of ethnicity as a factor. Young studied native Chinese speakers' production of English plurals. While Young (like Beebe & Zuengler, 1983) illustrates the influence of the L2 speakers' identification with their interlocutor, he suggests that what is important is not simply whether the interlocutor is from the L2 speaker's ethnic group or not, but how much the speaker identifies more generally with the interlocutor. Identification, according to Young, is the result of the speaker and interlocutor converging socially on a number of factors (e.g., education, native country, gender, etc.), of which only one may be shared ethnicity. Young found that ethnicity of the interlocutor alone did not lead to significant L2 variation in plural production.

Research by Zuengler (1985, 1987) differed from that just reported in that it investigated the speech performance of both NNSs and NSs who were interacting with each other. Outcomes of this research is explained below. The one remaining study which was conducted within an SAT framework is that of Berkowitz, which is discussed in Chapter 7 of this volume.

3. ASSESSING SAT WITH RESPECT TO L2 DATA

The discussion which follows is based on research reported in detail in Zuengler (1985). The study was originally conducted to address questions concerning phonological variation (see also Zuengler, 1987). In addition, further analyses of the same data set were conducted on other measures of language use. The expanded analysis enables us to critically assess the limits of a theory such as SAT within the context of the study in question.

3.1. Background and Procedure of the Study

The study which produced the data to be discussed was a partial replication of a set of L1 studies conducted by Thakerar, Giles, and Cheshire (1982), which followed the SAT paradigm. Thakerar *et al.* sought to determine whether unequal status (i.e., relative to one's interlocutor) had an effect on speech. They operationalized status as relative conversance with the conversational topic or task. Setting up dyads of equal-status interlocutors and dyads of unequal-status interlocutors, the researchers analyzed several speech measures. Results showed an effect of relative status on speech. The low-status interlocutors shifted toward more standard speech, while the high-status interlocutors shifted toward less standard speech. Using SAT for their explanation, the researchers concluded that the shifts reflected the interlocutors' attempts to converge toward each other's speech.

The present study was an effort to determine whether status imbalance would affect NS–NNS interactions as it affected the NS–NS interactions in the Thakerar *et al.* research. Following one of the Thakerar *et al.* studies, "status" was operationalized as relative expertise on a task. Four of the hypotheses of the study stemmed from the outcomes of the phonological analysis in the Thakerar *et al.* research. It was predicted that, relative to a control group in which subjects were not informed of their expertise,

(1) NSs who were "experts" in NS–NSS dyads would show a decrease in L1 standardness.
(2) NSs who were "nonexperts" in NS–NNS dyads would show an increase in L1 standardness.
(3) NNSs who were "experts" in NS–NNS dyads would show a decrease in L2 correctness.
(4) NNSs who were "nonexperts" in NS–NNS dyads would show an increase in L2 correctness.

The rationale for constructing parallel hypotheses for NSs and NNSs was that the research literature illustrates that some of the same factors which cause NSs to shift along a continuum of standardness (e.g., attention to speech, characteristics of the interlocutor) will cause NNSs to shift along a continuum of correctness (see e.g., Beebe, 1980; Dickerson, 1974; Tarone, 1979, 1984). What was of interest was determining whether relative "expertise" was another such factor.

Ninety adult subjects, comprising 45 NS–NNS dyads, participated in the study. All were female, and the NNSs were native speakers of Spanish. An effort was made to include only NSs who had acquired, as their vernacular, the dialect of the greater New York City area. Additionally, none of them were involved in the teaching profession. The NNSs were judged to be at intermediate level or above in English. Insofar as possible, each NS–NNS pair was matched according to social class (using the Hall–Jones Scale of Occupational Prestige; see Oppenheim, 1966, pp. 275–284). The interlocutors were strangers to each other, and, for reasons which will become obvious, none were art majors.

Each member of each dyad performed, individually, a section of the Meier Art Test of Aesthetic Perception (1963). This involves aesthetic judgments of sets of four slightly different pictures; the subject is asked to rank them from "best" to "worst." Following that, each NS–NNS dyad had a 10- minute conversation about the pictures (without their answer sheets). Then, each member was asked to complete a second section of the test, again individually. When they finished, the dyads were randomly assigned to one of two experimental conditions or to the control group. "Expertise" was induced by telling each of the subjects in the experimental conditions how they had performed on the test. In Condition A, the NS was told, in her partner's presence, that she (the NS) had gotten a low score on the test (41% of 100%)—low with respect to the judgments of the art experts who constructed the test. Her NNS partner was told that she (the NNS) had gotten a high score, 86%, on the test. (These scores were manipulations and did not reflect the subjects' actual performance.) The low scorer, that is, the relative "nonexpert," was the NS in Condition A. Her NNS partner was the relative "expert." Condition B was the opposite: the NS was the relative expert, while the NNS was the relative nonexpert. Dyads in the control group were not told how they had performed on the test.

Then, each dyad was asked to have a second 10- minute conversation about the pictures (again, without their answer sheets). Both Conversations 1 and 2 were audiotaped.[1] After the conversation ended, subjects filled out a questionnaire (in Spanish for the NNSs, English for the NSs), which asked them, among other things, to rate how they had performed on the test, relative to their partner. This question was included to ascertain whether the subjects believed the score manipulations. Results revealed that they had; the reader desiring additional information is referred to Zuengler (1985).

To test the hypotheses, four phonological variables were selected for the NSs and five for the NNSs. The NS variables, drawn from Labov (1966), were (dh)[2] and (th), the voiced and voiceless interdental fricatives, respectively; (r) in preconsonantal and word-final positions; and (oh), the midback vowel found

---

[1] The audio recorder used for the taping was a reel-to-reel Uher Report Stereo IC. Two external, standing microphones (one, a Uher M517, and the other, a SONY) were positioned within view of the subjects, about 12–16 inches from their side.

[2] In referring to linguistic variables, we follow Labov (1966, 1972). The symbols ( ) and [ ] are used; ( ) represents a phonological variable which has various phonetic realizations. The actual phonetic realizations exist along a continuum; [ ] represents a given phonetic realization of the variable. The symbols as used here are sociolinguistic symbols.

in such words as *off*. In the NNS speech, the five variables were (dh); (r); (CC), word-final consonant clusters; the central vowel (uh), found in *up;* and the low front vowel (eh), found in *ask*. (The first three were selected because previous literature indicates they can undergo social conditioning, while the remaining items were chosen when a preliminary analysis revealed that they exhibited variation.) Data were analyzed by determining each subject's degree of standardness/correctness on the selected variable in Conversation 1 and Conversation 2 and the comparing performance in each experimental group with that of the control group. The total NS corpus analyzed exceeded 12,000 tokens, while the NNS corpus exceeded 18,000 tokens.

3.2. Results

The outcome of the phonological analysis was that relative expertise exerted an effect on only one variable produced by the NSs and one produced by the NNSs; for both groups, the effect was confined to the relative nonexperts. In other words, the significant shifts which occurred related to only two of the four hypotheses, namely, (2) and (4), and they only involved two of the variables. Of the four variables analyzed for the NSs, it was only the (oh), among the nonexperts, which underwent significant change. That is, a significant proportion of "perceived nonexperts" increased in standardness of (oh).[3] The Fisher Test of Exact Probability (see Siegel, 1956) indicated $p = .0535698$ (cell freqs = 2, 13, 14, 3; marginal freqs = 7, 15, 6, 16; total $N = 22$). Shifts in (dh), (th), and (r) were nonsignificant. Figure 1 illustrates the limited support found for hypothesis (2) in performance on (oh). Note the difference in proportions of group which increased in standardness.

With respect to the NNS nonexperts, only one of the five variables analyzed, (r), revealed a significant pattern. However, the pattern was not that which was predicted by hypothesis (4). Instead of shifting toward greater L2 correctness on (r), the NNS nonexperts significantly *failed to increase* in correctness (Fisher test, using a table of approximations: $p < .05$; cell freqs = 0, 13, 4, 7; marginal freqs = 13, 11, 4, 20; total $N = 24$). Figure 2 illustrates the NNSs' performance. Note the difference in proportions of group increasing in correctness.

Relative expertise, as we have seen, did have an effect on the pronunciation of both the NSs and NNSs in this study, although the effect was limited.

---

[3] "Perceived" refers to one of two ways in which the subjects were grouped for analysis. To take individual differences into account, it was decided to group the subjects according to the original research design (i.e., Conditions A and B as induced by the researcher), as well as according to how the subjects themselves reported their performance on the questionnaire (i.e., their "perceived" expertise). In the case of (oh), which we are reporting here, it was only the "perceived" grouping (and not the induced grouping) which produced noteworthy results.

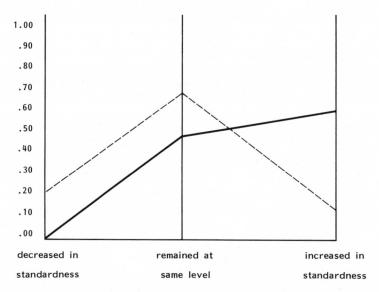

Figure 1. Comparison of NS "perceived nonexperts' " performance ($n = 7$; solid line) with the control group's performance ($n = 15$; dashed line) on (oh), Conversation 1 to 2 (n is small for perceived nonexperts because for some NSs, there were insufficient tokens for analysis).

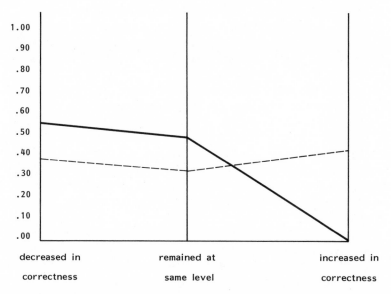

Figure 2. Comparison of NNS "nonexperts' " performance ($n = 13$; solid line) with the control group's performance ($n = 11$; dashed line) on (r), Conversation 1 to 2.

It only affected subjects who were nonexperts, and it led to a change in performance on only two of the nine variables analyzed. In the case of the NSs, the
significant pattern of shift on (oh) supported hypothesis (2), and as such, was
consistent with the outcome of the phonological analysis in Thakerar *et al.*
(1982). However, the pattern of performance on (r), which was significant for
the NN nonexperts, did not correspond to the predicted pattern in hypothesis
(4). In significantly *failing* to increase in correctness, the NNSs in this study
differed from both the NSs in this study and the NSs in the Thakerar *et al.*
(1982) study.

More recently, analyses were undertaken of additional performance measures in the NS–NNS interactions. Admittedly, phonological performance represents only a part of the subjects' overall performance. It is possible that though
there was not much significant shifting phonologically, subjects might have
made accommodative adjustments in other aspects of performance (H. Giles,
personal communication, April 16, 1986).

The next measure to be reported is speech rate, which was also analyzed
in the Thakerar *et al.* research. It will be recalled that their high-status subjects
decreased their speech rate, while their low-status subjects increased their speech
rate. Though it was not explicitly stated, one can assume that the subjects, all
L1 speakers, had similar speech rates prior to their increase or decrease in rate.
Not surprisingly, the present data reveal differences in rate for NNSs versus
NSs. Speech rate was calculated for the present data by following Thakerar *et
al.*'s formula: total number of words spoken divided by the total time spent
speaking. Comparisons of NNSs with NSs reveal that in both Conversations 1
and 2, the NNSs in the control group, Condition A, and Condition B spoke
significantly more slowly than the NSs. Table 1 lists the average speech rate
for each group in each conversation.

What was important to determine in the present data, however, was not
NS–NNS speech-rate differences but whether there were changes in rate by the
NNSs, and NSs, from Conversation 1 to Conversation 2. If the subjects in this
study followed a pattern similar to those in Thakerar *et al.*, we would expect
to see the nonexperts (i.e., the NSs in Condition A and NNSs in Condition B)
increasing their speech rate from Conversation 1 to 2 and the experts (i.e., the
NNSs in Condition A and NSs in Condition B) decreasing their speech rate
from the first conversation to the second. Table 2 charts the results of the
analysis.

As we can see, there are no clear differences between the control group
and conditions; nor are there any apparent differences between NSs and NNSs.

Table 2, however, fails to show possible patterns of shift within dyads.
That is, taking the NSs in Condition A as an example, we see that there were
four NSs who increased in speech rate; the existing information, though, does
not tell us what their particular NNS partners did. The figures for overall NSs

Table 1. Average Speech Rates in Words per Second

	Control group		Condition A (NNS "experts")		Condition B (NS "experts")	
	NSs	NNSs	NSs	NNSs	NSs	NNSs
Conversation 1	2.90	2.21**	2.97	2.24**	3.08	2.29*
	(.329)	(.403)	(.320)	(.498)	(.540)	(.493)
Conversation 2	2.84	2.23*	2.85	2.29*	2.98	2.36*
	(.403)	(.379)	(.263)	(.681)	(.473)	(.421)

Note. $n = 12$ in each cell; standard deviations are in parentheses.
*$p < .005$, one-tailed t test of correlated groups.
**$p < .0005$, one-tailed t test of correlated groups.

and NNSs in each group might mask patterns of convergence of divergence occurring within dyads. Therefore, the analysis of speech rate was carried further to investigate possible convergence or divergence. Figures 3 and 4 schematize patterns of convergence and divergence we would expect to find if our subjects performed similar to those in Thakerar et al. (1982).

As Figure 3 shows, linguistic divergence would be the outcome if our subjects' performance in Condition A corresponded to that of Thakerar et al. In Condition B, however, due to the different baseline speech rates, linguistic convergence would be predicted (Figure 4).

With the predicted patterns in mind, 12 dyads each in conditions A and B were analyzed for speech-rate divergence in the former and convergence in the latter. Results showed no tendencies as predicted (or opposite those predicted): only 1 of the 12 dyads in Condition A exhibited divergence, and only 3 of the 12 dyads in Condition B exhibited convergence.

Table 2. Number of Subjects Shifting Their Speech Rate by an Increase or a Decrease from Conversation 1 to 2

	Control group		Condition A (NNS "experts")		Condition B (NS "experts")	
	Increase	Decrease	Increase	Decrease	Increase	Decrease
NSs	7	5	4	8	5	6
					(No change = 1)	
NNSs	7	5	6	6	6	6

Note. $n = 12$ in each cell.

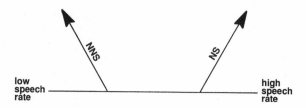

Figure 3. Predicted patterns of shift in speech rate in Condition A (with NNS "experts").

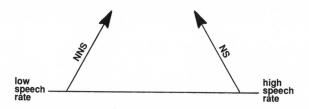

Figure 4. Predicted patterns of shift in speech rate in Condition B (with NS "experts").

3.3. Discussion

The results of the analyses of phonological variables and speech rate enable us to argue that (at least with respect to subjects in the present study) important differences between NS–NNS interactions and NS–NS interactions call into question the applicability of an SAT paradigm as conceptualized in the Thakerar *et al.* (1982) study. Phonological variation and speech rate, the two measures of objective speech performance which Thakerar *et al.* argue undergo modification in their NS–NS dyads, revealed limited, or very different, outcomes in the data just presented.

Speech rate, you will recall, did not undergo any significant modification in the present study. That is because the differences illustrated in Figure 3 might be fundamental. Whereas the subjects in Thakerar *et al.* presumably started out with approximately the same speech rate (i.e., their baseline was the same), the subjects in the present study had clearly different baseline speech rates. We saw, in Table 1, that the NNSs consistently spoke significantly more slowly than the NSs. The different speech rates exhibited in Conversation 1 put constraints on the performance of both NSs and NNSs, which they were, at some level, aware of. While we cannot prove it, there is no reason to believe that the NNSs were speaking more slowly out of choice; they paused often, and many made remarks like "this is difficult for me," and "I don't know how to say this." It seems that many were simply not able to speak as quickly as their NS partners. If so, this constraint would explain why the NNS nonexperts did not increase their speech rate (they couldn't), and it might also explain why the NS nonexperts did not increase theirs: they were already speaking significantly faster than the NNSs. The NNS experts wouldn't be motivated to decrease their speech rate when they were already speaking much more slowly than their partners. The only subjects whom we might still expect to modify their speech rate are the NS experts, but they did not reduce it as predicted. Perhaps that is because, given all of the foregoing reasons, speech rate was not "chosen" by the NS–NNS dyads in this study as a mechanism of speech accommodation.

Phonological modifications, as we saw, occurred to a limited extent, and not solely as predicted. These results, like the data on speech rate, reflect important differences between NS–NNS and NS–NS interactions, and they point up consequent limitations in the applicability of SAT. None of the subjects who were experts (NSs or NNSs) made the decreases in standardness/correctness which were predicted. Thakerar et al.'s explanation for a decrease was that those in a higher status position, having the self-esteem which accompanies it, would attempt to make their speech more comprehensible to their partners. However, for the NS experts in the present study, the nonnativeness of their partners may have been a consideration. Making their speech less standard wouldn't necessarily have made it more comprehensible to the NNSs. In fact, it might have caused less comprehension. And, for the NNS experts as well, a decrease (in correctness) could have led to less comprehensibility, not more. In the interests of maintaining comprehensibility, the experts might have refrained from shifting phonologically.

It was only the nonexpert position which showed (albeit limited) effects of relative "expertise." And, the effect was different for the NNSs than it was for the NSs. That the effect was limited, and was manifested in dissimilar patterns for NNSs and NSs, may indicate that a different dynamic is operating in NS–NNS interactions. Intergroup dynamics may have become more salient. Beebe and Giles (1984) suggest that a dynamic affecting NS–NNS interactions is that of differential linguistic status. Interlocutors may be unequal with respect to different levels of proficiency in the language; NSs' native command of the language might give them the controlling position in an interaction with NNSs. If the NSs in the present study did indeed perceive the NNSs as lower in linguistic status, while the NNSs perceived the NSs as higher, then any other potential status determinants (such as relative expertise) could have been weakened. That could explain why we found only a very limited effect among the NSs.

The different and limited pattern that we found for the NNSs could also be explained by taking ethnolinguistic differences into account. The significant failure to increase correctness of (r) by NNS nonexperts could be a manifestation of the NNSs' simply "giving up." As we suggested above, NNSs in many

NS–NNS interactions may be automatically assigned lower linguistic status. Additionally, we have evidence that native English speakers tend to judge Hispanic speakers as being less competent in general (e.g., Carranza, 1982). Consequently, being told that they did less well than their NS interlocutors may have seemed, for the NNS nonexperts, just another confirmation of their lower status. Hence, they might have simply given up with respect to their pronunciation of correct (r). (Though it was statistically nonsignificant, there was a similar pattern, for the other variables, of failure to increase in correctness.)

What the analyses of phonology and speech rate reveal is that, for the reasons given above, there are important qualitative differences between NS–NNS and NS–NS interactions. The existence of such differences means that the dynamics which are salient in NS–NNS interactions are not necessarily the same as those salient in NS–NS interactions. Consequently, SAT appears limited in its applicability to the present data.

3.4. A Further Analysis

The assertion by Beebe and Giles (1984) that, due to ethnolingusitic differences, NS–NNS interactions exhibit NS control led to our suggesting above that that might explain why the measures important in Thakerar *et al* (1982) exhibited little or no accommodative patterns in the present study. That is, dominance (supposedly by the NS) may be a more influential dynamic in our NS–NNS dyads than accommodation is. To ascertain this, an analysis of measures of dominance is underway, and some preliminary results of the ongoing analysis is presented here.

It is beyond the scope of this chapter to review the literature on dominance. There is a large body of research, conducted from the perspectives of sociology, psychology, social psychology, and communications. However, almost all of it focuses on native speakers. The measures of dominance chosen for the present study are those which have the largest supporting literature, that is, amount of talk and interruptions (e.g., Ferguson, 1977; Leet-Pellegrini, 1980; Owsley & Scotton, 1984; Scherer, 1979; Wenzl, 1982; Wiemann, 1985; Zimmerman & West, 1975). In addition, several measures considered in a recent NNS–NNS study by Gass and Varonis (1986) are included.

Amount of talk was calculated for the NSs and NNSs, as part of the calculation of speech rate which we reported above. Since amount of talk is a well-established measure of dominance, it was also analyzed separately. The results are displayed as Table 3. What the table reveals is that in all groups and in both Conversations 1 and 2, the NSs talked significantly more than their NNS partners.

In addition, gaining 'expert'' status led a significant number of NSs to increase their already greater amount of talk. Relative to the control group, a

Table 3. Average Amount of Talk in Number of Words

	Control group		Condition A (NNS "experts")		Condition B (NS "experts")	
	NSs	NNSs	NSs	NNSs	NSs	NNSs
Conversation 1	782	414***	782	461***	785	566*
	(193)	(207)	(206)	(232)	(199)	(221)
Conversation 2	708	384***	655	414**	775	445***
	(184)	(208)	(227)	(129)	(251)	(227)

Note. $n = 15$ in each cell; standard deviations are in parentheses.
*$p < .01$, one-tailed t test of correlated groups.
**$p < .005$, one-tailed t test of correlated groups.
***$p < .0005$, one-tailed t test of correlated groups.

significantly greater number of NS experts (i.e., Condition B) talked more in Conversation 2 than in Conversation 1 (Fisher test, using a table of approximations: $p < .005$; cell freqs $= 10, 5, 0, 15$; marginal freqs $= 15, 15, 10, 20$; total $N = 30$). (No such tendency occurred among NNS experts, however.)

Another measure of dominance is interruptions. The operational definition of interruptions was taken from West and Zimmerman (1977) and Scarcella (1983). To be classified as an interruption, the second speaker needed to begin at least one syllable away from a proper turn transition place. Overlaps and back-channel cues are not counted, as they are not considered dominance manifestations. Table 4 displays preliminary results. Successful as well as total interruptions have been calculated, as there is some argument that it is only successful interruptions which are valid indicators of dominance (e.g., Kennedy & Camden, 1983).

Preliminary outcomes displayed in Table 4 suggest that in the control group and Condition B (NS experts), the NNSs interrupt more often than their NS interlocutors, but they do so less successfully. However, when the NNSs became the relative experts (i.e., Condition A), they not only were more successful interrupters than they were in Conversation 1, but they succeeded beyond that of their NS partners (i.e., 93% successful versus 76% for the NSs).

The next measure to be reported is "moving the task along." In each conversation, it will be recalled, subjects were asked to discuss the various sets of pictures they had judged. The present analysis took note of which interlocutor moved the discussion to the next set of pictures (saying, for example, "What did you think of the next set?" or "Okay, now what about these?"). Sometimes this was done nonverbally (by paging ahead); in these cases, the analysis noted which interlocutor began talking about the set they had just turned to. Support for moving the task along can be found in Gass and Varonis (1986;

Table 4. Number of Interruptions by NSs and NNSs

	Conversation 1		Conversation 2	
	Total	Proportion successful	Total	Proportion successful
Control group				
by NSs	54	.70	37	.73
by NNSs	87	.66	59	.61
Condition A				
by NSs	82	.89	58	.76
by NNSs	116	.81	87	.93
Condition B				
by NSs	48	.65	45	.80
by NNSs	73	.56	55	.67

Note. Control group, $n = 10$ dyads; Condition A, $n = 15$ dyads; Condition B, $n = 10$ dyads.

they refer to it as "leading") and Scollon and Scollon (1981). Results are listed in Table 5 (due to small numbers, no statistical tests have been conducted).

What the table illustrates is that in the control group and in Condition B, more NSs than NNSs moved the task along. They displayed this dominating behavior in both conversations. When the NNSs were made experts, though, the pattern was reversed. Then, a greater number of NNSs than NSs moved the task along (9 versus 6).

Table 5. Number of Subjects Moving the Task Along

	Conversation 1	Conversation 2
Control group		
NSs	9	8
NNSs	5	5
Equal[a]	1	2
Condition A		
NSs	6	6
NNSs	7	9
Equal	2	0
Condition B		
NSs	9	11
NNSs	4	3
Equal	2	1

[a] "Equal" refers to the number of dyads in which the task was moved along an equal number of times by the NS and NNS.

The final measure of dominance to be reported concerns who won the speaking turn when both interlocutors started speaking simultaneously (see Gass & Varonis, 1986). The results are listed in Table 6. The numbers are small because simultaneous turn initiation was not that frequent an occurrence. Nevertheless, one can see that, generally, the "turn winners" were quite evenly divided, with the exception of the NNS experts (i.e., Condition A). In Conversation 2, the NNS experts clearly dominated with respect to winning more turns (i.e., 8 of 10 simultaneously initiated turns).

3.5. Discussion

In the foregoing discussion of the data on phonological variables and speech rate, it was suggested that important qualitative differences between NS–NNS and NS–NS interactions might explain why so few effects were found in the accommodative measures which were analyzed. Limitations in NNS proficiency could explain the minimal (or absent) effects on pronunciation and speech rate. Additionally, it was suggested that what may be operating is an ethnolinguistic status differential which favors the NS (see Beebe & Giles, 1984) and thus represents a fundamental difference between NS–NNS and NS–NS interactions. Such a differential might prevent, or at least limit, any accommodative tendencies.

The results of the analysis just reported suggest that NS dominance was indeed apparent in many of the NS–NNS dyads. The data from the control group clearly reveal that when NSs and NNSs talked about a task, and were completely uninformed about their performance on it, the NSs dominated the conversation. The control group NSs talked more (Table 3), interrupted more successfully (Table 4), and took over with respect to moving the task along (Table 5). Such displays lend support to Beebe and Giles' (1984) assertion that

Table 6. Number of Subjects Who Won Simultaneous
Initiation of Turns

	Conversation 1	Conversation 2
Control group		
NSs	3	4
NNSs	2	2
Condition A		
NSs	4	2
NNSs	4	8
Condition B		
NSs	3	3
NNSs	5	3

ethnolinguistic differences lead to a status differential. It is this differential which was manifested in dominance behavior by the NSs in the control group. As such, it typifies an important difference between NS–NNS and NS–NS interactions.

However, dominance by the NSs in the control group does not in itself point up limitations of SAT in explaining performance in the present study. What must be considered is whether performance in the experimental conditions is different from that in the control group and, if so, whether SAT provides the best explanation. What the second set of results reveals is that (greater) "expertise" affects both NSs and NNSs, but it does so through dominance behavior rather than accommodative behavior.

First of all, there is evidence of dominating behavior by the NNS experts in Condition A. NNS experts led in moving the task along (Table 5), produced a greater proportion of successful interruptions than their NS partners did (Table 4), and almost won out when both interlocutors began a turn at the same time (Table 6). They did not speak more than their NS partners, however (Table 3). That was probably due to constraints on their proficiency, which was mentioned in the earlier analysis.

There was dominating behavior, as well, among the NS experts of Condition B. While their behavior may have been due to the same ethnolinguistic dynamic which, as suggested above, was operating among NSs in the control group, it appears that (greater) expertise exerted at least some effect as well. That is because there is evidence that the NSs in Condition B displayed even more dominating behavior than they did in the control group. Significantly more NS experts than controls increased their amount of talk from Conversation 1 to 2. In Conversation 2, more NS experts than controls moved the task along (Table 5). The preliminary results of the analysis of interruptions (Table 4) shows that NS experts produced a greater proportion of successful interruptions in Conversation 2 than the NS controls did.

All of the foregoing point up two main limitations of SAT in explaining performance in the present study or in the Thakerar *et al.* (1982) study. The first limitation is due to differences between NS–NNS and NS–NS interactions. In the present study, it was only the NS nonexperts who showed evidence of accommodation (and it was very limited), at least with respect to the measures on which Thakerar *et al.* built their accommodation argument, namely, speech rate and pronunciation standardness. The lack of much effect was probably due to the more limited linguistic proficiency of the NNS which, as argued, prevented the NNS from making accommodative moves. The ethnolinguistic differential affected the NSs' performance as well. It explains why the NSs did not display any accommodative behavior in terms of speech rate and only very limited accommodative behavior with respect to pronunciation. The ethnolinguistic differential also explains the NS dominance behavior which was observed in the control group. Clearly, linguistic proficiency is a factor differentiating NS–NNS from NS–NS interactions, and it may prevent or weaken any tendency toward accommodation.

A second limitation to SAT is one which is suggested by our NS–NNS results, but it needs to be investigated in NS–NS dyads as well. The dominating behavior exhibited by both NS and NNSs experts in the present study suggests that there might be several dynamics operating in expertise-salient interactions. One is dominance and another may be accommodation. The latter could be competing with, or stifled by, the former. Consequently, to explain performance in such interactions in accommodative terms alone, as Thakerar *et al.* (1982) have, is to risk missing an equally, or more important, dynamic underlying the subjects' language performance.

There is no reason to believe that NS–NNS interactions are any different from NS–NS interactions, with respect to a connection between relative expert status and displays of dominance. There is research on NS–NS interactions which shows at least some link between knowing more than one's interlocutor and displaying dominating behavior (see, e.g., Leet-Pellegrini, 1980). If Thakerar *et al.* (1982) had expanded their analysis beyond the boundaries of SAT, it is quite possible that dominance behavior could provide an important explanation for their subjects' performance as well.

4. CONCLUSION

Before drawing conclusions, several limitations to the study must be kept in mind. For control purposes, all of the subjects were women. However, research on NS–NS interactions indicates a relationship between dominance and gender (e.g., Leet-Pellegrini, 1980; Thorne & Henley, 1975). Therefore, NS–NNS dyads composed of males, or of both genders, might lead to quite different results. Outcomes concerning dominance behavior in the NS–NNS dyads of this study must remain tentative, since they are limited to females. Another limitation concerns the data on simultaneous turn initiation (Table 6). This measure did not occur very frequently, and consequently, any patterns apparent should be considered inconclusive.

Nevertheless, it is possible to suggest, at this point, some limitations in applying SAT to performance in NS–NNS interactions. One limitation stems from differences between NS–NNS and NS–NS interactions, while the other limitation is one which both types of interactions may share. While SAT may be one of the most explanatory theories for L2 performance variation (Beebe & Zuengler, 1983; Zuengler, 1982), it does not offer a comprehensive explanation if other dynamics are operating within the same interaction. To capture the extent of L2 performance variation and ultimately attempt to explain it, we must consider multiple language measures, and multiple, interaction-based theories as explanations. It is misguided to search for one comprehensive theory, since one theory will most likely be insufficient in explaining the complexity of performance variation we are already beginning to see in NS–NNS interactions.

REFERENCES

Beebe, L. M. (1980). Sociolinguistic variation and style shifting in second language acquisition. *Language Learning, 30*, 433–448.

Beebe, L. M., & Giles, H. (1984). Speech-accommodation theories: a discussion in terms of second-language acquisition. *International Journal of the Sociology of Language, 46*, 5–32.

Beebe, L. M., & Zuengler, J. (1983). Accommodation Theory: an explanation for style shifting in second language dialects. In N. Wolfson & E. Judd (Eds.), *Sociolinguistics and language acquisition* (pp. 195–213). Rowley, MA: Newbury House.

Bourhis, R. Y., & Giles, H. (1977). The language of intergroup distinctiveness. In H. Giles (Ed.), *Language, ethnicity and intergroup relations* (pp. 119–135). London: Academic Press.

Carranza, M. Z. (1982). Attitudinal research on Hispanic language varieties. In E. B. Ryan & H. Giles (Eds.), *Attitudes towards language variation* (pp. 63–83). London: Edward Arnold.

Dickerson, L. J. (1974). *Internal and external patterning of phonological variability in the speech of Japanese learners of English: toward a theory of second-language acquisition.* Unpublished doctoral dissertation, University of Illinois at Urbana-Champaign.

Ferguson, N. (1977). Simultaneous speech, interruptions and dominance. *Journal of Social and Clinical Psychology, 16*, 295–302.

Gass, S. M., & Varonis, E. M. (1986). Sex differences in nonnative speaker–nonnative speaker interactions. In R. R. Day (Ed.), *Talking to learn: Conversation in second language acquisition* (pp. 327–351). Rowley, MA: Newbury House.

Giles, H. (1973). Accent mobility: A model and some data. *Anthropological Linguistics, 15*, 87–105.

Giles, H., & Smith, P. (1979). Accommodation theory: Optimal levels of convergence. In H. Giles & R. N. St. Clair (Eds.), *Language and social psychology* (pp. 45–65). Baltimore: University Park Press.

Kennedy, C. W., & Camden, C. T. (1983). A new look at interruptions. *Western Journal of Speech Communication, 47*, 45–58.

Labov, W. (1966). *The social stratification of English in New York City.* Washington, DC: Center for Applied Linguistics.

Labov, W. (1972). *Sociolinguistic patterns.* Philadelphia: University of Pennsylvania Press.

Leet-Pellegrini, H. M. (1980). Conversational dominance as a function of gender and expertise. In H. Giles, W. P. Robinson, & P. Smith (Eds.), *Language: Social psychological perspectives* (pp. 97–104). Elmsford, NY: Pergamon Press.

The Meier Art Tests. II. Aesthetic perception. (1963). Based on research of N. C. Meier, Ph.D., University of Iowa. Chicago: Stoelting Co. (Preliminary Manual, 1967).

Oppenheim, A. N. (1966). *Questionnaire design and attitude measurement.* New York: McGraw-Hill.

Owsley, H. H., & Scotton, C. M. (1984). The conversational expression of power by television interviewers. *The Journal of Social Psychology, 123*(2), 261–271.

Scarcella, R. C. (1983). Discourse accent in second language performance. In S. M. Gass & L. Selinker (Eds.), *Language transfer in language learning* (pp. 306–326). Rowley, MA: Newbury House.

Scherer, K. R. (1979). Personality markers in speech. In K. R. Scherer & H. Giles (Eds.), *Social markers in speech* (pp. 147–209). Cambridge: Cambridge University Press.

Scollon, R., & Scollon, S. B. K. (1981). *Narrative, literacy and face in interethnic communication.* Norwood, NJ: Ablex.

Siegel, S. (1956). *Nonparametric statistics for the behavioral sciences.* New York: Mcgraw-Hill.

Tarone, E. (1979). Interlanguage as chameleon. *Language Learning, 29,* 181–191.

Tarone, E. (1984). On the variability of interlanguage systems. In F. R. Eckman, L. H. Bell, & D. Nelson (Eds.), *Universals of second language acquisition* (pp. 3–23). Rowley, MA: Newbury House.

Thakerar, J. N., Giles, H., & Cheshire, J. (1982). Psychological and linguistic parameters of speech accommodation theory. In C. Fraser & K. R. Scherer (Eds.), *Advances in the social psychology of language* (pp. 205–255). Cambridge: Cambridge University Press.

Thorne, B., & Henley, N. (Eds.) (1975). *Language and sex: Difference and dominance.* Rowley, MA: Newbury House.

Wenzl, P. A. (1982). *An investigation of the interrelationships of four measures of human dominance.* Unpublished doctoral dissertation, Tulane University, New Orleans.

West. C., & Zimmerman, D. H. (1977). Woman's place in everyday talk: Reflections on parent–child interactions. *Social Problems, 24,* 521–529.

Wiemann, J. M. (1985). Power, status and dominance: interpersonal control and regulation in conversation. In R. L. Street & J. N. Cappella (Eds.), *Sequence and pattern in communicative behaviour* (pp. 85–102). London: Edward Arnold.

Young, R. (1987, April). *Variation and the interlanguage hypothesis.* Paper presented at the Annual TESOL Conference, Miami, Florida.

Zimmerman, D. H., & West, C. (1975). Sex roles, interruptions and silences in conversation. In B. Thorne & N. Henley (Eds.), *Language and sex: Difference and dominance* (pp. 105–129). Rowley, MA: Newbury House.

Zuengler, J. (1982). Applying Accommodation Theory to variable performance data in L2. *Studies in Second Language Acquisition, 4,* 181–192.

Zuengler, J. (1985). *The effect of induced and perceived expertise on the language performance of native and nonnative speakers.* Unpublished doctoral dissertation, Teachers College, Columbia University.

Zuengler, J. (1987). Effects of "expertise" in interactions between native and non-native speakers. *Language & Communication, 7*(2), 123–137.

PART II

Adjustment in Native and Nonnative Discourse

CHAPTER 5

Incorporated Repairs in
Nonnative Discourse

SUSAN M. GASS AND EVANGELINE MARLOS VARONIS

1. INTRODUCTION

Nearly a century ago, Henry Sweet[1] noted that

> conversation in a foreign language may be regarded from two very different points
> of view: (1) as an end in itself, and (2) as a means of learning the language and
> testing the pupil's knowledge of it. But there is, of course, no reason why the second
> process should not be regarded as being at the same time a preparation for the first.
> (1899/1964, p. 219)

While the importance of conversation to second-language (L2) acquisition has
long been recognized, it is only recently that it has been the major focus of
analysis. In particular, current research in L2 acquisition emphasizes the role
of negotiated interaction between native speaker (NS) and nonnative (NNS)
speaker in the development of a second language (Brock, Crookes, Day, &
Long, 1986; Bruton & Samuda, 1980; Chun, Day, Chenoweth, & Luppescu,
1982; Day, Chenoweth, Chun, & Luppescu, 1984; Ellis, 1985; Long, 1983;
Long & Porter, 1985; Pica, 1988; Scarcella & Higa, 1981; Varonis & Gass,
1985a and 1985b). Thus, the current view of the role of conversation in L2
learning differs noticeably from an earlier view of acquisition that held that
learners learned grammatical rules and then practiced them within a conversa-

---

[1]We thank Kumar Balsabrumanian (n.d.) for bringing the work of Sweet and others to our
attention.

SUSAN M. GASS • Department of English, Michigan State University, East Lansing, Michigan
48824.   EVANGELINE MARLOS VARONIS • University of Akron, Akron, Ohio 44325.

tional setting; classroom drills, classroom interactions, and daily interactions with NSs were considered important only as a means of reinforcing the grammatical rules acquired by a learner.

In 1975, Wagner-Gough and Hatch suggested a different role for conversation in second-language acquisition. They argued that conversational interaction forms the *basis* for the development of syntax rather than being only a forum for practice of grammatical structures. Syntax, they claimed, developed out of conversation rather than the reverse. Hatch, Flashner, and Hunt (1986) argue that

> language clarifies and organizes experience and, conversely, that language grows out of experience. That is, the development of language is not completely preordained and internally driven. Thus, language is developed as a way of structuring experience as that experience takes place. In interactions, the discourse frames, the scripts for interactions develop: the language appropriate to the interaction builds on this development; and the language, in turn, refines the frame. (pp. 5–6)

Example (1) illustrates the way learning can take place within a conversational setting, as the learner in this case uses the conversation to further her own grammatical development. The example (from Ellis, 1985) is an excerpt from a conversation in which a teacher, a native speaker of English, is conversing in English with a native-speaking Punjabi child:

(1)

    NS: Do you want to look at the next picture? Yeah?
    NNS: Man
    NS: A man. And do you know what this is? A wall.
    NNS: A wall
    NS: Like that one there. A wall
    NNS: A wall, a wall
    NS: Yes. Now, can you see what the man is doing?
    NNS: A man wall
    NS: He's going into the wall

Prior to this point in time there were no examples of two-constituent utterances in this child's L2 discourse. As can be seen, the conversation itself provides the framework, or as Ellis states, "the breakthrough points," for a two-constituent utterance to develop. The teacher broke the task into parts and helped with the crucial vocabulary which finally enabled the child to juxtapose *man* and *wall,* as can be seen in her final utterance.

Ellis (1984) further states that

> interaction contributes to development because it is the means by which the learner is able to crack the code. This takes place when the learner can infer what is said even though the message contains linguistic items that are not yet part of his competence and when the learner can use the discourse to help him modify or supplement the linguistic knowledge he has already used in production. (p. 95)

From this perspective, namely, that of language development arising from conversation, stems a number of studies in which second-language conversational interactions are the object of investigation. At the center of this research is Krashen's (1980) notion of comprehensible input. He claims that in order for acquisition to take place, the input to the learner has to be comprehensible at the $i+1$ level, where i represents the current linguistic stage of the learner and $i+1$, the stage just beyond. Given the central role of input in acquisition, it becomes increasingly important in L2 research to understand the nature of the input. To that end a number of recent studies have investigated the modified input directed to NNSs, a phenomenon also referred to as foreigner talk (see Hatch, 1983, for a list of many of the most salient features).

The importance of the role of comprehensible input is not in dispute; however, the degree to which second-language development can be attributed to comprehensible input alone is a matter of continuing debate. Gass (1988) argues that the significant concept is not comprehensible input but comprehend*ed* input (see also Krashen, 1982, p. 33), shifting the focus, therefore, from the speaker (usually a NS) to the hearer. Swain (1985) similarly argues that comprehensible input is not a sufficient condition for successful language learning as Krashen (e.g., 1982) claims. She proposes that what is needed is comprehensible *output*. By this she means that without the opportunity for language production (in particular, interaction), successful learning will not take place. Speaking in a second language provides an opportunity for the learner to test hypotheses he or she may have about the L2 (Schachter, 1984). Additionally, as Swain points out, in production the learner is pushed from semantic to syntactic processing of the language. In comprehending language, it is possible for a learner not to "understand" the syntax of a comprehended utterance, while in production, the learner is forced to impose some syntactic structure on an utterance.

In 1980, Long made an important distinction between modified input and modified interaction, thus differentiating between the modified talk directed to the learner and the modified structure of the conversation itself. His interactional features include such aspects of conversation as comprehension checks, topic shifts, and clarification requests. Examples (2) and (3) show modified input and modified interaction, respectively:

(2) Modified input (from Gass & Varonis, 1985):

    (a) Greater specificity

        NNS: How have increasing food costs changed your eating habits?

        NS: Well, I don't know that it's changed *them*. I try to adjust.

        NNS: Pardon me?

        NS: I don't think it's changed *my eating habits*. (emphasis ours)

    (b) Greater elaboration

        NNS: There has been a lot of talk lately about additives and preservatives in food. In what ways has this changed your eating habits?

NS: I try to stay away from nitrites.

NNS: Pardon me?

NS: Uh, from nitrites in uh *like lunch meats and that sort of thing.* I don't eat those. (emphasis ours)

(3) Examples of modified interaction:

(a) Abrupt topic shift (from Long, 1983)

NS: Are you going to visit San Francisco? Or Las Vegas?

NNS: Yes, I went to Disneyland and to Knottsberry Farm.[2]

NS: Oh, yeah?

(b) *Or*-choice questions (from Long, 1983)

NS: Well, what are you doing in the United States? Are you just studying? Or do you have a job?

Or—

NNS: No, I have a job.

(c) Comprehension check (from Varonis & Gass, 1985a)

NNS(1): . . . declares her ingress

NNS(2): Ingless?

NNS(1): Yes, if for example, if you, when you work you had an ingress.[3] You know?

In his work, Long showed that conversations involving NNSs show a greater incidence of interactional modifications than do conversations between only NSs. He argues that this is so for two reasons: first, these devices aid in avoiding conversational trouble, and second, they serve the function of repairing the discourse when trouble does occur. This work has been furthered by Scarcella and Higa (1981), and Varonis and Gass (1985a), who have argued that the interactional feature of negotiation of meaning is important to the second-language acquisition process.

Varonis and Gass (1985a) found that conversational dyads involving NNSs included significantly more instances of negotiation than did dyads including only NSs of a language. Furthermore, the greatest frequency of negotiation occurred in dyads involving NNSs of both divergent language background and divergent proficiency level. In that paper we argued that NNS dyads provide learners with a nonthreatening environment in which to receive comprehensible input and produce comprehensible output. In interactions that involve only NNSs, interlocutors have to "work harder" to negotiate meaning, given the paucity of shared linguistic (and/or cultural) background. Stevick (1976) argues that acquisition is facilitated precisely by such active involvement in the discourse, since the input becomes "charged," allowing it to penetrate. (See Long & Porter, 1985, for further arguments concerning the significance of NNS–NNS interactions in the form of group work in the classroom.)

[2] These amusement parks are both near Los Angeles, hence, far from both San Francisco and Las Vegas.

[3] The actual targeted word was "ingress," from Spanish *ingreso,* meaning income.

This chapter further explores NNS–NNS discourse by focusing specifically on incorporated repairs in NNS speech. We argue that not only do learners repair deviant forms in the speech of other learners but that as a result of these repairs, the "repaired" learners incorporate standard language forms into their own speech. The corrected forms may appear immediately or after considerable delay.

2. NS–NNS CONVERSATION AND LANGUAGE DEVELOPMENT

The first question we consider is the role of NS corrective feedback for a NNS. Vigil and Oller (1976) claim that a certain amount of corrective feedback is necessary for the continuing development of a NNS's second language. Schachter (1984) suggests that it is necessary to consider a broad range of "negative input" provided to a NNS from a NS, negative input being an indication to the learner that

> her utterance was in some way deviant or unacceptable to the native speaker, i.e., that it wasn't understandable, wasn't grammatically correct, wasn't situationally appropriate, etc. (p. 168)

This negative input can range from explicit corrective feedback about the form of an utterance to a general indication that the NNS's utterance was not comprehended. Interestingly, despite the usual assumption about the importance of NS–NNS conversation, Chun et al. (1982) report relatively little "on-record" (Brown & Levinson, 1978) corrective feedback in free conversation between NSs and NNSs. Since NSs corrected only 8.9% of a NNS's errors, they question the value of correction as an integral part of successful acquisition.

In another study, Day et al. (1984) differentiate between corrective and noncorrective feedback, analyzing only corrective feedback that occurs when a NS, in response to what is perceived to be an error by the NNS, supplies an appropriate item. They find that NSs provide more on-record than off-record feedback to NNS friends. Here, too, they further question the role of error correction in L2 acquisition, noting that out of 1,595 student errors in the corpus, only 119 (7.3%) were singled out for corrective feedback.

In a follow-up study, Brock et al. (1986) investigated a broader range of negative input in NS–NNS speaker free conversations, examining short-term effects of negative input on the NNS's language development. They found surprisingly little change, with only 26 out of 152 instances (17.1%) in which learners clearly responded to the NS's corrective input by incorporating it into their next turn. However, they point out that there may be an effect for task type, since there were examples of observable effects and apparent incorporations of NS-provided corrective feedback following error when communication took place in the context of communication games. In other words, learners may respond more to feedback, and their grammar may be more quickly destabilized, if they give sufficient attention to the area in question, with the assumption that they would give more attention in the context of a game as opposed to free conversation. Similar claims are made in Gass (1988), where it is argued that selective attention plays a central role in second-language development. In addition, it is important to bear in mind that the absence of short-term effects does not exclude the possibility of long-term effects, when the learner has had sufficient processing time to incorporate the feedback.

Crookes and Rulon (1985) consider NS–NNS dyads to further examine the issue of the incorporation of corrective feedback in three situations: free conversation and two 2-way communication tasks. Feedback was defined as the correct usage by a NS of a word or construction incorrectly used in the *immediately preceding* NNS utterance. They found significantly more feedback in task-related conversation than in free conversation. Because the difference was significant for only one of the two tasks, they suggest that it may be the case that for maximum grammatical destabilization, linguistic material should be slightly unfamiliar to the NNS, and the structure of the task should require the maximum use of this same material by both parties.

Finally, Pica (1988) specifically examines the output of second-language learners as a consequence of a negotiated interaction with a NS. She finds some evidence of modifications in a learner's output in the direction of the target language as a result of a given interaction, although the reason why a particular utterance serves as a stimulus for change is unclear.

While this research into the nature of NS–NNS repairs has added to our knowledge of the role corrective feedback may play in L2 production, there has been no similar systematic investigation into the nature or function of repairs that occur in NNS–NNS dyads. It is clear that this is an important forum for gaining input, since, in general, learners spend a great deal of time conversing with other NNSs.

3. NNS–NNS CONVERSATION AND LANGUAGE DEVELOPMENT

We begin this discussion with an example of a modification of a NNS's speech toward a target-language (TL) norm which took place as a result of input from another NNS.[4] Two NNSs of different language backgrounds were

---

[4] It is important to bear in mind that the NNSs in this study were in the United States in an intensive English program. As a result, they had numerous native-speaking models from which other language information was obtained. Wong-Fillmore (1987) points out that in the absence of such models, learners develop a language which diverges from standard norms.

given the task of going out in Ann Arbor, Michigan, with a tape recorder to ask people for directions to the train station. These students left the tape recorder on during the entire time they were engaged in this task, so that the whole conversation between them was also recorded, even when they were not specifically engaged in stopping passersby to ask for directions. They alternated stopping strangers on the street. The form of the requests is given in (4):

(4)

    (a) NNS (1):   Can you tell me where is the train station?
    (b) NNS (2):   Can you tell me where the train station is?
    (c) NNS (1):   Can you tell me where is the train station?
    (d) NNS (2):   Can you tell me where the train station is?
    (e) NNS (1):   Can you tell me where is the train station?
    (f) NNS (2):   Can you tell me where the train station is?
    (g) NNS (1):   Can you tell me where the train station is?
    (h) NNS (2):   Can you tell me where the train station is?
    (i) NNS (1):   Can you tell me where the train station is?

In understanding the significance of this example, it is important to note that nowhere in the entire conversation between requests for directions did the students discuss the correct grammatical form of English indirect questions. Nonetheless, NNS (1) made an unprompted change in the form of her utterance (4g), from incorrect to correct, while the other made no change. What is particularly interesting is that the change was in the direction of the TL, and not from a correct TL form to an incorrect one. This is similar to what has been referred to by Bruton and Samuda (1980) as "correction by permeation," with the correct form gradually permeating the learner's grammar over time. In 10 hours of taped conversations, they found only one example of a change from a correct to an incorrect form. In other words, errors of one's partner are generally not incorporated, whereas there were examples of modifications in the direction of the correct TL forms. These findings have implications for the way L2 knowledge is internalized, a point to which we return later.

4. THE STUDY

4.1. Data Base

The present study was designed to investigate repairs in NNS–NNS dyads. We examined data from 10 NNS–NNS dyads, all consisting of native Japanese-speaking students enrolled in intermediate-level classes of an intensive English-language program at an American university. There were three male–male pairs, three female–female pairs, and four male–female pairs. Each dyad participated in two tasks: free conversation and a picture description task. In the picture description task, one interlocutor had to describe a simple picture, while the other attempted to draw it. During the second trial of this task, the roles were reversed. Each of the dyads was tape-recorded using lavaliere microphones. The first 10 minutes of each task was transcribed and used in the present study for a corpus comprising 5 hours of conversation.

4.2. Data Analysis

In what follows we present examples from the data and discuss the implications of NNS–NNS interactions for second-language development. We limit our discussion to those repairs which resulted from an exchange between the participants, as opposed to unprompted self-repairs which might more appropriately be termed "mistakes," in Corder's (1967) sense.

The examples below illustrate the range of the phenomenon we are concerned with. In particular, we present examples of output modifications which relate to syntax, phonetics, and the lexicon. In these examples, the NNS who originally produced a deviant form incorporates a repair or a model provided by the interlocutor. Interestingly, we have no examples of discourse or pragmatic modifications, a point we return to later.

4.2.1. Phonetic Modification

Examples (5) and (6) show phonetic modification, which, as can be seen, results from a significant amount of negotiation:

(5) Prompted repair (see Varonis & Gass, 1985b):

    Chinatsu: . . . woman has a [dək]
    Yoko: duck? (surprised)
    Chinatsu: [dɔk]
    Yoko: [dɔk] ah, I see—
    Chinatsu: a [dək]
    Yoko: What kind of dog?[5]
    (eight turns)
    Chinatsu: The dog wear s-some clothe. . . .

(6) Lapsed repair (see Varonis & Gass, 1985b):

    Atsuko: uh holding the [kəp]
    Toshi: holding the cup?
    Atsuko: hmm hmmm . . .
    (seventeen turns)
    Toshi: holding a cup
    Atsuko: yes
    Toshi: coffee cup?

[5] When standard English orthography is used in the targeted words, assume standard pronunciation.

Atsuko: coffee? oh yeah, tea, coffee cup, tea cup
Toshi: hm hm

In (5), Chinatsu attempts to say *dog,* but her phonetic output more closely resembles the English word *duck.* Yoko responds with an indication of nonunderstanding: "duck?" Chinatsu tries again, this time coming a little closer to producing a back vowel in the word [dɔk]. Yoko seems to repeat the utterance, lowering the vowel even more but also pronouncing a voiceless velar stop [k] instead of the correct voiced velar stop [g].[6] Having repeated the utterance, she seems to understand Chinatsu's intention: "ah, I see," at which point Chinatsu overlaps with the end of her utterance, repeating the utterance yet reverting to her original incorrect pronunciation: [dək]. It seems that once Yoko's comprehension is assured, Chinatsu is free to continue with her old mistake. However, an interesting phenomenon occurs somewhat later in the conversation. Yoko continues with, "What kind of dog?" and eight turns later Chinatsu uses the word again for the first time, this time pronouncing it correctly: "the dog wear s-some clothe."

In example (6), Atsuko incorrectly pronounces *cup* as [kəp]. Toshi checks his understanding with a confirmation check: "holding the cup?" Atsuko responds affirmatively but does not repair her utterance, and the conversation continues. After another 17 turns, Toshi uses the word again: "holding a cup," to which Atsuko simply replies "yes." Up to this point she has not again attempted to use the word in question. Toshi requests more information: "coffee cup?" And here at last Atsuko responds, "coffee? oh yeah, tea, coffee cup, tea cup," correctly pronouncing the word for the first time. Thus, although Toshi offered the correct form immediately after Atsuko mispronounced it, she did not incorporate the correction until some 20 turns later, and only after there had been two more instances of the correct model.

4.2.2. Syntactic Modification

In (7) and (8) we present syntactic incorporations. In (7) they result from a negotiation and in (8), from an earlier model:

(7)

Toshi: He stands up? He stands, you mean?
           He stands up?
Tomoko: He stand. He is standing and—
Toshi: he's standing.

(8)

Shizuka: When will you get married?
Akihito: When? I don't know. Maybe . . . uh . . . after thirty.

[6]We are in actuality simplifying the difference between the final consonants in *dog* and *duck,* a difference which in English is more likely due to preceding vowel length.

Shizuka: Thirty?
Akihito: Yeah, after thirty I'll get marriage—I'll get married . . .
(3 turns)
Akihito: . . . then if I fall in lover with her, I'll get marriage with her . . .
(11 turns)
Akihito: And . . . uh . . . when I saw her, I liked to get married with a Chinese girl
          because she's so beautiful.

In (7), Tomoko self-corrects, thus providing an appropriate model for Toshi, who incorporates the corrected form into his next turn. It is particularly interesting that Tomoko's correct form results from a self-repair. It may be that it is precisely this act of modified repetition which focused Toshi's attention on the form.

In (8), Akihito hears the correct form (''get married'') at the beginning of the exchange. One can hypothesize that the form which he initially offered, ''get marriage,'' was his learner-language form and that the correct model, which Shizuka offered, resulted in the confusion seen in Akihito's second utterance. It is only 16 turns later in which we see the correct form ''winning out.''

4.2.3. Lexical Modification

Examples of lexical corrections and incorporated repairs are shown in examples (9) and (10):

(9)

Hiroko: Ah, the dog is barking to—
Izumi: at
Hiroko: at the woman

(10)

Arai: Well, which part in left or right?
Hiroshi: To the right
Arai: To the right, OK.

In (9), Hiroko is incorrectly using the preposition *to*. Izumi simultaneously offers the correct preposition *at*. Hiroko incorporates this information immediately, as she continues her utterance: ''at the woman.''

In (10), Arai incorrectly asks ''Well, which part in left or right?'' Hiroshi seems to respond to the information content of the question, but his response also constitutes a corrected form of the utterance: ''to the right.'' Arai immediately incorporates this form in his reply: ''to the right, OK.''

In looking at all examples of this type, we find that, although they are not frequent—only nine in the entire corpus—the large majority of the repairs that occur are in the direction of the TL. In fact, eight out of nine of the incorporations are made in the direction of the TL. This includes incorporated changes which occur immediately as well as those which occur after a period of time. The single modification which a learner made in the incorrect direction is given in (11):

(11)

Tadahiro:	Her leg is straight?
Kenichiro:	Uh, her?
Tadahiro:	Her, uh she

In this case, Kenichiro questions Tadahiro's utterance presumably because of the gender (up until this point they had been talking about the man in the picture), but Tadahiro mistakenly changes the case of the pronominal form.

4.2.4. Incorrections

Another source of modification in our data stems from what we call "incorrections," in which one of the NNSs offered an incorrect repair. Despite the fact that there were only four instances, it is noteworthy that in *all* four of these cases the NNS did not accept the repair and maintained the form which he or she had originally used. An example is given in (12):

(12)

Hiroko:	A man is uh drinking c-coffee or tea uh with uh the saucer of the uh uh coffee set is uh in his uh knee.
Izumi:	in *him* knee
Hiroko:	uh on *his* knee
Izumi:	yeah
Hiroko:	on *his* knee
Izumi:	so sorry. On *his* knee
	(emphasis ours)

Hiroko says "in his knee," with Izumi responding with an incorrect form, "in him knee." Note that Hiroko maintains the original form in terms of the pronominal case but changes the preposition from "in" to "on." Both finally finish the negotiation with the correct form. It may be that Izumi's first response forced Hiroko to focus on the form of the utterance, thus triggering the resulting modification. In (13), on the other hand, after an incorrection, the learner used an entirely different construction:

(13)

Yoshi:	and uhm will she's uhm mouth *is* open
Keiko:	mouth *are* open
Yoshi:	She has a rather wide jaw
	(emphasis ours)

5. DISCUSSION

These findings are important for at least two reasons. First, they provide evidence for the direct positive effect of conversational interaction on second-language acquisition, even between two NNSs of a language. Second, they provide evidence for the way learners internalize second-language knowledge.

The first issue, we and others have discussed elsewhere, so we simply point out here that our results bear out the findings of Long (1980), Crookes and Rulon (1985), and others who argue that tasks requiring the negotiation of meaning optimize the opportunities for acquisition. In fact, in Varonis and Gass (1985b), there were significantly more repairs (including other repairs and self-repairs) in the picture task than in free conversation.

The second issue, that of learner internalization of knowledge, is what concerns us in the remainder of this chapter. If, in fact, repairs are accepted primarily in the direction of the TL, we assume that in dealing with learner internalization of second-language knowledge, one must refer to the notion of grammatical and ungrammatical knowledge and to the strength of that knowledge (for related notions see MacWhinney, 1985, and Slobin, 1985). Gass (1983) investigated the grammatical intuitions of second-language learners, asking them to judge sentences they had produced and to repair those sentences they felt were ungrammatical English sentences. For both intermediate and advanced learners, the changes which were made rarely affected the actual grammaticality of a sentence. That is, although students could judge sentences as ungrammatical, those same sentences remained ungrammatical after they attempted to correct them. As is to be expected, advanced learners were better able to make appropriate changes than were intermediate learners. Thus, there is some evidence, based on Gass (1983), as well as the results from this study, that different parts of learners' grammars are more or less susceptible to external influence. What we suggest is that susceptibility is determined by the strength of knowledge which learners have over given forms.

A related notion comes from Bialystok (1979, 1981) and Bialystok and Sharwood Smith (1985), who propose that language proficiency consists of many disparate skills that can be characterized by the amount of control a learner has over them. Language information can be viewed along two dimensions: (1) the explicit–implicit dimension, reflecting the learner's ability to view the language information as an abstract entity, and (2) the automatic–analyzed dimension, reflecting the learner's ability to access that information. In Bialystok and Sharwood Smith's terms, these are referred to as knowledge representation and control procedures, that is, procedures for accessing the information. In our framework, we argue that strength of knowledge representation is crucial in determining the control that learners have over given forms. We further argue that learners have an ability to recognize what is correct and what is incorrect even in the absence of a NS and even when their own forms are not in conformity with the TL form. Consider, for example, the train station utterances, where one NNS incorporated the correct form of the other. The speaker who eventually changed the form of her utterance may have had only a weak representation of that form, allowing external feedback to filter through; in contrast, the other speaker, more confident that the form she was using was correct, had that grammatical information more strongly represented and, thus, did not allow external (incorrect) feedback to interfere. This is also the case for the four examples we mentioned in which "incorrections" were made, but were not accepted.

A related phenomenon has been noted by Eisenstein, Shuller, and Bodman (1987). In a pedagogical experiment in which NNSs learned English by viewing videotapes of other learners involved in learning English using the Silent Way methodology, the authors found that a significant amount of learning did take place during 100 hours of instruction, despite the fact that there was a minimal amount of access to NS models.[7] As Eisenstein *et al.* (1987) stated, "viewers (i.e., learners) must develop criteria for deciding when the learners on the tapes are accurately representing the structure and phonology of the target language . . ." (p. 215) and when they are not. The question then remains: what criteria are being used?

Swain (1985) provides an example from an eighth-grade immersion student who says, "I can hear in my head how I should sound when I talk, but it never comes out that way." Additionally, many second-language learners report dreams in which their TL mastery is far more advanced than it is when they are awake. These examples are compatible with a position which claims that strength of knowledge representation may in part determine what output will result, the means by which output takes place, and what changes in a learner's grammar will take place. In other words, there are limitations on the translation of knowledge into output, since it is possible to have a target in mind, but not necessarily have a plan available to implement it.

One final point we mention has to do with the nature of the repairs that are offered. We noted that there were no examples of either discourse or pragmatic repairs. Thus, when there is a breakdown or possible breakdown in communication, interlocutors focus on local rather than global aspects of the message. This is inherent in the nature of conversation and is consistent with the general tendency to keep a conversation going in as smooth a manner as possible. Commenting on an inappropriate remark is often considered rude, as is the case in (14):

(14)

        NNS: You're Jewish, aren't you?
         NS: Yes. [pause] How did you know?
        NNS: Your big nose betrays you. I read it in a book . . .

In this case, given American cultural norms, the NNS made an inappropriate remark. A remark from the NS would have been even more rude than the

[7] Given that these learners were in an ESL program in the United States, there is the possibility that, indeed, the learners had exposure to native-speaking models outside of the classroom.

NNS's original comment. Nonetheless, the paucity of this kind of repair may contribute to the eventual delay in acquisition of discourse or sociolinguistic features compared to the acquisition of grammatical features stemming from situations in which there is ample opportunity for the type of feedback we have been discussing.

Clearly, a caveat is in order. We have been talking quite loosely about "changes in one's grammar," without having any way of knowing what happens at a later point in time, as complete follow-up was not undertaken. Are the changes signaled by incorporation of feedback true changes, or are they only temporary ones? In actuality, it is likely that some changes are more lasting than others. An interesting question is what determines whether modifications are long term or temporary? Do changes form the basis for hypotheses which await confirmation from native speakers, a textbook, or a teacher? That incorporation is not simply imitative can be seen in some of the examples presented here in which there was a time lapse between the initial correct utterance and the change. However, there does not seem to be any adequate way of measuring interlanguage destabilization as a result of repair that does not depend on immediately—or almost immediately—observable performance.

Despite this methodological problem, we believe that it is premature to argue, as some have suggested, that corrective feedback is of little value in acquisition. It seems that a crucial difference between studies reporting little versus great corrective feedback is the task in which the interlocutors are engaged, as well as the nature of the interlocutors (e.g., native versus nonnative, experienced versus inexperienced in subject matter, or high versus low status). We claim that it is of theoretical interest to understand the source and importance of the external feedback available to learners and the way external information interacts with a learner's internalized grammatical system.

ACKNOWLEDGMENTS

We would like to thank Orestes Varonis for his assistance on all aspects of this chapter.

REFERENCES

Balasubramaniam, K. (n.d.). Macro-strategies for ELT teacher preparation.
Bialystok, E. (1979). Explicit and implicit judgments of L2 grammaticality. *Language Learning,* *29,* 81–104.
Bialystok, E. (1981). The role of linguistic knowledge in second language use. *Studies in Second Language Acquisition, 4,* 31–45.
Bialystok, E., & Sharwood Smith, M. (1985). Interlanguage is not a state of mind: An evaluation of the construct for second-language acquisition. *Applied Linguistics, 6,* 101–117.

Brock, C., Crookes, G., Day, R., & Long, M. (1986). The differential effects of corrective feedback in native speaker–nonnative speaker conversation. In R. Day (Ed.), *Talking to learn: Conversations in second language acquisition* (pp. 229–236). Rowley, MA: Newbury House.

Brown, P., & Levinson, S. (1978). Universals in language usage: Politeness phenomena. In E. Goody (Ed.), *Questions and politeness: Strategies in social interaction* (pp. 256–289). Cambridge: Cambridge University Press.

Bruton, A., & Samuda, V. (1980). Learner and teacher roles in the treatment of error in group work. *RELC Journal, 11,* 49–63.

Chun, A., Day, R., Chenoweth, A., & Luppescu, S. (1982). Errors, interaction and correction: A study of native–nonnative conversations. *TESOL Quarterly, 16,* 537–547.

Corder, S. P. (1967). The significance of learners' errors. *IRAL, 4,* 161–170.

Crookes, G., & Rulon, K. (1985). Incorporation of corrective feedback in native speaker/nonnative speaker conversation. Paper presented at the Second Language Research Forum, UCLA.

Day, R., Chenoweth, A., Chun, A., & Luppescu, S. (1984). Corrective feedback in native–nonnative discourse. *Language Learning, 34,* 19–46.

Eisenstein, M., Shuller, S., & Bodman, J. (1987). Learning English with an invisible teacher: An experimental video approach. *System, 15,* 209–216.

Ellis, R. (1984). *Classroom second language development.* Oxford: Pergamon Press.

Ellis, R. (1985). *Understanding second language acquisition.* Oxford: Oxford University Press.

Gass, S. (1983). The development of L2 intuitions. *TESOL Quarterly, 17,* 273–291.

Gass, S. (1988). Integrating research areas: A framework for second language studies. *Applied Linguistics, 9*(2), 198–217.

Gass, S., & Varonis, E. (1985). Variation in native speaker speech modification to non-native speakers. *Studies in Second Language Acquisition, 7,* 37–58.

Hatch, E. (1983). *Psycholinguistics: A second language perspective.* Rowley, MA: Newbury House.

Hatch, E., Flashner, V., & Hunt, L. (1986). The experience model and language teaching. In R. Day (Ed.), *Talking to learn: Conversation in second language acquisition* (pp. 5–22). Rowley, MA: Newbury House.

Krashen, S. (1980). The input hypothesis. In J. Alatis (Ed.), *Current issues in bilingual education.* Washington, DC: Georgetown University Press.

Krashen, S. (1982). *Principles and practice in second language acquisition.* Oxford: Pergamon Press.

Long, M. (1980). *Input, interaction and second language acquisition.* Unpublished doctoral dissertation, University of California at Los Angeles.

Long, M. (1983). Linguistic and conversational adjustments to non-native speakers. *Studies in Second Language Acquisition, 5,* 177–249.

Long, M., & Porter, P. (1985). Group work, interlanguage and second language acquisition. *TESOL Quarterly, 19,* 207–228.

MacWhinney, B. (1985). Hungarian language acquisition as an exemplification of a general model of grammatical development. In D. Slobin (Ed.), *The crosslinguistic study of language acquisition, Volume 2: Theoretical issues* (pp. 1069–1156). Hillsdale, NJ: Lawrence Erlbaum.

Pica, T. (1988). *Interlanguage adjustments as an outcome of NS–NNS negotiated interaction. Language Learning, 38,* 45–73.

Scarcella, R., & Higa, C. (1981). Input, negotiation and age differences in second language acquisition. *Language Learning, 31,* 409–437.

Schachter, J. (1984). A universal input condition. In W. Rutherford (Ed.), *Universals and second language acquisition* (pp. 167–183). Amsterdam: John Benjamins.

Slobin, D. (1985). Crosslinguistic evidence for the language-making capacity. In D. Slobin (Ed.), *The crosslinguistic study of language acquisition, Volume 2: Theoretical issues* (pp. 1157–1249). Hillsdale, NJ: Lawrence Erlbaum.

Stevick, E. (1976). *Memory, meaning and method*. Rowley, MA: Newbury House.

Swain, M. (1985). Communicative competence: Some roles of comprehensible input and comprehensible output in its development. In S. Gass & C. Madden (Eds.), *Input in second language acquisition*. Rowley, MA: Newbury House.

Sweet, H. (1964). *The practical study of language*. London: Oxford University Press. (Original work published 1899)

Varonis, E., & Gass, S. (1985a). Non-native/non-native conversations: A model for negotiation of meaning. *Applied Linguistics, 6,* 71–90.

Varonis, E., & Gass, S. (1985b, July). *Repairs in NNS discourse and the evidence for second language development*. Paper presented at TESOL Summer Meeting, Washington, DC.

Vigil, N., & Oller, J. (1976). Rule fossilization: A tentative model. *Language Learning, 26,* 281–296.

Wagner-Gough, J., & Hatch, E. (1975). The importance of input data in second language acquisition studies. *Language Learning, 25,* 297–307.

Wong-Fillmore, L. (1987, November). *Learning a second language from learners*. Plenary, TESL 1987, Toronto.

CHAPTER 6

Interlinguistic Variation and Similarity in Foreigner Talk
Illustrated with Respect to English-Speaking and German-Speaking Contexts

ELSA LATTEY

1. INTRODUCTION AND DEFINITIONS

Foreigner talk (FT), a speech variety often discussed together with broken language, pidginization, or simplification, is seen as a sociolinguistic phenomenon involving speech adjustment in the presence of foreign speakers. Much of the research to date has been on English foreigner talk, for which syntactic as well as functional analyses have been put forward (e.g., Clyne, 1981; Ferguson, 1971, 1975, 1977, 1981; Freed, 1979, 1981a, 1981b; Hatch, Schapira, & Gough, 1978). But other languages have been studied as well (e.g., Czech by Henzl, 1974, 1979; Dutch by Snow, van Eeden, & Muysken, 1981; French by Valdman, 1981; German by Hinnenkamp, 1981, 1982, 1984, 1985; Meisel, 1977, 1980; and Roche, 1982; Tok Masta by Muehlhaeusler, 1981; Turkish by Hinnenkamp, 1982). Gass and Varonis (1985) discuss native-speaker reaction to FT, and Gass and Madden (1985) consider the effects of FT on language learning.

Two primary aspects of FT have been mentioned in defining the term: FT has been characterized as "the variety of language that is regarded by a speech community as primarily appropriate for addressing foreigners" (Ferguson & DeBose, 1977, p. 103) and as "used by speakers of a language to outsiders

ELSA LATTEY • Seminar fuer Englische Philologie, University of Tübingen, Tübingen, Federal Republic of Germany.

who are felt to have very limited command of a language or no knowledge of it at all" (Ferguson, 1971, p. 43). The concepts *regarded by a speech community as appropriate* and *used by speakers* are worth distinguishing. The first refers to reflection on what one might say in a particular imagined context, while the other refers to actual use of language in a communication situation.

2. DATA COLLECTION AND STRATEGIC COMPETENCE

2.1. Methodologies

These two ways of viewing FT are also reflected in the methods of data collection that have been employed:

1. *Primary FT:*[1] This can be collected by (1) "experimental investigation in which investigators play the role of foreigners" and elicit language actually used by native speakers or by (2) "recordings of native–foreign interaction in a natural communicative setting," which also yields language actually used by speakers.
2. *Secondary FT:* What Ferguson and DeBose (1977, p. 104) describe as "elicitation from informants who report on how they or others . . . speak to foreigners," that is, what the speech community regards as appropriate; included here is also the use of FT in comics, cartoons, jokes, and stereotypical material written about foreigners, such as the following citation by Hinnenkamp (1981, p. 173, and 1982, p. 178) of an excerpt from the newspaper *Welt am Sonntag* of July 13, 1980, that appeared in a discussion of the right of political asylum and the extent to which foreigners seek to be caught up in the Federal Republic of Germany's social net:

(1)

Ali Baba Bumbum hat sich braune Haut und große, schwarze Schnurrbart. Er steigt in Frankfurt aus der Boeing, die aus Lumumbashi kommt, zieht noch auf der Gangway einen Zettel aus seinem Turban und liest laut vor: "Ich sein politisch Verfolgter. Ich wollen in Deutschland Republik Asyl."

Ali Baba Bumbum has him brown skin and big black moustache. He alights in Frankfurt from a Boeing that has just come from Lumumbashi, pulls a slip of paper out of his turban while still on the gangway and reads aloud: "Me political refugee. Me want in Germany Republic asylum." (trans. by E. Lattey)

---

[1] The terms *primary FT* and *secondary FT* are taken from Hinnenkamp (1981, p. 174 & 1982, pp. 40–41).

The two approaches to the variety of language under consideration yield basically different types of data, as can be seen when we look at what is collected by implementing one or the other of these methods. Elicitation of secondary FT yields data that provide information about how native speakers regard their language, what they consider to be complex, and where they feel that simplification can be fruitfully attempted in order to facilitate communication. To a great extent this capacity of native speakers is akin to their ability to write telegrams or, better yet, to take notes. On the other hand, there is a negative side to this view, for secondary FT is also the characterization of a stereotypical linguistic variety that is definitely "a component of our linguistic repertoire, at least passively, for every speaker immediately catches on as to *who* is being addressed and *what feelings* are to be evoked, when this variety is switched into" (Hinnenkamp, 1981, p. 173; trans. by E. Lattey).

Experimental investigation and recording in natural communicative settings, in contrast, yield data that provide information about one's functioning in *communicative interaction,* the ability to hone in on the interlocutor's level and style of understanding. To some extent native speakers, when actually speaking with foreigners, make use of the products of a self-analysis such as that gotten via the elicitation method mentioned above, but beyond this they respond to the actual demands of the communication situation, to feedback— or lack of it—they get from the foreigner.

They thus exhibit a *strategic competence* as described by Canale and Swain (1980): "verbal and non-verbal communication strategies that may be called into action to compensate for breakdowns in communication due to performance variables or to insufficient competence" (p. 30). Tarone (1980), who suggests that this strategic competence must have some universal aspect because "it is used to bridge the gaps between two linguistic or sociolinguistic systems," characterized it as follows: "the ability to employ strategies of language use in the attempt to reach communicative goals" (p. 422).

Thus the two approaches mentioned above differ with respect to the role of strategic competence—in the case of secondary FT, it is primarily grammatical and sociolinguistic competence that play a role, while in primary FT, strategic competence also significantly determines utterance production.

Canale and Swain (1980) identify two main types of communication strategy:

> those that relate primarily to grammatical competence (e.g., how to paraphrase grammatical forms that one has not mastered or cannot recall momentarily) and those that relate more to sociolinguistic competence (e.g., various role-playing strategies, or how to address strangers when unsure of their social status). (pp. 30–31)

Users of FT will be motivated in the development and use of both types of strategy by their assessment of their interlocutors' mastery of the language.

This assumes that the native speaker has the capability of reducing the information to be communicated to a minimum and to keep the conversation going using the least possible amount of lexical material (Heyder, 1986, p. 69).

A further distinction between the two types of data can be found in the occurrence of simplifying and clarifying processes, as discussed in Ferguson (1977), and Ferguson and DeBose (1977).

2.2. Data Samples

My own research into FT (Lattey, 1981, 1985) was motivated by the lack of information in the linguistic literature on which a comparison of English and German FT could be based. I had observed that German FT was quite obvious, while that in the United States had never been particularly obtrusive—the stereotypes and caricatures of such talk occurring in films, in the media, and in literary texts (secondary FT) notwithstanding.

The goal of the investigations reported on here was to discover, by means of a comparison of English and German FT and the situational contexts in which they are used, why the impact of the two varieties should differ so greatly. In pursuit of this goal, several corpora were examined:

1. *Primary FT:*

a. Secretly recorded FT responses to requests for directions by two foreign students, a Brazilian and a black African, who pretended to have a very limited knowledge of German—and secretly recorded FT responses to requests for directions by a German student in Dublin, Ireland, who pretended not to speak English very well.

b. Openly recorded native–foreigner interactions in a "natural" setting, the municipal office for foreigner matters in a university town in SW Germany. Here evidence of *pronounced* FT behavior was found only in interaction with a Turkish couple (Turks rank lowest among foreigners in Germany on the hierarchy of perceived status and so are most likely to elicit FT).[2] Conversations

---

[2]This hierarchy of perceived status has been corroborated by Bert Hardin and Bernd Estel, two sociologists at the University of Tuebingen. Though it appears that there has been no detailed, quantitative scientific study of this phenomenon, it is taken for granted in many domains of German culture and can be plausibly explained in terms of a social distance scale, the Turks being farthest removed from the Germans in terms of culture, religion, role of women in society, and the like. (Sociologically speaking, the refugees—*Asylanten*—have now usurped the bottom-of-the-scale position; however, no refugees were addressed in the German data being considered here.)

A 1970s study of the language of the *Gastarbeiter* in Germany concentrated on the Turks, because of all the nationalities of foreign workers "they are the most disadvantaged group (the only non-Europeans; the degree of social distance between country of origin and the Fed. Rep. of Germany being the greatest; lower standard of education compared to the other foreign nationals,

with other foreigners—Americans, Greeks, and the like—were conducted in standard German. The data gathered by Roche (1982) and Hinnenkamp (1981, 1982) are similar and are included in the discussion below. The English counterpart is openly recorded conversation among American natives and Spanish-speaking foreigners in the United States, where the foreigners spoke quite fluent English that was, however, noticeably foreign in its phonology.

2. *Secondary FT:*

Ferguson (1975) gave American students 10 sentences, asking them to rephrase them as they would imagine people to speak to foreigners who do not know the language well. I carried out a self-analysis elicitation similar to Ferguson's, using translations into German of Ferguson's stimulus sentences.

Although there are many foreigners in each of the countries under consideration, the cultural setting of the Federal Republic of Germany (FRG) is somewhat different from that of the USA and Ireland. The bulk of the foreign workers who came to the German context were originally welcomed as a desirable expansion of the labor force during the industrial boom but subsequently merely tolerated (if that) as unemployment rose. The German language has a term for its foreign labor force that can be heard or read almost daily in the media: *Gastarbeiter*, or 'guest workers.' One can perhaps surmise a subliminal undercurrent in this designation that reflects the thoughts of many in the FRG today: guests shouldn't overstay their welcome.

Be that as it may, the bulk of the foreign population in the FRG is comparable in status to the Mexican workers in the USA; that is, a foreign labor force seeking employment in a more prosperous neighboring country because the labor market—and chances for good wages—is so poor at home. Immigration into the USA and into other English-speaking countries in the West is, however, not largely restricted to this type. This may very well account for a differential in the sociolinguistic situation between our English-speaking and German-speaking contexts.

3. CHARACTERISTIC FEATURES OF FT

Ferguson (1977, p. 28) and Hatch *et al.* (1978) list a number of features characteristic of English FT. These and others from the German data can be grouped into three major categories:

- Simplifying processes
- Clarifying processes

---

etc.). A 1972 report by the BfA [Bundesanstalt fuer Arbeit = Federal Employment Institute] indicates that their level of proficiency in German is also the lowest" (Keim, 1978, p. 223, note 1; trans. by E. Lattey).

• Expressive–identifying processes (e.g., greater use of diminutives or frequent use of status markers; cf. Ferguson, 1977, pp. 30–31; Hinnenkamp, 1984, pp. 51–52).[3]

3.1. Simplifying Processes

The first of these categories, the *simplifying processes,* is where the overt
differences between English and German FT are primarily to be found. Included here is the use of (1) short sentences, (2) simple sentences (i.e., little
embedding), (3) various kinds of omission, and (4) readjustment of word order;
(1) and (2) are modifications of native-speaker speech that are nevertheless
grammatical, while (3)—and sometimes (4)—generally leads to *ungrammatical*
utterances (see Long, 1983, for a discussion of grammatical versus ungrammatical speech to nonnative speakers).

Let us take a closer look at one of these simplifying processes, namely,
omission:

1. *Omission of articles*

(2)

When you get right down to [0] extreme end there, you go round . . .

(3)

Dienstag, ja. Mit [0] Arbeitsbescheinigung.
'Tuesday, yes. With [0] work permit.'

Examples such as the above occurred repeatedly in the data. They were
counted and the instances of omission were quantified relative to the total number of potential articles to yield the percentage of omission. In the following,
the English (E) percentages are derived from Ferguson, 1975; the German (G)
figures are from my analogous study; the German, Hinnenkamp (GH) percentage is taken from a résumé of a German interview cited in Hinnenkamp, 1982,
p. 54; and the German communicative interaction (GCI) data are from the interviews recorded on the street and in the municipal office in Germany:

E: 89% omission   G: 50%   GH: 50%   GCI: 64%

The observable percentage distinction between German and English has a plau-
sible language-specific explanation. .

English has an indefinite and a definite article: *a/an* and *the,* while German
has the following correspondences: *ein* (masc.) / *eine* (fem.) / *ein* (neut.) and
der (masc.) / *die* (fem.) / *das* (neut.), which exhibit further distinctions to

---

[3] Hinnenkamp finds Ferguson's term somewhat confusing and prefers to call these "direct status-
marking" characteristics (1982, p. 61).

indicate different relationships among the participants in an event—what has traditionally been discussed in terms of case but is more coherently seen in terms of a ranking of participants (Zubin, 1978; Lattey, 1980). The German articles therefore carry the higher functional load. While the English articles indicate only definite versus indefinite reference, the inflection of the German articles additionally signals gender of the nouns and the relationships among the participants in the event. German speakers are thus more reluctant to omit the articles because to do so would be to sacrifice considerably more communicative information.

It is interesting to note, however, that—despite the self-analysis hypothesis that articles are omissible in English—in communicative interaction (e.g., in my Dublin and U.S. data), there is almost no omission of articles. It appears that this phenomenon is one in which English speakers recognize a potential for simplification that is not made much use of in practice.

    2. *Omission of verbs: to be*

(4)

        NS: Where are you from anyway?
     NNS: From Germany.
        NS: Oh, you're kidding. Yeah, lovely.
             You [0] here before, no?

(5)

    I [0] nix Chef. (see also Ex. 13)
    I [0] not boss.

Here, too, the instances of omission (of a form of the verb *be*) were counted and quantified relative to the total number of potential (or expected) occurrences (of *be*) in the data to yield the percentage of omission:

        E: 89% omission   G: 50%   GH: 27%   GCI: 42%

Again the difference in percentages can be explained on the basis of language-specific features, namely, the English data's inclusion of progressive occurrences of *be;* German has no such progressive.[4] As far as the GCI percentage is concerned, it should be pointed out that quantification is more difficult in communicative interaction, as it is not always clear what a nonoccurring verb would have been had it been supplied (doubtful cases were not counted).

    3. *Omission of verb inflection.* The loss of inflectional endings results in the neutralization of—that is, the loss of information regarding—*person, number,* and *tense.* In English there is not a great deal of information to lose via loss of inflectional endings on the verb, because not much information is carried in this way. Nevertheless, Ferguson (1975) shows us that in one example,

---

[4] A similar auxiliary omission in German FT occurs in the perfect, but with the auxiliary *haben* 'have.'

(6a)

I haven't seen the man you're talking about (Ferguson's Ex. 1)

83% of the respondents replaced the perfect form of the verb—*have(n't) seen*—
with the infinitive—*see*. In the same example in my parallel German study,

(6b)

Ich habe den Mann, von dem Sie sprechen, nicht gesehen

a total of 90% of the respondents replaced the perfect—*habe gesehen*—but only
30% did so with the infinitive *sehen*.[5] The remaining 60% used the participle
gesehen, in effect omitting only the auxiliary. This is an example of a tendency
found in the rest of my German data as well: a tendency to constrain verbal
forms to the nonfinite infinitives and participles; where inflected forms do appear, they occur in the present. This tendency of German FT speakers, which
can be interpreted as a strategy to avoid complicating the communicative event
with additional information the hearer would need to process and, rather, to
resort to *grammarless lexicon*,[6]—that is, to employ bare stems of verbs and
nouns, without inflectional morphology—undoubtedly also exists in English FT.

It is a strategy that is, however, considerably more obvious in German.
With the exception of *to be*, the English infinitive is identical to the conjugated
present tense verb form for all persons except third-person singular, whereas in
German the infinitive is the same form as only first- and third-person plural.
Consequently, when the inflected verb form is replaced by the infinitive, there
are many more instances in German where this leads to a deviant utterance.
This is, therefore, an example of how language-specific features of form can
in the context of identical communicative strategies produce language that differs greatly as to degree of deviance and, consequently, differs equally greatly
in impact on the observer.

The reader may well ask: How is it that the percentage of omission (and
consequently deviation from the norm) is greater for English FT and yet it is
German FT that gives the impression of greater deviance? A first answer was
already given above, when I pointed out that English speakers fail to make
much use of the potential article deletion in actual communicative interaction
(despite their cognitive recognition of this as a potential simplification device).
With respect to verb deletion, too, part of the answer is given above. In addition, speakers of German FT, when they retain the copula, often use the infinitive *sein* (see example 1 above), which is conspicuously obvious.

We might even hazard a guess that the presence of an ungrammatical form
is more stigmatized than the absence of that form. A feeling for this can also

---

[5] In Hinnenkamp's data there is 29% replacement of an inflected verb by the infinitive.
[6] Term suggested by Erica C. García.

be gotten from example 1, if one compares the missing English copula with the ungrammatical German copula present. If this hypothesis as to linguistic attitude (hearer's response to absence versus ungrammatical presence) is correct, it would also explain why German speakers who are evaluating their potential FT would prefer to replace a perfect form with the participle rather than the infinitive, as that would amount to a less stigmatized auxiliary omission rather than replacement by an ungrammatical form.

In addition to the above examples of simplifying processes, named by researchers working with English FT but applicable as well to German FT, the German respondents suggested the following as characteristic of FT as they imagine it: use of nouns instead of pronouns as an attempt at concretizing, simplification of the lexicon, and adjustment of word order to subject + object(s) + infinitive.[7]

3.2. Clarifying Processes

The second category of adjustments in speech are the *clarifying processes,* described in considerable detail for English in Hatch *et al.* (1978). They include repetition; restatement; simple and analytical paraphrase; padding, that is, including what is normally omitted (e.g., imperative subjects); separating elements normally fused (e.g., avoiding contractions); confirmation checking; and suprasegmental phenomena, such as slow, loud, or distinct pronunciation. This particular category of processes appears to have a relatively low salience. In response to the question of how they would most likely adjust their speech in communicating with someone whose knowledge of the language was limited, only 15% of the German respondents said they would speak slowly, and only 5% mentioned repetition and stress.

Yet it is this category in which the differences between English and German FT seem to disappear (as observed in communicative interaction). All of the processes mentioned for English also occur in German. The first two, repetition and restatement, are especially frequent, as seen in the following native-speaker attempts at giving directions to nonnatives:

(7)

Hier Auto durch und hier Ammergasse. Hier durch. Hier durch.
Here car through and here Ammer Lane. Here through. Here through.

---

[7]This sequence is normal for utterances with auxiliaries and modals—where the auxiliary occurs between subject and object—but not for present or simple past, where the sequence is SVO. The infinitive and final position are both also reminiscent of the form of public commands and requests (cf. Ferguson, 1977; e.g., *Nicht hinauslehnen* 'do not lean out', *drücken* 'push', *ziehen* 'pull').

(8)

> *Wirtschaft. Lokal. Kneipe. Verstehen? Nix. Ah, Wirtschaft. Lokal. Café.*
> Bar. Tavern. Pub. Understand? No, ah, bar. Tavern. Café.

(9)

> *Ueber die Ammer weg. Ueber das Wasser weg. Ueber den Fluß, den*
> *Bach.*
> Across the Ammer. Across the water. Across the river, the stream.

Restatement sometimes gives way to a kind of analytic paraphrase, as in
the communicative interaction utterances,

(10)

> *Und wie heißen die Kinder? Name von Kinder?*
> And what are the children called?[8] Name of children?

where the verb *heißen* 'be called' is analyzed into something like 'what is the
name of', and .

(11)

> Now, the English people, people who live in England . . . (this example
> from Heyder, 1986)

Varonis and Gass (1982) also discuss an interactional repetition, namely, the
"overwhelming tendency on the part of native speakers to begin their responses
to nonnative speakers by echoing a part of the question" (p. 116). The same
is observable in the German data: 90% of the German natives who were asked
for directions responded with a repetition of part of the question, most frequently the target destination. For example,

(12)

> *Hautklinik, Hautklinik, wo die isch?*
> Skin clinic, skin clinic, (you want to know) where it is?

Other speakers delayed the repetition of the question, but got there eventually, anyway:

(13)

> NNS: Verzeihen Sie . . . Am . . . Ammergasse.
> NS: *I, ah, Moment. Warten bis Chef kommen. Bin nix Chef. I nix*
> *Chef. Chef kommen, gleich. Se verstehen?!*
> NNS: Nh—
> NS: *Was suchen, Ammergasse.*

---

[8] It should be pointed out that the more natural English translation of this question is: "What are
the children's names?" But that would have obscured the analytical paraphrase.

NNS: Excuse me . . . Am . . . Ammer Lane.

NS: I, ah, just a moment. Wait until boss come. Am not boss. I not boss. Boss come, right away. Ya understand?

NNS: Nh—

NS: What look for, Ammergasse.

Varonis and Gass suggest that this repetition of the question could be a stalling for time, a request for confirmation, or a negotiating of the topic. In the communicative situation of asking directions, it is the first two of these strategies that are likely explanations.

We find differences between the English and German communicative interaction data collected with respect to these strategies. Most of the native speakers in my German study did not use question intonation in their repetition of the question, which would have suggested that it was a request for information, while in the Dublin data 50% of the respondents repeated part of the question asked, and 75% of these used question intonation in their repetition. Since the experimenters in the German context appeared to be performing at a lower level of language acquisition than the German student experimenter in Dublin, this might suggest that when the level of linguistic performance is lower, the native speaker either needs time to decide on a strategy for formulating an answer, doesn't expect the nonnative interlocutor to be able to manage a confirmation response, or—and this is another possible explanation for the repetition—is taking an expressive, empathetic, conversation-moving turn.

3.3. Expressive–Identifying Processes

The third and final category suggested by Ferguson (1977) is a type of empathetic communication. Among the primary indicators are: lexical items like *savvy* in English (in the German data *Kotschen,* derived from the Spanish for *Autos* 'cars', is an expression of empathy, "a temporary fusion of self/object boundaries," according to Hatch *et al.,* 1978, p. 58)[9] or status markers, usually in the form of "talking down" to the foreigner. (An American English example of talking down is the use of "sweetie" or "honey" by men in speaking to a woman they do not know.) In German the use of the familiar pronoun *du* rather than the polite *Sie* in talking to foreigners has been cited as an example of an expressive process (Ferguson, 1977, p. 31) and is consequently used more frequently to those national groups lower down on the perceived hierarchy of foreigners.

This phenomenon in German, however, is potentially relevant to the simplifying category as well, for the use of *du* avoids the ambiguity of *Sie/sie:* the latter, especially when co-occurring with what looks like an infinitive form of the verb, may be equivalent to English *you* (polite), *she,* or *they. Du* can be

[9] This notion is derived from A. Guiora (1965).

only second-person singular. Although the substitution of *du* for *Sie* is one of the stereotypes of German FT, the above mentioned communicative interaction conversations recorded in Germany contained no instances of *du*. When present, however, this is another feature that accounts for the pronounced difference in impact of the English and German FTs, another feature deriving from differences in the two linguistic systems, English having no opportunity to make this pronominal distinction.

4. CONCLUSION

We have seen that there are differences in the processes involved in FT and that these differences are variously reflected in different languages.

Simplifying processes, while proceeding in similar ways in English and German, lead to language-specific variation, the impact of which on the hearer depends in part on structural features of each language (see also Lattey, 1986, for a further discussion of speaker attitudes in native–nonnative interaction).

Clarifying processes, on the other hand, dealing as they do more with communicative interaction than with language analysis, appear to be the same, at least for these two languages—although it is likely that this similarity holds true for other languages as well.

Expressive–identifying processes, though as yet the least well defined of the three categories, also seem to operate in similar ways for both languages, yet here, too, language-specific phenomena will give different overt realizations to what may be similar strategies. Additional data involving many more topics and conversational contexts need to be examined in order to extend the comparison begun in the current investigation.

REFERENCES

Canale, M., & Swain, M. (1980). Theoretical bases of communicative approaches to second language teaching and testing. *Applied Linguistics, 1*(1), 1–17.
Clyne, M. (1981). 'Second generation' foreigner talk in Australia. *International Journal of the Sociology of Language, 28,* 69–80.
Ferguson, C. A. (1971). Absence of copula and the notion of simplicity: A study of normal speech, baby talk, foreigner talk and pidgins. In D. Hymes (Ed.), *Pidginization and creolization of languages* (pp. 141–150). Cambridge: Cambridge University Press.
Ferguson, C. A. (1975). Towards a characterization of English foreigner talk. *Anthropological Linguistics, 17,* 1–14.
Ferguson, C. A. (1977). Simplified registers, broken language, and Gastarbeiterdeutsch. In C. Molony, H. Zobl, & W. Stoelting (Eds.), *German in contact with other languages* (pp. 25–39). Kronberg/Ts.: Scriptor Verlag.
Ferguson, C. A. (1981). 'Foreigner talk' as the name of a simplified register. *International Journal of the Sociology of Language, 28,* 9–18.

Ferguson, C. A., & DeBose, C. E. (1977). Simplified registers, broken language, and pidginization. In A. Valdman (Ed.), *Pidgin and creole linguistics* (pp. 99–125). Bloomington: Indiana University Press.

Freed, B. (1979, Feb.–Mar.). *Foreigner talk and conversational interaction.* Paper presented at the TESOL Convention, Boston.

Freed, B. (1981a). Talking to foreigners versus talking to children. In R. Scarcella & S. Krashen (Eds.), *Research in second language acquisition* (pp. 19–27). Rowley, MA: Newbury House.

Freed, B. (1981b). Foreigner talk, baby talk, native talk. *International Journal of the Sociology of Language, 28,* 19–39.

Gass, S. M., & Madden, C. G. (Eds.). (1985). *Input in second language acquisition.* Rowley, MA: Newbury House.

Gass, S. M., & Varonis, E. M. (1985). Variation in native speaker speech modification to non-native speakers. *Studies in Second Language Acquisition, 7*(1), 37–57.

Guiora, A. (1965). On clinical diagnosis and prediction. *Psychological Reports, 17,* 779–784.

Hatch, E., Shapira, R., & Gough, J. (1978). Foreigner talk discourse. *ITL Review of Applied Linguistics, 39,* 39–60.

Henzl, V. M. (1974). Linguistic register of foreign language instruction. *Language Learning, 23,* 207–222.

Henzl, V. M. (1979). Foreign talk in the classroom. *ITL Review of Applied Linguistics, 17,* 159–167.

Heyder, U. (1986). *Untersuchungen zur sprachlichen Simplifikation im Englischen.* Unpublished master's thesis, University of Tübingen.

Hinnenkamp, V. (1981). "Tuerkish Mann, Du?"—Sprechverhalten von Deutschen gegenueber Gastarbeitern. In K. G. Bausch (Ed.), *Mehrsprachigkeit in der Stadtregion.* Jahrbuch des Instituts fuer Deutsche Sprache (pp. 171–193). Duesseldorf: Schwann.

Hinnenkamp, V. (1982). *Foreigner Talk und Tarzanisch.* Hamburg: Buske Verlag.

Hinnenkamp, V. (1984). "Infantilisierung" oder "funktionale Anpassung"?—Fragen zum "Foreigner Talk" der Deutschen gegenueber "Gastarbeitern". In W. Kuehlwein (Ed.), *Sprache, Kultur und Gesellschaft.* Kongressberichte der 14. Jahrestagung der GAL (pp. 51–52). Tübingen: Gunter Narr Verlag.

Hinnenkamp, V. (1985). Zwangskommunikative Interaktion zwischen Gastarbeitern und deutscher Behoerde. In J. Rehbein (Ed.), *Interkulturelle Kommunikation* (pp. 276–298). Tübingen: Gunter Narr Verlag.

Keim, I. (1978). *Gastarbeiterdeutsch.* Tübingen: TBL Verlag Gunter Narr.

Lattey, E. (1980). *Grammatical systems across languages. A Study of participation in English, German and Spanish.* Unpublished doctoral dissertation, City University of New York.

Lattey, E. (1981). *Foreigner talk in the U.S.A. and Germany: Contrast and comparison.* Washington, DC: ERIC Clearinghouse on Languages & Linguistics. (ED 221 064)

Lattey, E. (1985). From sign to text and from text to understanding. In Y. Tobin (Ed.) (in press). *From sign to text: A semiotic view of communication.* Amsterdam: John Benjamins.

Lattey, E. (1986). Sprachen im Kontakt. In H. Bausinger (Ed.), *Auslaender—Inlaender* (pp. 111–128). Tübingen: Tübinger Vereinigung fuer Volkskunde, e.V.

Long, M. H. (1983). Linguistic and conversational adjustments to non-native speakers. *Studies in Second Language Acquisition, 5*(2), 177–193.

Meisel, J. M. (1977). Linguistic simplification: A study of immigrant workers' speech and foreigner talk. In S. P. Corder & E. Roulet (Eds.), *The notions of simplification, interlanguages and pidgins and their relation to second language pedagogy* (pp. 88–113). Geneva: Librarie Droz.

Meisel, J. M. (1980). Linguistic simplification. In S. W. Felix (Ed.), *Second-language development. Trends and issues* (pp. 57–79). Tübingen: Gunter Narr.

Muehlhaeusler, P. (1981). Foreigner talk: Tok masta in New Guinea. *International Journal of the Sociology of Language, 28*, 93–113.

Roche, J. (1982). *Merkmale des foreigner talk im Deutschen.* Unpublished master's thesis, University of Munich, 1982.

Snow, C. E., van Eeden, R., & Muysken, P. (1981). The interactional origins of foreigner talk: Municipal employees and foreign workers. *International Journal of the Sociology of Language, 28*, 81–91.

Tarone, E. (1980). Communication strategies, foreigner talk, and repair in interlanguage. *Language Learning, 30*, 417–431.

Valdman, A. (1981). Sociolinguistic aspects of foreigner talk. *International Journal of the Sociology of Language, 28*, 41–52.

Varonis, E. M. & Gass, S. (1982). The comprehensibility of non-native speech. *Studies in Second Language Acquisition, 4*(2), 114–136.

Zubin, D. (1978). *Semantic substance and value relations: A grammatical analysis of case morphology in modern standard German.* Unpublished doctoral dissertation, Columbia University.

CHAPTER 7

The Effect of Cultural Empathy on Second-Language Phonological Production

DIANA BERKOWITZ

1. INTRODUCTION

As the field of second-language acquisition (SLA) research is still relatively young, it frequently looks to related disciplines such as first-language acquisition, theoretical linguistics, or psychology for much of its research methods, approaches, and models. In very recent years, a great deal of interest has been generated among second-language researchers in applying a sociolinguistic framework to SLA research. Some of these researchers, dissatisfied with the static nature of sociolinguistic descriptions, have been seeking to extend second-language (L2) sociolinguistic models by incorporating social psychological theories which seem better able to explain the dynamics of human verbal interaction. Some of these theories, however, account for first-language (L1) data better than they do for L2 data. As Beebe and Giles (1984) note, the L2 learner is a special case compared to the monolingual or fluent bilingual. The linguistic competence of the L2 learner is constantly in flux. Consequently, there is a more complex set of factors affecting L2 performance. The present study was undertaken with the goal of further exploring the social psychological dynamics that affect L2 production and seeing how well theories originally developed to explain L1 data fit within an L2 model.

DIANA BERKOWITZ • English Language Program, Hofstra University, Hempstead, New York 11550.

The study looked at an English speaker's culturally empathic treatment of adult Dominican ESL learners and at the effect their perceptions of this empathy had upon their phonological production. Since ESL teachers by nature tend to respond to their students on an empathic level (and teacher education programs reinforce this kind of response), it is particularly important to confirm that this kind of interlocutor behavior has the positive effect that it is assumed to have.

The study also sought to determine which of two L1 models of speech behavior, having been applied to L2 data, would more adequately account for the linguistic behavior of L2 speakers in response to cultural empathy: Giles' social psychological theory of speech accommodation (Giles & Powesland, 1975; Giles & Smith, 1979) or the Labovian sociolinguistic paradigm of attention to speech (Labov, 1972).

Speech accommodation theory is basically concerned with accounting for speech style-shifts in terms of social psychological variables which are relevant to interactions between interlocutors. These variables can be strong enough to influence speakers to move either closer to (i.e., converge) or further away (i.e., diverge) from each other on any number of linguistic or paralinguistic levels. Convergence, the most general case, is considered to be the one in which speech shifts take place in order to encourage further interaction between interlocutors as well as to reduce the perceived discrepancies between them (Giles & Smith, 1979). According to Giles and Powesland (1975), the desire for social approval is at the heart of such speech accommodation. Cultural empathy is related to social approval in that showing understanding of an ethnic group's cultural orientation (as cultural empathy was operationally defined) may be interpreted as an expression of social approval by acknowledging that the group has a positive social identity since it is one which is worth understanding. According to accommodation theory, the recipients of this expression of social approval tend to respond positively and wish to reciprocate by returning social approval to their interlocutor. Therefore, we can expect that if a member of the target culture displays cultural empathy or sensitivity towards L2 learners by trying to understand their culture, customs, and traditions better, the L2 learners may feel more accepted by this target-culture member and may want to show their appreciation through accommodation.

However, it is also possible that once an individual has already secured social approval from others and with it a positive social identity, he or she will feel no further need to continue to actively seek out such approval or positive identity. Rogers (1971) feels that fearful and insecure individuals will act in terms of those values which bring them social approval. In the opposite situation, where individuals already feel secure, socially accepted, and approved of, we could expect that these same individuals would feel more at ease about being themselves. Thus, there would no longer be any need to explicitly converge on a linquistic level in order to seek that approval. Speakers would also feel free to use their vernaculars or casual styles, as they would with peers from their own group. Responding in this way would result in linguistic differences not only in native speaker–native speaker (NS–NS) settings (LaFerriere, 1979) but also in native speaker–nonnative speaker (NS–NNS) interactions. Dickerson (1974), using the Labovian attention to speech paradigm, has shown that the more casual the speech style used by the L2 learner, the lower the percentage there is of correct or standard target-language (TL) forms. If the L2 learners used their most casual styles in the interaction described above, they would, at the same time, be diverging from the TL speaker. This linguistic phenomenon may occur even though on a psychological level their intention might actually be to reduce the social distance rather than increase it through linguistic divergence. This sociolinguistic prediction of divergence in a situation involving the expression of social approval is a possibility which Giles does 'not discuss in his accommodation theory.

The investigation of L2 phonology within a social psychological context is also important because it considers that variable phonological performance can be a function of social psychological factors. Since biological factors have been posited to account for the failure of many adults to achieve a more native-like L2 production (Scovel, 1969; Seliger, 1978, 1981), recognition of these factors is especially important with regard to adult learners. As a result, in many instances pronunciation teaching has been all but neglected, since pedagogical intervention has been felt to be futile. This has been unfortunate since speakers are evaluated socially on their speech (Eisenstein, 1983; Giles & Powesland, 1975).

2. THE STUDY

The study addressed the following question: Will Dominican L2 learners linguistically converge toward or diverge from the pronunciation of a TL speaker who responds to them in a culturally empathic manner?

It was hypothesized that in terms of specific phonological variables, L2 learners would linguistically diverge from the pronunciation of a TL interlocutor whom they perceived to be culturally empathic toward them. It was felt that the effects of the perception of empathy would override the general need to seek social approval. No longer needing to seek approval, since it had already been bestowed, the learners would feel less need to linguistically converge and instead would seek to reduce the formality of the situation and also the social distance between themselves and the TL group member. They would then address the TL speaker in the same way they would speak to peers, that is, through use of their vernacular styles.

2.1. Subjects

Subjects for the study, 52 intermediate to advanced adult female Dominican ESL learners, were selected from ESL programs at the City University of
New York. The women ranged in age from 18 to 46, with a median age of 22.
The median age at arrival in the United States was 18 years, with a range from
10 to 43 years of age. The average length of residence in the United States was
6 years. The residence patterns of these students in New York City indicated
that they lived in relatively similar neighborhoods in terms of socioeconomic
status ranging from lower working class to lower middle class.

Information was gathered on the students' motivational orientations to
learning English, since it was felt that this was a factor which could affect an
individual's reactions to cultural empathy. Instrumental motivation was strongly
suggested by the fact that the students had generally chosen rather practical
majors in college in the sense that their academic studies would clearly prepare
them for jobs after graduation (e.g., business, computers, nursing, etc.) Forty-
three learners, in fact, said they were studying English for school or job-related
reasons. Furthermore, two of these said that they planned to return to the Dominican Republic after finishing their studies to bring back to their people the
knowledge and skills they had gained. Only two claimed to be learning English
for integrative reasons, yet even they were also considering returning to their
countries after their studies. In any case, each student certainly needed English
in order to succeed in her studies here.

2.2. Design

After an initial interview (pretest), students viewed a videotape (treatment), were interviewed a second time (posttest), and, lastly, filled out questionnaires, both as a check on their perceptions and for additional attitudinal
information. After the initial interview, each subject was randomly assigned to
either a control group receiving the neutral treatment or an experimental group
receiving the empathic treatment. The only constraint on the randomization
procedure was that experimental and control subjects were blocked or matched
for equal numbers of low L2 phonological proficiency (or heavily Spanish-
accented English) and high L2 phonological proficiency (or moderately to slightly
accented English). This procedure was necessitated by the following factors.
Since they were being interviewed orally, it was necessary that the subjects had
some minimal level of fluency in English. For this reason they had been chosen
from the intermediate and advanced proficiency levels of the various ESL programs. However, most of these programs placed heaviest emphasis on teaching
the skill of writing, and it was felt that their placement procedures did not
reflect the students' levels of phonological accuracy in English. Since this was

a study on phonological performance, the interviewer made an impressionistic assessment of each subject's L2 phonological proficiency during the first interview. On this basis, subjects were categorized in the experimental design according to degree of accentedness (i.e., as having high or low degrees of Spanish-accented English). In this way, equal numbers of subjects in each category could be represented in the control and experimental conditions. Furthermore, it could be determined if there was a difference in style-shifting between the two proficiency levels.

2.3. Materials

The initial interview consisted of a biographical questionnaire which allowed three kinds of data to be obtained:
1. Baseline data on the subjects' L2 phonological systems.
2. Speech samples upon which to judge the subjects' relative degrees of accent in order to categorize them according to L2 proficiency level for purposes of the research design.
3. Background biographical information.

The control and experimental conditions were established through the use of videotapes which portrayed the investigator teaching a small group of female Dominican ESL students. The lesson consisted of the reading and discussion of a story about a young Dominican woman who returns to the Dominican Republic and becomes aware that she has changed as a result of living in the United States for a number of years. This story theme was chosen because it provided the opportunity for an empathic treatment by the teacher. In the neutral tape, the investigator's aim was to appear as neutral as possible by reading the story to the class in a matter-of-fact manner and subsequently going over vocabulary items and factual comprehension questions using a fairly even tone of voice and a limited number of nonverbal cues. In contrast, in the empathic tape the investigator's aim was to appear culturally empathic toward the students by involving them more in the discussion of the story and asking them if they had ever experienced feelings of anomie, as had the main character of the story. In general, the teacher expressed a desire to understand the difficulties stemming from specific cultural differences that immigrants often have to overcome when coming to a new land or when returning to their homelands. The investigator used response modes that are considered to be effective ways of communicating empathy (Curran, 1972; Horwitz & Horwitz, 1979) and aimed at using appropriate nonverbal cues as well (e.g., eye contact, smiling, etc.).

After the tapes were made, they were shown to two sets of judges, American graduate students and Dominican ESL students, who were asked to rate the teacher according to the same empathy scales which were to be given to the subjects in the study. In addition, the investigator herself viewed the tapes and coded them for nonverbal cues using Gabriel's (1980) study, *Dominican Migrant Nonverbal Behavior,* as a guide. On the basis of all of the judgments as well as additional comments and suggestions made by many of the judges, the tapes were edited to their final versions.

The posttreatment interview questions asked each student her opinion about certain aspects of the lesson she had just observed on tape and ways of improving the ESL instruction. Since the study looked at phonological style-shifting in response to cultural empathy, the main concern in choosing the questions was that they be fairly neutral and identical from condition to condition so as not to introduce any other social psychological factors. The topic concerning ESL instruction was also chosen because it was natural within the context of the experiment. In order to maintain consistency in the interviewer's behavior from the treatment to the end of the interview session, she attempted to act in a reserved and businesslike manner among the students who had seen the neutral tape. In contrast, during the interviews with the students who had been assigned to the empathic condition, the interviewer looked for opportunities to be supportive both verbally and nonverbally.

To determine if the interviewer was indeed perceived as more empathic in the empathic condition, a research assistant administered two self-report written questionnaires in the subjects' L1 at the end of the entire session. The subjects were told that the research assistant was an independent researcher in the hope that this explanation would encourage the women to be more honest in filling out the questionnaries. The format of the first questionnaire was based on Davis' (1983) Interpersonal Reactivity Index, a self-report measure of empathy. The second scale was simply a series of statements describing the interviewer according to different adjectives which could be said to typify an empathic person (P. Tirone, personal communication, 1984). On each questionnaire the students were asked to indicate on a Likert scale how much they agreed or disagreed with each statement.

A written attitudinal questionnaire was also administered by the research assistant to obtain some additional background information which might aid in the interpretation of the results of the study. This questionnaire also took the form of a Likert scale. The statements used were based on part of an attitudinal questionnaire used by Pierson, Fu, and Lee (1980). All of the written questionnaires had been refined on the basis of pilot test results.

Each subject was interviewed and audiotaped separately, shown the appropriate videotape while the investigator left the room, interviewed again, and then directed into a different room where the research assistant was waiting to administer the written questionnaires. The whole procedure generally took about 45 minutes.

2.4. Analysis of Data

The investigator phonetically transcribed the following variables for each subject: prevocalic /r/, stressed /Λ/, unstressed /ə/, initial /s/ consonant clusters (/##sC__/), and final consonant clusters (/__CC##/). The rationale for choosing these variables for the study was that they have been found to vary stylistically and/or correlate significantly with social variables among Hispanic L2 speakers (see e.g., Anisman, 1975; Brennan & Brennan, 1981; Fishman, Cooper, & Ma, 1975). In addition, the investigator phonetically transcribed her own final consonant clusters to see if she had been accommodating to the learners. Only consonant clusters were analyzed since native speakers of English tend to simplify these clusters in final position along a style continuum according to socioeconomic status as well as the degree of situational formality (Labov, 1972; Wolfram, 1969). However, it is highly unlikely that a monolingual native speaker of English would use Spanish-influenced variants, such as [r] or substitute [o] for [Λ] to accommodate toward a Hispanic L2 learner of English.

A decision had to be made as to what would constitute convergence and divergence. Since this was a performance study, it seemed appropriate to measure the subjects' phonological productions against the investigator's. However, there was no way of knowing if the subjects would have enough exposure to the investigator's idiolect to know what TL norms to move toward or away from. An assumption was made that the investigator's speech was representative of Standard New York English and that the learners would recognize this TL variety, as L2 learners have been shown to have an awareness of standardness in the L2 as distinct from nonstandardness (Eisenstein, 1979). Since the analysis consisted of a tabulation of TL versus non-TL productions, it was felt that a range of TL acceptability according to this abstract TL norm, as judged by the investigator, would suffice.

An intrarater reliability test indicated that all variables met the criterion for reliability with scores higher than .80 (see Table 1). However, interrater reliability judgments failed to achieve this criterion for /r/ and the two vowels. (See Table 2). It is likely that this failure was due more to the acoustic and phonetic nature of these sounds than to an actual disagreement between raters as to what sound was actually produced. The investigator used a particular set of criteria for labeling each sound as either TL or non-TL. It is relatively easy to communicate this set of criteria to other raters when the task is to judge consonants. A consonant cluster is either simplified or it is not, just as a consonantal sound is either substituted or it is not. However, with respect to liquids (e.g., /r/) or vowels, it is very difficult to clearly explain at what point along a continuum of possible variants the sound produced is no longer to be considered TL. This interpretation of the reliability test results is supported by the

Table 1. Intrarater Reliability

Variable	Total agreed / Total # tokens	Percent agreement
/r/	$\dfrac{43}{51}$	84
/ʌ/	$\dfrac{40}{42}$	95
/ə/	$\dfrac{41}{50}$	82
/##sC__/	$\dfrac{40}{42}$	95
/__CC##/ (Subjects')	$\dfrac{109}{123}$	88
/__CC##/ (Investigator's)	$\dfrac{92}{93}$	98

failure of a second independent rater to reach the criterion level of agreement with the first independent rater on these three variables (see Table 3).

2.5. Results

For each subject the percentage of TL correctness was calculated for each of the interviews by simply dividing the number of TL productions for each variable by the total number of tokens for that variable. The mean percentages of TL correctness across subjects for each variable were then calculated, and an analysis of covariance was performed on the data to test the hypothesis that the L2 learners would linguistically diverge in response to a culturally empathic TL speaker. While the analysis of covariance procedure yielded no significant results which were directly related to the hypothesis, there were significant effects for proficiency level for final consonant clusters ($p < .05$; see Table 4).

A t test for independent samples was performed on the mean scores of the empathy scales. While there was no significant difference between the two groups in terms of their perceptions of the interviewer, significant correlations (Pearson Product-Moment) were found between such perceptions and the raw gain scores for /r/, /##sC__/, and final clusters ($p < .05$ for each). There was a positive correlation for the first two variables and a negative correlation for the third (see Table 5). In other words, the more the subjects perceived cultural empathy on their interlocutor's part, the more they increased their TL production of /r/ and /##sC__/. In contrast, the more they perceived cultural empathy, the more they decreased their TL production of final clusters. The empathy scale scores also correlated significantly with the factors of length of residence

Table 2. Interrater Reliability

Variable	Total agreed / Total # tokens	Percent agreement
/r/	$\frac{78}{101}$	77
/ʌ/	$\frac{69}{96}$	72
/ə/	$\frac{51}{87}$	58
/##sC__/	$\frac{88}{99}$	88
/__CC##/ (Subjects')	$\frac{92}{109}$	84
/__CC##/ (Investigator's)	$\frac{78}{82}$	91

($r = -.26$, $p < .05$) and attitudes toward the target culture ($r = .29$, $p < .05$). In other words, the longer the women lived in the United States, the lower they rated their American interviewer in terms of culturally empathic qualities. However, the more favorably disposed they were toward American culture, as measured by their attitudinal scale scores, the higher they rated their interviewer on these qualities.

3. DISCUSSION

The subjects' perceptions of the interviewer's degree of cultural empathy varied, but not according to the experimental design. Therefore, this study failed

Table 3. Interrater Reliability between First and Second Raters

Variable	Total agreed / Total # tokens	Percent agreement
/r/	$\frac{94}{148}$	64
/ʌ/	$\frac{109}{139}$	78
/ə/	$\frac{96}{157}$	61

Table 4. Analysis of Covariance for /__CC##/

Source of variation	Sum of squares	df	Mean square	F	p
Covariates					
/__CC##/1	0.974	1	0.974	47.052	<.000
Main effects					
Proficiency	0.136	1	0.136	6.569	<.014
Condition	0.006	1	0.006	0.299	n.s.
2-way interactions					
Proficiency/condition	0.005	1	0.005	0.250	n.s.

in its attempt to experimentally manipulate the perception of cultural empathy. However, it did succeed in revealing significant relationships between such perception and the amount of phonological variation exhibited by female Dominican ESL learners in terms of increases and decreases in TL production. That such a relationship exists strongly suggests that some of these variables function, to different extents and in different ways, as social markers for these nonnative English speakers. Thus, the study did achieve its more general goal of gaining further insight into the social psychological dynamics of L1–L2 interactions.

The failure of the experiment to successfully manipulate cultural empathy was probably due to difficulties in maintaining the neutral treatment. During the posttreatment interviews, particularly in the neutral condition, it was very difficult for the interviewer to maintain the appropriate behavior, in contrast to the great deal of control which could be achieved in the videotapes. It was very difficult during these actual interviews to maintain a neutral stance with women who often tended to appear very friendly with a lot of smiles and laughter.

Table 5. Correlation Coefficients between Raw Gain Scores and Perceived Empathy Scores

Phonological variable	Correlation with empathy score
Raw gain /r/	.29*
Raw gain /ʌ/	.15
Raw gain /ə/	.19
Raw gain /##sC__/	.31*
Raw gain /__CC##/	−.23*

*$p < .05$

During the audiotape transcription process, it was noticed that the interviewer had sometimes unconsciously accommodated toward the interviewees in terms of laughter or supportive feedback. Indeed, it was a lack of neutral or low ratings of cultural empathy that resulted in the similarity in the empathy scores between the two groups. However, as stated above, the interviewer was perceived as culturally empathic to varying degrees by the subjects, but not necessarily in a pattern consistent with the experimental design.

Another likely cause for failure was the unnatural laboratory nature of the experiment. There is a lack of congruity between experimental manipulation and empathic behavior. Therefore, to manipulate empathy in order to achieve the effects sought after in this study is a very delicate matter indeed.

In spite of the problems with the experimental design, a relationship was found between the perception of a TL speaker as being culturally empathic and phonological variation in L2. The overall correlations between the raw gain scores of the dependent variables and the empathy scores were both positive and negative, indicating that different phonological variables are sensitive to a given social psychological factor in differing ways. This finding suggests that the variables showing significant relationships with perceived cultural empathy may be identified as social markers for female Dominican learners of English although these variables behave differently in response to the same social psychological stimulus. (Markers are used here in the sense of speech cues that potentially provide the listener with information about the speaker's social characteristics; see Scherer & Giles, 1979.)

The analysis of covariance revealed a significant effect for phonological proficiency level. The fact that the relationships between phonological variation and perception of cultural empathy were found to a larger extent among the less phonologically proficient learners rather than the highly proficient ones is in keeping with Dowd's (1984) findings with regard to female Mexican learners of English. She found a significantly greater amount of variation among the beginning learners in her study as compared to the intermediate and advanced learners. These two studies provide evidence that less proficient learners exhibit more phonological variability than more proficient ones do with respect to sociolinguistically and/or social psychologically motivated variation. It may be expected that the interlanguage of low-proficiency learners would have more instability than that of more highly proficient learners, since the TL has been acquired to a far more limited degree.

The perception of cultural empathy was also significantly related to length of residence in the United States and attitudes toward American culture. The relationship with length of residence was a negative one, while the relationship with attitudes was positive. The results indicate that the longer the subjects had lived in the United States, the less they tended to perceive their interviewer as culturally empathic. It is possible that the longer L2 learners live in a foreign country, the more they lose tolerance for being treated empathically by members of the target culture. A number of studies (Savignon, 1972; Gardner, Smythe, & Clement, 1979) found that with increasing exposure to the target culture there may be increasingly negative attitudes toward the culture. In contrast, the relationship found between perceived cultural empathy and attitudes was a positive one, suggesting that the more positive the women felt toward American culture, the higher they tended to rate their interviewer as culturally empathic. However, it is also possible that answers on the attitudinal questionnaire were influenced by the students' perceptions of the last American with whom they had interacted, that is, the investigator.

As far as applying L1 theories to L2 data is concerned, the fact that the variables did not behave consistently with respect to increasing or decreasing TL correctness suggests (along with other studies in this volume) that not all L2 style-shifting can be adequately accounted for by Labov's principle of attention to speech. Attention to speech predicts shifting in one or the other direction. In this data, shifting was found to occur in opposite directions in response to the same social situation. We may have to look for psycholinguistic explanations such as perceptual saliency in order to account for some L2 variation, as Beebe and Giles (1984) assert. Furthermore, it appears that some kind of social psychological dynamic which is not encompassed by speech accommodation theory may underlie L2 phonological performance. These women exhibited divergence on a variable while perceiving or claiming to perceive their interlocutor to be culturally empathic toward them. Speech accommodation theory would not predict divergence under this circumstance. A tentative conclusion of this study is that both Labov's principle of attention to speech and Giles' speech accommodation theory do not always account for L2 speech behavior. The findings of this study point toward caution when designing research based on L1 models.

4. IMPLICATIONS

Wong (1983) claims that empathy for students' cultural backgrounds establishes the necessary foundation for a good relationship between teacher and students. It would be difficult to find an ESL teacher who disagrees with such a common sense belief. However, while most teachers would agree that empathy toward one's students is a good thing, the findings of this study suggest the possibility that those L2 learners who have lived in the target culture longer may react negatively to a display of empathy. It is almost as if they lose appreciation for what may seem to them to be naively optimistic attitudes of their teachers about their social and linguistic progress. Perhaps some L2 learners become jaded over time. Teachers need to understand and be prepared to deal with this possible reaction.

Teachers should also be made aware of the effects they may have on their own students and should understand that they themselves may be a source of variation in their students' speech. The L2 learners' perceptions of the teacher's cultural empathy toward them may result in more or less targetlike production at any given time.

Finally, the most important implication is that social psychological factors should be dealt with in any approach to pronunciation teaching. The fact that adult ESL learners can vary their levels of TL production should indicate to teachers that their students are capable of improving their TL production rates if they feel they have a good reason or a need to do so. Students may be concerned with a number of problems such as intelligibility or communicative effectiveness, but they should also be concerned with social evaluations based on their speech. Pronunciation could be taught after an assessment of learners' needs with respect to what they want to communicate about themselves and what they want to communicate to their interlocutors on a phonological level. Certain discrepancies could be pointed out between what learners actually produce and what they wish to produce in order to achieve a particular social psychological purpose, for example, returning social approval to an interlocutor through convergence in a formal situation. Students must first be made aware of the social markers in their L2 speech. Then they must become aware of the social evaluations they receive as a result of using these markers. Only after such awareness occurs can they decide if they wish to make a change in their L2 speech patterns.

REFERENCES

Anisman, P. (1975). Some aspects of code switching in New York Puerto Rican English. *Bilinqual Review, 2*(1 & 2), 56–86.

Beebe, L., & Giles, H. (1984). Speech accommodation theories: A discussion in terms of second language acquisition. *International Journal of the Sociology of Language, 46*, 5–32.

Brennan, E. M., & Brennan, J. S. (1981). Measurements of accent and attitude toward Mexican-American speech. *Journal of Psycholinquistic Research, 10*(5), 487–501.

Curran, C. (1972). *Counseling learning: A whole person model for education.* New York: Grune and Stratton.

Davis, M. H. (1983). Measuring individual differences in empathy: Evidence for a multidimensional approach. *Journal of Personality and Social Psychology, 44*(1), 113–126.

Dickerson, L. J. (1974). *Internal and external patterning of phonological variability in the speech of Japanese learners of English: Toward a theory of second language acquisition.* Unpublished doctoral dissertation, University of Illinois.

Dowd, J. (1984). *Phonological variation in L2 speech: The effects of emotional questions and field-dependence/field-independence on second language performance.* Unpublished doctoral dissertation, Teachers College, Columbia University.

Eisenstein, M. (1979). *The development of dialect discrimination and stereo-typing in adult learners of English as a second language.* Unpublished doctoral dissertation, The Graduate Center, City University of New York.

Eisenstein, M. (1983). *Language variation and the ESL curriculum.* Washington, DC: Center for Applied Linguistics.

Fishman, J. A., Cooper, R. L., & Ma, R. (1975). *Bilingualism in the barrio* (2nd ed.). Bloomington: Indiana University Press.

Gabriel, G. (1980). *Dominican migrant nonverbal behavior.* Unpublished doctoral dissertation, Fordham University.

Gardner, R. C., Smythe, P., & Clement, R. (1979). Intensive second language study in a bicultural milieu: An investigation of attitudes, motivation and language proficiency. *Language Learning, 29*(2), 305–320.

Giles, H., & Powesland, P. F. (1975). *Speech style and social evaluation.* London: Academic Press.

Giles, H., & Smith, P. M. (1979). Accommodation theory: Optimal levels of convergence. In H. Giles & R. St. Clair (Eds.), *Language and social psychology* (pp. 1–20). Baltimore: University Park Press.

Horwitz, E., & Horwitz, M. (1979). Bridging individual differences: Empathy and communicative competence. In H. Trueba & C. Barnett-Mizrachi (Eds.), *Bilinqual milti-cultural education and the professional. From theory to practice.* (pp. 351–359). Rowley, MA: Newbury House.

Labov, W. (1972). *Sociolinguistic patterns.* Philadelphia: University of Pennsylvania Press.

La Ferriere, M. (1979). Ethnicity in phonological variation and change. *Language, 55*(3), 603–617.

Pierson, H. D., Fu, G. S., & Lee, S. (1980). An analysis of the relationship between language attitudes and English attainment of secondary students in Hong Kong. *Language Learning, 30*(2), 289–316.

Rogers, C. (1971). The interpersonal relationship: The core of guidance. In C. R. Rogers & B. Stevens (Eds.), *Person to person: The problem of being human.* (pp. 85–101). New York: Pocket Book.

Savignon, S. (1972). *Communicative competence: An experiment in foreign language teaching.* Montreal: Marcel Dider.

Scherer, K., & Giles, H. (1979). *Social markers in speech.* New York: Cambridge University Press.

Scovel, T. (1969). Foreign accents, language acquisition and cerebral dominance. *Language Learning, 19,* 245–254.

Seliger, H. (1978). Implications of a multiple critical-periods hypothesis for second language learning. In W. C. Ritchie (Ed.), *Second language acquisition research* (pp. 11–19). New York: Academic Press.

Seliger, H. (1981). Exceptions to critical period predictions: A sinister plot. In R. W. Andersen (Ed.), *New dimensions in second language acquisition research* (pp. 47–57). Rowley, MA: Newbury House.

Wolfram, W. (1969). *A sociolinguistic description of Detroit negro speech.* Washington, DC: Center for Applied Linguistics.

Wong, A. (1983, March). *Beyond empathy: Helping ESL instructors cope with cross-cultural differences.* Paper presented at the Seventeenth Annual TESOL Convention, Toronto.

PART III

Alternative Varieties and Second-Language Acquisition

CHAPTER 8

Variation and Convergence in Nonnative Institutionalized Englishes

JESSICA WILLIAMS

1. NONNATIVE INSTITUTIONALIZED ENGLISH AND SECOND-LANGUAGE ACQUISITION

The study of language variation within second-language acquisition research generally includes variation across learners as well as within the production of a single learner. An area which is less often addressed is the variation which is found across nonnative institutional varieties. It is important that this be done both because of the huge numbers of people who speak these nonnative varieties and because of the wide-ranging implications that this area of research has for the study of second-language acquisition in general. A number of descriptive studies of nonnative institutionalized varieties of English (NIVEs) have been reported (Bailey & Görlach, 1982; Görlach, 1984; Kachru, 1982b; Lowenberg, 1986; Platt, Weber, & Ho, 1984; Smith, 1981; Williams, 1987a).

Spoken in such diverse settings as Fiji, Ghana, India, Nigeria, Singapore, and Sri Lanka, NIVEs are used as both international and intranational languages. Yet for very few speakers is English chronologically the first language. Platt *et al.* (1984) refer to development through the educational system as the single most important criterion for classification as a NIVE. In nations where NIVEs are spoken, depending on educational level, English may be taught as a subject or used as a medium of instruction. In virtually none of them, however, is English a mother tongue which is brought to the classroom by a substantial portion of the population.

JESSICA WILLIAMS • Department of Linguistics, University of Illinois at Chicago, Chicago, Illinois 60680.

A second attribute of NIVEs is their broad functional and sociolinguistic range. As mentioned above, NIVEs are used intranationally, both between and among ethnic groups. Like their external native speakers (NS) counterparts, NIVE speakers can style-shift depending on social context. This shifting often takes place along a continuum which has been compared to the post-creole continuum (Platt & Weber, 1980). The acrolect is the closest to external norms, while the basilect is the most divergent. A third characteristic, and the focus of this analysis, is that NIVEs have undergone certain changes which have resulted in linguistic features quite different from NS varieties such as American and British English. These modifications may range from phonological and syntactic innovations to new rules for conversational interaction. Kachru (1982a) has attibuted these changes to the process of *nativization*, that is, an adaptation to a new sociocultural and linguistic context.[1] It is undoubtedly the case that this process accounts for many of the features which differ from variety to variety; however, there are also many features which are similar across NIVEs, a phenomenon which cannot be explained by individual processes of nativization. Certain forms which are found in NIVEs strongly resemble forms found in learner languages and, at one time, may in fact have been the result of individual second-language acquisition. However, these varieties, which contain many such modifications, have spread throughout the population and become institutionalized. As a result, they can no longer be considered learner varieties of their NS counterparts.

While the genesis of NIVEs necessarily entailed second-language acquisition, there are a number of important differences between their development and more familiar cases of second-language acquisition, where the learner is surrounded by NSs. For most second-language learners (SLLs), for whom the NS target is available, some progression in the direction of that target is possible. Even in foreign language learning settings, the NS target is used as a model for learning and teaching. In NIVE situations, the nature of the target is somewhat different. The original target is often no longer easily accessible—or even desirable—for most speakers. Instead, NIVEs have become the standard and the target of second-language acquisition.

Any comparison between NIVEs and second-language acquisition data should in no way imply that NIVEs are linguistically or expressively deficient versions of some NS standard. Several researchers (Kachru, 1982a; Lowenberg, 1986) have urged that the innovations in localized speech, rather than its deviations from some exonormative standard, be noted. Many of the innovations found in NIVEs, particularly lexical ones, were indeed created to meet

---

[1] Nativization, as used here, should not be confused with the work of Roger Andersen (1979). Andersen defines *nativization* as the creation of an individual, internal autonomous linguistic system. It bears little resemblance to Kachru's conception of the term.

the needs of the new sociocultural settings and cannot be construed as steps along the way toward acquisition of some NS target. Thus, to compare NIVEs to other acquisitional phenomena is not to deny their legitimacy; rather, it is to explore the diversity as well as the similarities which can be found in language acquisition and production data across a wide range of settings, as a contribution to the general knowledge of language and language learning.

2. VARIATION AND CONVERGENCE IN NIVES

Descriptions of NIVEs from around the world reveal that there are many differences, both across NIVEs and between NIVEs and NS varieties. However, NIVEs, which are found in a wide range of geographical settings and used by speakers of diverse first languages, also exhibit a number of interesting similarities. Williams (1987a) and Platt *et al.* (1984) show similar findings regarding some of these cross-NIVE features. The following analysis examines syntactic and some morphological features in NIVE production.

There are a number of modifications typical particularly of lower sociolects of NIVEs which render NIVEs both more regular and less redundant than their NS counterparts. One of the most immediately apparent features of NIVEs in this category is the use of the invariant tag question:

(1)

   a. He will come tomorrow, *not so?*
      (Cameroon: Todd, 1982)
   b. You are coming to the meeting, *isn't it?*
      (India: Das, 1982)

Another area which shows evidence of a shift to a more regular system is in the distinction between mass and count nouns:

(2)

   a. hardware*s; (a)* trouser
      (Kenya: Zuengler, 1982)
   b. stuff*s:* dandruff*s*
      (Singapore: Williams, 1987a)

The verbal system of NIVEs is also more regular in some respects. Progressive aspect has been extended to verbs which, in most NS English contexts, cannot co-occur with *-ing:*

(3)

   a. I *am having* a cold.
      (West Africa: Hancock & Angogo, 1982)

b. Ram was *knowing* that he would come.
   (India: Kachru, 1982c)

The redundancy which is inherent in NS English may be reduced in a variety of ways. Platt *et al.* (1984) report that past is often marked lexically in NIVEs by expressions such as *already* and *last time,* which could make the production of morphological marking semantically redundant. Another way of expressing pastness is to establish a time frame at the beginning of a stretch of speech and let it serve for the balance of the narrative or conversation. This has been found in the production of SLLs (Klein, 1986; Sato, 1986) as well as in NIVEs (Williams, 1987b). Thus, marking may be overt, as in the case of adverbials, or implicit, if the sequencing of events in discourse is meant to follow an actual event line.

A final instance of the reduction of contextual redundancy is the omission of subject pronouns or the extended use of zero anaphora. Where the referent is firmly established in the discourse, NIVE speakers frequently omit further marking (Williams, 1989):

(4)

They make you run round and round and round until you can't take it. You sit down and you know, you are giddy, but *the fellows* still push you, Ø say,'' I give you another ten more second to do the—the circle—to do again.'' That kind of torture, you know. And Ø ask you to carry rifle overhead and do duck walk. (Singapore: Williams, 1987a)

While the modifications mentioned so far tend to increase ambiguity, there are other NIVE features which appear to be less ambiguous than their NS counterparts. One way this can occur is through an increase in transparency. *Transparency* is defined as the one-to-one mapping of form and meaning (Slobin 1980). Lexicalization of various elements of meaning in NIVEs demonstrates this heightened transparency. Some studies (Platt & Weber, 1980; Platt *et al.* 1984; Williams, 1987a) have indicated that the tense-aspect-modality systems of some NIVEs show some evidence of lexicalization, which is generally thought to be a more transparent mapping of meaning than bound morphology. Platt *et al.* (1984) have made the strongest case for lexicalization of aspectual distinctions for Singapore English, although they claim that the same is true of other NIVEs as well. They maintain that the aspectual, and not the tense, system is more important in NIVEs and thus a more likely candidate for such lexicalization. The following are examples from diverse NIVEs of NS lexical items and, in some cases, auxiliary and modal verbs, taking on the role of aspect marking. In no case, however, is this grammaticization process complete, nor is the use of these markers categorical. However, their use is sufficiently distinct from NS norms to merit closer examination.

Lexicalization of the completive aspect is perhaps the clearest example of this kind in NIVEs. The completive aspect is not a notion which is explicitly marked in NS English. It is generally marked more overtly in NIVEs. However, it is not always obvious that the aspectual, as opposed to the temporal, distinction is being marked, because often the surface forms which are used to mark completion are neither new nor different from NS forms. They are often taken from the target verb phrase and simply used in novel ways. It is only where the resultant production is judged ungrammatical by NS standards that it attracts attention:

(5)

    a. It *has been* established many years ago.
       (Ghana: Tingley, 1981)
    b. I *have read* this book last month.
       (India: Das, 1982; Verma, 1982)

In Singapore and Malaysian English, *already* is commonly used to mark completion. *Already* appears with, but also often without, a verb marked morphologically for past:

(6)

    a. So I was walking and I saw the tree, you know. A figure, you know? And it was dark, completely dark because I think it must be overnight *already*. The blood clot *already*. (Singapore: Williams, 1987a)

In Singapore English, *already* can also mark completion in the future, as well as the anterior past, without simultaneous morphological marking of tense:

    c. I'm so scared because by next week, I think I'm on night shift *already*. (Singapore: Williams, 1987a)
    d. She asked me to go—to go out to lunch with her. I agreed *already* that day. Then I think it rained. After it rained, I cancelled, (anterior past) (Singapore: Williams, 1987a)

It is even used for negative completion, equivalent to the NS construction *not . . . anymore:*

    e. That was when the first national library, 25 years ago. Now, they don't have mobile libraries *already,* uh? (Singapore: Williams, 1987a)
    f. Everywhere if you scared, then you don't have to go out and work *already,* wa. (Singapore: Williams, 1987a)

The habitual aspect, according to Platt *et al.* (1984), is marked in Singapore and Malaysian English by *used to* or *usually:*

(7):

    a. We *use(d)*[2] to speak Hokkien at home (now).
    b. She *usually* go shopping every Saturday. (Malaysia: Wong, 1981)

Remote habitual is usually marked by *last time* in Singapore English, equivalent to NS English *before:*

(8)

Last time, it's not like now. *Last time* all you have to do is just go there and register. Whatever you said, counts. Right now, no (not a reference to a single incident, but to the previous practice of registration of ethnic group by self-report). (Singapore: Williams, 1987a)

3. A DETAILED LOOK AT ONE NIVE: SINGAPORE ENGLISH

The description above gives a very general picture of the ways in which NIVEs diverge form external NS models of English, as well as ways in which modifications in various NIVEs converge. The following is a more detailed look at one NIVE, Singapore English (SingE), and at one aspect of production in particular: yes/no questions. Singapore English is perhaps unique even among NIVE nations in that there is a comparatively high level of English proficiency and use. Although there are four official languages in Singapore—Mandarin Chinese, Malay, Tamil, and English—English is the "de facto national language and the dominant working language" of Singapore (Foley, 1984, p. 29). On the one hand, it is almost never the language that a Singaporean learns first. On the other hand, for many, especially those under 45 who have been educated in English-medium schools, it is the language in which they profess to be most proficient and the one which they use the most.

Not all Singaporeans fall into this category of the proficient speaker of SingE. Rather, there is a cline of proficiency (Kachru, 1982a). The participants in this study were drawn from the middle of this linguistic cline. They were all educated at English-medium schools and have the equivalent of a high school diploma. Their occupations include clerks, secretaries, policemen, military men, and factory workers. These jobs do not often bring them into contact with NSs of external varieties of English. None of the participants has ever traveled outside of Asia. Their first language (L1) backgrounds reflect the languages of Singapore: Malay, Tamil, and four dialects of Chinese.

[2]It is possible that this usage is the result of some confusion between NS *used to* and *to be used to*, since both connote habituation. In Singapore English, the final *d* is not enunciated. It is unclear, therefore, whether this is the effect of a phonological deletion rule on the former, or if it is an innovation in the use of the latter. Because of this uncertainty, the form is transcribed as *use(d).*

The study examines the spoken production of second-language English speakers in Singapore and compares it to similar production by NSs of English living in a large city in the eastern United States. Data consist of six 45-minute audiotaped unguided conversations (see Perdue, 1984) between two members of each group, a total of 12 participants for each group. The speakers were selected from the two groups on the basis of educational and occupational status. Six participants were located initially by field assistants who were recruited from within each speech community. These six were then asked to choose a partner with whom to converse. The relationship between the two speakers was thus established prior to the study. In the case of the SingE speakers, members of the conversational pairs did not share a first language or dialect.

The SingE and NS participants were matched as closely as possible for educational and occupational status. The NSs in this study are high school graduates, but none has a university education. Their jobs—waiters, salespeople, housewives, and the like—are similar to those of the Singaporeans. The speakers were chosen in the same way as the Singaporeans; that is, a research assistant was hired from within the speech community to recruit participants.

3.1. Yes/No Questions in Second-Language Acquisition Research

Research on the development of interrogatives in second-language acquisition was a focus of several early studies (Bailey, Eisenstein, & Madden, 1976; Cancino, Rosansky, & Schumann, 1978; Hatch, 1974; Wode, 1978). One difficulty which is apparent in these studies is that most elicitation techniques fail to capture any spontaneous production of questions. This lack of authentic question data may result in an analysis which obscures both the forms and functions of questions in naturally occurring discourse. Longitudinal studies (Cancino et al., 1978; Ravem, 1978; Wode, 1978) indicate that, in general, learners acquire WH questions and yes/no questions simultaneously, but they reach targetlike performance of yes/no questions first. Acquisition of inverted questions involving copula or modals generally precedes that of questions requiring do support. Intonation was found to be a frequently used method of marking interrogative status among all subjects (Cancino et al., 1978; Felix, 1980; Hatch, 1974). Subject–main-verb inversion was found to be relatively rare, even in questions produced by speakers whose L1s use this device to mark interrogation (Cancino et al., 1978; Ravem, 1978) while subject–copula and subject–modal inversions were far more frequent.

Another significant hurdle in the investigation of the production of questions is to establish a working definition of the term *question. Interrogative* is the term which is usually used to identify a question using structural criteria. Ultan (1978) describes three basic ways of forming interrogatives: (1) some change in intonation which will differentiate the question from a declarative statement; (2) a change from declarative word order, usually subject–verb inversion; and (3) the insertion of segmental elements, such as question words, particles, tags, or affixes. These devices may be combined in a single utterance.

In addition to structural criteria, questions can be defined by function. Quirk, Greenbaum, Leech, and Svartvik (1985) define questions functionally as utterances which seek information (including a yes/no answer). In spite of these attempts to clarify the term, both formal and functional definitions of questions remain vague. It has been shown that constructions which are considered canonical forms for questions, such as those involving subject–verb inversion, have a wide range of discourse and pragmatic functions (Grice, 1975; Searle, 1976). Conversely, the elicitation of information, which is the traditional view of question function, can be performed by a variety of other constructions. Any analysis which seeks to establish the factors which determine the syntactic structure of these utterances will have to take into account their function as well as their form. However, since the range and variety of question function is huge, this analysis is limited to only a small portion of these. Specifically, only those utterances which seek new information or those which attempt to confirm or clarify shared or known information are considered.

Among those utterances which have an information-seeking function, a basic distinction can be made between those which seek new information, as in (9), and those which seek to confirm or clarify old information, as in (10):

(9)

   Do you like living in Los Angeles?[3]

(10)

   a. What a day.
   b. *You just got in?*

Vander Brook, Schlue, and Campbell (1980) point out that these two types of questions represent part of a continuum of speaker presupposition. Questions such as (9) correspond to a low presupposition of a known answer, while questions like that in (10), correspond to high presupposition.

The corpus was subdivided by function into those questions which seek new information (NIQs) and those which seek confirmation or clarification of old information (CCQs). Some examples from SingE may help to illustrate this distinction. Example (11) is a NIQ, while (12) is a CCQ:

(11)

   Ra: *Are you taking any food along the way?*
   Rz: I don't think so. (SE6-005)

---

[3] Those examples which are followed by "NS" (native speaker) or "SE" (SingE speaker) refer to actual transcripts. Those which are not keyed to transcripts are fabricated.

(12)

    L: Okay, lah, you just going to get a letter from principal.
    M: Why?
    L: Because I failed it.
    M: *You failed uh?* (SE2-050)

It is not necessarily the case that NIQs and CCQs correspond strictly to inverted and uninverted word order, respectively. The correlation between question structure and function is a matter for empirical investigation. First, some criteria must be established in order to classify questions as either NIQ or CCQ. This distinction is not always clear, since it is often difficult to determine when new information becomes stale and when given information becomes so far removed in the discourse that it must be once again considered new (Chafe, 1987). The criteria which were used to differentiate between the two types of questions are: (1) the presence of the questioned information in the preceding discourse, and (2) information or knowledge which was shared between the two interlocutors. If a question addressed either of these, it was judged to be a CCQ. All others were counted as NIQs. New information is defined negatively as that which does not appear in the preceding discourse and which was not judged to be shared by the interlocutors. Clearly, the second criterion is more difficult to judge than the first. In order to make these judgments as objective as possible, question classification was made on the basis of evaluations by the researcher and three assistants who were familiar with both local and standard varieties of English. Only questions which could be classified as either a NIQ or a CCQ by three or more raters were retained for analysis.

Questions are analyzed in terms of two basic characteristics: first, basic word order, and second, the presence or absence of the essential syntactic elements of the English interrogative, namely *do* support. Since these features are frequently dependent on verb type, questions are subdivided into those containing (1) main verbs, (2) lexical *be,* (3) lexical *have,* (4) auxiliary *be* and *have,* and (5) modals.[4] Finally, a number of devices are identified and described which were used by subjects in both groups and which mark as questions utterances which contain neither inversion nor *do* support.

---

[4]Lexical *have* presents something of a problem for analysis in that there are differences between British and American English usage. British English, as well as SingE, allows inversion without *do* support with lexical *have,* while American English requires the use of *do* support (compare *Have you any money?* [BrE] with *Do you have any money?* [AE]. Since the SingE speakers have had exposure to both U.S. and British varieties, it is difficult to determine which exonormative model would be most influential. For this reason, questions containing lexical *have* are kept separate from other main verbs.

3.2. Results

From the point of view of word order and the presence of basic syntactic elements, SingE and NS usage is actually surprisingly similar. In particular, every form of yes/no question produced by the SingE speakers can also be found in the speech of the NSs and vice versa. There are, however, sometimes significant quantitative differences in the use of certain question forms. Table 1 gives the figures comparing the use of three question forms in new information questions (NIQs). Table 2 gives the same information for clarification/ confirmation questions (CCQs). The first column consists of those questions which are produced complete with the *do* support. The second column applies to those verbs which require inversion but not *do* support. The last column represents those utterances which include neither inversion nor *do* support, although one or the other may be required by prescriptive standards. These can be found in the production of both speaker groups, although they are technically ungrammatical. Without comparable data from NSs, this usage might be considered characteristic of nonnative varieties in particular. However, it is clear that the inversion and *do* support are frequently absent from the production of NSs as well.

Tables 1 and 2 display the use of inversion and *do* support by the two speaker groups in NIQs and CCQs. In NIQs, it is the main verb which shows the most evidence of inversion plus *do* support. This would be expected, since questions with main verbs are the only interrogatives in the NS target in which

Table 1. Number of Participants Using New Information Yes/No Questions (NIQs)[a]

	+ *do* support/ inversion		+ inversion		− inversion/ *do* support	
	SingE	NS	SingE	NS	SingE	NS
Main verb	8 (89)	20 (65)	—	—	50 (36)	26 (45)
Lexical *be*	—	—	8 (25)	8 (13)	16 (11)	9 (17)
Lexical *have*	1 (11)	11 (35)	2 (6)	0 (0)	28 (20)	6 (11)
Aux *be/have*	—	—	14 (44)	27 (43)	40 (28)	7 (13)
Modals	—	—	8 (25)	26 (42)	4 (3)	5 (10
Total	9	31	32	61	138	49
Percent of total NIQs for each group of speakers:	5	21	18	42	77	36

Note. Numbers in parentheses are percentages.
[a]For Singapore English speakers (SingE), $n = 179$; for native speakers (NS), $n = 141$.

Table 2. Number of Participants Using Confirmation/Clarification Yes/No Questions (CCQs)[a]

	$+ do$ support/ inversion		$+$ inversion		$-$ inversion/ do support	
	SingE	NS	SingE	NS	SingE	NS
Main verb	5 (100)	12 (71)	—	—	37 (32)	64 (48)
Lexical be	—	—	1 (9)	9 (36)	7 (56)	27 (21)
Lexical have	0 (0)	5 (29)	0 (0)	0 (0)	23 (21)	13 (10)
Aux be/have	—	—	3 (27)	10 (40)	45 (40)	20 (15)
Modals	—	—	7 (64)	6 (24)	4 (4)	9 (7)
Total	5	17	11	25	116	133
Percent of total CCQs for each group of speakers:	4	10	8	15	88	75

Note. Numbers in parentheses are percentages.
[a]For Singapore English speakers (SingE), $n = 131$; for native speakers (NS), $n = 176$.

both of these changes from declarative order are found. Modals, copula, and auxiliary verbs are the most frequently inverted. Again, this is not surprising considering prescriptive standards for questions containing these verbs in NS English. Tables 3 and 4 show the differences in the use of inversion according to question function. In these tables, the first two columns in Tables 1 and 2 are combined into one category. In other words, $(1) + do$ support $/ +$ inversion and $(2) +$ inversion form the category "Inverted" in the first row of Tables 3 and 4. Together, these constitute those questions in the corpora which conform to prescriptive norms. Row 2, "Uninverted," corresponds to the third column of Tables 1 and 2. These forms include those which can be found in both the NS and SingE data, yet are not considered strictly grammatical.

3.2.1. Question Function

In NIQs, the difference between the two speaker groups is significant ($X^2 = 4.36$, $p < .05$, $df = 1$). In contrast, in CCQs, the difference between the use of inverted and uninverted order between speaker groups is much smaller ($X^2 = 0.54$, $df = 1$), not even reaching significance. Both speaker groups primarily use SVO order in CCQs: 78% (NS) and 88% (SingE). It appears, then, that the use of SVO questions by the SingE speakers must be considered NS-like for this function, where NS-like use is described in terms of the production of the NSs in this study. Indeed, the uninverted form in CCQ context is typical. Some examples of the more frequent uninverted CCQ from the SingE corpus include:

Table 3. Use of Inversion in New Information Questions

	SingE		NS	
	n	%	*n*	%
Inverted	41	23	92	65
Uninverted	138	77	49	35
	179		141	

$$\chi^2 = 4.36, \, p < .05$$

Table 4. Use of Inversion in Clarification Questions

	SingE		NS	
	n	%	*n*	%
Inverted	16	12	42	24
Uninverted	116	88	133	76
	132		175	

$$\chi^2 = 0.54, \, \text{n.s.}$$

(13)

> L: You go down there and then you pass a market. All the chicken down there, lah. After you pass that, you go further down until you come to one shop that sells paint.
>
> M: *I have to* pass a market? (SE2-298)

(14)

> R: Okay, I give you three minutes, alright? Run to that tree there and bite the bark.
>
> P: *You bite* the bark? What the hell for? (SE5-320)

There is a significant, although smaller number of uninverted NIQs found in the SingE corpus, as seen in the following examples:

(15)

> L: You have money or?
>
> M: I have. Steven give me the room rent already. The bursary money *they give you yet?* (SE2-319)

(16)

    A: She's fair. My whole family is fair, especially my sisters, what. They are even fairer. I just keep myself tan.

    P: Burnt.

    A: They are fair.

    PL *Your sisters they speak the Chinese language—dialect?* (SE3-500)

It appears that SingE speakers have generalized a question form, which in NS English corresponds fairly closely to a specific function (confirmation/clarification), to a wider range of functions. In SingE, not only is the SVO-order question used to make confirmation checks, it is used to elicit new information as well.

3.2.2. Question Form

In the previous section, it was shown that when question function is taken into account, in some cases, NS and SingE question production appears to be quite similar in terms of subject–verb inversion and the use of *do* support. However, this only appears to be true for CCQs. The production of NIQs by the two speaker groups is quite different. Specifically, the SingE speakers use SVO order and fail to use *do* support in NIQs to a far greater extent than do NSs. The following sections examine the ways in which these questions are marked as questions without the aid of standard interrogative syntax.

Tables 1 and 2 indicate that there are large numbers of questions in the data which appear in uninverted SVO order and without *do* support. Among the SingE subjects, 82% of all questions are in uninverted form. For the NSs, the figure is still quite high at 58%. Even when a declarative sentence is used as a question, however, some indication is generally needed to mark the fact that the utterance is indeed a question rather than a statement. There are a wide variety of devices which help to indicate question status and at the same time preclude the necessity of rearranging major constituents and of using *do* insertion. These are seen in Table 5.

    3.2.2a. Tag Questions. One of the most productive forms of uninverted yes/no questions in the SingE data, in terms of number of tokens, includes a question tag. This form constitutes fully one-third of all SVO questions. Question words and particles are frequent in Chinese dialects, Malay, and Tamil. In these languages, the particles are not restricted to any one position in the sentence, although the final position is a common one. In SingE, tags take a number of forms, including the invariant tag (17)—where the tag does not reflect the verb in the main clause—and fixed phrases such as *huh, right, ah* (18).

JESSICA WILLIAMS

Table 5. Devices Used to Indicate Question Status in Uninverted
Yes/No Questions

	SingE		NS	
	n	%	n	%
Tags	89	35	28	16
Intonation	81	32	116	64
Lack of noun phrase	20	8	15	8
Lack of auxiliary verb	14	6	9	5
Alternative questions	49	19	14	8
	253		182	
Total questions (uninverted + inverted)	310		317	
Uninverted questions/ total questions (%)	82		57	

(17)

> P: What's the course for?
> R: What course?
> P: PTI one.
> R: PTI?
> P: They going to train the army people, *is it?* (SE5-016)

(18)

> M: Don't know how long they been keeping the bottle.
> L: It's preserved, *right?*
> M: Preserved? How do you know for how long? (SE2-026)

From the point of view of production, the tag question has three major advantages. First and most important, it maintains the order of constituents used in the declarative sentence. The addition of the tag renders the rearrangement of elements unnecessary because the tag itself, rather than word order, indicates communicative function. Psycholinguistic research (Fodor, Bever, & Garrett, 1974; Kempen, 1977; Slobin, 1973) indicates that the language processing system, from the point of view of both production and comprehension, prefers a standard order. Interruption and rearrangement of sentential elements hinder processing. There have been similar findings in second-language acquisition studies (Clahsen, 1984; Meisel, Clahsen, & Pienemann, 1981). Since the maintenance of SVO order is a basic production strategy, it is necessary to relegate the marking of communicative function to a position outside of this canonical sequence. This is precisely what occurs with the addition of the question tag. This external position is the second major production advantage of the tag question construction. It has been shown that the utterance-final and utterance-initial positions are particularly salient ones (Klein, 1986; Neisser, 1967; Osgood & Bock, 1977; Slobin, 1973). The tag occupies this salient final position, clearly expressing the information-seeking function of the utterance, without disturbing the basic word order. Any ambiguity in communicative function which is created by the preservation of canonical SVO order is compensated by the addition of the question tag. In SingE, the tag has the further production advantage of appearing in invariant forms, which are generally considered to be easier to process than variables ones (Slobin, 1973).

   3.2.2b. Intonation. Another form of SVO-order yes/no question which appears in the data with high frequency is the intonation question, that is, a declarative sentence with rising final intonation. In all three of the L1s of the Singaporeans, a change in pitch or intonation can be used to mark interrogativity. Intonation as a marker of interrogativity has also been noted as characteristic of the pragmatic principles which SLLs follow, particularly in the early stages of acquisition (Cancino *et al.*, 1978; Hatch, 1974; Klein, 1986). Many of the observations made above regarding the tag question are also relevant in the case of intonation questions. As in the case of tag questions, canonical SVO order is preserved, and the only indication of the interrogative status of the utterance is intonation contour and context, as in these SingE examples:

(19)

   A: She still owe me one belacan (shrimp paste) from Malaysia.
   P: How come?
   A: Hm?
   P: *She promised* you? (SE-015)

(20)

   E: Hey, how much interest they charge you, man?
   S: You know what happen? I tell you that—terrible—I hate administration there—
   E: *You purchase* already?
   S: Ya. (SE4-444)

   The intonation question is also highly productive, however, in the NS data. Over half of the uninverted questions in the NS corpus use intonation alone to mark question status. Over one-third of *all* yes/no questions produced by NSs in this sample are marked solely by rising intonation, an even higher figure than was found in the SingE corpus.

   3.2.2c. Lack of Subject NP. In some questions, both *do* support and the subject NP are omitted. The omission of the NP precludes the need for subject–verb inversion:

(21)

> L: Uh—must pass the market. Quite far down.
> M: That means *I* don't have to take the 216 bus, uh? *Drop* at the main one?
> L: No no. Don't go. It's not the same. (SE2-299)

(22)

> S: I already see it. The guy—the performer, you see—was here.
> E: Was he good? Negro uh?
> S: Negro uh. Good!
> E: How *he* dance? *Spin* his leg?
> S: His movements really pro, lah. (SE4-130)

From discourse context, these missing NPs referents (in italics) appear likely to be pronouns. In SingE, when referents are clear in the context of the discourse, subject NPs are deleted as redundant (Williams, 1989). It is possible, then, that these are examples of intonation questions with redundant referents omitted.

3.2.2d. Lack of Auxiliary. In a number of questions in the data, the auxiliary *be* or *have* appear to be absent:

(23)

> R: I really sweat it out, you know. And take a lot of vegetarian—vegetable—sort of vegetarian diet, lah. No meat really—and uh—smoke a lot.
> P: *You trying* to say something?
> R: No. Ya. Smoke a lot. Two big packet a day. (SE5-081)

(24)

> S: Oh, yeah—"Against all Odds" or "All against Odds" or whatever. They say it's very nice or what?
> C: They say the movie's very nice, sure. *You seen* that show?
> S: Noo. (SE1-074)

It is difficult to say whether these were originally SVO or VSO sentences. The fact that they are NIQs implies that an inverted question would be appropriate. However, in the SingE data, auxiliary *be* and *have* are inverted in only 25% of all yes/no questions, suggesting that all omissions may not be from the uninverted form. Omission of auxiliary verbs also occurs regularly in NS English:

(25)

> L: Nobody was down this weekend and I think I would have been invited to the wedding.

B: *Your mother and father still going* down every week? *They staying* down there or what?

L: My father just went down today to get away. My mother's a bitch anymore. (NS6-605)

Perhaps similar surface structures are produced as the result of different strategies in the two speaker groups. It is unfortunately impossible to give a well-founded answer to this question. It does seem clear from the extensive use of these devices, however, that preserving a regular order of constituents and the avoidance of *do* support are high priorities in the production of yes/no questions, particularly by SingE speakers.

There is yet another question form prevalent in SingE production, which is noted in Table 5—the disjunctive or alternative question. This form also maintains SVO order, avoids semantically redundant interrogative syntax, and mirrors similar structures in Chinese. The disjunctive question offers two alternatives within the yes/no question. A full treatment of this topic is beyond the scope of this chapter (see Williams, 1987b), but some examples from the SingE corpus include:

(26)

a. You want to buy country guitar *or classic guitar?* (SE2-008)

b. That one you scared *or not?* (SE1-314)

c. The material is very soft *or what?* (SE2-368)

In general, then, both the NSs and the SingE speakers make extensive use of constructions which do not disturb canonical SVO order. The omission of potentially redundant constituents is also common. This usage is especially frequent in CCQs, although the SingE group in particular has extended it to new contexts. The maintenance of SVO order and the reduction of redundancy are "shortcuts" which shape the spoken production of all the speakers in this study, indicating that usage which is frequently attributed to L2 varieties may sometimes also be found in the production of NSs.

4. CONCLUSION

This brief glimpse at nonnative institutionalized varieties of English can only begin to describe the diversity among them, as well as a number of striking similarities. Both the variation and the convergence among them can provide insights into language acquisition and production processes. The influence of local languages on these new varieties is clear. In the case of SingE, it is evident that Chinese has been a powerful force, creating a unique variety of English. There is continuous innovation in NIVEs; some of these innovations become institutionalized, accounting for some of the modifications which have been examined here. It is this institutionalized status which makes NIVEs a particularly rich area for research in second-language acquisition. What is often elusive in second-language development may be more readily apparent in these stable varieties. At the same time, we can see evidence of some production processes, found across many NIVEs, which may not be limited to these NIVEs at all. On the contrary, it appears that at the level of production at least, SLLs, NIVEs speakers, and NSs have much in common.

REFERENCES

Andersen, R. (1979). Expanding Schumann's pidginization hypothesis. *Language Learning, 29,* 105–119.

Bailey, N., Eisenstein, M., & Madden, C. (1976). The development of WH questions in adult second language learners. In J. Fanselow & R. Crymes (Eds.), *ON TESOL 1976* (pp. 1–17). Washington, DC: TESOL.

Bailey, R., & Görlach, M. (Eds.). (1982). *English as a world language.* Cambridge: Cambridge University Press.

Cancino, H., Rosansky, E., & Schumann, J. (1978). The acquisition of English negatives and interrogatives. In E. Hatch (Ed.), *Second language acquisition: A book of readings* (pp. 207–230).

Chafe, W. (1987). Cognitive constraints on information flow. In R. Tomlin (Ed.), *Coherence and grounding in discourse* (pp. 21–51). Amsterdam: John Benjamins.

Clahsen, H. (1984). The acquisition of German word order: A test case for cognitive approaches to L2 development. In R. Andersen (Ed.), *Second languages: A cross-linguistic perspective* (pp. 219–242). Rowley, MA: Newbury House.

Das, S. (1982). Indian English. In J. Pride (Ed.), *New Englishes* (pp. 141–149).

Felix, S. (1980). Interference, interlanguage and related issues. In S. Felix (Ed.), *Second language development: Trends and issues* (pp. 93–107). Tübingen: Gunter Narr Verlag.

Fodor, J., Bever, T., & Garret, M. (1974). *The psychology of language.* New York: McGraw Hill.

Foley, J. (1984). A study of the development of language among pre-school children in Singapore with particular reference to English. In P. Larson, E. Judd, & D. Messerschmidt (Eds.), *On TESOL 84* (pp. 29–44). Washington, DC: TESOL.

Görlach, M. (1984). A selective bibliography of English as a world language (1965–1983). In W. Viereck, E. Schneider, & M. Görlach (Compilers), *A bibliography of writings on varieties of English, 1965–1983* (pp. 225–319). Amsterdam: John Benjamins.

Grice, H. P. (1975). Logic in conversation. In P. Cole & J. Morgan (Eds.), *Syntax and semantics: Vol. 3. Speech acts* (pp. 41–58). New York: Academic Press.

Hancock, I., & Angogo, R. (1982). English in East Africa. In R. Bailey & M. Görlach (Eds.), *English as a world language* (pp. 306–323).

Hatch, E. (1974). Second language learning—universal? *Working Papers on Bilingualism, 3,* 1–17.

Hatch, E. (Ed.). (1978). *Second language acquisition: A book of readings.* Rowley, MA: Newbury House.

Kachru, B. (1982a). Models for non-native English. In B. Kachru (Ed.), *The other tongue: English across cultures* (pp. 31–57). Urbana: University of Illinois Press.

Kachru, B. (Ed.). (1982b). *The other tongue: English across cultures.* Urbana: University of Illinois Press.

Kachru, B. (1982c). South Asian English. In R. Bailey & M. Görlach (Eds.), *English as a world language* (pp. 353–383).

Kempen, G. (1977). Conceptualizing and formulating sentence production. In S. Rosenberg (Ed.), *Sentence production: Developments in research and theory* (pp. 259–274).

Klein, W. (1986). *Second language acquisition.* Cambridge: Cambridge University Press.

Lowenberg, P. (1986). Non-native varieties of English: Nativization, norms and implications. *Studies in Second Language Acquisition, 8,* 1–18.

Meisel, J., Clahsen, H., & Pienemann, M. (1981). On determining developmental stages in second language acquisition. *Studies in Second Language Acquisition, 3,* 109–135.

Neisser, U. (1967). *Cognitive psychology.* New York: Appleton-Century Crofts.

Osgood, C., & Bock, J. (1977). Salience and sentence processing: Some production principles. In S. Rosenberg (Ed.), *Sentence production: Developments in research and theory* (pp. 89–140).

Perdue, C. (Ed.). (1984). *Second language acquisition by adult immigrants: A field manual.* Rowley, MA: Newbury House.

Platt, J., & Weber, H. (1980). *English in Singapore and Malaysia: Status, features, functions.* Kuala Lumpur: Oxford University Press.

Platt, J., Weber, H., & Ho, M. (1984). *The new Englishes.* London: Routledge and Kegan Paul.

Pride, J. (Ed.). (1982). *New Englishes.* Rowley, MA: Newbury House.

Quirk, R., Greenbaum, S., Leech, G., & Svartvik, J. (1985). *A comprehensive grammar of the English language.* London: Longman.

Ravem, R. (1978). Two Norwegian children's acquisition of English syntax. In E. Hatch. (Ed.), *Second language acquisition: A book of readings* (pp. 148–154).

Rosenberg, S. (Ed.). (1977). *Sentence production: Developments in research and theory.* Hillsdale, NJ: Erlbaum.

Sato, C. (1986). Conversation and interlanguage development: Rethinking the connection. In R. Day (Ed.), *Talking to learn* (pp. 23–45). Rowley, MA: Newbury House.

Searle, J. (1976). A classification of illocutionary acts. *Language in Society, 5,* 1–23.

Slobin, D. (1973). Cognitive prerequisites for the development of grammar. In C. Ferguson & D. Slobin (Eds.), *Studies in child language development* (pp. 23–45). New York: Holt, Rinehart and Winston.

Slobin, D. (1980). The repeated path between transparency and opacity in language. In U. Bellugi & M. Studdert-Kennedy (Eds.), *Signed and spoken language: Biological constraints on linguistic form* (pp. 229–243). Wenheim: Verlag Chemie GmbH.

Smith, L. (Ed.). (1981). *English for cross-cultural communication.* New York: St. Martins Press.

Tingley, C. (1981). Deviance in English in Ghanaian newspapers. *English World-Wide, 2,* 39–62.

Todd, L. (1982). *Cameroon: Varieties of English around the world.* Heidelberg: Julius Groos Verlag.

Ultan, R. (1978). Some general characteristics of interrogative systems. In J. Greenberg (Ed.), *Universals of human language. Vol. 4: Syntax* (pp. 211–248). Stanford: Stanford University Press.

Vander Brook, S., Schlue, K., & Campbell, C. (1980). Discourse and second language acquisition of yes/no questions. In D. Larsen-Freeman (Ed.), *Discourse analysis in second language research* (pp. 56–74). Rowley, MA: Newbury House.

Verma, S. (1982). Swadeshi English: Form and function. In J. Pride (Ed.), *New Englishes* (pp. 174–187).

Williams, J. (1987a). Non-native varieties of English: A special case of language acquisition. *English World-Wide, 8,* 161–199.

Williams, J. (1987b). *Production principles in non-native institutionalized varieties of English.* Unpublished Ph.D. dissertation, University of Pennsylvania.

Williams, J. (1989). Pronoun copies, pronominal and zero anaphora. In S. Gass & C. Madden (Eds.), *Variation in second language acquisition: Discourse and pragmatics.* Clevedon, Avon: Multilingual Matters.

Wode, H. (1978). The L1 vs. L2 acquisition of English interrogation. *Papers in Bilingualism, 15,* 38–57.

Wong, I. (1981). *Malaysian English as a new variety of English: The structural aspect.* Paper presented at 16th SEAMEO Seminar, RELC, Singapore.

Zuengler, J. (1982). Kenyan English. In B. Kachru (Ed.), *The other tongue: English across cultures* (pp. 112–140). Urbana: University of Illinois Press.

CHAPTER 9

Different Paths to Writing Proficiency in a Second Language?

A Preliminary Investigation of ESL Writers of Short-Term and Long-Term Residence in the United States

ROBIN SCARCELLA AND CHUNOK LEE

One source of language variation sometimes discussed in the second-language (L2) literature is tied to the ESL learners' length of residence in the United States. ESL learners who have lived in the United States a short time seem to have a somewhat different set of social values and norms than learners who have lived in the United States many years. These different sets of values and norms may lead to specific differences in L2 writing practices. Is it possible that different groups of learners follow somewhat different paths on their way to becoming proficient writers of a second language? More specifically, do ESL writers acquire the rhetorical, morpho-syntactic, and lexical features of their L2 along different routes? Or do these different groups merely travel the same roads at different speeds?

1. INTRODUCTION

Linguistic practices are always tied to a specific set of beliefs of a particular social group (Gee, 1986; Heath, 1983; Ochs, 1987; Street, 1984). Anglo-

ROBIN SCARCELLA AND CHUNOK LEE • ESL/Linguistics, University of California, Irvine, California 92717.

Americans are likely to consider ESL learners who have acquired Anglo-American values more competent writers of American English than ESL learners who have not acquired these beliefs. In a classic, though controversial, paper, Kaplan (1966) took a similar view, arguing that cultural thought patterns and rhetorical organization are closely related. Like Kaplan, a number of applied linguists have provided evidence that specific rhetorical structures may be culturally determined. (For recent collections on contrastive rhetoric, see Connor & Kaplan, 1987; Kaplan, 1983; see also Ricento, 1987.)

Along different lines, a number of researchers have attempted to document aspects of the writing practices of ESL learners of various lengths of residence in the United States. For example, Perkins and Scarcella (1986) compared the essays of 60 international, university students who had lived in the United States 1 to 2 years with the essays of 60 permanent residents who had lived in the United States 5 to 10 years. Both groups were acquiring English as a second language. Students were matched for first-language background and L2 proficiency level. Perkins and Scarcella reported that, in comparison to international students, permanent residents tended to communicate in writing much as native English speakers would in speech. In addition, Scarcella and Perkins found that international students sometimes transferred the literacy practices of their first language into their second.

A number of other studies have examined the effect of length of residence on grammatical aspects of L2 writing production. For example, Ahrens (1984) and Phillips (1984) showed that ESL students who have lived in the United States longer than 3 years generally attain higher holistic scores on university essay exams than students who are only recent arrivals to the United States. Yet Phillips (1984), who examined Korean junior high school students of short- and long-term duration in the United States, found no evidence that the kinds of grammatical and lexical errors made by the two groups of ESL learners were different. It should be noted, however, that there was a difference of 1½ years between the number of years Phillips' long-term "immigrants" and "recent arrivals" had lived in the United States. In a different type of study (an analysis of natural spoken data), Wolfram and Hatfield (1985) found that Vietnamese adolescents who had lived in the United States from 1 to 3 years and their peers who had lived in the United States 5 to 7 years used English verb tense markers similarly. Thus, like Phillips and Ahrens, Wolfram and Hatfield found that length of residence in the United States alone did not appear to affect the grammatical development of their subjects.

The research on the L2 development of learners of varying *lengths of residence* in the United States is a response to the growing numbers of students with Asian ancestry who are enrolling in university ESL programs across the nation. Koreans are among the fastest growing of the Asian groups in the United States; numerically, the Korean population already surpasses Chinese communities in Los Angeles and San Francisco (Kitano & Daniels, 1988; see also Choy, 1979). Korean-American college students have, for the most part, lived in the United States less than 10 years, and are in various stages of acculturation and English-language development. Kim (1977) reports that almost half of all Korean-American college students are prevented from obtaining academic success because of English-language difficulties. Writing is one of their most difficult problems. Although many Korean students complete their entire junior and high school educations in the United States, they are often required to complete ESL course work before taking other university courses. Unfortunately, however, despite the growth in the number of Korean-American university students and the growing body of literature on writing in an L2, little research has described the rhetorical practices of Korean ESL writers (see Chang, 1983, and Eggington, 1987, for some preliminary investigation).

2. THE STUDY

This study attempts to document the English writing practices of Korean students of varying lengths of residence in the United States. More specifically, we compare the expository writing of Korean-born university students who have lived in the United States 3 years or less with the expository writing of their peers who have lived in the United States over 5 years. Our study consists of two parts: an investigation of the rhetoric produced by the two different groups of learners and an analysis of the morpho-syntactic and lexical errors made by the two groups.

2.1. Subjects

One hundred thirty-four university expository essays were examined. Of these essays, 27 came from Korean ESL students who had lived in the United States less than 3 years (hereafter termed *short-term L2 learners* [STs]), 29 came from Korean ESL students who had lived in the United States for 5 years or longer (hereafter termed *long-term L2 learners* [LTs]), and 20 came from a group of native English students, providing baseline data for this study. For the investigation of rhetoric, we also included 58 essays from monolingual Korean students from Seoul, Korea. All the ESL students spoke Korean as a first language and were at an advanced L2 proficiency level, as judged by TOEFL scores (above 500), Michigan Test of English Language Proficiency scores (above 85), and an essay exam, judged holistically by two to three ESL instructors. Both native English and nonnative students were undergraduates (freshmen and sophomores) at the University of California. Native Korean students were graduating seniors in a high school in Seoul, Korea. The mean age of the native

ESL students was 19, while the mean age of the native Korean students was 17.

2.2. Task

The nonnative students wrote a 50-minute timed essay as part of their ESL placement procedure for the University of California. The native English students wrote the same essay as part of their freshmen writing exams, while the native Korean students wrote the same essay as part of their regular Korean class work. The directions were as follows: Write an essay in which you describe a significant change which took place in the United States (or in Korea) during the last 10 years. Be sure to explain at least three effects that the change had on Americans (or Koreans).

2.3. Analysis

The essays were typed and analyzed by two investigators who coded them independently. Following Kroll (1984), the essays were analyzed for morpho-syntactic errors, lexical errors, and rhetoric. In addition, we analyzed a number of rhetorical aspects, including the use of personal opinions, directness, reference to past events, and what we referred to as "putting your best foot forward." (Measures and definitions used in the analysis of rhetoric are given in the Appendix at the end of the chapter.) Measures and definitions of morpho-syntactic and lexical errors appear in Kroll (1984) and Lee and Scarcella (1988). To control for essay length, numbers of morpho-syntactic and lexical errors are given in proportion to number of total words. Following Andersen and Johnson (1973), a word was defined as "a standard orthographic unit including proper names, contractions, and exclamatory expressions, but not concatenate forms such as *kinda,* which counted as two words" (p. 151). Group means and standard deviations were calculated for rhetorical organization, rhetorical aspects, and morpho-syntactic and lexical features; chi-square tests were used to test differences between group means for significance.

3. RESULTS

In general, we found that although LTs made about the same types of morpho-syntactic errors as STs, LTs' essays were significantly better organized (from the point of view of native English-speaking raters) and contained fewer lexical errors. While it is clear that length of residence is not an accurate predictor of acculturation, it appears that, in many cases, it may be a rough indicator of a learner's experiences in a given culture. Perhaps the organization

Table 1. Mean Holistic Scores on the Rhetorical
Organization of the Essays[a]

Groups[b]	Mean	n	t
ST	20.6	27	-5.35*
LT	31	29	

[a]Holistic scores range from 10 (the lowest score) to 60 (the highest score).
[b]LT refers to Korean ESL students who have lived in the U.S. over 5 years; ST refers to Korean ESL students who have lived in the U.S. less than 3 years.
*$p < .001$

score earned by the LTs reflects the LTs' experiences in the United States. In the discussion which follows, we examine the effect of length of residence on the rhetorical development, grammar, and lexicon of LTs and STs.

3.1. Rhetoric

As expected, the LTs received significantly higher scores on the rhetorical organization of their essays than the STs (see Table 1). On a scale from 10 to 60, LTs received an average holistic score of 31, and STs received an average holistic score of 21. The difference between the two groups is significant ($t_{36} = -5.35$, $p < .001$). However, both groups as a whole scored poorly compared to the native English students, who received an average score of 50. Thus, the data indicate that LTs tended to write more like native English students than recent arrivals.

In the next section of the analysis, we examined specific rhetorical aspects. The results are given in Table 2.

3.1.1. Personal Opinions

The STs were particularly reluctant to state their own opinions. Whereas 69% (20/29) of the LTs made personal statements, only 26% (7/27) of the STs made these statements. This difference is significant ($X^2 = 19.46$, $p < .001$). Consider, for instance, example (1), in which one Korean student wrote about the bombing of Libia. Although she discussed the Americans' reactions to this incident, she failed to give any of her own opinions. She states:

(1)

There were different reactions toward the bombing of Libia. There were many outraged Americans and many other Americans who agreed and applauded the bombing. Still, some didn't care what happened. . . . The

Table 2. Analysis of Rhetorical Characteristics of the Essays

	Rhetorical aspects		
Groups[a]	Personal opinion[b]	Statement of thesis[c]	Reference to past events
LTs	69 (20/29)	79 (23/29)	7 (2/29)
STs	26 (7/27)	48 (13/27)	59 (16/27)
NESs	90 (18/20)	100 (20/20)	0 (0/20)
NKSs	0 (0/58)	0 (0/58)	3 (2/58)

Note. Numbers are percentages of students who expressed the rhetorical aspect in their writing.
[a]LT, Korean ESL students who have lived in the U.S. over 5 years; ST, Korean ESL students who have lived in the U.S. less than 3 years; NES, native English students; NKSs, native Korean students.
[b]$\chi^2 = 34.51$, $df = 2$, $p < .001$ for STs, LTs, and NESs; $\chi^2 = 19.46$, $df = 1$, $p < .001$ for STs and NESs.
[c]$\chi^2 = 18.09$, $df = 2$, $p < .001$ for STs, LTs, and NESs; $\chi^2 = 7.56$, $df = 1$, $p < .01$ for STs and LTs.

bombing of Libia shook the citizens of the United States, whether they were for or against it. (JYi; LT) (Names in parentheses are used to identify subjects.)

Although native Korean students never stated their own opinion and STs frequently failed to give their own point of view, most LTs and native English students did state their opinions. The reluctance to state one's opinion seems closely tied to Korean social values. To Koreans, stating one's own opinion too strongly is usually considered arrogant (Romaine, 1986). In addition, the risk involved in stating a personal opinion may not be as valued by Koreans as it is by Americans. According to Cheng (1987), Asians do not like to take social risks. They have not grown up with the traditions of verbal play, debate, show-and-tell or bedtime storytelling. Within the home, most Asian children are often expected to listen and obey rather than express their personal opinions (Cheng, 1987). Classroom size in Korea (usually about 60 students) also discourages active communication between teachers and students (Lee, 1982). Added to this, Cheng (1987) suggests that the expectations of parents and teachers seem to prevent Asian students from stating their own opinions. Parents and teachers may exert such great pressure on these students that the students may be unwilling to risk expressing an opinion which might subject them to ridicule in peer-editing sessions or cause them to receive low evaluations from their teachers.

Our findings are consistent with those of Iwasaki and Hayasaka (1984), who noted that the "Japanese tend to express their personal opinion at the very end in expository writing, whereas native English speakers [Americans] express it at the beginning or both the beginning and the end" (p. 66). Like Japanese

ESL writers, the Korean STs often postponed a personal conclusion or general statement until after giving all the specifics. (For discussions of this phenomenon in Japanese-English expository essays, refer to Achiba & Kuromiya, 1983; Inoue, 1986; Iwasaki & Hayasaka, 1984, 1985; and Kobayashi, 1984.)

3.1.2. Directness

The essays written by STs (and, again, to a lesser extent LTs) also tended to be more indirect than those written by the LTs and native English students. Compared to the native Korean students and STs, native English students were direct. In fact, all 20 of the native English writers wrote their thesis statement in the first sentence of the essays. In contrast, none of the native Korean writers and only 48% (13/27) of the STs wrote a thesis statement at all. It was as if some writers expected the reader to guess what they were writing about. Perhaps this is because indirectness is valued by Koreans, whereas directness is valued by Anglo-Americans. Such directness may be seen as inappropriate or rude by Koreans because it may seem distancing, blunt, or condescending to the reader's intelligence. Thus, Korean readers seem to play a far more active role than English readers. Example (2) illustrates the indirectness used by a Korean ESL student in this study:

(2)

The biggest political difference between the 19th century and the 20th century would probably be that the world has moved towards democracy much more in the 20th century. A lot of countries have gone from a dictatorship to a democracy in the 20th century. About a year ago Phillipine islands kicked out the dictatorship of Marcos and replaced it with democracy of Aquino government, but it is not the latest democracy movement in the world.

The most recent democracy movement hit South Korea when hundred thousands of students and civilians protested against the military dictatorship of President Chun last month. (Y. Jun; LT)

In this passage, the student seems to write *around* her topic, the demonstration against President Chun. Before introducing her thesis statement, she discusses political differences between the nineteenth and twentieth centuries and the rise of Corazon Aquino in the Philippines. The data are consistent with Kaplan's (1966) observations that Korean discourse is "marked by what may be called an approach of indirection" (p. 46). According to Kaplan, Korean writers show the subject, "from a variety of tangential views, but the subject is never looked at directly. Things are developed in terms of what they are not, rather than in terms of what they are" (p. 46; see also Eggington, 1987). In contrast, American writers often value directness. In general, in good college writing, the thesis statement is stated early on in expository prose, and paragraphs are tightly connected and directly support the thesis (Scarcella, 1984).

In a similar vein, Hinds (1987) proposes a related explanation for indirectness. He states:

> In Japan, perhaps in Korea, and certainly in ancient China, there is a different way of looking at the communication process. In Japan it is the responsibility of the listener/reader to understand what it is that the speaker or author intended to say. (p. 144)

Hinds points out that in a reader-responsible language (such as Japanese), there is greater tolerance for ambiguity, imprecision of statement, and an entirely different attitude toward the writer "such that English-speaking writers go through draft after draft to come up with a final product, while Japanese authors frequently compose exactly one draft which becomes the finished product" (p. 145). We propose that Korean, like Japanese, is a reader-responsible language. Good Korean writers tend not to edit and revise to the same extent as good English writers, and, like good Japanese writers, good Korean writers are capable of composing a finished product the first time around (see also Hinds, 1983, 1987).

3.1.3. Reference to Past Events

A closer analysis of the essays also reveals that unlike the LT and native English essays, the ST essays contained frequent reference to past events. Of the ST essays, 59% (16/27) referred to events which occurred over 20 years ago, while only 7% (2/29) of the LT essays and none of the native English essays referred to such events. Many STs referred to the Japanese and Chinese invasions and World War II, and one student even discussed the Dan Gun dynasty (established 5,000 years ago). Examples (3) and (4) are illustrative:

(3)

> To begin with, I would like to introduce the historical background of our country briefly. Korea, with its excessive population and small territory, has a long history of 5,000 years.
> Because of its geological environment, it has been attacked many times by China during the 17th and 18th centuries and it was sometimes dominated as an adopted-country. At the beginning of 20th century, Korea was governed by Japan and this period lasted about 36 years. (Kim, T; LT; the student continues to discuss the Korean War before introducing his thesis, industrial development in Korea.)

(4)

> The political dreams of leaders in Korea are always to give their people peaceful life and wealth. Our country, Korea, have been invaded many

times by China and Japan because Korea is located in very important area in the Far East. And also from 1950 to 1953 Korea was severely destroyed through Korean War.

Despite most Korean people wanted to live peacefully without war enjoyed their life. Early in the morning in 1961 a military revolution was leaded by young ambitious generals to give people what they wanted to have. Their aims were to develop our country economically and to rule people with democracy. *They made 5 years developing plans and completed them successfully.* (Shin; ST; thesis statement italicized)

The past is notably more important to Koreans than Americans (Kalton, 1979; see also Cheng, 1987, and Stewart, 1973). Perhaps this is why the STs referred to the past as a strategy for engaging and sustaining the reader's attention. LTs rarely used this strategy, and native English students did not use this strategy at all.

3.1.4. "Putting Your Best Foot Forward"

More observationally, we found that native English students and LTs used a different strategy to engage their readers' attention. We refer to this strategy as "putting your best foot forward." Although difficult to quantify, it appeared that native English speakers frequently informed their readers that their essays were worth reading (example (5) is illustrative):

(5)

The most interesting event in the last ten years was the invention of the video game. (Atkins)

This suggests that an additional difference between Korean and Native English rhetoric might be tied to how writers display themselves. In general, Koreans do not display, show off, or boast of their knowledge of a topic; the idea of putting your best foot forward seems to conflict directly with a Korean taboo. In situations in which English writers try to display themselves in the best possible light, Korean writers usually do not. When they do, they may do so in very subtle ways, such as using the strategy of mentioning past events. In contrast to the native English students, STs (and to some extent, LTs) appeared to be reluctant to put their best foot forward.

The differences between Korean and Anglo-American social practices, though subtle, appear to have a powerful influence on the writing practices of Korean ESL students. Our study suggests that these practices affect the writing of the ST essays to a greater extent than they do the writing of the LT essays. It appears that students who have lived in the United States for a lengthy time period develop American English rhetorical skills to a greater extent than recent arrivals in the United States. This may be because such skills are embedded in cultural practices which are acquired through exposure to cultural norms. As Ochs (1987) points out, "the process of acquiring language is embedded in the process of acquiring culture" (p. 305). In general, LTs appear to have acquired Anglo-American cultural norms to a greater extent than STs. Morphological and syntactic development may be less affected by cultural norms. In the next portion of our analysis we examine the effect of length of residence on morphological and syntactic development.

3.2. Analysis of Morpho-Syntactic and Lexical Errors

Results of our preliminary analysis of morpho-syntactic errors are reported in Table 3. These results indicate that claims for large morpho-syntactic differences between the LT and ST essays cannot be substantiated; LTs and STs make about the same number and type of morpho-syntactic errors. Like Phillips (1984), we did not find differences in morpho-syntactic categories related to the ESL learners' length of residence in the United States. As indicated by Table 4, the order of error difficulty for the LTs and STs is also similar. Thus, the data come close to suggesting that morpho-syntactic development (or at least error difficulty) is similar for both LTs and STs. It appears then that, for these learners, interlanguage morphology and syntax may be the same regardless of length of residence in the host country.

Despite these morpho-syntactic similarities, the two groups differed with respect to the frequency with which they used incorrect lexical items. As seen

Table 3. Analysis of Morpho-Syntactic Errors[a]

Error categories	Subjects[b]	
	ST	LT
Articles	.03 (248)	.03 (266)
Verb tense	.01 (85)	.01 (116)
Prepositions	.01 (90)	.01 (85)
Singular/plural	.01 (101)	.01 (72)
Pronoun reference	.01 (107)	.01 (72)
Subject/verb agreement	.004 (32)	.003 (28)
Run-on sentences	.002 (16)	.002 (17)
Sentence fragments	.001 (4)	.002 (13)
Relative clauses	.001 (4)	.001 (8)
Quantifiers	.001 (5)	.001 (7)

[a]Total number of errors in each category (in parentheses) divided by total number of words in the essays of 27 STs (7,383 words) and 29 LTs (8,173 words).
[b]ST, Korean ESL students who have lived in the U.S less than 3 years; LT, Korean ESL students who have lived in the U.S. over 5 years.

Table 4. Comparison of the Difficulty Orders of the Errors in
27 ST and 29 LT Essays

ST	LT
1. Missing/extra/wrong article	1. Missing/extra wrong article
2. Pronoun reference	2. Verb tense
3. Singular/plural	3. Preposition
4. Preposition	4. Singular/plural
5. Verb tense	5. Pronoun reference
6. Run-on sentence	6. Subject/verb agreement
7. Relative clause formation	7. Run-on sentence
8. Quantifier	8. Sentence fragment
9. Sentence fragment	9. Relative clause formation

in Table 5, LTs made significantly fewer lexical errors than STs ($p < .05$). This may be because the LTs have been exposed to much more English input than the STs.

In line with this finding, although both LTs and STs made translation errors, STs made significantly more. In fact, they made 2.5 times more than the LTs (compare the ST translation rate of .005 to the LT translation rate of .002). In addition, the percentage of translation errors to total lexical errors is significantly lower for the LTs than the STs (13% of the STs' lexical errors were translations, whereas 10% of the LTs' lexical errors were translations). Examples of translation errors are given in examples (6) and (7):

(6)

So the students might wear their own *private clothes* in the high school. (H, S-K; ST; student probably intended to write "casual clothes")

Table 5. Analysis of Lexical Errors[a]

Error category	Subjects	
	ST	LT
Wrong word	.03 (211)	.02 (123)
Incorrect word forms	.006 (47)	.005 (42)
Translations	.005 (40)	.002 (18)
Total number of errors[b]	.04 (298)	.02 (183)

[a]Total number of lexical errors (in parentheses) divided by total number of words in the essays of 27 STs (7,383 words) and 29 LTs (8,173 words).
[b]This difference is significant at $p < .05$; $t = -2.54$, $df = 26$, two-tailed.

(7)

As a result of that, the citizens *level of lives* also has been increased. (N, B; ST; student probably intended to write "standard of living")

In explaining this type of lexical transfer, Ijaz (1986) states that

> second-language acquisition, unlike first-language acquisition, involves the mapping of two lexical and conceptual systems onto each other. Across two languages many words may roughly correspond in meaning, but few word pairs completely overlap in all their lexical functions. (p. 405)

We also found that, in contrast to STs, LTs used more *acoustic approximations*. We define this term as lexical items which approximate what the learner has heard. Examples (8–11) illustrate the error type:

(8)

It had some *succession* in the peace talk with North Koreans. (Y, C; LT; student probably meant to write "success")

(9)

It was a very big *shot* to all of us. (K, CS; ST; student probably meant to write "shock")

(10)

First of all, it was learning to live many kind of different *ratios*. (H, J; LT; student probably meant to write "races")

(11)

The people of Korea live a better life *then* they used to. (K, JH; LT; student probably meant to write "than")

Krashen (1985) suggests one explanation for these errors. He states:

> The learner's own input can serve as comprehensible input to his own language acquisition device . . . the learner's own imperfect versions of English enter into "permanent storage" (Stevick, 1982) when the appropriate English forms are not available in the input. (p. 42)

In contrast to STs, LTs clearly seemed to display a more complete "inventory of possible alternatives, recognize the sociolinguistic constraints on those alternatives and the sorts of constraints a choice imposes on the text which follows" (Kaplan, 1987, p. 11). Thus, LTs may have a greater control of diverse registers. Perhaps increased exposure to lexical items in a variety of contexts led to the LTs' more accurate and varied use of vocabulary.

In sum, these data suggest that while LTs and STs may be in different lexical and rhetorical stages, they may be in similar morpho-syntactic stages. The data also suggest that lexical and rhetorical acquisition might, at least to some extent, be acquired independently of morpho-syntactic structure, a view consistent with current linguistic theory.

4. FUTURE DIRECTIONS

To confirm and generalize these findings, further studies are needed. For example, we have to allow for the fact that within each group there may be considerable variation. Whether a learner belongs to the LT or ST group may depend on a number of sociopsychological factors. As Krashen (1976) points out, length of residence is not an accurate predictor of amount of input or interaction with native speakers. Nor is length of residence an accurate indicator of degree of acculturation. Future studies should carefully control input, interaction, and acculturation. It should also be mentioned that error analyses are, necessarily, limited, and they cannot be used as evidence of a learner's actual competence, since a learner may avoid using structures not yet acquired (Schachter, 1974; Kellerman, 1978, 1983). Longitudinal and ethnographic studies are also needed to confirm these findings since grammar does not develop uniformly, and certain structural properties can be known only if one knows of the L2 learners' preceding and following stages of L2 development. Larger numbers of students are also needed to generalize the findings. Finally, as Anglo-American writing practices spread across the world, they may in the future replace Korean practices, and the writing of both STs and LTs may come to resemble that of native Anglo-American writers.

Clearly this is just a beginning. Yet, the large numbers of Koreans entering American schools make it imperative that studies of Korean ESL acquisition and production be undertaken now. We have found significant linguistic variation in the writing practices of LTs and STs. Our results call into question the practice of examining large groups of students without first considering their diverse social values and norms. In addition, our results suggest that while LTs and STs probably follow the same path with respect to L2 morpho-syntactic development, LTs are considerably further down the road when it comes to lexical and rhetorical development; or, taking a different perspective, the LTs' morphological and syntactic development may have slowed (or even ceased!), while their lexical and rhetorical skills continued to develop independently.

APPENDIX

Measures and definitions

Scoring for Rhetoric (From Kroll, 1984, pp. 166–168)

A 60 paper is a top paper. It does not have to be perfect, but it will do all or most of the following well:

- Clearly limit the discussion to something which can be reasonably handled in a short essay

- Follow through on what it sets out to do
- Stick to the topic throughout the essay and in each paragraph
- Effectively use paragraphs to break up the topic into unified parts
- Maintain a consistent point of view
- Sequence ideas logically within paragraphs and in the essay
- Use overt markers/transitions artfully to signal relationships between and within paragraphs
- Use reference markers appropriately

A 50 paper is a less consistent version of a 60 paper. It will be distinctively above average, but will have noticeable slip ups. The paper may do one of the following:

- Begin discussion without stating or implying overall topic
- Omit a conclusion where called for
- Present the argument in unbalanced proportions to clearly stated thesis

A 40 paper shows adequate but undistinguished control over both paragraph structure and essay structure. It is an upper-half paper which shows organizational competence and general competence, but does one or more of the following:

- Relies heavily on juxtaposition to show relationships rather than spelling them out
- Uses overt transitions in inappropriate ways
- Fails to adequately develop a major point of the argument

A 30 paper is a lower half paper. It may show either clear ability to set up the major building blocks of an essay OR clear ability to construct a unified, coherent paragraph, but it will not show clear competency in both areas. It may be a paper that shows weak abilities in both areas. Reasons for assigning a 30 include:

- Noticeable introduction of irrelevant ideas
- Failure to provide a clear sense of purpose
- Shifting point of view
- Use of transition signals in a mechanical or heavy-handed way
- Some inconsistencies in argument

A 20 paper shows some minimal ability to organize a paper, but is rather poorly presented. It may do some of the following:

- Go around in circles
- Have little or no connection between parts either stated or implied
- Use transitions that don't work in context
- Assume the validity of statements which are never developed

A 10 paper shows little or no skill at setting up major sections of the paper and developing paragraphs. It may stray and wander from the topic or it may simply never get beyond the most superficial statements so that there is no sense of awareness of expository conventions.

Aspects of Rhetorical Development

Giving Personal Opinions: essays which contained personal statements having one or more of the following characteristics:

- Containing personal statements preceded by "I think," "I believe," "In my opinion"
- Containing summary statements which summarized the writer's personal point of view (usually, though not always, beginning with a transition such as "In sum," "Therefore," or "In summary" and followed by a statement of the writer's belief
- Containing a major personal viewpoint

Examples:

Thus, Park's assassination had a detrimental effect on Korea.
In my opinion, the recession was the most significant event of the last ten years.

Being Direct: statements of identifiable theses; theses which were merely implied by the text were not considered "direct." Theses statements which addressed broad topics, such as, "This essay examines politics," were also excluded from our count of thesis statements.

Examples:

One of the most significant changes in the last ten years was the new school uniform.
This paper discusses the importance of political reform in the last ten years.

Putting Your Best Foot Forward: explicit statements asserting the writer's belief that the reader should be interested in his or her essay.

- Containing adjectives such as "interesting" or "fascinating" with reference to the writer's thesis

Example:

This essay discussed an interesting topic, Reagan's presidency.
All Americans should be fascinated by the problem of gang wars.

Reference to Past Events: reference to an event which occurred fifty or more years ago which was not essential to the development of the essay.

Example:

During World War II, Korean politics developed. The death of President
Park brought sorrow to the Korean people. (The essay continues to discuss
Park's death. The connection between World War II and Park is un-
known.)

REFERENCES

Achiba, M., & Kuromiya, Y. (1983). Rhetorical patterns extant in the English compositions of
   Japanese students. *JALT Journal, 5*, 1–13.
Ahrens, C. (1984). *Comparing composition skills of native and non-native born students at the
   junior high school level.* Unpublished master's thesis, UCLA.
Andersen, E. S., & Johnson, C. (1973). Modifications in the speech of an eight-year-old as a
   reflection of age of listener. *Stanford Occasional Papers in Linguistics, 3*, 149–160.
Chang, S. J. (1983). English and Korean. In R. Kaplan (Ed.), *Annual Review of Applied Linguis-
   tics* (pp. 85–98). Rowley, MA: Newbury House.
Cheng, L.-R. (1987). *Assessing Asian language performance: Guidelines for evaluating limited-
   English-proficient students.* Rockville, MD: An Aspen Production.
Choy, B.-Y. (1979). *Koreans in America.* Chicago: Nelson-Hall.
Connor, U., & Kaplan, R. (Eds.). (1987). *Writing across languages: Analysis of L2 text.* Reading,
   MA: Addison Wesley.
Eggington, W. (1987). Written academic discourse in Korean: Implications for effective commu-
   nication. In U. Connor & R. Kaplan (Eds.), *Writing across languages: Analysis of L2 text*
   (pp. 153–168). Reading, MA: Addison Wesley.
Gee, J. (1986). Orality and literacy: From the *Savage Mind* to *Ways with Words. TESOL Quar-
   terly, 20* (4), 719–746.
Heath, S. B. (1983). *Ways with words.* Cambridge: Cambridge University Press.
Hinds, J. (1983). Japanese and English. In R. Kaplan (Ed.), *Annual review of applied linguistics*
   (pp. 78–84). Rowley, MA: Newbury House.
Hinds, J. (1987). Reader versus writer responsibility: A new typology. In U. Connor & R. Kaplan
   (Eds.), *Writing across languages: Analysis of L2 text* (pp. 9–22). Reading, MA: Addison
   Wesley.
Ijaz, I. H. (1986). Linguistic and cognitive determinants of lexical acquisition in a second lan-
   guage. *Language Learning, 36*(4), 401–451.
Inoue, N. (1986). Japanese and English rhetorical patterns. *Tsukuba English Education Journal,
   7*, 69–81.
Iwasaki, M., & Hayasaka, K. (1984). Unique logic patterns found in English compositions written
   by Japanese students—reconsideration of "Cultural thought patterns in intercultural educa-
   tion" by Robert Kaplan. *Speech Education, 11*, 60–67.
Iwasaki, M., & Hayasaka, K. (1985). Unique logic patterns found in English compositions written
   by Japanese students, II. *Speech Education, 12*, 21–27.
Kalton, M. C. (1979). *Korean ideas and values.* Elkins Park, PA: Philip Jaisohn Memorial Foundation.
Kaplan, R. (1966). Cultural thought patterns in intercultural education. *Language Learning, 16*,
   1–20.
Kaplan, R. (Ed.). (1983). *Annual review of applied linguistics.* Rowley, MA: Newbury House.
Kaplan, R. (1987). Cultural thought patterns revisited. In U. Connor & R. Kaplan (Eds.), *Writing
   across languages: Analysis of L2 text* (pp. 9–22). Reading, MA: Addison Wesley.

Kellerman, E. (1978). Giving learners a break: Native language intuitions as a source of predictions about transferability. *Working Papers on Bilingualism, 15*, 60–92.

Kellerman, E. (1983). Now you see it, now you don't. In S. Gass & L. Selinker (Eds.), *Language transfer in language learning.* (pp. 112–319). Rowley, MA: Newbury House.

Kim, D. S. (1977). How they fared in American homes: A follow-up study of adopted Korean children. *Children Today, 6*, 2–6.

Kitano, H., & Daniels, R. (1988). *Asian Americans: Emerging minorities.* Englewood Cliffs, NJ: Prentice Hall.

Kobayashi, H. (1984). *Rhetorical patterns in English and Japanese.* Unpublished doctoral dissertation, Columbia University Teachers College, New York.

Krashen, S. D. (1976). Formal and informal linguistic environments in language acquisition and language learning. *TESOL Quarterly, 10*(2), 157–168.

Krashen, S. D. (1985). *The input hypothesis: Issues and implications.* New York: Longman.

Kroll, B. (1984). *Levels of error in ESL essays.* Unpublished doctoral dissertation, University of Southern California.

Lee, K. (1982). Students from Korea. In *Asian bilingual education* (pp. 105–114). Cambridge, MA: Evaluation, Dissemination, and Assessment Center.

Lee, C., & Scarcella, R. (1988, March). *Helping Korean university students overcome ESL writing problems.* Paper presented at the TESOL convention, Chicago.

Ochs, E. (1987). Input: A socio-cultural perspective. In M. Hickman (Ed.), *Social and functional approaches to language and thought* (pp. 305–319). New York: Academic Press.

Perkins, L., & Scarcella, R. (1986). Coming out of the cabbage badge: Relying on what you've got. *TECFORS* Research Report. Los Angeles: University of Southern California.

Philips, J. (1984). *The Effect of morphological and syntactic errors on the holistic scores of native and non-native composition.* Unpublished master's thesis, UCLA.

Ricento, T. (1987). *Aspects of coherence in English and Japanese expository prose.* Unpublished doctoral dissertation, UCLA.

Romaine, S. (1986). *The language of children and adolescents: The acquisition of communicative competence.* New York: Basil Blackwell.

Scarcella, R. (1984). How readers orient their writers. *TESOL Quarterly, 18*(4), 671–688.

Schachter, J. (1974). An error in error analysis. *Language Learning, 24*, 205–214.

Stewart, E. (1973). *American cultural patterns: A cross-cultural perspective.* Yarmouth, ME: Intercultural Press.

Street, B. V. (1984). *Literacy in theory and practice.* Cambridge: Cambridge University Press.

Wolfram, W., & Hatfield, D. (1985). Interlanguage fads and linguistic reality: The case of tense marking. In D. Tannen and J. Alatis (Eds.), *Proceedings of the Georgetown round table* (pp. 17–34). Washington, DC.

CHAPTER 10

Variation and Transfer in English Creole–Standard English Language Learning

LISE WINER

1. INTRODUCTION

This chapter examines the nature of errors in the written standard English of native speakers of an English Creole, with particular attention to the sources of variation in errors. Presented are the findings of a previous macrostudy on the number and nature of errors in written English compositions of secondary school students in Trinidad, West Indies. A microstudy of a small subset of these compositions is then used to illustrate sources of errors, particularly negative transfer, in a creole/related standard language situation. Implications for appropriate language teaching approaches in this situation are discussed.

The questions investigated are (1) What is the amount and nature of error variation and transfer in this type of situation?, and (2) What implications do the findings have for determining approaches to language teaching, with specific reference to the question of language distance?

2. BACKGROUND TO THE STUDY

The official language of Trinidad, Trinidad and Tobago, West Indies, is English, but the vast majority of the population speaks Trinidadian English Creole (TEC) as a first, primary, or only language. While varieties of interna-

LISE WINER • Department of Linguistics, Southern Illinois University, Carbondale, Illinois 62901.

tional standard English, Trinidadian standard English, and TEC overlap in lexicon, phonology, and grammar, TEC has a basically different grammatical system, not always recognized as distinct because of superficial formal similarities (Carrington, 1983; Solomon, 1972; Winford, 1974, 1979).

Although other L1–L2 language sets may share cognates, rules, and "faux amis," the high degree of overlap in a creole/related standard pair, as also in dialect/standard pairs, presents a very significant difficulty for the language learner in distinguishing language boundaries. In many cases, it is not just that the L1 and L2 are similar, but that the *same* words—not translations—used in exactly the same syntactic and collocational contexts can have very different meanings. Examples of such "form counterparts" include: *He does wait for bus* 'He waits for the bus' (i.e., every morning), where the TEC *does* marks habitual aspect rather than emphasis; and *The melon in flower* 'The melon has flower buds'. In some cases, word and meaning are virtually identical in the two languages, but syntactic or collocational constraints are different, for example, *I reach 8 o'clock* 'I reached (place) at/by 8 o'clock'. This relationship between English and TEC has several implications for the learning of English in Trinidad. The major problem to be faced is that while the similarities of TEC and English encourage successful positive transfer of language forms and structures from the L1 to the L2, they also facilitate negative transfer, that is, transfer from L1 resulting in error in the target L2.

Attitudes toward TEC in Trinidad are now very different from the virtually total rejection of even 10 years ago, but it is still common to hear teachers or other native TEC speakers talk about the language as "bad" or "broken" English, or to state that you can "mix up" the language any way you want because it "has no rules." Although the recognition of the vernacular as a real language of some sort, often as a "dialect" of English, is much greater now, there is still a widespread lack of understanding of the language and, especially on the part of teachers, tremendous insecurity about language use and a lack of conscious awareness and understanding of the ways in which TEC works (Winford, 1974, 1979).

There is a difference, of course, between a "lack of rules" and acceptable variation. This can be illustrated with "must be," a modal form most equivalent to English "must" or "must have," as in: *He must be do it already* 'He must have done it already'. Variability in TEC negation means that you could say either *He must be eh do it* or *He eh must be do it* 'He must not have done it'. Even speakers who claim the language has no rules will laugh at and not accept *He must eh be do it*, which would, in fact, correspond most closely to the English pattern, even as "broken English."

Normal variation in creole/standard situations is usually manifested through variants described as "lects"—basilect, mesolect, and acrolect—defined primarily in terms of their relative closeness to the lexically related standard, that is, with the basilect being the "deepest," "broadest," or most "conservative" creole and the acrolect being different from standard English in only minor ways. Because variation in this situation is closely tied to differences in social class, the use, avoidance, and judgment of particular variants in each lect are often highly charged. For negation, in various lects it would be possible to say: *me eh like it, I eh like it, I doh like it,* or *I don't like it.* The last one is identical to standard English, and the third is virtually identical to the *phonological* form of colloquial spoken North American standard English. In the first two, the similarity of TEC *eh* to nonstandard English *ain't* is noticeable (although it is not, in fact, the same), but the first variant is clearly not English.

Many Trinidadian secondary school students have serious problems with local and international standardized examinations, including the junior secondary entrance exam taken at about age 11, and the O Level secondary matriculation exams. Problems stem in part from inadequate overall language skills in English, particularly in its written forms. Given the relatively low present international and even national status of TEC (Carrington, 1978), it is unlikely that the need for students to attain competence in reading and writing standard English will soon diminish. Therefore, it is important to develop adequate analyses of problem areas in the learning of English in order to design measures to cope with such difficulties effectively.

On the other hand, there is increasing pressure for a policy of "extending the official use of Creole to areas of direct and immediate concern to the mass of the Creole speaking population" (Devonish, 1986, p. 113). Both sets of concerns and goals are relevant to an area specifically addressed by this chapter, namely, that much of the variation seen as error vis-à-vis English is in fact acceptable and correct in forms of the Creole and that many real errors, particularly those which can be termed "hypercorrections," are in fact encouraged by a teaching approach which is inadequately contrastive and which emphasizes literacy in standard English only rather than in TEC and English.

3. THE ORIGINAL STUDY

3.1. The Corpus

The original studies (Winer, 1982, 1983, 1986b) on which this chapter is based, were analyses of the errors in the written compositions of Trinidadian secondary school students. The data consisted of 896 compositions of three discourse types (narrative, letter of complaint, and instructions) from 13 Form 1 (first-year secondary) and 11 Form 5 (last-year secondary) classes in 16 secondary schools, chosen so that the subject population reflected the social and linguistic variables characteristic of both the educational system and the national population. Three types of secondary schools were included: the prestige (government-assisted); government 5-year; and comprehensive (junior secondary plus senior secondary). Female and male students in single-sex and coeducational schools were included; residence categories were urban, semi-urban, rural, and moved (more than one); ethnicity categories (self-identified by subjects) were African, Indian, Mixed, and Other.

3.2. Description of Errors

The texts were scored for errors; correctness comprised both "acceptability" or "well-formedness" and "appropriateness" or "textual and situational suitability." Each error was categorized by Error Type (morphology, syntax, lexicon, spelling, and punctuation, plus combinations) and by Attribution of Error (English, Transfer, English and Transfer, and Indeterminate). The separation of error description and attribution was crucial, to avoid the nested or confounded criteria used in many studies—for example, both "overgeneralization of the definite article" and "misuse of article" (Richards, 1974).

3.3. Definitions of Transfer

Kellerman (1983) has pointed out, in reference to any language learning situation:

> It is of course quite true that what at first glance appear to be interference errors may be etiologically ambiguous on the basis of their linguistic form alone . . . since it is logically possible for one and the same form to have multiple psychological origins which to some extent reinforce each other. (pp. 112–113)

This phenomenon obtains even more strongly in a L1–L2 situation in which, as noted above, there is a very high percentage of "form counterparts."

Schachter's (1983) characterization of language transfer is also relevant to the analytic framework used here. She correctly describes transfer within an overall interaction of strategy and knowledge/competence in which "the learner infers from previous knowledge the domain within the universe from which the solution to the current target language problem will be taken. Then, the learner samples hypotheses from that domain" (pp. 103–104). Her model of possible results, as follows, is very close to the guidelines described below for determining negative transfer (interference) in this study:

1. The learner may choose the wrong domain:
   (a) because the input has provided conflicting signs (not transfer); or
   (b) because the learner has assumed that a preestablished domain of the L1 is the relevant domain for the L2 (negative transfer).
2. The learner may choose both the correct domain and the correct hypothesis:

    (a) because the learner has done a good job of analyzing input (not transfer); or

    (b) because the L1 and L2 structures are identical and the learner has recognized this (positive transfer).

3. The learner may choose the correct domain but the wrong hypothesis

    (a) because of a partly mistaken analysis of the input (not transfer); or

    (b) because of correctly equating domains but not hypotheses (negative transfer).

It is not clear how rigidly Schachter has applied the criterion of the learner's conscious recognition or awareness of transfer possibilities, but in the current analysis, such conscious awareness is not necessary. The determination of possible cause of an error should ideally include introspection by the learner as well as analysis by the researcher, but this is impossible on a large scale. In light of this, the following guidelines, used in both the previous and current studies, have proven reasonably operational for a bilingual analyst.

3.3.1. English Error

Such nontransfer errors reflect intrinsic difficulties in analyzing and learning English, the target language, which arise primarily as a result of the nature of that language. For both L1 and L2 learners of English, such intrinsically difficult areas include: modals, auxiliaries, use of articles, expression of aspect, prepositions in phrasal verbs, and many orthographic patterns.

Generally speaking, an English error involves the supply of an English element or pattern in an area where English rules are irregular, highly complex, or subject to perceived arbitrariness, or where words are phonologically similar.[1] Errors labeled English Writing involve all punctuation conventions and

---

[1] Although many areas of English, like any language, can be considered intrinsically difficult, a definition of intrinsic error cannot be so broad as to include all errors. The present and past tense markers are good examples of the process of determining attribution. Given the very limited inflectional system of English, it might be thought easy for language learners to grasp. However, numerous studies have found that the present tense third-person singular -s is among the last features to be acquired completely by both L1 and L2 learners of English, perhaps due to its degree of markedness and its obvious redundancy. Thus, any error in the use of -s involves intrinsic English difficulty. However, when a TEC speaker produces *she go* for 'she goes' in English, the error is considered both English and Transfer, as (1) no distinction is made in TEC for marking number and person in the verb and (2) the tenses in English and TEC are marked by an overlapping but distinct set of morphemes, such that *she go* is correct TEC, corresponding to English past tense *she went*, not to the present tense, which in TEC would be either *she does go* (habitual) or *she goin* (continuous).

In the case of the English past tense, the morpheme -d is a very regular and common pattern and does not constitute intrinsic difficulty except, of course, for irregular verbs. The simple past tense in TEC is, except for *be*, an unmarked verb form. Therefore, an error involving the use of the unmarked verb form for the inflected past tense form of a regular verb was attributed to Transfer alone.

most spelling ones. (A Transfer Writing category is possible between languages
with different written conventions.) Examples of EE are:

He was intent *to* build up his business. ('on [building]')
He *telled* them. ('told')
Many people are *illegitimate*. ('illiterate')

Examples of English Writing errors (EWE) are:

dont ('don't')
help us do something *a bout it stop* this water situation ('about' 'it. Stop')

3.3.2. Positive Transfer

When the forms, structures, and rules of the L1 and the L2 coincide, the
application or transfer of these L1 features to L2 situations results in positive
transfer, that is, the correct domain and the correct hypothesis, in the L2. Such
transfer is often unremarked in learner language, but it clearly plays an important role, particularly in a creole/standard situation where much of the two
languages overlap. In writing, high levels of positive transfer from TEC to
English (E) are found in vocabulary, grammar, and rhetorical style. Positive
transfer was not expressly marked in this study, but it could have been, utiliz-
ing the same principles as for negative transfer.

3.3.3. Negative Transfer Error

When the forms, structures, and rules of the L1 and the L2 do not coincide, the learner's attempts to transfer an L1 element to the L2 result in language behavior which does not conform to the norms of the L2, but which do
correspond, in *precisely statable ways*, to structures, forms, or rules in the L1.
When a sentence contained what appeared to be a possible transfer error, the
sentence was translated into (spoken) TEC. If the correspondence between the
L1 and the L2 expressions was *exact*, the error was classified as Transfer.
Examples of transfer error are:

From that day he never *advantage* the other monkeys. ('took advantage
of', 'bullied')
It have too much dogs in our village. ('There are')
The frog *turn* prince. ('turned into a')

Examples of transfer of phonology errors are:

deat (E: 'death' /dɛθ/; TEC: /dɛt/)
This may *song* foolish. (E: 'sound' /saʊnd/; TEC: /sɔŋ/)

3.3.4. English and Transfer Error

Applying the same procedure as used to determine Transfer error, the sentence in question was translated into (spoken) TEC. If this showed that the learner had modified the syntax, morphology, or lexicon of the TEC equivalent when transferring it to English, the error was classified as both English and Transfer. Most of these errors are characterized by the inappropriate contextual use of a well-formed English form or structure, that is, the correct domain but the wrong hypothesis. This results in a sentence which is *neither* correct TEC *nor* correct English (E):

My problem *are* about the water. (TEC: *is*; E: *is*; the form *are* is E only)
It has too much cars on our street. (TEC: *it have*; E: *there are*; the form *has* is E only)
The bus *is coming* morning and evening. (TEC: *does come*; E: *comes*, the form *is coming* is E only)
Then the frog *turn to* princess. (TEC: *turn*, E: *turned into a*)

3.3.5. Indeterminate Error

Without extensive learner introspection and elicitation, researchers should avoid categories such as "carelessness." The Indeterminate category covers all currently unanalyzable errors, including metathesis of letters and word repetition.

3.4. Results

Overall error rates (ER) for each student and each text were obtained by dividing the number of errors per student and per text by the number of running words for that student or text. Almost half of the 19,878 errors in the corpus were errors in spelling (20%) and punctuation (25%); that is, English Writing errors constituted 45% of all errors. Lexicon (20%), morphology (17%), and syntax (18%) together constituted the remaining 55% of all errors.

Statistically significant differences in ER were found between groups for the following variables (Winer, 1982, pp. 159–160):[2] grade, sex, school type, residence, and ethnicity (see Table 1).

[2] Several tests of variance were used to analyze the coded data, using SPSS (non-proportional cell sizes in some cases did not affect the analysis). For one nominal (i.e., nonmetric) variable of no more than two groups and one dependent measure, the t test was used. For one nominal variable including more than two groups and one dependent measure, a One-way was used. If significant differences were found, a Scheffé test of between groups variance was used in post hoc analysis to determine which groups differed from each other. With one dependent measure and more than one independent variable, an ANOVA was used and breakdowns obtained.

Table 1. Overall Error Rate by Social
Variables

Variable	Mean	SD
Grade		
Form 1	.135	.066
Form 5	.087	.048
t test, *df* 446, *F* = 1.89, *p* < .001		
Sex		
Female	.106	.055
Male	.127	.071
t test, *df* 446, *F* = 1.66, *p* < .001		
School type		
Prestige	.078	.041
Government	.110	.044
Comprehensive	.165	.073
One-way: *F* (2,445) = 97.424, *p* < .001		
Scheffé: Prestige/Government/Comprehensive		
Residence		
Urban	.091	.046
Semi-urban	.109	.052
Moved around	.118	.053
Rural	.142	.076
One-way: *F* (3,444) = 20.112, *p* < .001		
Scheffé: Urban, Semi-urban, Moved Around/Rural		
Ethnicity		
African	.132	.069
Indian	.121	.070
Mixed	.103	.050
Other	.083	.045
One-way: *F* (3,444) = 5.964, *p* < .001		
Scheffé: Other, Mixed, Indian/African		

The frequencies for categories of Attribution of Error were: English Writing (all punctuation errors and 70% of all spelling errors), 40%; English, 19%; English and Transfer, 16%; Transfer, 19%; and Indeterminate, 6%. If the English Writing errors are excluded from consideration, the attributions for the remaining (non-English writing) were: English, 36%; English and Transfer, 30%; and Transfer, 35%. If the latter two categories are combined, then Transfer from L1 accounts wholly or in part for 65% of all errors, excluding English Writing errors. This is clearly a considerable proportion.

Because overall ER and rate for Transfer error were generally higher for rural than urban students, a further analysis was carried out to determine the nature of these differences. For grade, it was found that as the ER decreased

Table 2. Overall Error Rate by Residence and
School Type

Group	Mean	SD
Urban prestige	.073	.036
Rural prestige	.079	.043
Urban government	.110	.041
Rural government	.112	.048
Urban comprehensive	.142	.058
Rural comprehensive	.183	.076

ANOVA: F (5,317) = 42.618, $p < .0001$
Scheffé: Urban Prestige, Rural Prestige/Urban Government/
Rural Government/Urban Comprehensive/
Rural Comprehensive

from Form 1 to Form 5, the proportion of Transfer errors also decreased. With additional tests (ANOVA plus Scheffé), the variables of residence and school type proved to be significant at all levels (Winer, 1986, p. 103). (See Table 2.)

It was further determined that, although slightly higher levels of Transfer were found in rural students and in high-ER students, generally speaking, rural students made more errors of the same types than did urban students, thus leading to higher overall ERs. This lower ER accounted at least in part for the much higher proportion of urban students in prestige schools.[3]

4. DETAILED MICROSTUDY OF SELECTED TEXTS

An analysis of errors resulting from Transfer and English and Transfer was carried out for the current study and is presented here. The subset of texts chosen were all letters of complaint about shortages—usually of water or transportation—from Form 1 classes in two junior secondary schools, one a government 5-year and one a comprehensive type. These texts were chosen because (1) the letter and narrative discourse types had the same ER (lower than that

---

[3] The situation of rural students is difficult to clarify. Given that high-competence rural students, lower in absolute number than high-competence urban students, have tended to go to prestige schools, the effect of introducing rural students into prestige schools is to skim off the high-competence, low-ER students from government and comprehensive schools, without "dragging down" the prestige schools, thereby increasing the mean ER of students who are left to continue in government and comprehensive schools. Furthermore, student ER improvement by grade, particularly for rural students, may be related more to the dropping out of high-ER students than to general improvement in language skills.

for instructions), (2) they had the widest variety of tense and structure usage, and (3) the narrowing to choice of similar topics ensured even greater comparability. This class level was chosen because Form 1 students had much higher rates of both overall error and of transfer error than Form 5 students. The particular schools were chosen as representative of the high and middle range of ER and because their populations had a fairly even representation of urban and rural residents. Of the 18 texts thus identified, a sample of 10 was made by choosing every other text and a final one at random.

4.1. The Texts

In the following texts, analysis is limited to a discussion of types of negative transfer elements appearing in the L2 and suggested attributions for error and variation. The texts are provided in their entirety; only return addresses, salutations, and closings are omitted.

T1: I am writing this letter because of the water problems. The water problems is not only bad in the area where I live, but all over. I think something should be done about it.

T2: For the past two months the road situation at [village] have been getting worse evry day. People have been writing on many occasion but notting have been done about it I would like something to be done about it.

T3: I am living verry far away in the country. And I have plenty troable to come to school. It have no busses running in the country at [village]. Some times I have to go back home, and can not get transport in time to attend school. Then and again, I reach home verry late and can not have enought time to do my home lesson.

T4: I would gradually like to say WASA [Water and Sewerage Authority] mens does take to long to give somebody connection. Because so many pipe lines they have to fix and they can't fix all at one time they have to fix one at a time. When we was going to fix our pipe we did have to wait almost seven or eight months before we get our pipe fix. Thank you.

T5: I wish to draw to your attention, of the drains of both sides of [name] Street is cloded and its houseing stagnant water. Therefore, creating a situation appropriate for the breathing of mosquito. I wish to thank you in anticipation should you draw this to the greater attention.

T6: When pipe lines are burst the Water and Sewerage Authority do not fix it and when they do fix it they dig up the place and when they are finished they filled it up any how and when rain fall the place get muddy and so vehicles get trouble to cross the place where the people fix.

T7: I will like to tele you abught the water in [village] sum tim we don get water for two three days in [village] and the animals are ding and if water don full we done get ane water.

T8: I hope you are well and enjoying best of life in our villiage there is no water some time there is no water for a week or two there is a pipe line burst I want the WASA to come and fix the pipe lines please people have to go to another villiage to get water and the farm as lock off the water to wash the farm the people in my villiage had to walk from home to a far distance to get water please give us water regular the people animal are dying for water some time there is no water ane tall please supply us water regular please.

T9: I don't like WASA because the water in the pipe line comes red. During Saturday and Sunday the water comes clear. The presure comes slow on evening. We have a tank and the water go up once a week. Every morninge we has to go and full water do our work and we reached to school late every day.

My father go to the WASA head office nealy every week but they don't take note of it. The community decided to take note of this because no one can used the water in the pipe line and if you have to used it.

T10: I am not pleased with the water shortage. And pleased let there be water in [village]. The other areas has water day and night, water wasting. So make sure there are water in [village].

4.2. Transfer and Variability in the Texts

Sources of error in the texts can be described in the following categories (the examples do not include all examples of a given type).

1. *Negative Transfer.* There is a considerable amount of straightforward Transfer of L1 features into the L2, inappropriately, resulting in L2 error. It is important to keep in mind that in all of these examples, the learner's text is *correct* TEC:

Transfer lexicon:
    (T3) It have 'There are'
    (T3) transport 'transportation'
Transfer phonology:
    (T2) notting 'nothing'
Transfer morphology and syntax:
        (T2) on many occasion 'on many occasions'
        (T3) plenty troable 'plenty of trouble'
        (T4) can not have 'do not have'
        (T4) does take 'take'

(T4) to give somebody connection 'to give somebody a connection' or 'to give people connections'

(T4) we was going 'we were going'

(T4) we did have to wait 'we had to wait'

(T6) vehicles get trouble to cross 'vehicles have trouble crossing'

(T7) I will like to tell you abught 'I would like to tell you about'

(T7) for two three days 'for two or three days'

(T8) the people animal 'the people's animals'

(T8) animal are dying for water 'animals are dying from lack of water'

(T8) please supply us water regular 'please supply us water regularly'

(T9) the water in the pipe line comes red 'the water in the pipe line comes out red'

(T9) to go and full water 'to go and fill water containers'

(T10) water wasting 'water is being wasted' or 'people are wasting water'

2. *English and Transfer.* In some cases the forms used are correct, but the context is inappropriate. In all cases, the resulting language is an error in both the L1 and the L2.

Spelling:

(T5) the breathing 'the breeding' TEC 'breeding', E 'breeding', plus hypercorrective strategy for partial correspondence of TEC /d/ to E th /ð/.

Phonology:

(T7) we don get water (TEC: 'doh'; E: 'don't')

Morphology and syntax:

(T1) the water problems is bad (TEC: 'the water problem (is) bad'; E: 'the water problem is bad' or 'the water problems are bad')

(T2) the road situation have been getting worse (TEC: 'the road situation getting worse'; E: 'the road situation has been getting worse')

(T4) Because so many pipe lines they have to fix and they can't fix all at one time they have to fix one at a time. (TEC: 'Because it have so much pipe line to fix and they can't fix all one time, they have to/must be fix one one time'; E: 'Because they have to fix so many pipe lines, they can't fix all of them at one time. They have to fix one at a time'.

(T10) make sure there are water (TEC: 'make sure it have water'; E: 'make sure there is water')

3. *English*

Lexicon:

(T3) then and again (E: 'then again', influenced by E 'now and again; TEC: 'too besides')

Spelling:
   (T3) verry 'very'
   (T4) to 'too'

There are other areas, not always errors, which show evidence of other strategies at work. Schachter (1983, p. 120) refers to the learner's use of "unanalyzed chunks" of language, particularly as the learner learns the variability involved in language, "one semantic area at a time." Since all the above texts are in the discourse/semantic areas of "letter to a newspaper," and "complaint," certain formulaic-type expressions appear which seem to be beyond the morpho-syntactic control evident in the rest of the texts:

   (T1) I think something should be done about it.
   (T2) I would like something to be done about it.

That this domain is not fully controlled by this group of writers is seen in lexical and syntactic errors resulting from incomplete learning of such phrasing:

   (T4) I would gradually like to say
   (T5) I wish to draw to your attention, of the drains of both sides of [name] Street is cloded and its houseing stagnant water.

Another factor which appears to be involved here is the traditional Trinidadian preference for what I have called "Rococo English" (Winer, 1986a, p. 123), that is, long, Latinate, flowery language. Places where this style appears to be influencing the learner's production include:

   (T8) I hope you are well and enjoying best of life in our village there is no water
   (T5) I wish to thank you in anticipation should you draw this to the greater attention.

Lowenberg (1986), in discussing strategies developed and used by speakers of nativized varieties of English such as Indian English, has pointed out that certain features regarded as "errors" in such langauge may be deliberate acts of social-cultural-ethnic identity arising from native language traditions; the transfer from indigenous literacy and cultural traditions lead to new styles of formal prose in English characterized by a "deferential, indirect, and highly ornamental style" rather than directness, little stylistic ornamentation, and emphasis on information content (Lowenberg, 1986, p. 10). This tendency is certainly still operative in Trinidadian linguistic orientation, particularly in circumstances perceived as formal—certainly including letters to a newspaper. (No examples of this type of language occurred in the narrative or instruction texts.)

5. DISCUSSION OF TEXT ANALYSIS

In addition to direct transfer of L1 features to L2, with both positive and negative results, several factors appeared to be involved in the production of these texts. Some problems arose from English intrinsic developmental errors, and some from a combination of elements of both languages. Overall, however, the level of communicative competence of the texts is striking, reflecting a high degree of positive transfer.[4] It is partly for this reason that English Creole-speaking students in North American schools who are placed in English as a second language classes with speakers of very different L1s, such as Greek, Spanish, or Chinese, generally exhibit much higher entry level English, particularly in comprehension. However, they are also more apt to hit a plateau (Craig, 1978), and to continue producing English which has persistent errors, lagging behind native English-speaking students and even ESL students in mainstream English classes. This clearly supports Kellerman's and Zobl's claims, discussed below, about the relationship between language distance and speed of learning.

As Kellerman (1983) noted:

> The L1 (or other L2s) may affect the L2 in ways that do not lead to convenient calques for the analyst. Unless one already has a fairly shrewd idea of what one is looking for, some most interesting transfer phenomena might remain invisible. (p. 113)

Thus, the analyst must be suspicious of closely related forms and must be aware of which elements classified as errors in terms of the target language are accepted variants at some level—basilectal, mesolectal, or acrolectal—of the creole L1.

This problem is found in the current situation, and it is increased in effect by the form counterpart similarities noted above. That is, in cases of a very high degree of linguistic relatedness, *both* positive transfer (facilitation) and

---

[4]Given the sometimes overwhelming incoherence apparent in most "basic" or "immature" writers (Shaughnessy, 1977), a higher level comprehensibility of texts was expected than found. A large sample of texts, in computer printout form, was shown to teachers in Canada, England, and the United States for comment. In general, they found no difficulties in understanding the students' messages; problems cited were mainly a lack of comprehension of particular TEC lexical items. The problems they described in the texts were for the most part discrete errors in grammar, spelling, lexicon, and punctuation; overall organization and development were rated highly. Teachers of English as a second language said that the writers exhibited language difficulties similar to those of students of ESL but within a native English rhetorical framework. Teachers of native English speakers found the compositions much like their own students' [compositions], but with some "peculiar" differences in types of linguistic errors.

negative transfer (interference) will be greater than in cases of lower degrees of relatedness. As Kellerman (1983) pointed out:[5]

> The general typological closeness of L1 to L2 would be capitalized on by learners as the result of a relatively immediatae opportunity to identify cognate forms and structures across the two languages . . . one would anticipate both facilitation and interference. However, certain interference errors would be resistant to eradication, particularly in environments of minimal linguistic difference. . . . Conversely, if L1 and L2 were very different, the lack of available correspondences would, in the initial stages at least, act as a bar to transfer, since the learner is unable to make the necessary cross-lingual tie-ups. (p. 114)

It is not difficult to see that the very high degree of real correspondence, and the even higher degree of perceived correspondence, between TEC and English would lead TEC L1 learners of English L2 to use transfer as a primary, long-term general strategy. In most cases, this strategy will result in positive transfer, thus reinforcing the learner's hypothesis about close language distance and the effect of this strategy. In some cases, use of the transfer strategy results in negative transfer. However, such errors in English are not always analyzed correctly—or even noticed—by either the learner or the teacher because of their low contrastive saliency or because of the difficulty of analysis; as a result, such errors tend to support further the tendency for potential slowing down of learning and high rate of fossilization at points of L1–L2 similarity.

Similarly, Zobl (1980) has claimed that

> Errors which seem to show influence from the L1 presumably begin as L2-developmental errors which are subsequently reinforced by an L1 structure compatible with the developmental error. . . . Structural properties of the L2 which give rise to developmental errors may also activate influence from the learner's L1 when an L1 structure is compatible with the developmental error. . . . Although there is a crucial degree of overlap between developmental and transfer errors with respect to the factors involved in their genesis, transfer errors may prolong restructuring of the rule underlying the error. It is hypothesized that this tendency toward fossilization results from the use of a common rule in a mature linguistic system (the L1) and in a developing linguistic system (the L2 developmental stage the learner has attained). (p. 470)

[5] Kellerman (1983) illustrated this hypothesis with the example of Swedish and Finnish learners of English as a second language. The Finns made mostly L2-intrinsic overgeneralizations, apparently judging that their L1 was "not a useful basis for making predictions about the form of English utterances," whereas the Swedes made many errors attributable to their L1, which they perceived as being more similar to English. As further support, he noted that the Finns made errors in English attributable to their Swedish L2, whereas the Swedes did not make errors from their Finnish L2 to their English L2. That is, even speakers of Finnish and Swedish as second languages recognized, as did speakers of these as first languages, that the degree of relatedness to the shared target language—English—was different, and used similar strategies of transfer.

Furthermore, given the claims of some creolists, such as Bickerton (1981), that creole languages are closest to the universal "bioprogram" for developing language (discussed by Adamson, Chapter 3, this volume), one might well posit that the creole L1 rules are closer to universal developmental sequences and, therefore, have an even stronger tendency to encourage deferment of replacement by L2 rules.

However, Schachter's claim (1983, p. 104))—that phenomena such as slower learning, overproduction, avoidance, and choice of wrong domain should be relatively *more* evident in the data of a learner of an unrelated target, whereas interference and positive transfer should be more evident in the data of one learning a related language—is only partially supported. Slower learning may not proceed at an equal pace in all domains, and it may result from greater similarity as well as greater distance.

6. IMPLICATIONS

In light of the findings relating to ER and social variables, it is clear that more attention needs to be given to particular groups of students, for example, rural residents and those in comprehensive schools. Reasons for higher ER among these students should be investigated; possible explanations include (1) less regular attendance by rural students because of problems in getting reliable, cheap transportation to school or because their labor is needed by the family and (2) a higher quality of teacher in the prestige and government schools. Remediation of this situation should then be attempted.

In light of the finding that levels of Transfer error are very significant, especially in high ER-students, and in light of the discussion of the possible effects of (perception of) language closeness, two approaches to the teaching of "language arts" should be seriously considered in this situation: (1) an overtly contrastive method of comparing TEC and English and (2) the development of true TEC L1 literacy.

Devonish (1986) has urged the greater acceptance of creole languages in the Caribbean, particularly in official domains. He points out the need for a "description of the range of intermediate varieties of Creole along the continuum, [a variety of lects] all of which would be considered as acceptable forms" (p. 115), and the identification of "certain forms which are most common and likely to [be] widely known" (p. 115), and advocates the use of creole in education.

Adequate descriptive studies of TEC are desperately needed in order to establish the kinds of variation which exist in the language as spoken currently. TEC has, from its very beginnings, been characterized by a high degree of variability (Winer, 1984). It is important to note, however, that the recognition of variation in a language is very closely related to ideas of "correctness" and "proper" status; without significant changes in both attitude and overt knowledge about TEC as an L1, such recognition will be difficult to achieve, and a consistent, accurate, and helpful contrastive approach will be hampered. Similarly, a much higher degree of teacher linguistic knowledge and training in language teaching will have to be achieved.

Much language now considered "error" is in fact a result of what might be considered inadequate or inappropriate code-switching. A teaching approach which consciously used positive transfer and focused on areas of overlap which are difficult for learners to disentangle on their own should serve to decrease hypercorrections and negative transfer in English by increasing the perception of language distance and by facilitating recognition of differences as well as true similarities between the two languages.

A second, more controversial, suggestion is L1 literacy in TEC. Although research evidence is not conclusive (e.g., Cummins & Swain, 1986), there is strong support amongst many educators, most notably perhaps Paolo Freire, for literacy in L1 vernacular as crucial to educational, social, and political development. In the Caribbean, higher social prestige for creoles has developed over the last 20 years or so (Carrington, 1978, p. 10). However, marked increases in creole L1 literacy are probably only significant in French Creole L1 in Haiti and in St. Lucia (Dalphinis, 1985, pp. 204–210), where consistent, workable standardized orthographies have been developed, where printed materials in the creole are available, and where there is political, social, and educational commitment to this aim.

First-language literacy in the English–English Creole areas is less developed. The most politically progressive and socially committed literacy campaign in the region, during the short-lived regime of the People's Revolutionary Government in Grenada, aimed at literacy in English, not Grenadian English Creole, using Freirian-type content and a modified English phonics and whole-word recognition approach (Centre for Popular Education, 1980).

Since 1979, the regionally indigenous Caribbean Examinations Council O Level (secondary matriculation) English tests have included questions which elicit or depend on the written use of creole in dialogue, poems, song lyrics, and other limited areas. Although TEC, for example, has a long history of being written, and although many writers use it today, it has been and generally is used in fairly circumscribed areas, and the lack of an "official" standardized orthography and official Ministry of Education support for L1 literacy has helped hamper efforts in this area.

Kephart's (1987) preliminary work in Carriacou, Grenada, is the only example of a study of the use of a phonemically based orthographic system used to teach reading and writing to native speakers of a Caribbean English Creole who were otherwise taught in English. He found that L1 literacy was accepted, understood, and liked by the students and was accepted by parents and teachers once they were assured that it would not hamper their children's educational progress in English, which it apparently did not. A stronger position to investigate is that L1 literacy would in fact develop general reading skills *more easily*, without the burden of concurrent L2 learning, and that the skills could be transferred to L2 literacy as well.

As Devonish points out (1986, p. 119), the validity of the creole must be established in the society at large before its use as a medium for acquiring literacy will be seen as valid by teachers, students, and parents. Other factors include the development of a standardized creole writing system, considerations of oral versus written discourse styles, and methods of encouraging creole use in wider contexts (Devonish, 1986, chap. 6; Winer, 1988).

7. CONCLUSION

This study reports that overall ER for Trinidadian English–Creole-speaking students varied significantly by social variables such as school type and residence. High rates of negative transfer from TEC to English were found, particularly in high ER compositions. The analysis suggests that real and perceived closeness of language distance between TEC and English contributes greatly to persistent difficulties students have in writing English and suggests that overall strategies of contrastive language teaching and TEC L1 literacy be considered as appropriate and useful pedagogical approaches.

REFERENCES

Bickerton, D. (1981). *The roots of language.* Ann Arbor, MI: Karoma Press.
Carrington, L. D. (1978). Education and development in the English-speaking Caribbean: A contemporary survey. UNESCO, ECLA, DEALC/16.
Carrington, L. D. (1983). The challenge of Caribbean language in the Canadian classroom. *TESL Talk, 14*,(4), 15–28.
Centre for Popular Education. (1980). *Forward ever.* Grenada: Ministry of Education.
Craig, D. R. (1978). Bidialectal education: Creole and standard in the West Indies. *International Journal of the Sociology of Language, 8*, 93–134.
Cummins, J., & Swain, M. (1986). *Bilingualism in education.* London: Longman.
Dalphinis, M. (1985). *Caribbean and African languages: Social history, language, literature and education.* London: Karia Press.
Devonish, H. (1986). *Language and liberation: Creole language politics in the Caribbean.* London: Karia Press.
Kellerman, E. (1983). Now you see it, now you don't. In S. Gass & L. Selinker (Eds.), *Language transfer in language learning* (pp. 112–134). Rowley, MA: Newbury House.
Kephart, R. (1987, April). *Reading Creole English does not destroy your brain cells.* Paper presented at TESOL '87, Miami.

Lowenberg, P. H. (1986). Non-native varieties of English: Nativization, norms, and implications. *Studies in Second Language Acquisition, 8*(1), 1–18.

Richards, J. C. (1974). *Error analysis: perspectives on second language acquisition.* London: Longman.

Schachter, J. (1983). A new account of language transfer. In S. Gass & L. Selinker (Eds.), *Language transfer in language learning* (pp. 98–111). Rowley, MA: Newbury House.

Schachter, J. (1986). In search of systematicity in interlanguage production. *Studies in Second Language Acquisition, 8*(2), 119–133.

Shaughnessy, M. P. (1977). *Errors and expectations.* New York: Oxford University Press.

Solomon, D. (1972). *Form, content and the post-creole continuum.* Paper presented at the Conference on Creole Languages and Educational Development, St. Augustine, Trinidad.

Winer, L. (1982). *An analysis of errors in the written compositions of Trinidadian English Creole speakers.* Ph.D. dissertation, University of the West Indies, St. Augustine, Trinidad. (University Microfilms No. 83-12,214)

Winer, L. (1983). Factors affecting error rate in written English in an English Creole context: Residence and school type. *York Papers in Linguistics, 11,* 323–333.

Winer, L. (1984). Early Trinidadian English Creole: The *Spectator* texts. *English World-Wide, 5*(2), 181–210.

Winer, L. (1986a). Socio-cultural change and the language of calypso. *New West Indian Guide, 60* (3 & 4), 113–148.

Winer, L. (1986b). An analysis of errors in written compositions of Trinidadian secondary school students. *Caribbean Journal of Education, 13*(1 & 2), 88–109.

Winer, L. (1988, April). *Standardization of orthography for the English Creole of Trinidad and Tobago: Linguistic and political considerations.* Paper presented at the Linguistics and Literacy Symposium, University of Wisconsin, Milwaukee.

Winford, D. (1974). Aspects of the social differentiation of language in Trinidad. *Caribbean Issues, 1*(3), 1–16.

Winford, D. (1979). Grammatical hypercorrection and the notion of ''system'' in creole language studies. *CARIB, 1,* 67–83.

Zobl, H. (1980). Developmental and transfer errors: Their common bases and (possibly) differential effects on subsequent learning. *TESOL Quarterly, 14*(4), 469–479.

CHAPTER 11

Dialect Variation and Second-Language Intelligibility

MIRIAM R. EISENSTEIN

1. INTRODUCTION

Despite our growing awareness of variation and its role in second-language acquisition, and the recent attention given to variability in the learner's interlanguage (see Ellis, 1986), much current research and pedagogy presumes a single dialect of the target language as a baseline for the analysis of the learner's comprehension and production. The limitations imposed by such an assumption are particularly inappropriate for the consideration of second-language acquisition in urban centers, which are likely to contain speakers representing a range of social and regional dialects. Hyltenstam (1981) and Kachru (1982) have emphasized the fact that many learners must communicate in an environment that involves contact with speakers of diverse target-language varieties.

   This chapter addresses the challenge of learning English as a second language in the New York Metropolitan area and focuses on the nonnative's ability to comprehend three of the major English dialects spoken there: Black English, New Yorkese (New York nonstandard English), and the regional standard. The importance of comprehensible input in the development of interlanguage (Krashen, 1981) has underscored our need to help learners interpret the range of second-language speakers with whom they converse. A greater understanding of the extent to which the various dialects which contribute to a learner's input are comprehended and assimilated will allow us to more effectively inter-

MIRIAM R. EISENSTEIN • Department of Communication Arts and Sciences, New York University, New York, New York 10003.

pret interlanguage data and make more informed recommendations for the improvement of second-language methodology and material.

2. BACKGROUND

Kachru (1976) considered models of English for the Third World and emphasized that the concept of intelligibility is relevant for all levels of language. Nelson (1981) found that the syllable-timed nature of Indian English contrasts with the stress-timed framework of American English and causes processing difficulties for individuals who must interpret each other's speech. Bansal (1969) reported that the relative intelligibility of Received Pronunciation and Indian dialects of English depended on word stress, sentence stress, rhythm, and intonation.

Intelligibility was also investigated by d'Anglejan (1975), and Tucker and Sarofim (1979), who found that the learner's ability to recognize deviant sentences improves along with proficiency in the target language. To the extent that the variety of dialects in a learner's input represents deviance from a perceived norm, this work has relevance for the current study.

Smith and Rafiqzad (1979) studied the intelligibility of different forms of accented English for ESL populations around the world and found that the order of difficulty for the varieties tested was similar for listeners from different native language backgrounds. Smith and Bisazza (1982) reported that the inherent difficulty or ease of comprehension for various dialects was also significantly affected by the extent of the learner's exposure to them. This provided confirmation of Brodkey's (1972) finding that prior listener experience with the voice of a particular speaker may also be a crucial factor in promoting comprehension.

In addition to the role of intelligibility in interlanguage development, the ease or difficulty in comprehending native models may influence the development of dialect discrimination and sociolinguistic stereotyping. Swacker (1977) noted that advanced English learners make judgments of various dialect speakers which are consistent with native views of the same speakers. Eisenstein (1979, 1982) studied learners at a range of proficiency levels and found that the ability to recognize dialect differences occurs early in the English-learning process, while the ability to correctly identify specific varieties develops more grradually. She also confirmed that the dialect-mediated attitudes reported by Swacker were shared by native and advanced nonnative speakers to a significant degree. The question of how such attitudes develop remained to be answered. One possible clue was contained in open-ended interviews conducted by Eisenstein. English learners characterized tape recordings of nonstandard speech as hard to understand and claimed that the same was true of their actual experience with similar speakers.

Eisenstein and Berkowitz (1981) investigated the role of phonological deviance in the comprehension by beginning and intermediate learners of individual sentences and a reading passage read aloud in New Yorkese and foreign-accented English. Significant findings pointed toward greater ease of comprehension of Standard English, with a stronger effect for the higher-level learners and the reading passage.

3. PROCEDURE

Since context has been found to be a crucial element for comprehension (Garrod, 1986) and has been identified as a necessary condition for testing listening comprehension (Douglas, 1988), a task was designed to provide a realistic setting for listening. Contextualized monologues were developed consisting of short narratives in which speakers related unusual or humorous experiences that had ostensibly occurred to them in the recent past. Each narrative was placed in a setting for the listener so that it would be more like a natural language experience. Topics and situations were selected which would be familiar to the learners. (For greater detail on task development, see Eisenstein & Hopper, 1983.) Six monologues were selected, with eight comprehension questions each, and balanced so that all monologues and questions did not differ significantly in difficulty when presented in Standard English to intermediate-level learners. Thus, comprehension difficulties for learners when listening to narratives with the same content presented in different dialects are likely to reflect elements specific to the language variety rather than the content and context of the monologues.

The monologues were randomly assigned to one of the three dialects under investigation; the regional standard, New Yorkese English, and Black English. One male and one female speaker performed each narrative on audiotape.

Subjects were 163 adult learners studying English at a private university in New York City. The learners, 80 females and 83 males, were mostly middle class and represented 23 different language backgrounds. Their English proficiency ranged from high beginning to advanced, with classes at Levels 3 through 8 represented. Level 3 learners had been in the United States for an average of 2½ years, although some learners had recently arrived. Level 8 learners had been in the United States for an average of 3½ years. Many learners had studied English prior to their arrival.

The contextualized monologues were presented to subjects in groups of 10 to 15 students in one of four different orders. Students heard each monologue only once and were given as much time as needed (up to 5 minutes per tape was sufficient) to answer written multiple-choice comprehension questions.

Afterwards debriefing sessions were held for the students in order to elicit their responses to the experience and to assess their familiarity with the dialects presented.

This procedure was later repeated with working-class and lower middle-class learners attending classes at three public universities in the New York area which have less affluent populations and include a significant number of native speakers of New Yorkese and Black English. One hundred and thirteen learners from nine different native backgrounds listened to the monologues. Their proficiency in English was rated by a cloze procedure which had been given to learners at the private university mentioned above. This made it possible to compare the responses of these learners with those of approximately the same proficiency level at the other institution.

After the comprehension procedure, students from this group were asked to describe what each speaker might be like by rating each one on a job scale (adapted from Shuy, Baratz, & Wolfram, 1968) and two 7-point semantic differential scales relating to friendliness and appearance. It was hoped that this would provide additional information for the interpretation of the intelligibility data.

Finally, a discussion and debriefing session was held, as explained above.

4. RESULTS

Mean scores for the middle-class learners are presented in Table 1. Average comprehension scores for the dialects considered were: Standard English, 5.47; New Yorkese, 5.23; Black English, 2.79. An ANOVA with repeated measures on dialect and sex of speaker was performed with learners' proficiency level and sex as the independent variables and comprehension score as the dependent variable (see Table 2).

Significant effects at the .001 level were found for proficiency of learner and dialect of speaker. An interaction effect for level by dialect by sex of speaker at the .01 level was found. Sex of learner was not significant.

Post hoc Scheffé tests revealed significant differences in comprehension between proficiency Levels 8 and 4 ($p < .05$) and between Levels 6 and 7 ($p < .01$).

In general, middle-class learners found Standard English easiest to comprehend, New Yorkese was a bit more difficult, and Black English the most difficult. Post hoc Scheffé tests showed these between-dialect differences were significant at the .01 level. The comprehension of all dialects increased with the development of learners overall proficiency but was not uniform for all three dialects. The extent of these between-dialect differences remained relatively constant for Standard English and New Yorkese as learners progressed

Table 1. Comprehension Scores: Middle-Class Learners

Level	Sex	SE			NYE			BE			Average total score
		M	F	All SE	M	F	All NYE	M	F	All BE	
3	m	4.78	3.56	4.17	3.89	4.11	4.00	2.44	2.33	2.39	
	f	4.22	3.56	3.89	2.33	4.89	3.61	2.44	1.89	2.17	
All L_3		4.50	3.56	4.03	3.11	4.50	3.81	2.44	2.11	2.28	3.37
4	m	4.83	4.50	4.67	4.83	5.00	4.92	2.33	1.83	2.08	
	f	5.73	4.80	5.27	4.73	5.27	5.00	2.93	1.93	2.43	
All L_4		5.28	4.65	4.97	4.78	5.13	4.96	2.63	1.88	2.26	4.06
5	m	5.07	4.00	4.54	5.07	5.00	5.04	2.00	2.77	2.39	
	f	6.17	5.17	5.67	5.89	5.29	5.58	2.56	2.78	2.67	
All L_5		5.62	4.58	5.10	5.48	5.14	5.31	2.28	2.77	2.53	4.31
6	m	6.00	4.39	5.20	4.46	5.46	4.96	3.18	2.54	2.86	
	f	6.25	5.00	5.63	4.83	5.25	5.04	2.92	2.92	2.92	
All L_6		6.13	4.70	5.41	4.65	5.36	5.00	3.05	2.73	2.89	4.43
7	m	6.47	6.33	6.40	5.93	6.80	6.37	3.87	3.07	3.47	
	f	6.75	6.92	6.83	5.50	6.50	6.00	3.83	2.92	3.38	
All L_7		6.61	6.63	6.62	5.72	6.65	6.18	3.85	2.99	3.42	5.41
8	m	6.67	7.25	6.96	6.75	6.33	6.54	4.17	3.50	3.83	
	f	6.50	6.29	6.39	5.36	6.14	5.80	2.86	2.93	2.89	
All L_8		6.58	6.77	6.68	6.05	6.24	6.15	3.51	3.21	3.36	5.40
All levels	m	5.64	5.01	5.32	5.16	5.45	5.31	3.00	2.67	2.84	
	f	5.94	5.29	5.61	4.77	5.55	5.16	2.92	2.56	2.74	
All levels		5.79	5.15	5.47	4.97	5.50	5.23	2.96	2.62	2.79	

Note. M, male speaker; m, male learner; SE, Standard English; BE, Black English; F, female speaker; f, female learner; NYE, New Yorkese; L, level.

Table 2. Analysis of Variance: Middle-Class Learners[a]

Source	df	F test	Significance
Level	5	16.465	<.001
SX	1	0.014	>.500
Level X SX	5	1.645	0.152
Dialect	2	356.967	<.001
Level X Dialect	10	2.988	0.002
SX X Dialect	2	2.274	0.125
Level X SX X Dialect	10	0.229	>.500
Sexspk	1	2.804	0.097
Level X Sexspk	5	0.821	>.500
SX X Sexspk	1	0.648	0.423
Level X SX X Sexspk	5	0.931	0.463
Dialect X Sexspk	2	15.000	<.001
Level X Dialect X Sexspk	10	2.921	0.002
SX X Dialect X Sexspk	2	0.882	0.415
Level X SX X Dialect X Sexspk	10	1.137	0.335

[a]Classifying factors: Level, level of English proficiency; SX, sex of learner; Dialect, dialect of speaker; Sexspk, sex of speaker; Unit, subjects or units of analysis.

from Levels 3 to 8. However, the comprehension of Black English improved to a much more limited extent. Level 3 scores for Standard English and New Yorkese were 4.03 and 3.81, respectively, and Level 8 scores for these dialects were 6.68 and 6.15. Black English scores, however, ranged from 2.28 at Level 3 to only 3.42 at Level 7 and 3.36 at Level 8.

Results for working-class learners with greater exposure to nonstandard speakers revealed both similarities and differences in the relative intelligibility of the dialects under consideration. Comprehension scores for speaker and dialect are listed in Table 3 (Standard English, 5.07; New Yorkese, 4.77; Black English, 3.05). The order of difficulty is the same as that for the middle-class learners, but there are differences in degree.

Table 3. Comprehension Scores: Working-Class Learners

Speaker		Dialect	
Standard English male	5.75	Standard English	5.07
Standard English female	4.40		
New Yorkese male	4.63	New Yorkese	4.77
New Yorkese female	4.91		
Black English male	3.06	Black English	3.05
Black English female	3.04		

Table 4. Analysis of Variance: Working-Class Learners

Source	df	F test	Significance
Between subjects			
Sex (of listener)	1	0.001	n.s.
Subjects within groups	98		
Within subjects			
Dialect	2	130.109	<.001
Sex X Dialect	2	0.803	n.s.
Dialect X Subject within groups	196		
Speaker	3	14.116	<.001
Sex X Speaker	3	1.519	n.s.
Speaker X Subject within groups	294		
	599		

An ANOVA for repeated measures was performed with one between-group factor, sex of listener, and two within-group factors, dialect and speaker. Once again, the dependent variable was each learner's intelligibility score on the tapes (see Table 4). An analysis of covariance was also performed using the cloze test scores as the covariate. Results were vitually identical to the original ANOVA with respect to the effects being tested (see Eisenstein & Verdi, 1985, for the analysis of covariance). However, proficiency as measured by the cloze procedure did account for a large amount of between-subject variability. Dialect of speaker was significant at the .001 level. Sex of listener was not significant. Post hoc Scheffé tests showed the Black English tapes to be significantly less intelligible than the standard tapes ($p < .05$). The major difference between these students and middle-class subjects is that for the working class learners the difference between the comprehensibility of Standard English and New Yorkese did not reach statistical significance.

Group discussions revealed that many of the learners had developed the concept of dialect differences in English and the differing status associated with such varieties. In the course of the discussions, it also became clear that some students evidenced patterns typical of Black English in their interlanguage. None of these students, however, indicated an awareness of this in their own speech. Learners said they heard speakers like those on the New Yorkese and Black English tapes frequently in the school setting.

The surprising result of the working-class data is that these learners with considerable exposure to Black English should find it so much more difficult to understand than Standard English or New Yorkese. The learners' judgments of speaker characteristics in terms of friendliness, appearance, and job status closely paralleled relative intelligibility with most favorable judgments at-

Table 5. Speaker Judgments: Working-Class Learners

	Standard English		New Yorkese		Black English	
	Male	Female	Male	Female	Male	Female
Job status	5.23	3.72	3.13	4.89	3.08	2.69
Friendliness	5.67	5.07	4.80	5.34	4.41	4.23
Appearance	5.41	4.94	4.60	5.21	3.84	3.59

tributed to Standard English speakers and least favorable qualities perceived for the Black English speakers (see Table 5).

5. DISCUSSION

Results of this study show clearly that Black English creates serious intelligibility problems for ESL learners in New York City regardless of the extent of its prevalence in the English they hear around them. Virtually all learners interviewed reported at least some familiarity with all three dialects represented on the tapes. Consequences for the students tested include difficulties in some exchanges with natives and communication problems with a significant portion of the English speakers with whom they have the possibility of interaction.

The barriers to intelligibility of local English dialects may do more than interfere with communication and reduce the opportunity for comprehensible input for learners. In the case of the working-class learners, it appears that they may be isolated from at least part of the English-speaking community around them and that lower intelligibility could be associated with negative sociolinguistic stereotypes. In an earlier study (Eisenstein, 1982), learners with a Standard English target reported that their first clue to the difference of nonstandard dialects was the greater difficulty they experienced in early encounters with nonstandard speakers, as mentioned above. These learners also developed negative stereotypes of New Yorkese and Black English speakers which became stronger as their English proficiency increased.

A striking aspect of the results reported here is that working-class learners with considerable exposure to Black English found it much more difficult to understand than Standard English or New Yorkese to a degree similar to that of middle-class learners whose exposure to Black English was much more limited. It is possible that Black English has relatively more complex phonological, syntactic, and/or semantic elements in universal terms, but other factors should be taken into account. Joshua Fishman (personal communication, 1984) notes that intelligibility and linguistic perceptions may be affected by a variety of psychosocial factors. Nelson (1982) also points out that both linguistic and nonlinguistic factors may influence intelligibility. A further element with relevance to the comprehension process is elucidated by Brown (1986), namely, the cooperativeness of the hearer in processing the message. Is it possible, she points out, for a listener to "just let the words flow past while one thinks one's own thoughts . . ." (p. 288). Does some aspect of Black English cause the ESL learners to take a different stance as listeners than they do in response to Standard English or New Yorkese? A clearer understanding of how linguistic, social, and psychological variables influence intelligibility in this case awaits further investigation.

This research also has implications for second-language acquisition research and pedagogy. The role of different target-language varieties in the comprehensibility of input must be taken into account in the analysis of second-language data and should likewise be incorporated into models of the language acquisition process. And finally, teachers and materials developers must address the challenge of how to help learners become more receptive to nonstandard varieties while maintaining an accurate appraisal of how dialects are valued by the larger speech community. Some approaches for incorporating target-language variation into the second-language curriculum appear in Eisenstein (1983) and in the section of this book devoted to pedagogical issues (Part V). However, this is an area which is crucial to the second-language development of many learners and, as such, requires considerably more attention than it has received to date.

REFERENCES

d'Anglejan, A. (1975). *Dynamics of second language development*. Unpublished doctoral dissertation. McGill University, Montreal.

Bansal, R. K. (1969). The intelligibility of Indian English. Hyderabad: Central Institute of English and Foreign Languages (Monograph no. 4).

Brodkey, D. (1972). Dictation as a measure of mutual intelligibility. *Language Learning, 22*, 203–220.

Brown, G. (1986). Investigating listening comprehension in context. *Applied Linguistics, 7*, 284–302.

Douglas, D. (1988). Testing listening comprehension in the context of the ACTFL proficiency guidelines. *Studies in Second Language Acquisition, 10*, 245–261.

Eisenstein, M. (1979). *The development of dialect discrimination and stereotyping in adult learners of English as a second language*. Unpublished doctoral dissertation. The Graduate Center, C.U.N.Y., New York.

Eisenstein, M. (1982). A study of social variation in adult second language acquisition. *Language Learning, 32*, 367–392.

Eisenstein, M. (1983). *Language Variation and the ESL Curriculum*. Washington, DC: Center for Applied Linguistics.

Eisenstein, M., & Berkowitz, D. (1981). The effect of phonological variation on adult learner comprehension. *Studies in Second Language Acquisition, 5,* 75–80.

Eisenstein, M., & Hopper, S. (1983). The intelligibility of English social dialects for adult learners of English as a second language. *Indian Journal of Applied Linguistics. 9,* 43–52.

Eisenstein, M., & Verdi, G. (1985). The intelligibility of social dialects for working-class adult learners of English. *Language Learning. 35,* 287–298.

Ellis, R. (1986). *Understanding second language acquisition.* Oxford: Oxford University Press.

Garrod, S. (1986). Language comprehension in context: A psychological perspective. *Applied Linguistics, 7,* 226–238.

Hyltenstam, K. (1981). Understanding varieties of the target language. *Working Papers, 20,* 1–26 (Lund University, Dept. of Linguistics).

Kachru, B. (1976). Models of English for the third world: White man's burden or language pragmatics. *TESOL Quarterly, 10,* 221–240.

Kachru, B. (1982). *The other tongue.* Urbana: University of Illinois Press.

Krashen, S. (1981). *Second language acquisition and second language learning.* Oxford: Pergamon Press.

Nelson, C. (1981, March). *Rhythm in non-native varieties of English.* Paper presented at the International TESOL Conference. Detroit, Michigan.

Nelson, C. (1982). Intelligibility and non-native varieties of English. In B. Kachru (Ed.), *The other tongue* (pp. 58–73). Urbana: University of Illinois Press.

Shuy, R., Baratz, J., & Wolfram, W. (1968). *Field techniques in urban language study.* Washington, DC: Center for Applied Psychology.

Smith, L., & Bisazza, J. (1982). The comprehensibility of three varieties of English for college students in seven countries. *Language Learning, 32,* 259–269.

Smith, L., & Rafiqzad, K. (1979). English for cross-cultural communication: The question of intelligibility. *TESOL Quarterly, 13,* 371–382.

Swacker, J. (1977). *Attitudes of native and non-native speakers toward varieties of American English.* Unpublished doctoral dissertation, Texas A&M University.

Tucker, G. R., & Sarofim, M. (1979). *Investigating linguistic acceptability with Egyptian ESL students.* (ERIC Document Reproduction Service No. ED 152 106)

PART IV

Aspects of Variation in
Language Learning

CHAPTER 12

Systematic Variability in Second-Language Tense Marking

WALT WOLFRAM

1. INTRODUCTION

The absence of morphologically marked tense in sentences such as *Last year we visit my friend* or *Yesterday he is sick* is among the most prominent characteristics of second-language acquisition (SLA) studies in English. Its status as an interlanguage structure is secure (Burt & Kiparsky, 1972; Dulay & Burt, 1974; Krashen, 1982), and its pedagogical and descriptive significance is unchallenged (Riddle, 1986). Regardless of source language background, it is a feature to be expected in SLA in English.

There is ample evidence which also suggests that tense marking in SLA is a highly variable phenomenon, in the sense that sometimes a sentence requiring overt tense marking in standard English will be marked for tense, and sometimes it will not. In other words, the same speaker may fluctuate between saying *Last year we visit my friend* and *Last year we visited my friend*. While just about all researchers who study tense in SLA recognize this variation between marked and unmarked tense, some of the explanations of this fluctuation seem almost as varied as the fluctuation itself. The bottom line in many attempts to account for this variation, however, seems to be the desire to explain each instance in which an interlanguage speaker shifts between marked and unmarked tense forms. In a number of recent studies (Ellis, 1987; Godfrey, 1980; Kumpf, 1984; Larsen-Freeman, 1980), researchers have turned to discourse-

WALT WOLFRAM • University of the District of Columbia, Washington, DC, and Center for Applied Linguistics, 1118 22nd Street NW, Washington, DC 20037.

187

level constraints to help account for shifts in tense marking. As Godfrey (1980)
put it:

> It is not the case, however, that speakers can switch indiscriminately from one tense
> to the other; they must obey discourse level constraints on tense continuity if their
> production is to be acceptable. (p. 93)

Such an attempt to explain shifting forms is commendable in the sense
that it typifies the consummate search for at least descriptive explanation in
SLA studies; unfortunately, at the same time it represents an unrealistic view
on the nature of variation that presently represents some attempts to account
for shifting tense forms. In the following sections, we show that individual
cases of marking and unmarking cannot be accounted for invariantly but that
there is a set of constraints that affects the relative incidence of tense marking
in a systematic way.

2. SYSTEMATIC VARIATION IN SLA STUDIES

One of the important discoveries to emerge from the systematic study of
linguistic variation pioneered by Labov (1969, 1972) was the understanding
that this variation could be an inherent part of a unitary linguistic system. Furthermore, it was shown that this variation could be systematically constrained
by both internal linguistic factors and external social factors. In other words,
the relative frequency of fluctuating forms could be enhanced or inhibited by
"independent" linguistic factors such as linguistic composition and linguistic
context in addition to social factors such as status, style, ethnicity, and so forth.
From this perspective, a particular variant could not necessarily be predicted to
occur at a given point, but a consideration of the linguistic and social constraints could raise or lower the "likelihood" of different variants in a fluctuating set. Further investigation of variation in SLA indicated that this framework was quite applicable to the study of interlanguage as well (e.g., L.
Dickerson, 1975; W. Dickerson, 1976; Wolfram, 1978), as the relative incidence of fluctuating interlanguage forms could be shown to be "inhibited" or
"favored" by particular linguistic factors as well as social conditions. This
perspective is critical for the study of variability in tense marking as well, and
various studies from this vantage point (e.g., Wolfram, 1985; Hatfield, 1986;
Wolfram & Hatfield, 1986) have supported the case for systematic variability
in the face of proposals that purport to account categorically for each particular
shift in the marking of tense.

In the following account, we review some of the systematic linguistic constraints on variation in tense marking, based on our extensive studies (Wolfram
& Hatfield, 1984) of this phenomenon in a Vietnamese community in Northern

Virginia. In the context of this community, we conducted over 90 interviews with subjects representing four different age groups (10–12, 15–18, 20–25, and 35–55) and two length of residency (LOR) groups (1–3 years and 4–7 years). In practically all cases, knowledge of English prior to the subjects' entry into the United States was nonexistent, so that the distinction of speakers on the basis of LOR correlates in an approximative way with their exposure to and their relative proficiency in English. Each of the subjects was interviewed, following loosely the kind of sociolinguistic interview described in Wolfram and Fasold (1974). In the interviews, lasting approximately an hour for each subject, many of the questions concerned past time events, such as the nature of the subjects' activities in their homeland and events leading to their resettlement in the United States. In the discussion that follows, a subsection of this original sample consisting of 32 subjects is used as the basis for the cumulative tabulations of variation between marked and unmarked tense forms. In our earlier reports (e.g., Wolfram & Hatfield, 1984), tabulations are given for each subject individually and broken down on the basis of age, sex, and LOR.

3. SURFACE CONSTRAINTS ON VARIABILITY

Our initial tabulations of the incidence of tense marking followed some fairly traditional lines of classification, with somewhat more refined subclasses of items and linguistic environments than those found in most earlier morpheme acquisition studies (e.g., Dulay & Burt, 1974).

Morphological tense marking in English takes a number of different surface forms, including three forms of the regular: /t/ following voiceless nonalveolar stops as in /mIst/ 'missed' or /kIkt/ 'kicked'; /d/ following a voiced nonalveolar stop as in /peyd/ 'paid' or /lind/ 'leaned'; and /Id/ following an alveolar stop, as in /tritId/ 'treated' or /reyded/ 'raided'. Irregular forms of past tense marking also fall into some distinct categories of formation. These include (1) suppletive forms (e.g., go/went, am/was), (2) internal vowel change (e.g., come/came, run/ran), (3) internal vowel change plus a suffix (e.g., keep/kept, do/did), and (4) replacive final consonants (e.g., have/had, make/made).

In Figure 1, the incidence of tense marking in our subsample of 32 speakers is given for the different kinds of regular forms and the irregular forms as a single set. As mentioned previously, these are cumulative figures, based upon the individual tabulations done for each subject in Wolfram and Hatfield (1984). The figures are, however, delimited on the basis of the two primary LOR groups distinguished in this study. The figures represent the number of unmarked past tense forms in relation to all those cases where Standard English would require a marked form. The percentages therefore represent the relative frequency of unmarking.

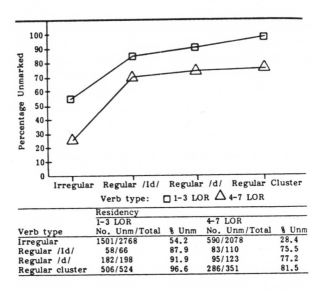

	Residency			
	1-3 LOR		4-7 LOR	
Verb type	No. Unm/Total	% Unm	No. Unm/Total	% Unm
Irregular	1501/2768	54.2	590/2078	28.4
Regular /Id/	58/66	87.9	83/110	75.5
Regular /d/	182/198	91.9	95/123	77.2
Regular cluster	506/524	96.6	286/351	81.5

Figure 1. Incidence of unmarked tense (Unm) for different regular verb forms versus irregular verbs, by length of residency (LOR). (Reprinted from Wolfram & Hatfield, 1986, p. 20.)

As indicated in Figure 1, there is a distinction in the marking of tense based upon the different phonetic forms of past tense. It is that regular forms of the past tense, regardless of the phonetic form, are less likely to be marked for tense than irregular forms. The primary constraint of regular versus irregular forms of the past tense is supported by virtually all studies that have recognized this structural distinction in their tabulations, as irregularity favors marking in SLA (e.g., Dulay & Burt, 1974; Ellis, 1987). There also appears to be a constraint based on the phonetic composition of the regular past tense and the surrounding phonological context. Thus, the surface unmarking of past tense is more likely to be found when the form ends in a phonetic cluster (e.g., reduction in an item such as /mIst→mIs/ 'missed' or /kIkt→kIk/ 'kicked') as opposed to a singleton consonant /d/ (e.g., /peyd→pey/ 'paid').

The variability of tense marking for past tense forms composed of phonetic clusters (e.g., /mIst/ 'missed', /kIkt/ 'kicked') is also constrained by the kind of segment which follows the cluster—in this case whether the following word begins with a consonant or nonconsonant. Thus, if we break down the figures for regular clusters in Figure 1 on the basis of whether the form is followed by a consonant (e.g., *missed school, kicked people*) versus a nonconsonant (e.g., *missed autumn, kicked air*), we find that the tense is more likely to be realized when the following item is a nonconsonant than a consonant. Tabulations for the 4-7 LOR group, for example, show that 75% of the past tense forms are unmarked when followed by a nonconsonant, but 91% are unmarked when followed by a consonant (Hatfield, 1986, p. 124). The important point that derives from this observation is that both the phonetic composition of the past tense form and the phonological context in which it is found affect the relative frequency of past tense marking in a systematic way.

We have found further that the shape of the past tense irregular form may also have a systematic effect on the incidence of tense marking. In Figure 2, the incidence of unmarking is given for the four different shapes of the irregular mentioned above. In addition, the marking of past tense on modals (a special case of internal vowel change and suffix addition, as in *can/could, will/would*) is included among the types of irregular forms. Again, the tabulation combines the totals for all speakers in the 1–3 LOR group and those in the 4–7 LOR group based on the individual figures reported in Hatfield (1986, p. 76ff). The figures for past tense unmarking for regular forms are also included for comparison.

The incidence of tense marking again shows a systematic pattern of variation, in which replacive forms (e.g., *have/had, make/made*) are the least likely to be marked for tense, and suppletive forms (e.g., *go/went, am/was*) are the most likely to be marked. This pattern of systematic variability has been attributed to a "principle of perceptual saliency," in which the more distant

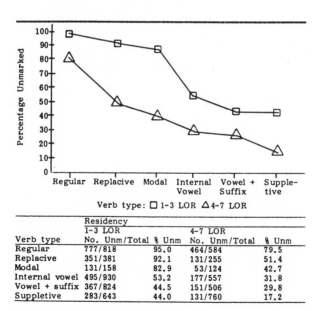

Verb type	Residency 1–3 LOR		Residency 4–7 LOR	
	No. Unm/Total	% Unm	No. Unm/Total	% Unm
Regular	777/818	95.0	464/584	79.5
Replacive	351/381	92.1	131/255	51.4
Modal	131/158	82.9	53/124	42.7
Internal vowel	495/930	53.2	177/557	31.8
Vowel + suffix	367/824	44.5	151/506	29.8
Suppletive	283/643	44.0	131/760	17.2

Figure 2. Incidence of unmarked tense (Unm) for different types of irregular verbs versus regular verbs, by length of residency (LOR). (Reprinted from Wolfram & Hatfield, 1986, p. 21.)

phonetically the past tense form is from the present tense form, the more likely it is to be marked for past tense (Wolfram, 1985, p. 247). We should, however, point out here that the overall pattern of systematic variation shows considerable individual variance, particularly for less proficient speakers (in this case, speakers in the 1–3 LOR group). In the incipient stages of learning English, speakers may show patterns of lexical preference. One speaker may thus acquire to some extent marking for the past tense of the irregular form of *go/went* while ignoring the marking of tense on *come/came*. Another speaker, at the same approximate state in SLA, may reverse this pattern of marking preference, maintaining a high degree of marking for *come/came* while ignoring *go/went*. Thus, there appears to be a strong lexical constraint on marking of irregular forms, at least in the earlier stages of SLA. As acquisition continues, however, the lexical basis of tense marking tends to be reduced, so that speakers in the 4–7 LOR group show less individual variance from the overall pattern. In Figure 2 the individual variation based upon lexical form for 1–3 LOR speakers is skewed by our reporting of the composite figures here, but it is clearly documented in Wolfram (1985).

One final constraint on tense marking with irregular verbs is considered here. This is the constraint based on verb frequency. Our rough, operational definition of a frequent verb in this study is based simply on the irregular verbs which occurred most frequently in our overall corpus. For replacive forms the most frequent form is *have/had*, for internal vowel change the most frequent form is *come/came*, and for internal vowel change plus a suffix it is *do(nt)/did(nt)*. Since *go/went* and the forms of *be* are, for all practical purposes, the only suppletive forms we find, these are not included in the tabulation. The most frequent verb form in each irregular verb category is compared with all other verbs in the same category to give a rough approximation of the effect of frequency on tense marking. From the standpoint of linguistic structure, this is a type of lexical constraint on variability, since it is the nature of the lexical item rather than a phonological or morpho-syntactic pattern which is at the basis of the distinction between classes of items. The figures for the frequently occurring verbs are given in Table 1.

The results for this tabulation are not quite as uniform as some of the figures reported for other structures, but they do suggest that at various points in SLA (e.g., internal vowel change for the 1–3 LOR group and replacives for the 4–7 LOR group), the frequent use of a verb systematically increases the likelihood of tense marking.

We may summarize our discussion of variability in tense marking up to this point by noting that there are a number of linguistic variables which seem to favor or inhibit the relative frequency of tense marking. A particular case of marking or unmarking is not predictable on this basis, but the *likelihood* of marking is systematically affected by these linguistic factors. The linguistic

Table 1. Incidence of Unmarked Tense for Frequent Irregular Verbs versus Others, by Irregular Verb Type and Residency

	Irregular verb type					
	Replacive (F = *have*)[a]		Internal vowel (F = *come*)[a]		Vowel + suffix (F = *do(n't)*)[a]	
LOR	No. unm. Total	% unm.	No. unm. Total	% unm.	No. unm. Total	% unm.
1–3 years						
Frequent	299/322	92.9	109/306	35.6	119/337	35.3
Other	52/59	88.1	386/624	61.9	248/487	50.9
4–7 years						
Frequent	111/227	48.9	62/151	41.0	67/215	31.2
Other	20/28	71.4	115/405	28.3	84/291	28.9

[a]F, most frequent form.

factors we have pointed to here seem to exist on the more superficial levels of language organization and include (1) whether the form of the past tense is regular or irregular, (2) the phonetic composition of a past tense regular form, (3) the phonological context of the items which may follow a regular form composing a consonant cluster, (4) the phonetic shape of an irregular past tense form, and (5) the relative frequency with which a particular irregular form may be used.

4. SURFACE CONSTRAINTS AND HIGHER-LEVEL LINGUISTIC ORGANIZATION

As mentioned at the outset, the current vogue in SLA studies on tense variation has centered on the examination of discourse organization rather than the kinds of surface variation scrutinized in the previous section. Thus, Kumpf (1984, p. 132) maintains that "it is the discourse which creates the conditions under which the forms appear, and in order to explain the forms, it is necessary to refer to this context." From Kumpf's perspective, the major constraint on interlanguage tense marking is that of narrative "foregrounding" and "backgrounding," in which foreground clauses push the event line forward and the background clauses set the scene, make digressions, or give evaluative remarks. According the Kumpf, clauses carrying the event line forward *do not* mark tense overtly, and those that are background have variable tense marking. While such a hypothesis is certainly seductive, the attempt to replicate Kumpf's analysis on the basis of our Vietnamese English sample has proven quite unproductive. For example, consider one attempt to replicate Kumpf's shifting of tense marking with a 4–7 LOR adult speaker (a 33-year-old female who is roughly comparable to the single subject Kumpf used as the basis of her analysis). This separation of tense marking on the basis of foregrounding and backgrounding for this subject is shown in Table 2. In order to see if the kinds of surface constraints mentioned above might interact with foregrounding and backgrounding, we have broken down the verbs on the basis of the regular form and the different kinds of irregular forms.

The pattern of tense marking shown in Table 2 does not remotely resemble the kind of distribution of tense marking found by Kumpf, in which foregound clauses have *no* tense marking and background clauses have variable marking. In fact, tense unmarking is more frequent for background than foreground clauses, but it is highly variable in both contexts. On the other hand, the breakdown by verb types clearly indicates the significance of the distinction between regular and different kinds of irregular forms. This attempt at replication of the discourse constraint should make us quite suspicious about a singular, unqualified hypothesis about tense-marking patterns as a manifestation of higher-level discourse schemes in interlanguage.

A similar attempt to replicate the "tense continuity" hypothesis of Godfrey (1980) was undertaken in Wolfram (1985) and Wolfram and Hatfield (1984). In brief, Godfrey proposes that patterns of tense marking occur in clustered series within a discourse. Due to internal and external constraints (e.g., episodic boundaries within the discourse or a difference in the amount of attention paid to speech), a speaker will shift tense, maintaining the marked or unmarked tense sequence until there is some reasoned basis for shifting to the opposite value. Thus, a speaker will use a series of marked forms, shift to a series of unmarked forms, and so forth. This observation, however, is offered without any qualification about the kind of surface forms involved. When we replicate Godfrey's study (Wolfram, 1985; Hatfield, 1986) while considering the different kinds of surface verb forms and contexts, however, we find that the analysis is seriously flawed by the failure to take into account even the most basic surface distinction such as regular and irregular past forms.

To say that Godfrey's proposal is seriously flawed by the failure to take into account the kinds of surface variables we detailed in the previous section should not be taken to mean that the hypothesis is totally without merit. In fact, our investigation of tense marking in some written samples of Vietnamese English (Wolfram & Hatfield, 1986) suggests that there may be some validity to the notion of tense clustering on the basis of episodic boundaries. However, we found this pattern does not exist as a singular explanation; instead, sequencing of tense marking is highly interactive with surface variables of the types we have specified here. In reality, no analysis of higher-order structuring in

Table 2. A Sample of Tense Unmarking for a Narrative Delimited by Foreground, Background, and Verb Type

	Clause type			
	Foreground		Background	
Verb type	No. unm./total	% unm.	No. unm./total	% unm.
Regular	5/5		12/12	
Suppletive	2/2		3/4	
Internal	0/8		7/15	
Replacive	—		9/9	
Modal	—		0/5	
Total	7/15	46.7	31/45	68.9

tense-marking patterns in interlanguage can hope to get very far without considering these kinds of constraints, however imaginative and suggestive the hypothesis appears to be at first glance.

This caution about interactive linguistic variables providing the basis for systematic variability is not, of course, limited to hypotheses related to discourse organization. Similar cautions have to be taken for any proposal to account for variation in tense marking. Thus, Ellis (1987) shows systematic differences in planned writing, planned speech, and unplanned speech with respect to patterns of tense marking, but his data also show a strong interaction based on the linguistic forms of the verb, in this case regular, irregular, and copula forms. That should not surprise us, for tense variation cannot be reduced to simplistic explanations regardless of the level of linguistic organization or the external variables appealed to as a basis of explanation. Studies of inherent variability in unitary linguistic systems have typically shown a number of linguistic and social constraints affecting variability in a regular way, and there is no reason to expect the case to be any different for systematic variability in interlanguage.

5. THE SIGNIFICANCE OF TENSE VARIABILITY

What does our empirical study of tense marking say about the underlying nature of interlanguage variability, and how might such information relate to the pedagogical world of second-language teaching? On a theoretical level, these data support the notion that there are regular, systematic effects on variability in SLA. Perhaps more importantly, it argues strongly against the reduction of fluctuation to a singular, categorical explanation, whether it is based upon surface form constraints or higher-level discourse organization. It also suggests a strong lexical variable in the incipient stages of SLA, as particular irregular verb forms take prominence over regular ones. The role of rote memorization as an early basis for a second-language pattern seems to be reinforced in studies of the type undertaken here. Although it has commonly been assumed that regular patterns should take prominence over irregular ones in the second-language instruction, the data offered here suggest that such a strategy does not recapitulate the natural acquisition process. To the extent that a pedagogical program might be plugged into the natural sequencing of SLA, we may have to reconsider the traditional consignment of rote, irregular items to language background noise which simply interferes with the acquisition of language patterns. Clearly, irregular forms play an important role in the incipient stages of learning the tense-marking system of English, and to deny their role in SLA seems pedagogically unwise as well as descriptively invalid. While I would not go so far as to suggest an early, exclusive focus on irregular tense marking, our materials ought to at least concede the empirical truth about tense marking and be prepared for the prominent role of irregular forms in the early stages of SLA.

REFERENCES

Burt, M., & Kiparsky, C. (1972). *The gooficon: A repair manual for English*. Rowley, MA: Newbury House.

Dickerson, L. (1975). The learner's interlanguage as a system of variable rules. *TESOL Quarterly, 9*, 401–407.

Dickerson, W. (1976). The psycholinguistic unity of language learning and language change. *Language Learning, 26*, 215–231.

Dulay, H., & Burt, M. (1974). Natural sequences in child second language acquisition. *Language Learning, 26*, 215–232.

Ellis, R. (1987). Interlanguage variability in narrative discourse: Style shifting in the use of the past tense. *Studies in Second Langauge Acquisition, 9*, 1–20.

Godfrey, D. L. (1980). A discourse analysis of tense in adult ESL monologues. In D. E. Larsen-Freeman (Ed.), *Discourse analysis in second language research*. (pp. 92–110). Rowley, MA: Newbury House.

Hatfield, D. (1986). *Tense marking in the spoken English of Vietnamese refugees*. Unpublished doctoral dissertation, Georgetown University.

Krashen, S. (1982). *Principles and practice in second language acquisition*. New York: Pergamon Press.

Kumpf, L. (1984). Temporal systems and universality in interlanguage: A case study. In F. Eckman, O. Bell, & O. Nelson (Eds.), *Universals of second language acquisition*. (pp. 132–143). Rowley, MA: Newbury House.

Labov, W. (1969). Contraction, deletion, and inherent variability of the English copula. *Language, 45*, 715–762.

Labov, W. (1972). *Sociolinguistic patterns*. Philadelphia; University of Pennsylvania Press.

Larsen-Freeman, D. E., (Ed.). (1980). *Discourse analysis in second language research*. Rowley, MA: Newbury Press.

Riddle, E. (1986). The meaning and discourse function of the past tense in English. *TESOL Quarterly, 20,* 267–286.

Wolfram, W. (1978). Contrastive linguistics and social lectology. *Language Learning, 28,* 1–28.

Wolfram, W. (1985). Variability in tense marking: A case for the obvious. *Language Learning, 35,* 229–253.

Wolfram, W., & Fasold, R. W. (1974). *The study of social dialects in American English.* Englewood-Cliffs, NJ: Prentice-Hall.

Wolfram, W., & Hatfield, D. (1984). *Tense marking in second language learning: Patterns of spoken and written English in a Vietnamese community.* Final Report, National Institute of Education Grant no. NIE-G-83-0035.

Wolfram, W., & Hatfield, D. (1986). Interlanguage fads and linguistic reality: The case of tense marking. In D. Tannen & J. E. Alatis (Eds.), *GURT '85 languages and linguistics: The interdependence of theory, data, and application* (pp. 17–34). Washington, DC: Georgetown University Press.

CHAPTER 13

Sociolinguistic Variation in Face-Threatening Speech Acts
Chastisement and Disagreement

LESLIE M. BEEBE AND TOMOKO TAKAHASHI

1. INTRODUCTION

The cross-cultural study of speech acts is vital to the understanding of international communication. In reviewing this area of research, we realize that face-threatening acts are particularly important to study because they are the source of so many cross-cultural miscommunications. Research has been done on a number of face-threatening speech acts[1]—for example, on apologies (Blum-Kulka & Olshtain, 1984; Blum-Kulka, House, & Kasper, in press; Borkin & Reinhart, 1978; Cohen & Olshtain, 1981, 1985; Coulmas, 1981; Godard 1977; Olshtain, 1983; Olshtain & Cohen, 1983); requests (Blum-Kulka 1982; Blum-Kulka & Olshtain, 1984; Blum-Kulka, House, & Kasper, in press; Tanaka & Kawade, 1982); refusals (Beebe & Cummings, 1985; Beebe, Takahashi, & Uliss-Weltz, in press; Takahashi & Beebe, 1986, 1987); complaints (Boni-kowska, 1985; Olshtain & Weinbach, 1986); disagreement (LoCastro, 1986; Pomerantz, 1984); expressions of disapproval (D'Amico-Reisner, 1983); and

This chapter overlaps with our paper "Do You Have a Bag?: Social Status and Patterned Variation in Second Language Acquisition," to appear in S. Gass, C. Madden, D. Preston, & L. Selinker (Eds.), *Variation in Second Language Acquisition: Discourse, Pragmatics and Communication.* Avon, England: Multilingual Matters. This chapter deals with chastisement and disagreement, while the paper deals with expressing disagreement and announcing embarrassing information.

LESLIE M. BEEBE AND TOMOKO TAKAHASHI • Department of Languages and Literature, Teachers College, Columbia University, New York, New York 10027.

199

expressions of gratitude (Eisenstein & Bodman, 1986).[1] The evidence provided in these studies suggests that second-language (L2) learners are faced with the great risk of offending their interlocutors or of miscommunication when performing face-threatening acts.

The problem in such situations is often due to differences between languages in the social rules of speaking (see Hymes, 1972, and Wolfson 1983a, for discussion of social rules of speaking). It is thus due to the L2 learner's lack of pragmatic competence in the target language, resulting in what Thomas (1983) calls ''pragmatic failure.'' Leech (1983) also points out that ''transfer of the norms of one community to another may well lead to 'pragmatic failure' and to the judgment that the speaker is in some way being impolite'' (p. 281). The chance of offending someone is also inherent in face-threatening acts. In performing face-threatening acts, therefore, speakers must integrate personal and societal values with linguistic competence and, most importantly, gain some knowledge of ''face-work'' (Goffman, 1967) and some experience using it in the L2 interaction.

As Brown and Levinson (1978) demonstrate, there exist universal strategies in performing face-threatening acts. At the same time, we are also aware of cross-cultural differences in the realization of speech acts. People may transfer some culturally specific politeness strategies from the native language into the target language. They may accurately or inaccurately perceive linguistic differences between their native language and the target language. Even if they accurately perceive differences, however, they may have difficulty producing what they perceive. And very often, the problem is that they do not perceive the differences accurately, or they exaggerate them.

Exaggeration and misperception lead to stereotypes: ''Americans are more direct than Japanese.'' ''Americans are more explicit than Japanese.'' ''Japanese do not make critical remarks to someone else's face. They avoid disagreement. And, they are constantly apologizing.'' These are stereotypes—stereotypes which many Americans and Japanese alike subscribe to. The stereotypes are claimed to apply to Japanese both when they speak their native language and when they speak English as a second language (ESL). Even the books on comparative culture seem to reinforce these views.

---

[1] It is, however, quite problematic to determine which speech acts are face threatening as well as whose face (the speaker's or hearer's) is being threatened. According to Brown and Levinson (1978), for instance, expressing thanks can be face threatening because in this act the speaker ''accepts a debt [and] humbles his own face'' (p. 72). Compliments can also be face threatening, predicting ''some desire of S [the speaker] toward H [the addressee] or H's goods, giving H reason to think that he may have to take action to protect the object of S's desire, or give it to S'' (Brown & Levinson, 1978, p.71). Scollon and Scollon (1981) are thus quite right in stating that ''any act of communication is a threat to face, that is, to the public self-image that a person seeks to maintain'' (p. 171). We may thus add to the list studies on compliments (Holmes & Brown, 1987; Manes, 1983; Manes & Wolfson, 1981; Wolfson, 1981, 1983b, 1984).

In this chapter we are investigating American and Japanese performance of face-threatening speech acts in English—especially, disagreement and chastisement. We are looking at how these face-threatening acts are performed with status unequals—a person of lower status talking to someone of higher status and a person of higher status talking to someone of lower status. Our primary purpose, therefore, is to present data describing the differences between native English responses and Japanese ESL responses in face-threatening situations and in an encounter of interlocutors of different status.

2. METHOD

The data for this study were gathered via two different data collection procedures. First, they consist of natural speech collected in notebooks by the researchers. A word-for-word transcription was made as soon after the interactions as possible. There are problems with these data: (1) Every situation is totally different sociolinguistically, (2) the number of interactions gathered is insufficient to make generalizations, and (3) word-for-word recall can be absolutely accurate only when the core speech act is very short. But is not possible to make a completely accurate transcription of long negotiated sequences. What can be recalled relatively accurately in long interchanges is the function of the utterances and the type of semantic formula used to fulfill the function (e.g., Sara refused Jack's invitation. She said she was sorry that she couldn't come and gave an excuse that her little daughter was sick). What is not always so reliable is the precise wording of what was said by each party.

For this reason, data were collected via a second procedure—a discourse completion test. This is a written role-play questionnaire where respondents write what they think they would say or indicate if they would say nothing—that is, they were allowed to "opt out" if they wished to do so (see Bonikowska, 1985).

The advantages of this approach are that one can collect a large amount of data in a relatively short period of time and all subjects are asked to respond in identical situations. There is no problem capturing what they give as a response because the data are written. As Beebe and Cummings (1985) have demonstrated for refusals, subjects' intuitions about what they would say correspond closely to what other subjects actually did say in the same situation. They correspond in terms of the stereotypical form of the speech act they give—that is, the semantic formulas which they find it necessary to use. They do not correspond completely where the psychosocial dynamics of the interaction become more heated. Real-life verbal interactions involve much more elaboration, especially in face-threatening situations. Written responses are streamlined, containing fillers for slots that the subject feels must necessarily be filled to fulfill a particular function.

The questionnaire used to collect the bulk of the data consisted of 12 items—two situations each of the following: correction, disagreement, chastisement, an embarrassing announcement, and two other speech acts as controls. In this chapter, we discuss only disagreement and chastisement. The situations were presented in randomized order. For each pair eliciting one type of speech act, one situation involved a person of lower status talking to someone in a higher position and one situation involved just the reverse—someone in a higher-status position talking to a person of lower status.

There were 30 subjects who filled out the questionnaire—15 native speakers of English and 15 native speakers of Japanese who responded in English. The Japanese speakers had high-intermediate to advanced levels of ESL proficiency.

All the responses were analyzed as consisting of a sequence of semantic formulas. For each of the subject groups (American and Japanese), the total number of semantic formulas of any kind used for each situation was obtained. In a few cases, some subjects described what they would do instead of giving what they would say (e.g., "I will go over the plan with him"). Such responses were excluded from the data.

The data are presented descriptively. The natural data we have do not permit statistical analysis. Descriptive statistics are used on the questionnaire data, but the primary purpose of this chapter is to describe the content of the responses—that is, to give the flavor of the Japanese ESL versus the American responses when speaking to a higher versus a lower status interlocutor.

3. RESULTS

3.1. Disagreement

From our natural data we have examples of a distinctively Japanese questioning strategy which was used in face-threatening speech acts, including disagreement. In one real-life situation, an American professor hired a Japanese student to act as editor on her research. On one occasion the student disagreed with the professor, but did not explicitly say so. Instead, he asked seemingly factual questions, getting the professor to go over her argument repeatedly in detail—four times in succession. After the fourth time, the desired self-discovery occurred—the professor finally heard the flaws in her own reasoning. She began to realize that the student was indirectly expressing disagreement. But after repeating her arguments four times in a row, she felt foolish. She wouldn't have been uncomfortable, however, if the student had expressed disagreement according to the "American" rules of speaking: "I see what you mean, but . . . ." or "I like the idea that X, but don't you think possibly Y?" What the

American professor found embarrassing was that she had said something illogical four times in a row, getting more and more explicit every time, thinking that clarification was being directly requested, not disagreement being indirectly suggested. And then she had to begin a questioning routine to find out the student's arguments because she still didn't have any idea what they were.

LoCastro (1986) captures the essence of a typical American pattern in the title of her paper on disagreement: "I agree with you, but . . ." Americans often preface their face-threatening speech acts with a statement of the exact opposite of what they mean to say. Similarly, based on his American data, Sacks (1973) reports the same phenomenon, where speakers tend to twist their utterances in order to hide disagreement by responding to a preceding utterance with "Yes, but . . ." (cited in Brown & Levinson, 1978, p. 119). We say "I agree with you, but . . ." as a "token agreement" (Brown & Levinson, 1978; Levinson, 1983) just before we disagree with an opinion. We say, "That was a great report, but . . ." just before we correct the student for giving the wrong date. So it is perhaps dangerous to stereotype American responses as "direct" while claiming that Japanese responses are "indirect."[2]

Still, Americans continue to complain that Japanese are so indirect that they don't understand what Japanese are saying, and Japanese continue to lament that Americans have to spell everything out ad nauseam when certain things would be better left unsaid. The Japanese use of the question as an expression of disagreement or a statement of opinion is a frequent source of misunderstanding. In another of our natural examples, an American professor was giving doctoral advisement to a Japanese student doing his dissertation. The professor made a suggestion that the student did not think it was advisable to follow. The student indicated this by an extended series of questions about the reasoning behind the suggestion. Finally, the professor retracted her suggestion, and the student was relieved that he did not have to take advice he didn't agree with. The problem was that the American professor felt that her time had been wasted. She would have considered it much simpler if the Japanese student had told her he thought another approach might be better. Also, the more the professor elaborated, the more she felt she had made herself appear foolish. The very strategy that the Japanese used to help the American professor save face is the same strategy that made the professor feel that she had lost it.

It is well known that Americans and Japanese have different strategies for expressing disagreement, but there is very little research explaining what ex-

---

[2]The study of directness/indirectness is a vast field where a great deal of work has been done. However, a great deal of work needs to be done even in defining the concepts. We are aware of definitional and other problems in the study of directness/indirectness, but they are beyond the scope of this chapter. Readers should see Blum-Kulka (1987), and Blum-Kulka and Olshtain (1984, 1986) on directness/indirectness.

actly the differences are. As mentioned above, the stereotype is that Japanese are indirect and Americans are direct. Deutsch (1983), for instance, advises the following to Americans doing business with the Japanese:

> It is not appropriate, according to Japanese custom, to criticize someone openly, thus causing him to lose face; embarrassment should be avoided whenever possible by refraining from negative or combative statements that will make the Japanese look wrong or foolish. (p. 182)

It is, however, an oversimplification to think that the Japanese are always indirect. Tatsuya Komatsu, one of the most famous simultaneous interpreters in Japan, explains that in talking to their superiors, Japanese try to avoid disagreement—not saying they disagree, saying nothing if possible, or if forced to state some disagreement, toning it down. They seek harmony with equals, but with their status inferiors, they essentially say, "I disagree. You are wrong" (T. Komatsu, personal communication, February 1987).

Let us now look at the results of the discourse completion data:

Disagreement Situation I (higher to lower status): You are a corporate executive. Your assistant submits a proposal for reassignment of secretarial duties in your division. Your assistant describes the benefits of this new plan, but you believe it will not work.

Disagreement is always a face-threatening act. In this situation we are dealing with disagreement between someone of a high status (a corporate executive) and someone of lower status (an assistant). The question is: do Japanese ESL speakers handle the situation differently from American native speakers? Are they blunter and more direct in a situation where they are in a higher status than their interlocutor? From our preliminary data, it seems that Komatsu is right. Japanese ESL speakers, playing the part of the corporate executive, were much more likely to state an explicit criticism of their assistant's proposal. Out of 13 Japanese, 11 (85%) criticized the lower-status person's plan, whereas only 7 out of 14 Americans (50%) did so. One Japanese gave two explicit criticisms: "I don't think that's a good idea; besides what you said about X doesn't seem to be making any sense here." Another one actually used the words "don't agree" (which American native speakers never did), saying: "I don't agree with you. I don't think your plan will work well." These examples can be explained in terms of the power of authority the speaker has; that is, the speaker with greater power chooses to assert his or her authority over the addressee (Thomas, 1984) and to go "on record" (Brown & Levinson, 1978) with the disagreement.

In this higher- to lower-status situation, many Japanese felt it appropriate to state criticism outright—that the plan would not work. They used softeners in every case of criticism, just as Americans did (in every case but one). Still, their responses did not sound as gentle to the "American ear" as the native

American ones did.[3] For one thing, what we coded as softeners were mostly just expressions (or hedges) like "I (don't) think," "I believe," "I think it's kind of doubtful" (see Brown & Levinson, 1978, pp. 276–278). And some of the intended softeners weren't particularly soft, such as "I'm afraid . . ." and "I hate to tell you that. . . ."

More importantly, the things that really soften disagreement the most in American English are other semantic formulas that we coded as positive remarks or expressions of gratitude. Five Americans (33%) expressed appreciation or gratitude at receiving the proposal from the lower-status person, whereas only two Japanese (15%) did. This is not significant quantitatively, but qualitatively, there seems to be a big difference. Americans said things like, "Thank you for your concern and efforts to . . ." or "I really appreciate your giving so much thought to this matter." The two Japanese said, "Thank you for giving me your proposal" and "Thank you very much for your proposal." Thus, the Japanese said a rather formulaic thank-you, whereas the Americans integrated positive remarks and tried to sound original in their statements of gratitude. Loveday (1982) supports this point, arguing that Japanese speakers of English are likely to transfer ceremonial formulas for thanks and other speech acts into English. He explains that in the Japanese community "politeness is closely connected with the use of ceremonial-like formulae which are unhesitantly used, without fear of sounding unoriginal"(Loveday, 1982, p. 83). The same point is made by Coulmas (1981) as follows:

> the Japanese are very particular about using the appropriate form in the appropriate context. There is not so much demand for originality as in Western cultures, and no fear of repeating the same formula others have just used. In many situations the choice of possible locutions is very limited. (p. 84)

Americans, on the other hand, seem to prefer "a 'formless' personal touch" (Goldstein & Tamura, 1975, p. 90) to a standard form (see Condon, 1984; Fukushima & Iwata, 1985; Sakamoto & Naotsuka, 1982, for similar views).

---

[3] We realize that there is no one subjective reaction to any English statement that all the speakers of American English would share. We use the somewhat vague term, "American ear," to reflect the fact that we have checked the response of many American native speakers to the data in this chapter, and we do find a commonality in their responses. We have asked graduate students in TESOL and Applied Linguistics at Columbia University Teachers College. We have also asked friends, acquaintances, relatives, and even a few strangers, for their reactions. There is a pattern in their responses (the details are not reported here) which gives us some empirical ground for saying the "American ear." We realize, however, it is an overgeneralization and an oversimplification.

Furthermore, the analysis presented in this study represents an examination of interlanguage, but it is not purely interlanguage analysis in the sense advocated by Selinker (1972) or Corder (1967, 1971). It compares Japanese ESL responses to American responses and gives American reactions to the interlanguage data. We do not attempt to discuss the interlanguage data in terms of the individual's interlanguage pragmatic system. We feel it is premature to do so at this stage of investigation.

Out of 14 Americans, 8 (57%) used a positive remark to accompany their criticism, whereas not one Japanese ESL speaker used a strictly positive remark. Japanese occasionally used gratitude (2/13) and occasionally used a statement of empathy (2/13), such as "I recognize your concern." But despite these expressions which admittedly have a softening effect, Japanese ESL responses did not sound gentle. Here are some typical Japanese statements that have no prefacing gratitude or empathy: "I think it will not work. Think it over again." "I'm sorry, but I'm afraid this won't work." "Well, it doesn't seem to work to me because . . ." When there *is* a prefacing formula, such as a statement of empathy, it sounds a bit short and perhaps perfunctory to the American ear: "I appreciate your concern. But I hate to tell you that I don't think it will work."

A major difference between American and Japanese responses was that Americans frequently made a suggestion or request to talk further, reconsider, rethink, and the like. Out of 14 Americans, 9 (64%) decided to go "off record" (Brown & Levinson, 1978) and used this strategy with the lower-status interlocutor, whereas only 2 out of 13 Japanese ESL speakers (15%) made suggestions. And when the American made suggestions, they seemed to be avoiding direct disagreement. When the Japanese made suggestions, they seemed to express disagreement. Americans typically said things like: "I think you've put a lot of thought into this plan and I appreciate that. I have a few ideas that I'd like to toss out as well, so let's set aside some time to go through this." Another said, "Thanks for your concern and efforts to streamline things but I think you and I ought to sit down and give this proposal thorough scrutiny before we implement the plan." These suggestions to talk or rethink are quite different from Japanese ESL answers. Japanese responses were shorter and blunter—more likely to criticize. One Japanese ESL speaker said, "Frankly speaking, I don't think it is fine. I will submit my plan better than this." Contrary to prevailing stereotypes, it is the Americans who sound indirect and the Japanese who take the disagreement with the lower-status person head on (see Table 1 for a summary of the data for the above situation).

Disagreement Situation II (lower to higher status): You work in a corporation. Your boss presents you with a plan for reorganization of the department that you are convinced will not work. Your boss says: "Isn't this a great plan?"

In this situation the disagreement is expressed from the lower-status employee to his or her boss. According to the stereotype that many American and Japanese have of Japanese disagreement, it should be very polite, hesitant, and indirect, even in English. Or it shouldn't be expressed at all. The data did not seem to confirm the stereotype, or at least not as completely as we might expect.

Table 1. Use of Major Semantic Formulas in the
Disagreement Situation I (Higher to Lower Status)

Semantic formulas	Groups[a]	
	Japanese (%)	American (%)
Criticism	85	50
Suggestion	15	64
Positive remark	—	57
Gratitude	15	33
Empathy	15	—

[a]For Japanese, $n = 13$; for American, $n = 14$.

It was true that in this situation where disagreement would have to be from the lower-status person to the higher-status person, 5 out of 15 (33%) of the Japanese ESL speakers said "yes," that the boss's plan was wonderful. All then proceeded to say "but . . ." and promptly criticized it or suggested doing something else. This could lead us to say that they were indirect, but that may not be a proper analysis. Out of 15 Japanese, 3 responded with an explicit "no" and then criticized the plan. American native speakers never once used an explicit "no," and only once used an explicit "yes." So they never resorted to the ultimate directness.

Beyond the question of saying an explicit "yes" or "no," Japanese responses simply sounded harsher and more direct. When the boss said, "Isn't this a great plan?" one Japanese ESL speaker said, "No, it isn't, I'm afraid." Another said, "No, I don't think it's a great plan." However, this type of minimalist answer, which sounds very blunt, is characteristic of ESL learners, not just Japanese speakers. It reflects lack of fluency and lack of proficiency in the target-language social rules of speaking. Therefore, we cannot simply assume that in this case it stems from native Japanese sociolinguistic transfer (see Takahashi & Beebe, 1987).

The major generalizations that we can make are that the Americans used more positive remarks, more softeners, and most importantly, fewer explicit criticisms to a higher-status interlocutor. Out of 15 Japanese, 10 (67%) made an explicit criticism in English, whereas only 5 out of 15 (33%) of the American did. So, at least on written role-play data, Japanese felt they could criticize even a higher-status person. This last finding is quite surprising. Is it true of natural situations as well? Or, is it an artifact of the data collection method? Questionnaires are known to favor shorter, less elaborated answers that give less attention to the psychosocial dynamics of the situation than natural speech does (see Beebe & Cummings, 1985). Does it reflect Japanese native language transfer, or is it a function of limited L2 proficiency? It could also be an accurate reflection of the Japanese ESL speakers' American personas. We are repeatedly told by Japanese people in the United States that ESL classes in Japan stress the need for Japanese to be more direct and explicit in ESL than they are in Japanese. Thus, some of their directness may be a transfer of training (Selinker, 1972). At this point, we know *what* the subjects did, but we do not yet know *why* they did it (see the "Conclusion" of the chapter for a discussion of "why" and Table 2 for a summary of the data).

Both groups generally chose between making positive remarks and criticisms. The very common American pattern of making a positive remark and then a subsequent criticism, which we saw in a higher- to lower-status interaction, did not show up in this situation, where a lower-status employee spoke to a higher-status person—the boss. Instead, Americans used very lukewarm positive remarks (e.g., "It has potential" or "It has possibilities") or they followed up their positive remark with a suggestion or request that looked very much like avoidance of direct disagreement. For instance, one American said, "It looks interesting. If you really want my opinion, I'd like to look it over more carefully, and maybe ask a few questions." Another said, "I really haven't had much time to look through it yet. Maybe we could sit down and talk about it after I've had a chance to look through it." These responses contain hedging and postponing tactics.

It was mentioned earlier that Japanese ESL speakers use a questioning strategy to show disagreement and that American native speakers often fail to pick up the pragmatic intent of the questions. Interestingly, one Japanese respondent wrote after her response to the boss's enthusiasm about his own plan: "I'll keep asking questions to convince him that there are things to be revised in the plan." It is helpful to have a Japanese explicitly state that she uses this strategy. However, we must be careful not to claim that the questioning strategy is totally alien to American culture. One American responded, "Uh. How do you see this being carried out? How do you think it will work?" But after that, he explicitly stated, "I guess I see problems . . ." Another American said, "You put a lot of time into this. Do you think it will really work?" So Americans also use questions to express doubts and disagreements, and they, too, can be very indirect. The question is: what are the differences between American and Japanese use of questioning to express disagreement?

One crucial difference may be that Japanese use a repeated questioning strategy when they fail to get results. Americans may resort to the statement of opinion (in this case, disagreement) when their initial questioning does not seem to work. Another difference may be that the Japanese question appears designed to solicit facts. The Americans who asked questions said, "Do you think it will really work?" The use of "think" clues the American listener that an opinion is being solicited, and the use of "really" suggests that there is some skepticism.

Table 2. Use of Major Semantic Formulas in the Disagreement
Situation II (Lower to Higher Status)

Semantic formulas	Groups[a]	
	Japanese (%)	American (%)
Criticism	67	33
Suggestion	20	33
Positive remark	40	47
Token agreement ("Yes")	33	7

[a]For Japanese, $n = 15$; for American, $n = 15$.

3.2. Chastisement

Some of the themes and linguistic patterns in the investigation of disagreement show up in the study of chastisement.

Chastisement Situation I (higher to lower status): You are a corporation president and you have asked your assistant to prepare xerox copies of essential documents for an important press conference. Your assistant arrives at the last moment with 100 copies of the wrong materials.

American native speakers were more likely to state the precise error that the assistant made (e.g., "You did X"), they specified more correction (e.g., "I needed Y"), and they more frequently made a request for repair (e.g., "Now do Z"). All in all, their statements were longer than Japanese ESL responses. What distinguished Japanese ESL chastisement was that although the whole statements were shorter, they contained many more explicit criticisms.

Elaborating on these points, 11 out of 15 Americans (73%) made an explicit statement of error, whereas only 5 out of 13 Japanese (39%) did so in their English. Out of 15 Americans, 7 (47%) stated a correction, that is, what they had wanted the assistant to do, whereas only 4 out of 13 Japanese (31%) did so. Out of 15 Americans, 11 (73%) made a specific request for repair (e.g., "Could you go make the copies now?"), whereas only 6 out of 13 Japanese (46%) did so in their English responses. One typical American response was: "Oh, dear. These are the Holloway reports. We need the Wall Street Journal articles. Could you go make copies now?" Another typical one said, "Oh, no! These are the wrong copies. I'd asked for 100 copies of the first page, not the second. Please, go back to the office as quickly as you can and see if you can make copies of the first page before the conference is over." Basically both said what was wrong, what was needed, and what should be done. Japanese frequently said these things, but only 1 out of 13 said all three of these things

together. Consequently, American responses were longer and seemed more explicit about the problem and the solution.

What is interesting about the Japanese responses is the prevalence of criticism. With regard to feelings, the Japanese seemed more explicit than the
Americans because they made 10 direct criticisms. Out of 13 Japanese, 7 (54%)
criticized the assistant, and 3 of the 7 made two critical statements in a row.
Only 3 Americans (20%) directly criticized the assistant, and none made double
criticisms. This use of criticism reminds us of the pattern found in disagreement. When a higher-status Japanese disagrees with a lower-status person, he
or she can say it right out. Americans feel the need to start out with something
positive before letting on that they disagree, whereas Japanese evidently find it
acceptable to say that the lower-status person is wrong and to criticize him or
her. Here, in chastisement, one Japanese said, "Oh my God! How silly you
are!" Another said, "Didn't I tell you how important they are? How careless
you are!" Americans never named the fault—carelessness, silliness, and so on.

From our natural data, we have an interesting example which is rather an
unusual case but seems to support the above observation. In the New York
office of a Japanese company, a Japanese top executive (the boss) and an
American manager were arguing over some important issues. It was almost the
end of the day at work. The argument went on, and the two got so involved in
the argument that they even became emotional. The Japanese boss started crit-
icizing the American manager for the mistakes he had made in the past. Finally, the American manager said, "Sorry, I have to go now. I have an ap-
pointment with my dentist." And, the Japanese boss said, "You'd better go
see a psychiatrist instead."

Thus, in general, Japanese (of higher status) seemed to let their displea-
sure show more than Americans, as seen in the following responses given by
our Japanese subjects: (1) "I never asked you for those! What do you think I
can do with them!" and (2) "No, not these! I want copies of [such and such].
Copy them right away." The second response also has a more commanding
tone of superior to inferior than any we found in the native English data. One
Japanese did not write what words she would say but responded, "I will get
angry and order him (her) to bring the original of the essential document as
soon as possible." That seems to capture the essence of the typical Japanese
response. It is neither inexplicit nor indirect when it comes to feelings (see
Table 3 for summary of data for Chastisement Situation I).

In this chapter we are concentrating on the first statement made in response to the discourse situation although the questionnaire allowed for two or
even three turns. Where we have a higher-status person chastising a lower-
status person, however, the second turn is particularly interesting, so it is mentioned here. The responses to chastisement from the boss suggested by Americans differed from the ones suggested by Japanese. Japanese assistants sounded

Table 3. Use of Major Semantic Formulas in the
Chastisement Situation I (Higher to Lower Status)

Semantic formulas	Groups[a]	
	Japanese (%)	American (%)
Statement of error	39	73
Correction	31	47
Request for repair	46	73
Criticism	54	20

[a]For Japanese, $n = 13$; for American, $n = 15$.

much more obedient and apologetic. As one Japanese said, "He (She) will apologize and follow my order." The obedient tone was seen in responses like, "I'll do right away," "I'm very sorry sir. I'll make new copies right away," "I'm sorry. I behave myself," and "Yes, sir."

According to stereotypes, Japanese apologize too much and Americans not enough. It is true that there are many places in the Japanese language where an apology is called for and where Americans in English would say nothing or use a thank-you (see Coulmas, 1981). These cross-linguistic differences have been found to be a source of transfer errors by Japanese speaking English and Americans speaking Japanese. It was said that the Japanese ESL responses sounded more apologetic than the American ones. It is therefore surprising to find out that 13 out of 15 Americans explicitly said that they were sorry and only 8 out of 15 Japanese said they were sorry (one of them using the transfer error "excuse me" for "I'm sorry").

Nevertheless, we interpret the data to show that the Japanese were more apologetic. It is more apologetic to say that you are sorry and that you will immediately do what was requested than to do what some Americans did: say you are sorry in the context of "but I thought you said . . ." Out of 15 Americans, 4 used self-defense as a response to their superior. Not one Japanese did. One American said, "I'm sorry too, but I'm sure that this is what you requested. I'll try to get the copies to you as fast as possible." another said, "Which articles? You told me to do the Holloway." Still another said, "I thought you said the second page! I'm sorry. I don't know if I can make them in time, but I'll try." And a fourth said, "All right. I'll be over at the hotel as soon as I possibly can. And I'm really sorry, but I did think you said you wanted these." These responses indicate that Americans were more likely to express self-defense and less likely to sound totally deferential.

Apologies and statements of self-defense were not the only indicators of a difference in deference. Two Japanese said they would say nothing. Not one American did. One Japanese said of the assistant, "She'll be shaking." All of this suggests a different degree of social distance between the boss and the assistant in the minds of Japanese and Americans.

All of these questionnaire data led us to wonder if these differences exist in the "real" world. Actually, it was a naturally occurring example that led us to write the questionnaire item on chastisement in the first place. A Japanese woman living in New York was stopped by a traffic cop for running a red light. She really didn't want to get a ticket. The policeman informed her of her infraction, and she just kept apologizing, saying "I'm sorry" over and over again. She used two Japanese strategies: (1) repeat the apology to demonstrate sincerity, and (2) stick to apology and don't use excuses, self-defense, or guilt-inducing strategies to a power superior. She didn't get a ticket. We suspect the the jaded New York cop who had heard just about every defense in the book was simply charmed by the deference in the Japanese rules of speaking.

Chastisement Situation II (lower to higher status): You are a middle manager in a large corporation and your boss hands you a 50-page document, asking you to make 30 copies of each page. Ten minutes later he comes back to get the copies because it turns out he only wanted 30 copes of the front page. You have just made 10 copies of the whole packet. Obviously he is angry with you.

Although this was intended to be a chastisement situation, only one American and one Japanese criticized the boss, even though the misunderstanding was his fault. Instead, both groups resorted to statements of self-defense. Americans always did (in all 15 cases), and Japanese did so in 9 out of 13 cases. Contrary to stereotypes about the ubiquitous Japanese apology, Americans again apologized more than Japanese ESL speakers, just as they did in the higher- to lower-status situation. Americans role-playing a middle manager talking to the boss apologized in 13 out of 15 cases (81% of the time), whereas Japanese apologized in only 4 out of 13 instances (31% of the time). Americans were more likely to talk about fault, and both groups occasionally added an offer of repair after their self-defense, but the basic element for both Japanese ESL and native English speakers was the statement of self-defense. As a general rule, for the Americans it had to be preceded by an apology (see Table 4 for summary of data for Chastisement Situation II).

The questionnaire did not reveal the rules of chastisement that we were hoping to discover. It should not be concluded from one role-play situation that lower-status Japanese or Americans do not chastise high-status people when speaking English. It may be that this behavior is just taboo enough that it is precisely what questionnaires can't get at. Despite our daydreams of telling off the boss, we aren't likely to advocate it. And questionnaires seem to elicit what we advocate we should say.

The most interesting example of chastisement we have in our natural data

Table 4. Use of Major Semantic Formulas in the
Chastisement Situation II (Lower to Higher Status)

Semantic formulas	Groups[a]	
	Japanese (%)	American (%)
Self-defense	69	100
Apology	31	87
Offer of repair	23	13
Criticism	15	7

[a]For Japanese, $n = 13$; for American, $n = 15$.

is from a Japanese student to an American professor. A doctoral student was taking a master's level course with a professor who lectured confidently about the subject matter of the class. After several classes, the student realized that the professor's lectures came straight out of a book published abroad that was not in the school library, but which he happened to have read. He complained repeatedly to a friend that credit for the lecture material was not being given. Feeling disapproval, he finally decided to say something. He went up after class and asked the professor, "Are you familiar with Smith's book (pseudonym used)?" According to the student, the professor became flustered and didn't give much of a response. He was satisfied with his move. Unfortunately, we don't have verification of the precise wording used by either of the participants, but the interesting point is that the student used such a seemingly innocent question to express challenge and chastisement. We know from D'Amico-Reisner's (1983) work on expressions of disapproval that native American English frequently uses questions to express criticism. We can say, "What are you, crazy?" or "Why don't you stop nagging me?" But the Japanese student's question is quite different from these: it sounds to the American ear strictly factual—devoid of judgment. It doesn't sound like chastisement; it sounds like a quest for information. It is not instantly recognizable as a rhetorical question unless you know the whole context. Somehow, it seems different from the American use of questions to express chastisement.

4. CONCLUSION

This research has been revealing in the way it contradicts prevalent stereotypes. With respect to how Americans and Japanese speak the English language, we make the following conclusions:

1. Americans are not always more direct than Japanese.
2. Americans are not always more explicit than Japanese.
3. Japanese do not always avoid disagreement.

4. Japanese do not always avoid critical remarks, especially when speaking to someone of lower status.
5. Japanese do not always apologize more than Americans.
6. Japanese and Americans can both use questions to function as warning, correction, disagreement, chastisement, and embarrassing information, but the questions they use can be significantly different in tone and content.
7. Americans tend to use positive remarks (compliments/praise) more frequently and in more places than Japanese.

We do not yet know why Japanese ESL speakers act as they do. First, we must investigate to what extent the characteristics of Japanese ESL described here are due to transfer from the native language. Our previous research has demonstrated a great deal of sociolinguistic transfer from the native language in Japanese ESL refusals (Beebe, Takahashi, & Uliss-Weltz, in press).

Another possible explanation for the data is that the directness described here is partly a function of the fact that the Japanese are using an L2 in which they do not have full native-like proficiency. Takahashi and Beebe (1987) found that higher-proficiency Japanese ESL speakers were more indirect in their refusals than lower-proficiency Japanese, who tended more frequently to say bluntly, "I can't." We have further evidence that ESL speakers from countries other than Japan sound blunt and direct (Takahashi & Beebe, unpublished data on international ESL refusals), apparently due to lack of native speaker competence in the social rules of speaking (Eisenstein & Bodman, 1986). Consequently, we must look both at other ESL groups and at the Japanese language before we claim that all findings are due to the fact that the subjects are Japanese.

In addition to the native language transfer and the limited proficiency explanations, there is the possibility, especially with advanced and relatively assimilated ESL speakers, that their directness and explicitness is an instance of psychological convergence (see Thakerar, Giles, & Cheshire, 1982). Psychological convergence occurs when speakers want and intend to converge linguistically but somehow go too far, and instead of succeeding in convergence (i.e., getting closer to the interlocutor), they end up diverging from (i.e., moving farther away from) the listener. In this case, the directness would be explained by an attempt to converge toward the stereotype or what is perceived to be the native American English norm—that is, a great deal of directness. In attempting to converge psychologically, the nonnative speaker "overshoots the mark," ending up diverging, in actual linguistic terms. This could be called "stereotype-induced error." In some instances, as discussed above, the student was formally taught the stereotype (e.g., "Americans are very direct, so be direct when talking to them''). In this case, we have psychological convergence, but it is also "transfer of training" (Selinker, 1972) and "teacher induced error" (Stenson, 1974). Many Japanese ESL learners have reported to us that they were, in fact, taught by their Japanese teachers of English to "be direct when using English." And since this stereotype is likely wrong for certain situations, these students may, at times, be striving toward a false goal.

There are other explanations for the data which lead us to avoid hypothesizing that transfer is the only answer. For one thing, stereotypes are overgeneralizations, but they are not always *completely* false. Japanese ESL speakers may not be transferring native Japanese directness but rather overgeneralizing accurately perceived American directness. Or, they may have wrongly concluded that softeners and politeness indicators are often not needed in English because they have not yet seen the American English counterparts to Japanese honorifics, particles, lexical selections, and formula choices. Of course, this latter explanation is a kind of transfer in the sense that it is a type of cross-linguistic influence. In addition to these explanations, there is always the possibility that Japanese ESL speakers simply made errors because they focused uniquely on their own message: directness, politeness, and effect on others were not even in their minds.

Finally, before any hard and fast conclusions can be drawn about either the findings themselves or the theoretical explanations for them, we need to amass more data on what Japanese and Americans do in natural conversation. Beebe and Cummings (1985) have shown that written role-play data can be extremely useful in creating an initial classification of semantic formulas used in natural speech and in studying the perceived requirements for a socially appropriate speech act. However, the data do not always reflect the full range of formulas or even the length of the response. They do not adequately show the depth of emotion, the amount of repetition, or the degree of elaboration. Consequently, we need more natural data.

We have, however, found problems with natural data. They are biased toward the linguistic preferences of our friends, relatives, and associates. They are biased toward short exchanges, because long ones are impossible to get down word for word in a notebook. And they are biased toward exchanges that the researcher finds especially typical, especially atypical, or especially non-native sounding. It is much harder to notice a native-like ESL example than a distinctively nonnative one. Moreover, natural data give us many examples that are not at all comparable in terms of speakers, hearers, and social situations, unless one or two situations are selected, and this poses other limitations.

Despite the unknowns and limitations of this study, we believe we have strong evidence that (1) Japanese and Americans are substantially different in the way they go about accomplishing face-threatening acts in English, and (2)

Japanese ESL speakers often do not conform to prevalent stereotypes about their indirectness and their inexplicitness.

ACKNOWLEDGMENTS

We would like to express our appreciation to Shoshana Blum-Kulka, Elite Olshtain, and Miriam Eisenstein (editor of this volume), whose comments were extremely helpful. We also wish to thank a large number of students in the TESOL and Applied Linguistics programs at Columbia University Teachers College who gave us many helpful suggestions. Special mention also goes to Patrick Aquilina of the American Language Program at Columbia University for his assistance in data collection, and all those who gave their time to answer the discourse completion questionnaire for the present research.

REFERENCES

Beebe, L., & Cummings, M. (1985, April). *Speech act performance: A function of the data collection procedure?* Paper presented at TESOL '85, New York.

Beebe, L., Takahashi, T., & Uliss-Weltz, R. (in press). Pragmatic transfer in ESL refusals. In R. C. Scarcella, E. Andersen, & S. D. Krashen (Eds.), *Developing communicative competence in a second language.* Cambridge, MA: Newbury House.

Blum-Kulka, S. (1982). Learning to say what you mean in a second language: A study of the speech act performance of learners of Hebrew as a second language. *Applied Linguistics, 3,* 29–59.

Blum-Kulka, S. (1987). Indirectness and politeness in requests: Same or different? *Journal of Pragmatics, 11,* 131–145.

Blum-Kulka, S., House, J., & Kasper, G. (Eds.) (in press). *Cross-cultural pragmatics: Requests and apologies.* Norwood, NJ: Ablex.

Blum-Kulka, S., & Olshtain, E. (1984). Requests and apologies: A cross-cultural study of speech act realization patterns (CCSARP). *Applied Linguistics, 5,* 196–213.

Blum-Kulka, S., & Olshtain, E. (1986). Too many words: Length of utterance and pragmatic failure. *Studies in Second Language Acquisition, 8,* 165–179.

Bonikowska, M. (1985). *Opting out from performing speech acts—pragmatic domain?* Unpublished manuscript, University of Warsaw, Poland.

Borkin, A., & Reinhart, S. M. (1978). Excuse me and I'm sorry. *TESOL Quarterly, 12,* 57–70.

Brown, P., & Levinson, S. (1978). Universals in language usage: Politeness phenomena. In E. N. Goody (Ed.), *Questions and politeness* (pp. 54–310). Cambridge: Cambridge University Press.

Cohen, A., & Olshtain, E. (1981). Developing a measure of sociocultural competence: The case of apology. *Language Learning, 31,* 113–134.

Cohen, A., & Olshtain, E. (1985). Comparing apologies across languages. In K. R. Janikowsky (Ed.), *Scientific and humanistic dimensions of language* (pp. 175–184). Amsterdam: John Benjamins.

Condon, J. C. (1984). *With respect to the Japanese.* Tokyo: Yohan Publications.

Corder, S. (1967). The significance of learners' errors. *International Review of Applied Linguistics (IRAL), 5,* 161–169.

Corder, S. (1971). Idiosyncratic dialects and error analysis. *IRAL, 9,* 149–159.

Coulmas, F. (1981). "Poison to your soul": Thanks and apologies contrastively viewed. In F. Coulmas (Ed.), *Conversational routines* (pp. 69-91). The Hague: Mouton.

D'Amico-Reisner, L. (1983). An analysis of the surface structure of disapproval exchanges. In N. Wolfson & E. Judd (Eds.), *Sociolinguistics and language acquisition* (pp. 103–115). Rowley MA: Newbury House.

Deutsch, M. F. (1983). *Doing business with the Japanese.* New York: New American Library.

Eisenstein, M., & Bodman, J. (1986). "I very appreciate": Expressions of gratitude by native and non-native speakers of American English. *Applied Linguistics, 7,* 167–185.

Fukushima, S., & Iwata, Y. (1985). Politeness in English. *JALT Journal, 7,* 1–14.

Godard, D. (1977). Same settings, different norms: Phone call beginnings in France and the United States. *Language in Society, 5,* 257–314.

Goffman, E. (1967). *Interaction ritual.* New York: Anchor Books.

Goldstein, B. Z., & Tamura, K. (1975). *Japan and America: A comparative study in language and culture.* Tokyo: Charles E. Tuttle.

Holmes, J., & Brown, D. R. (1987). Teachers and students learning about compliments. *TESOL Quarterly, 21,* 523–546.

Hymes, D. (1972). Models of the interaction of language and social setting. In J. J. Gumperz & D. Hymes (Eds.), *Directions in sociolinguistics: The ethnography of communication* (pp. 35–71). New York: Holt, Rinehart and Winston.

Leech, G. (1983). *Principles of pragmatics.* London: Longman.

Levinson, S. (1983). *Pragmatics.* Cambridge: Cambridge University Press.

LoCastro, V. (1986, November). *I agree with you, but . . .* Paper presented at JALT '86 Conference, Hamamatsu, Japan.

Loveday, L. (1982). *The sociolinguistics of learning and using a non-native language.* Oxford: Pergamon Press.

Manes, J. (1983). Compliments: A mirror of cultural values. In N. Wolfson & E. Judd (Eds.), *Sociolinguistics and language acquisition* (pp. 96–102). Rowley, MA: Newbury House.

Manes, J., & Wolfson, N. (1981). The compliment formula. In F. Coulmas (Ed.), *Conversational routines* (pp. 115–132). The Hague: Mouton.

Olshtain, E. (1983). Sociocultural competence and language transfer: The case of apology. In S. Gass & L. Selinker (Eds.), *Language transfer in language learning* (pp. 232–249). Rowley, MA: Newbury House.

Olshtain, E., & Cohen, A. (1983). Apology: A speech-act set. In N. Wolfson & E. Judd (Eds.), *Sociolinguistics and language acquisition* (pp. 18–35). Rowley, MA: Newbury House.

Olshtain, E., & Weinbach, L. 1986. Complaints—A study of speech act behavior among native and nonnative speakers of Hebrew. In M. B. Papi & J. Verschueren (Eds.), *The pragmatic perspective: Selected papers from the 1985 International Pragmatics Conference.* Amsterdam: John Benjamins.

Pomerantz, A. (1984). Agreeing and disagreeing with assessments: Some features of preferred/dispreferred twin shapes. In J. Maxwell Atkinson & J. Heritage (Eds.), *Structures in social action* (pp. 57–101). Cambridge University Press.

Sacks, H. (1973). Lecture notes. LSA Summer Institute, Ann Arbor, Michigan.

Sakamoto, N., & Naotsuka, R. (1982). *Polite fictions: Why Japanese and Americans seem rude to each other.* Tokyo: Kinseido.

Scollon, R., & Scollon, B. (1981). *Narrative, literacy and face in interethnic communication.* Norwood, NJ: Ablex.

Selinker, L. (1972). Interlanguage. *IRAL, 10,* 209–230.

Stenson, N. (1974). Induced errors. In J. Schumann & N. Stenson (Eds.), *New frontiers of second language learning* (pp. 54–70). Rowley, MA: Newbury House.

Takahashi, T., & Beebe, L. (1986). ESL teachers' evaluation of pragmatic vs. grammatical errors. *CUNY Forum, 12,* 172–203.

Takahashi, T., & Beebe, L. (1987). The development of pragmatic competence by Japanese learners of English. *JALT Journal, 8,* 131–155.

Tanaka, S., & Kawade, S. (1982). Politeness strategies and second language acquisition. *Studies in Second Language Acquisition, 5,* 18–33.

Thakerar, J. N., Giles, H., & Cheshire, J. (1982). Psychological and linguistic parameters of speech accommodation theory. In C. Fraeser & K. R. Scherer (Eds.), *Advances in social psychology of language* (pp. 205–255). Cambridge: Cambridge University Press.

Thomas, J. (1983). Cross-cultural pragmatic failure. *Applied Linguistics, 4,* 91–112.

Thomas, J. (1984). Cross-cultural discourse as "unequal encounter": Towards a pragmatic analysis. *Applied Linguistics, 5,* 226–235.

Wolfson, N. (1981). Compliments in cross-cultural perspective. *TESOL Quarterly, 15,* 117-124.

Wolfson, N. (1983a). Rules of speaking. In J. C. Richards & R. W. Schmidt (Eds.), *Language and communication* (pp. 61–87). London: Longman.

Wolfson, N. (1983b). An empirically based analysis of complimenting in American English. In N. Wolfson & E. Judd (Eds.), *Sociolinguistics and language acquisition* (pp. 82–95). Rowley, MA: Newbury House.

Wolfson, N. (1984). Pretty is as pretty does: A speech act view of sex roles. *Applied Linguistics, 5,* 236–244.

CHAPTER 14

The Social Dynamics of Native and Nonnative Variation in Complimenting Behavior

NESSA WOLFSON

1. INTRODUCTION

Over the past decade, sociolinguistics has come to have an increasing impact on the field of TESOL (Teachers of English to Speakers of Other Languages). To a great extent, this development has been due to the realization that second-language acquisition is, in fact, the acquisition of what Dell Hymes has called communicative competence. That is, becoming an effective speaker of a new language not only involves learning new vocabulary in addition to rules of pronunciation and grammar, but must also include the ability to use these linguistic resources in ways that are socially appropriate among speakers of the target language.

What has not always been recognized is that lack of such sociolinguistic competence can have serious consequences for a learner residing in a community where the target language is spoken. Unaware of the rules and patterns that condition the behavior of native speakers, the learner does not know how to interpret or respond to the often subtle conversational openings which could lead to increased interaction and even friendships with members of the society. Inappropriate or inadequate responses may well result in negative assessments and reactions on the part of native speakers. Even more damaging to learners is that lack of critical sociolinguistic information frequently makes it impossible

NESSA WOLFSON • Graduate School of Education, University of Pennsylvania, Philadelphia, Pennsylvania 19104.

for them to develop relationships with native speakers. This in turn prevents learners from gaining access to the very opportunities they need for input and practice in the target language. Thus, lack of sociolinguistic competence creates a vicious circle for learners, who, because they are unaware of the ways in which relationships are developed in the target society, have less opportunity to interact with its members and, consequently, less chance to learn the language and the sociolinguistic rules that are an integral part of it.

In order to better prepare students, members of the TESOL profession are therefore in critical need of empirically valid analyses upon which to base instruction. To be truly valuable, these analyses must deal not only with linguistic forms, but with the variation in functions and social rules that condition their use; such analyses of social variation in speech behavior can only be provided by sociolinguistic research. The results of such sociolinguistic investigation can give teachers of English necessary insights into the variation in speech behavior both within and among the many communities in which English is spoken as a native language, thus making it possible for them to present the relevant facts to their students.

To begin with, each speech act or act sequence, whether it be apologizing, thanking, scolding, complimenting, inviting, refusing, or greeting, is highly complex and variable, with important cultural information embedded in it. At the most superficial level, sociolinguistic data collected systematically and analyzed objectively can yield information as to what specific formulas and routines are in use in a particular speech community, as well their patterns of frequency and rules of appropriateness in different speech situations.

2. COMPLIMENTS: NATIVE SPEAKERS

An example of the sort of information to be gained by an examination of the surface structure of a speech act is the result of research on compliments in American English (Manes & Wolfson, 1981; Wolfson & Manes, 1980). In analyzing data collected from a wide range of spontaneous interactions, it was discovered that compliments are characteristically formulaic both in terms of semantics and of syntax.

If we take the definition of a compliment to be that of an utterance containing a positive evaluation by the speaker to the addressee, we find that while the number of words that could be chosen to evaluate positively, or compliment, is almost infinite, the fact is that our corpus contains a very restricted set of lexical items which carry the favorable evalutation, and the great majority of these are adjectives and verbs. Two-thirds of all compliments that use adjectives to carry the positive semantic load do so by means of only five adjectives: *nice, good, beautiful, pretty,* and *great.* Because *nice* and *good* lack specificity, they are usable with almost any subject. In present-day American English, *beautiful* seems to be widening its privilege of occurrence so that it too is losing its original specificity. The fact that *pretty* is used more than *great,* the more general adjective, reflects the much larger than equal number of compliments on appearance received by women.

In the 25% of compliments which make use of a verb rather than an adjective to carry the positive meaning, 90% make use of just two verbs: *like* and *love.* At the syntactic level the highly patterned nature of compliments is even more striking. In examining their syntax, we found that fully 50% of all compliments are characterized by the following formula:

NP {is/looks} (really) ADJ (e.g., "Your house is really beautiful.")

Two other syntactic patterns account for another 29% of the data:

I really {like/love} NP (e.g., "I really like your shirt.")
PRO is (really) (a) ADJ NP (e.g., "That was really a great paper.")

What this means is that only three patterns are needed to represent approximately 80% of all the compliments in our corpus of compliments given and received by middle-class speakers of American English. Furthermore, only nine syntactic patterns account for 95% of the well over 1,200 examples of compliments that make up the corpus.

The compliment formulas found in this analysis sound very familiar and, indeed, intuitively correct to native speakers. What was not obvious until the data were analyzed is that the way in which we give verbal expression to our approval and appreciation of one another's appearance and accomplishments is largely prepatterned. Like so much of our speech behavior, these patterns are below the level of speakers' conscious awareness. Thus, the tendency among middle-class Americans, interviewed about their perceptions of complimenting behavior, was to state the belief that if the speaker was sincere, the compliment would somehow be original rather than precoded. The fact that compliments, like so many other speech acts, may be formulaic, multifunctional, and at the same time quite sincere, was difficult for native speakers to accept; this was yet another example of the inadequacy of native speaker intuitions about the speech patterns which constrain their own behavior and that of the communities of which they are members.

It should be mentioned that after the original analysis (Manes & Wolfson, 1981; Wolfson & Manes, 1980), which was based on a corpus of 686 examples, additional data were collected, doubling the size of the corpus. When these new data were analyzed separately, it was found that the patterns matched those already discovered. Although our data were collected through ethnographic methods by female investigators in the United States (mainly in Virginia and Pennsylvania), more recent analyses by other researchers, both male and female, working in New York and Texas as well as in South Africa and New Zealand, have replicated our original findings (Herbert, 1986b, 1987, and personal communication; Holmes, 1988; Holmes & Brown, 1987; Knapp, Hopper, & Bell, 1984) regarding the frequency and distribution of the formulas. The fact that these researchers used a variety of different methods of data collection makes the high convergency in results all the more convincing. Thus, Knapp *et al.* (1984), in describing their collection of data through interviewing, report minimal differences in the syntax and semantics of compliment patterns despite quite different techniques in the gathering of their corpus. Holmes (1988), in a study of complimenting behavior in New Zealand, has replicated the compliment formulas first described by Manes and Wolfson (1981).

The consistent replication of our syntactic and semantic analysis by so many researchers working in such widely separated geographic areas is striking. However, it is critical to recognize that the description of a speech act's linguistic structure is relatively superficial in comparison to the sociocultural information that underlies the speech behavior being studied.

Looking beneath the surface structures, we can, through systematic data collection and analysis, learn a great deal about the rights and obligations that members of a community have toward one another, information which is culture specific and not necessarily available to the intuition of the native speaker. As we have already seen, the intuitions of native speakers may be very useful in interpreting the meaning of an interaction, but they are by no means sufficient in the sense of providing conscious access to patterns of behavior.

Insights into the variation inherent in speech behavior may be gained by investigating the way the social identities of interlocutors vis à vis one another condition what is said. In this respect, speech acts and sequences of all types appear to be equally informative. Thus, if we are interested in analyzing what the rights, obligations, and privileges of speakers are vis à vis one another, we can probably learn as much from studying greetings, partings, and invitations as we can from analyzing thanks, apologies, and compliments. And most interesting of all, if we look at the forms people use spontaneously with different interlocutors, we frequently find that the distribution, frequency, and elaboration involved in a specific type of speech behavior corresponds not only to speakers' roles and expectations but also to the manipulation of roles and the formation or reaffirmation of relationships (Wolfson, 1981, 1983).

A case in point is a consistent finding of mine that there is a qualitative difference between the speech behavior which middle-class Americans use to intimates, status unequals, and strangers, on the one hand, and to nonintimates, status-equal friends, coworkers, and acquaintances, on the other. That is, when we examine the ways in which different speech acts are realized in actual everyday speech, and when we compare these behaviors in terms of the social relationships of the interlocutors, we find again and again that the two extremes of social distance—minimum and maximum—seem to call forth very similar behavior, while relationships which are more toward the center show marked differences. I call this theory the Bulge, because of the way the frequencies of certain types of speech behavior plot out on a diagram, with the minimum and maximum degrees of social distance showing very similar patterns as opposed to the middle section (consisting of status equals), which displays a characteristic bulge (Wolfson, 1986, 1988, 1989). This may, on the face of it, seem very strange and even counterintuitive. What do intimates, status unequals, and strangers have in common that nonintimates, status-unequal friends, coworkers, and acquaintances do not share, and what do the last mentioned group have in common that the first do not share? Very simply, it is the relative certainty of the first relationships in contrast with the instability of the second. Put in other terms, the more status and social distance are seen as fixed, the easier it is for speakers to know what to expect of one another. In a complex urban society in which speakers may belong to a variety of nonoverlapping networks, relationships among speakers are often uncertain. These relationships are full of potential, are dynamic, and are open to negotiation. There is freedom here, but not security. And the dynamic nature of such relationships is manifested in speech behavior which is full of elaboration and negotiation.

For example, although compliments are exchanged between intimates and between total strangers, the great majority (the bulge) occur in interactions between speakers who are neither. This is a question of frequencies and not of absolutes. Compliments do, of course, occur in interactions between speakers at both ends of the social distance continuum, but they are relatively rare in such situations. For the purposes of this discussion, the important point is that the great majority of all compliments, no matter what their topic, occur between status equals who are, as has already been pointed out, potential friends.

Evidence for the validity of the Bulge Theory described here has recently emerged in the work of three separate investigators, all working independently on the speech behavior associated with compliments. In my own most recent work, I have been engaged in collecting and analyzing data not only on the speech act of complimenting, but on the speech sequence which includes the responses to compliments as well. During the fall of 1987, two of my classes at the University of Pennsylvania participated in some of the data collection and analysis, and examples from their data are cited below (Aratake *et al.*, 1987; Farah *et al.*, 1987; Jakar *et al.*, 1987; Okushi, 1987; Kim, 1987).

While Manes (1983) has reported on some of our earliest findings regarding compliment responses, and our original work certainly included the collection of responses along with the compliments that initiated them, it is only since 1985 that I myself began to focus specifically on the entire complimenting sequence as a speech event which might yield new and important insights into the underlying motivation of this aspect of speech behavior. My findings, while as yet incomplete, clearly indicate that the compliment–response sequence is a negotiated one in which two or more participants are involved in an often elaborated exchange. In the earliest of our joint reports on compliments (Manes & Wolfson, 1980; Wolfson & Manes, 1980), we suggested that the function of the act was to create or reaffirm solidarity. My own most recent work as well as that of others (Herbert, 1986a, 1986b; Holmes, 1987) has verified this hypothesis and provided additional results which add considerable depth and breadth to it. In my analysis (Wolfson, 1984), I have found that elaborated responses occur in the speech of both intimate and status-unequal females, but that the great majority of lengthy sequences are to be found in conversations among status-equal acquaintances. It is noteworthy that researchers have reported independent findings which lend strong support to the Bulge Theory put forward here, both by converging and by diverging with my analysis of complimenting behavior among speakers of American English.

Evidence for the Bulge Theory is found on a number of levels in the various studies conducted by researchers working in a number of different English-speaking communities. With respect to frequency and distribution, for example, the results of the research conducted in Texas (Knapp et al., 1984) show that people tend to compliment others of the same age, status, and to a lesser extent, gender.

With regard to compliment responses, Herbert (1986a, 1986b) reports on his analysis of a corpus of 1,062 native speaker compliment responses, both spontaneous and experimental, collected at the State University of New York at Binghamton. Herbert's focus was on the frequency of occurrence with which compliments were and were not accepted by addressees. His findings are striking in that speakers were "almost twice as likely to respond with some response other than acceptance" (Herbert, 1986a, p. 80). As Herbert points out, this finding disagrees with the U.S. societal norm requiring that compliments be accepted with thanks. Herbert (1986a) also raises the question as to whether native speakers of other varieties of English follow similar behavior patterns. In this connection, he says:

> In a study similar to this one conducted among a comparable university population in South Africa, a sharply different distributional profile emerged (Herbert, 1986b). Briefly, acceptances . . . accounted for fully seventy-six percent of the South African responses. (p. 82)

In a later paper (Herbert & Straight, in press) the authors posit an explanation for this phenomenon, pointing out that social stratification and inequality are intrinsic to South African ideology. Thus, the paucity of compliments given by South Africans in contrast to the frequency with which they occur in the speech of Americans, along with the fact that Americans tend to reject and the South Africans to accept compliments, has to do with the social systems in which the two groups interact. This supports the hypothesis put forth in Wolfson and Manes (1980) that Americans give compliments frequently because they are attempting to establish solidarity in a social context in which their own status is uncertain. For the same reason, say the authors, Americans tend not to accept the compliments they receive, thus further working toward the building of solidarity by stressing equality with their interlocutors. South Africans, in contrast, function in a society in which solidarity with status equals is assumed, and they have no need to make use of compliment negotiations to establish what they already have—certainty as to their relationships with one another. The analysis put forward by Herbert (1986a) and by Herbert and Straight (in press) fits neatly within the framework of the Bulge Theory, supporting it through their evidence and their explanation of why Americans and South Africans differ so sharply in their behavior regarding compliment–response sequences. The differences thus described provide yet another example of native speaker variation in speech behavior, in this case manifested by contrasts in rules of speaking in different speech communities within the English-speaking world.

In her report of compliment–response behavior in New Zealand, Holmes (1988) reports that "it is relatively rarely that New Zealanders overtly reject compliments." Holmes' ethnographic study, which includes a corpus of 484 New Zealand compliment–response sequences, yields many significant findings. Although she does not discuss the underlying ideology which may lead to this speech behavior from the same point of view as that addressed by Herbert (1986a) or by Herbert and Straight (in press), it is very possible that New Zealand society, like that in the United States, is sufficiently lacking in stratification to cause speakers to behave in similar ways for similar reasons. Indeed, Holmes' findings are so highly convergent with my own on virtually every level that is difficult to know how else to account for her findings. With respect to the frequency of occurrence of compliments among speakers of different social positions, for example, Holmes (1988) says:

> The New Zealand data used in this analysis consists predominantly of compliments
> between status-equals. . . . It is clear that compliments between equals are by far
> the most frequent in the New Zealand community sampled (79%). This finding is
> supported by Wolfson's data.

From the point of view of the theory under consideration, the most significant aspect of Holmes' study is the clear finding that most New Zealand compliments occur within what I have called the Bulge, thus lending further independent support to this analysis.

It should be mentioned in passing that while I, along with my students at
the University of Pennsylvania, have continued to investigate sex-related differences in compliment–response behavior (Wolfson, 1984), both Herbert (1986b)
and Holmes (1988) have conducted independent studies along the same lines.
What is most impressive about the findings and the analyses reported to date is
the high degree of convergence in all three studies. That is, it is clear from all
three investigations that women not only give and receive more compliments
than men do, but that their responses indicate that this speech activity functions
differently among men and women, with women making far greater use of such
compliment–response strategies to create and reaffirm solidarity. The fact that
all three studies indicate similar patterns among women as opposed to men may
well lead to some significant refinements of the Bulge Theory reflecting the
status-related social strategies of women. This is an area which demands further
attention since it goes to the heart of the entire issue, both reflecting and per-
petuating patterns of speech behavior and social dynamics.

The fact that urban middle-class Americans live in a complex and open
society means that individuals are members not of a single network in which
their own place is well defined, but rather belong to a number of networks,
both overlapping and nonoverlapping, in which they must continually negotiate
their roles and relationships with one another. The importance of the Bulge
Theory lies in what it tells us about how the very openness and potential for
mobility of American middle-class society is reflected in our everyday speech
behavior. The fact that very similar findings have emerged in research on complimenting behavior in Texas (Knapp *et al.*, 1984), New York (Herbert, 1986a,
1986b), and in New Zealand (Holmes, in press), as well as the report of very
different behavior patterns among native speakers of South African English
(Herbert & Straight, in press) provided additional evidence for the analysis
presented here.

3. COMPLIMENTS: NONNATIVE SPEAKERS

When we look at analyses of nonnative speaker data in English, it is immediately apparent that the great majority of learners of English are not aware
of the strong tendency of status-equal Americans to negotiate their roles through
opening speech sequences involving such behavior as complimenting, and that
they therefore do not know how to interpret or respond to native speaker compliments in a way that would lead to the formation of closer relationships. Part

of the problem is that learners tend to transfer their own sociolinguistic rules into the target-language interaction. As Daikuhara (1986) has said in reporting on the findings of her study of compliment–response sequences in Japanese:

> The analysis of a corpus of 115 examples of compliments has shown that there are both similarities and differences between Japanese and American compliments. . . . This may result in serious communicative interference if the interlocutor interprets such conduct as an insult according to his/her own rules. (pp. 128–129)

The problems encountered by nonnative speakers in responding to compliments given by Americans may be illustrated by examples of numerous types. It should be mentioned here that the examples given throughout this paper come from two sets of data, both collected through observation and recording of naturally occurring speech in everyday interactions in a wide variety of situations. The first source of data is my own extensive corpus of well over a thousand examples, gathered over the past 8 years. Included within it are compliments and responses given and responded to by both males and females of equal and unequal status. Speakers and addresses include both native and nonnative English speakers who come from a great variety of occupational, educational, and ethnic backgrounds, interacting in a wide range of settings, both public and private, formal and informal. In addition, for the purpose of this chapter, I have also made use of the ethnographic data collected through participant observation by my students.

From my own corpus and from the data collected by my students, many of whom are themselves international students from a variety of ethnolinguistic backgrounds, it is clear that sociolinguistic transfer accounts for only a portion of the miscommunication we find in the compliment–response behavior of nonnative speakers. Learners do, of course, transfer their own native sociolinguistic rules inappropriately in interactions with English speakers, especially when they have had little or no instruction in target-language sociolinguistic behavior. The following two examples, collected by Yoshiko Okushi, demonstrate the way in which transfer from Japanese sociolinguistic rules contrasts with typical American responses to compliments:

Two female graduate students are looking at photos. A is American, B is Japanese. The photos are of B's family.
A: Your brother is handsome.
B: Not so much.

Two American female graduate students are talking:
A: Your son is great.
B: Yes, I'm proud of my son.

While it is true that American speakers frequently seek to minimize compliments through their responses and sometimes even reject them completely, the means by which this downgrading is accomplished is very different from those used by nonnative speakers who are transferring their own sociolinguistic rules into the American English setting. Typically, Amerians respond to compliments by giving unfavorable information about the object (e.g., saying that it is old or cheap) or by transferring the credit for the accomplishment or the object complimented to someone or something for which they have no responsibility. An example of such an American response is the following:

Two female Americans meet, and A says to B:
A: I like your sweater.
B: It's so old, my sister brought it to me from Italy a long time ago.

This is very different from the nonnative speaker's attempt to demonstrate modesty by downgrading him or herself or by refusing to accept the compliment:

At a cocktail reception for foreign students, C has been introduced to A by her friend B. A and B are classmates, C is a friend of B's. A is an American male and C is an Oriental female. B is an Oriental male.
A: Do you know that he's the best student in the class?
B: No, no, no, that's not true.
A: It *is* true. You ask anyone in our class who the best student is, they'll say it's B.
C: Yeah. He studies all the time.
A: I study, but my results are poor.
C: That's not true.

A more pressing problem, however, is that even when learners do receive instruction in sociolinguistic patterns, the information they are given may well be inaccurate and therefore counterproductive, since much of it is not based upon results of empirical studies of the type just described. Because the area of sociolinguistics is itself still very young, and because there are still relatively few systematic investigations into patterns of speech behavior within English-speaking communities, materials writers and instructors are hampered by the dearth of information available to them. Thus, the field of TESOL is still very much in the situation of needing to apply information that does not yet exist. The lack of scientifically valid findings has forced instructors to rely on intuitive and often inaccurate impressions of sociolinguistic rules. As we have pointed out, native speaker communicative competence includes intuitions that are very useful in interpreting empirical data, but this does not mean that native speakers have conscious awareness of these patterns, much less the ability to describe them with any degree of accuracy. What native speakers know how to describe is what they perceive as the norms of speech behavior. That is, we can all describe what we believe people in our speech communities should do, but without scientific analysis, we are not able to say what they (or we ourselves) actually do. We have conscious access to the norms, but not to the actuality of our speech behavior. Indeed, the sociolinguistic literature is replete with empirical evidence of the inadequacy of native speaker intuitions (e.g., Blom & Gumperz, 1972; Brouwer, Gerritsen, & DeHann, 1979; Labov, 1966). Often incomplete or inaccurate information finds its way into the very textbooks we use, as Pica (1983) has so cogently pointed out with respect to the use of the definite and indefinite article in English.

An example of this problem, and one that goes to the heart of the issue we are dealing with here, is that language learners are usually taught that the appropriate response to a compliment in American English is to accept it with a simple thank-you. While this may seem correct in terms of the perceived norms of the target society, it does not take into account the social variation which motivates the very different response types found in the actual spontaneous behavior of native speakers. It is true that a simple thank-you is nearly always appropriate as a compliment response in American English. Indeed, it may even be the only appropriate response in certain contexts. When lower-status females are complimented by upper-status males or by strangers, a thank-you response is entirely appropriate, as the following example from Yoshiko Okushi's (1987) data shows:

Male dentist in his 40s speaks to female hygienist in her 20s, both are American:
A: Your hair looks good.
B: Thank you.

What has not been explained to language learners, largely because the information has until now been unavailable, is that the use of "thank you" is heavily conditioned by status and social distance. As we have seen, the compliment is often intended as an opening strategy to signal to the addressee that the speaker would like to engage in further conversation and, indeed, to create or enhance a relationship.

Taught to say "thank you" in situations where a native speaker would take the compliment as an opening to negotiate a relationship with a speaker, the learner is misled into making responses which have exactly the opposite of the desired effect—responses which create distance rather than solidarity between native and nonnative speakers. The following examples, the first two from data collected by Kyung Suk Kim (1987), the third from that of Paul Calzada, and the fourth from Yoshiko Okushi (1987), demonstrate this point.

American female student to her Korean male classmate:
A: Your English is good.
B: (little hesitation) Thank you.

An American female to a Korean male at church function:
A: Your pronunciation is so nice.
B: No response—topic change.

Two female students, one American, one Pakistani, are sitting alone in a classroom together waiting for the other students and the professor to arrive:
A: Your English is fluent.
B: No response.

Two women, a native speaker and a nonnative speaker of English meet for the first time at a cocktail party. The American says:
A: You have such a lovely accent.
B: No response.

In the above examples, the compliments about the addressee's English proficiency and/or pronunciation illustrate what may be regarded as almost a standard or formulaic conversation opener used by native to nonnative speakers, and this needs to be understood as such by nonnative speakers. Rather than a modest thank-you or no response at all—behavior which effectively blocks attempts at further interaction on the part of Americans—language learners need to know how to respond in ways that help to support a continuation of talk.

As we have seen, compliments on belongings and appearance are very frequently used by speakers of American English as leads into longer conversational sequences. This too is often misunderstood by nonnative speakers of English who, wishing to show modesty and having been taught that "thank you" is the proper response to a compliment, will often inadvertently resist such attempts at conversational openings made by Americans, either by closing the exchange by thanking or by not responding at all. As we see from the following example, the American may make a second attempt, but when this also is seemingly rejected, the effort is abandoned:

American female student to her Chinese female classmate:
A: Your blouse is beautiful.
B: Thank you.
A: Did you bring it from China?
B: Yeah.

Other, similar attempts to open conversations, however superficial, are typically met with little or no response:

A young nonnative-speaking woman stops at a street corner to buy fruit from an American black male peddler who has a stand there. She has bought from him before and he greets her saying:

A: Good to see you again. I'm glad—because you're so pretty.
B: Thank you.

Even in situations which are ripe for the initiation of conversations which the American speaker clearly wishes to engage in, nonnative speakers frequently fail to respond in a way which would allow for such interactions to take place. As the following examples illustrate, such openings, if responded to, could be of great benefit to the nonnative as a means of forming friendly relationships with neighbors or other members of the host community and thereby learning to interact with a variety of people and gaining the opportunity to practice using the target language:

A is a woman in her mid-70s and the landlady of the house where B, a Korean male student, lives. B had just returned from church on a Sunday and met A in the hallway. She stopped to have a chat and opened the conversation by saying:
A: You look very dressy today.
B: I used to wear like this way in church. (B then turned away and went to his room, leaving the landlady to wonder why he was so unfriendly.)

An American male in his 30s to a Japanese female student in her 20s:
A: That's a nice blouse.
B: Thank you.

In the following two examples of unsuccessful attempts by Americans to open conversations by means of complimenting, the addressees, either because of lack of proficiency or a desire to show modesty, do not respond at all to the speakers' compliments, even though in both cases they are at social gatherings designed (by a church organization to which all belong) to facilitate friendships among American and international members who are, in fact, co-workers in the organization:

At a crowded Thanksgiving dinner party for international students, A is an American male and B is a female Chinese student. Both work together for the religious organization which is hosting the party. A is in his mid-30s and B in her early 20s.
A: That's neat! (referring to a Chinese satin coat B is wearing)
B: No response.

Two Americans, a male and a female, meet a Chinese female at a traditional American holiday dinner arranged for international students by a religious organization to which all three belong. All are in their mid-20s

and have met before. The American male attempts to begin a conversation with the Chinese woman by commenting on her jewelry:
A: What's that necklace you're wearing?
B: It's a Chinese fan with a phoenix on it.
A: Oh, that's neat.
B: No response.

It is possible that since the American speakers in the above examples were male, while the nonnative addressees were female, some constraints concerning behavior between the sexes might have had a conditioning effect on the above responses, but no such argument can be made for the following examples:

A and B, who are both females in their mid-20s, are at a noisy monthly international church lunch. Both are staff members of the church organization, but B is also a student. A is American and B is Chinese. A is attempting to make friends, but B has no idea how to help develop the relationship.
A: It's pretty. I like this sweater.
B: Thank you.

American female dancing teacher to Japanese female student of approximately the same age:
A: You're doing good.
B: Thank you.

A is an elderly American woman, neighbor of B, who is a female Japanese student:
A: You talk good English.
B: Thank you.
A: You went to school to pick it up, right?
B: Uh-huh.
A: That's good.
B: No response

Two female graduate students, one American, one Japanese, meet in the cafeteria of International House. Both are in their late 20s.
A: This is a nice sweater. Nice color.
B: Oh, this? I brought it from Japan.
A: I like it. Nice color. Very nice.
B: Thank you.

In this connection, it is important for the learner to be aware that the use of the expression "thank you" among speakers of American English is subject to great variation, depending on the social distance of the interlocutors. Thus, "thank you" is usually followed or substituted by a very different response pattern when the interlocutors are equal in status, and particularly when they are both female. It is among these interlocutors (those in the bulge) that one finds responses that frequently lead to long and elaborated complimenting sequences which have the effect of establishing or reaffirming friendly relationships.

While many examples in the native speaker data concern performance and/or ability, the pattern of elaborated complimenting sequences is at least as typical of those which have to do with appearance or possessions. The next example demonstrates the marked difference in both form and function, typical of those which regularly occur between status-equal Americans:

A further point, illustrated in the example to follow, is that such interactions may involve more than two participants. It should be noted that the length of the sequence is not at all unusual:

> In this situation, A, B, and C are all American females.
> A: That's a nice sweater.
> B: Thanks.
>   (a few minutes pass)
> A: That really is a nice sweater.
> C: It really is—very nice. Where'd you get it?
> B: I got it at X in exchange for the red bag.
> C: Oh, you got rid of the red bag!
> B: Yeah, well what else could I do with it?
> C: I think you did exactly the right thing with it. That sweater is great.
> A: It really is.
> B: I like it too. I mean, I needed a new black sweater. But what makes it so great?
> A: The neckline is really good on you.
> C: And the weave is unusual and very elegant.
> A: It fits very well too.
> C: Does it have shoulder pads? (feeling) Yes, but they look good.
> A: They're not too big—they fit just right.
> B: Well, that's what I thought. I plan to wear it with a lot of dresses and I think it'll be practical.
> C: It will—it should go with most of your dresses.
> B: That was the idea.
> C: I'll have to look over at X's too. I could use something like that.
> B: They've got a good selection.

Not only does this sequence demonstrate the way a compliment, when the response of the addressee permits, may open into an elaborated affirmation of approval and solidarity, it also shows that complimenting is far from being a simple two-turn act but may comprise multiple turns.

While the above example is not atypical with respect to length, it is important to recognize that depending upon the setting, compliment sequences may also be considerably shorter and may be accepted or denied without losing their effect, as the following brief examples show:

A and B, female American colleagues, pass each other in the hallway of the building where they both work. Both are in a hurry. A points to B's dress:
A: That's a beautiful color.
B: I love it too.

Two female Americans meet, and A says to B:
A: I really like that dress.
B: I hate it. It looks like a bag.

4. CONCLUSION

Clearly, there is great variation in the rules and patterns which constrain both native and nonnative speech behavior in English. It has been the intention of this chapter to provide some insight into the complexity of this variation by focusing specifically on only one small aspect—that of complimenting behavior. That the analysis given here is representative of a much larger body of information, so far largely untapped, will, I hope, present a challenge to future research.

The research approach described here, as well as the Bulge Theory which derives from it, provides insights into American culture which could prove invaluable to language learners who are planning to live and/or work among U.S. English speakers. Once an overall picture of the dynamics of social interaction is gained, it will be much easier for nonnative speakers of English to interact effectively with members of the target-language community. Having seen the importance of negotiating personal relationships, both learners and native speakers will be able to avoid much of the miscommunication and frustration which so often result in dysfunctional interactions. The end result of gaining such insights into the way speakers of the new language behave is that learners will be able to interpret what is meant by what is said to them and, just as important, will gain control over the way in which they present themselves to others.

It is only through the dissemination of sociolinguistic findings regarding both the linguistic forms and the factors conditioning their use that we can hope to guide learners of English in their acquisition of the intricate variation involved in such speech behavior as that exemplified by the study of compliment–response sequences. The explanatory and predictive power of the Bulge

Theory has been shown to apply to all speech acts/sequences so far investigated in the context of U.S. English communities (Wolfson, 1986, 1988, 1989). Further, we have good reason to believe that the patterns it describes hold for many other English-speaking communities around the world. It is at this level—both in terms of concrete descriptions of sociolinguistic variation and of the more abstract sociocultural patterning which underlies it—that there is most hope of success in imparting the crucial facts which will enable language learners to achieve communicative competence in the target language.

From the point of view of native speakers, the insights to be gained from such analyses of the variation in their own speech behavior and the underlying sociocultural patterns it demonstrates provide a view of the way in which their own society is structured which may open the way to a new and deeper appreciation of the way their social world operates. It is only by bringing these patterns to the conscious attention of community members, and by comparing them to the very different patterns to be found in the speech behavior of people from different cultural backgrounds, that we can hope to avoid misunderstandings at both the individual and the societal level. It is through efforts such as these that we may work to attain true intercultural communication.

REFERENCES

Aratake, Y., Okushi, Y., & Susuki, N. (1987). *Analysis of observational data on compliment responses.* Paper presented in course on Cross-Cultural Variation in Speech Behavior, University of Pennsylvania.

Blom, J. P., & Gumperz, J. J. (1972). Social meaning in linguistic structures: Code-switching in Norway. In J. J. Gumperz & D. H. Hymes (Eds.), *Directions in sociolinguistics* (pp. 407–434). New York: Holt, Rinehart and Winston.

Brouwer, D., Gerritsen, M., & DeHann, D. (1979). Speech differences between men and women: On the wrong track? *Language in Society, 8*(1), 33–50.

Calzada, P. (1987). Unpublished research report. Philadelphia: University of Pennsylvania.

Daikuhara, M. (1986). A study of compliments from a cross-cultural perspective: Japanese vs. American English. *The PENN Working Papers in Educational Linguistics* (pp. 103–134). Philadelphia: University of Pennsylvania.

Farah, I., Chen, S.-C., Liao, G., Gallagher, W., & Boxer, D. (1987). *Ethnographic analysis of compliment data.* Paper presented in course on Cross-Cultural Variation in Speech Behavior, University of Pennsylvania.

Herbert, R. K. (1986a). Say 'thank you'—or something. *American Speech, 61*(1), 76–88.

Herbert, R. K. (1986b, December). *Sex-based differences in compliment behavior.* Paper presented at the American Anthropological Association meeting.

Herbert, R. K. (1987, October). *Form, frequency, and function in speech acts: Analyzing compliment structures.* Paper presented at Conference on New Ways of Analyzing Variation (NWAV-XVI).

Herbert, R. K., and Straight, H. S. (forthcoming). *Compliment-rejection versus compliment-avoidance: Listener-based versus speaker-based pragmatic strategies.* Paper presented at Sociolinguistics Symposium, April 1986, University of Newcastle Upon Tyne, England.

Holmes, J. (in press, 1988). Compliments and compliment responses in New Zealand English. *Anthropological Linguistics*.

Holmes, J. (1988). Paying compliments: A sex-preferential positive politeness strategy. Manuscript submitted for publication in the *Journal of Pragmatics*.

Jakar, V., Calzada, P., Qiu, S.-L., & Kim, K. (1987). *Summary of findings on compliment behavior*. Paper presented in course on Cross-Cultural Variation in Speech Behavior, University of Pennsylvania.

Kim, K. (1987). Unpublished research report. Philadelphia: University of Pennsylvania.

Knapp, M. L., Hopper, R., & Bell, R. A. (1984). Compliments: A descriptive taxonomy. *Journal of Communication*, autumn, 1984.

Labov, W. (1966). *The social stratification of English in New York City*. Washington, DC: Center for Applied Linguistics.

Manes, J. (1983). Compliments: A mirror of social values. In N. Wolfson & E. Judd (Eds.), *Sociolinguistics and language acquisition* (pp. 96–102). Rowley, MA: Newbury House.

Manes, J., & Wolfson, N. (1981). The compliment formula. In F. Coulmas (Ed.), *Conversational routine, Janua linguarum 96: Rasmus Rask studies in pragmatic linguistics*. The Hague: Mouton.

Okushi, Y. (1987). Unpublished research report. Philadelphia: University of Pennsylvania.

Pica, T. (1983). The article in American English: What the textbooks don't tell us. In N. Wolfson & E. Judd (Eds.), *Sociolinguistics and language acquisition* (pp. 222–233). Rowley, MA: Newbury House.

Wolfson, N. (1981a). Compliments in cross-cultural perspective. *TESOL Quarterly, 15*(2), 117–124.

Wolfson, N. (1983). An empirically based analysis of compliments. In N. Wolfson & E. Judd (Eds.), *Sociolinguistics and language acquisition* (pp. 82–95). Rowley, MA: Newbury House.

Wolfson, N. (1984). Pretty is as pretty does: A speech act view of sex roles. *Applied Linguistics, 5*(3), 236–244.

Wolfson, N. (1986). Research methodology and the question of validity. *TESOL Quarterly, 20*(4), 689–699.

Wolfson, N. (1988). The bulge: A theory of speech behavior and social distance. In J. Fine (Ed.), *Second language discourse: A textbook of current research*. Norwood, NJ: Ablex.

Wolfson, N. (1989). *Perspectives: Sociolinguistics and TESOL*. New York: Newbury House (Harper and Row).

Wolfson, N., & Judd, E. (Eds.). (1983). *Sociolinguistics and language acquisition*. Rowley, MA: Newbury House.

Wolfson, N., & Manes, J. (1980). The compliment as a social strategy. *Papers in Linguistics, 13*(3), 391–410.

Wolfson, N., Marmor, T., & Jones, S. (1989). Problems in the comparison of speech acts across cultures. In S. Blum-Kulka, J. House-Edmondsen, & G. Kasper (Eds.), *Cross-cultural pragmatics*. Norwood, NJ: Ablex.

CHAPTER 15

That Reminds Me of a Story
The Use of Language to Express Emotion by Second-Language Learners and Native Speakers

ELLEN M. RINTELL

1. INTRODUCTION

While there has been a great deal of interest in the variability of discrete aspects of the learner's interlanguage, such as specific syntactic or phonological patterns or of errors, this chapter focuses on variation which is motivated by pragmatics. One aspect of language use, namely, the way in which language is used to express emotion, is particularly interesting for the study of variation, but it has received little attention from linguists. As I try to show in what follows, the language of emotion varies on dimensions associated with pragmatic variation, such as directness, and it varies with respect to contextual variables pertaining to setting and speaker. There is also variation in the way emotional expression is embedded in discourse. In this chapter, I try to explore some of the variety of ways in which emotion is expressed through language, and I describe some research into how second-language acquirers interpret emotion in language they hear as well as attempt to produce language with emotional content.

2. THE STUDY OF EMOTION

The topic of human emotion has been studied from the perspectives of many disciplines. A recent collection of essays edited by Klaus Scherer and

ELLEN M. RINTELL • Linguistic Minority Education Resource Center, Lawrence, Massachusetts 01843, and University of Lowell, Lowell, Massachusetts 01854.

Paul Ekman, *Approaches to Emotion* (1984), reports work in biology, developmental and cognitive psychology, sociology, and anthropology. For psychologists and psychiatrists, emotion is at the very core of the study of human behavior, but the emotions themselves are unobservable and thus might be considered unavailable for study. That leaves as a solution a choice between abandoning the study of the emotions or relying on language as one window to the emotions.

The study of the language of emotion is still in very early stages. Current research comes mainly from the mental health field, where an attempt is being made to understand what the emotions are and how the language of emotion can be used as a way to look at the psychotherapeutic process; and from the field of psychosomatics, where the lack of ability to put one's emotions into words is believed to be linked to certain illnesses (Davitz, 1969; Knapp, 1980; Plutchik, 1962, 1980; Scherer & Ekman, 1984). Recently, some anthropologists have written about the expression of *affect,* where that term, often used as a synonym for emotion, is given a somewhat broader meaning to encompass not only emotional expression but the speaker's expression of attitudes of various sorts toward people and events. (Irvine, 1982; Ochs & Schieffelin, 1985). Levy (1984) is concerned with how language reveals the emotions in a particular society, that of Tahiti, and the more general relationship between culture and emotion.

Despite the apparent lack of research by linguists on the expression of emotion through language, the way in which emotion is expressed—the language speakers use to communicate their personal, inner states—has obvious interest for language researchers. To express affect (here, the terms *affect* and *emotion* are considered to be more or less synonymous) and to perceive affect in the speech of others are linguistic abilities which play an important role in the second-language learner's steps toward successful communication in the target language and within the target culture. But these are skills which are rarely included in second-language curricula to be explicitly taught, for reasons about which we can only conjecture.

Cross-cultural research often helps to illuminate how language is used in our own culture by contrast to another. Irvine (1982) describes some of the ways emotion is encoded into the Wolof language of Senegal. She cites exclamations, emphatic particles, syntactic devices, lexical devices, and others. In addition, she discusses some of the essential problems of interpreting emotional displays. A central issue is that a person's actual emotional state cannot be read directly from his or her emotional display; there is no simple one-to-one correspondence between the behavioral form and its pragmatic effect, which is the attribution of emotion of some particular type and intensity. She suggests that to assess affect, one must compare the speaker's actual display with what kind of behavior is expectable and appropriate from that kind of speaker in that kind of situation (Irvine, 1982). This principle applies in any culture. Emotional experience is internal; its expression will be tempered by cultural rules for its display. At the same time, there are aspects of emotional expression believed to be universal. Ekman (1984) describes research (Ekman & Friesen, 1969) which illuminates both the universality of facial expression of emotion and the cultural differences governing emotional display, which have led some researchers to believe (mistakenly, in his view) that culture is responsible for all emotional expression.

In earlier papers (Rintell, 1984a, 1984b), I argue that the expression of emotion is a pragmatic function, an illocutionary act. Indeed, to express emotion is to perform a speech act, and like other speech acts, emotion appears in some context in discourse. In this chapter, the linguistic expression of emotion is discussed as a pragmatic function and also with respect to its place in discourse. While the importance of intonation in conveying emotion is acknowledged, intonation is not treated here. Rather, an attempt is made to examine the use of that which is encoded in language. An empirical investigation which looks at the emotional expression of native English speakers and second-language learners is described, and the variation in strategies speakers use to talk about their emotional experience is discussed.

When we speak of speech acts, we are usually referring to the class of speech acts termed *illocutionary acts,* those which, according to Fraser (1985), are utterances in which the speaker attempts to bring to the hearer's awareness some state-of-the-world and a recognition of what communicative force the speaker intends the act of speaking to take on. According to this analysis, such an act is successfully performed when the hearer recognizes the speaker's intent to perform it. Communicative force often refers to that of requests, promises, and the like, acts which commonly require a certain kind of uptake on the part of the hearer. Utterances used to convey one's emotional state or one's emotional response to either an event or some state-of-the-world (to borrow Fraser's term) fall within the domain of this understanding of illocutionary acts.

It becomes even clearer that the act of revealing one's emotional state is an illocutionary act when we consider the fact that utterances which express emotion may simultaneously perform other speech acts with a variety of social and psychological functions. For example, one may indirectly perform the act of bragging while directly expressing happiness, such as when one makes a happy announcement about oneself or someone close. Other examples of indirect speech acts which result from directly expressing emotion are to confide, thereby creating intimacy, to evoke sympathy or support, and to complain.

In real conversation, a successful speech act is performed not only so that the speaker's intent is recognized by the hearer but also so that it is perceived as appropriate to the social and situational context. Research on another illocutionary act, that of requesting, has shown that appropriateness largely has to do with whether or not the speaker is heard as sufficiently polite, and the speaker's politeness seems to depend on the way language is adjusted to reflect what it is that is requested (the degree of imposition to the hearer) and the role relationship between speaker and addressee, with such factors as age, sex, status, and degree of intimacy included in the role relationship. In the case of the expression of emotion, politeness is not at issue. Rather, we can look at the range of strategies to express emotion as varying on the parameter of directness. Here, Ekman and Friesen's (1969) notion of display rules for expression of emotion appear to apply to linguistic expression; in this culture, we show emotion in culturally defined ways. Just as we seem to have a social convention that constrains us from making requests of other people, and that requires us if we *must* make a request to use appropriately deferent language to convey the request, there seems to be a convention that constrains us from directly expressing emotion, except in special circumstances.

Although indirectness is a common feature of conversation it is a strategy particularly characteristic of talk centering on topics which concern emotion.[1] When I speak here of indirectness, I am not talking about an intentional or unintentional way of speaking that is so unclear as to make understanding difficult but of the use of various lexical, syntactic, pragmatic, and discoursal features that allow a speaker to communicate without saying precisely what he or she means. There seems to be a social convention that says that to express one's feelings—especially strong or negative feelings—to another person is either an imposition on that person, causes loss of face to the speaker (and possibly the hearer as well), or both. Therefore, one must use whatever linguistic device one can to minimize or mitigate the expression of those feelings. Thus, variation in the linguistic expression of emotion can be seen as varying on the parameter of indirectness, and the extent to which an emotion-conveying utterance needs to be indirect seems to depend on the relationship between speaker and addressee, particularly the degree of initmacy between them. Other contextual factors play a role as well. Some of these are the setting of the conversation, the type of situation that elicited the emotion, and very likely, the sex of speaker and addressee.

Another important variable affecting the directness of emotional expression is which of the emotions is to be talked about. We do not have as strong a constraint against expressing positive emotion as negative, and speakers are freer both to express positive emotion and to be direct in so doing. Experiences

[1] Tannen (1984) claims that speakers do not ordinarily say what they mean. She agrees with Lakoff (1976), who says that they prefer indirectness for two reasons: to save face if their wants or opinions are not well received, and to achieve the sense of rapport that comes with being understood without saying what one means. Tannen adds that indirectness, by requiring the listener to fill in unstated information, contributes to the process of sense making by engendering audience participation in sense making. (Tannen, 1984, p. 156)

which evoke anger, anxiety, fear, and sadness are usually described only to intimates, or, as we shall see, to people who are designated, professionally or otherwise, as recipients of such stories. On the other hand, recounting events which make one happy is appropriate for almost any interlocutor.

In general, one can state that the more negative the emotion, the greater is the constraint against expressing it, and the greater the role contextual variables play in to what extent, how, and to whom this emotion may be expressed. Thus, in order to be heard as appropriate, the task of the second-language learner is to learn how to manipulate language so as to control the level of directness with which emotion can be expressed. At the same time, the learner has to become familiar with the way target-language speakers use indirect language to get an approximately correct reading on the emotional messages embedded in target-language utterances.

So far, contextual and social factors influencing what a speaker might say have been discussed, but no mention has been made of what the addressee answers in response. Naturally, speakers and addressees exchange roles over and over again in a conversation, each taking their turn at talk. A listener may elicit talk about emotion, even share in the speaker's expressed emotion, providing feedback which encourages the speaker to continue and to elaborate (in this case effectively weakening the constraint against directness in favor of Grice's maxim of clarity), or the listener, through a variety of linguistic or nonverbal cues, shows the speaker that he or she is not interested and uncomfortable with what the speaker is saying, thus discouraging any further talk on the subject. All of these possibilities, as well as others not mentioned here, contribute to the variation in the directness of emotional expresssion. Another important factor in tempering the level of emotional intensity, directness, and, perhaps, appropriateness is the time that the speech act is performed—that is, if the speaker is expressing emotion as it is experienced or recounting the experience at some later time. The level of intensity can be mitigated in either case, but there are important differences in the kind of discourse in which emotional expression occurs when it occurs in the context of telling about a past experience. Considering the delicacy and often the subtlety of the language of emotion, understanding and appropriately producing language which expresses emotion can be a difficult as well as essential skill for the learner to acquire, because getting a reading on the emotion of the speaker, especially when emotion is not the topic, can be crucial to communication.

3. THE SECOND-LANGUAGE LEARNER AND EMOTION IN SPEECH

Rintell (1984a) investigated the difficulty learners encountered in perceiving the emotional content of conversation in English. These subjects listened to a number of tape-recorded conversations in which one speaker described to another an experience which resulted in relatively strong emotion. For example, in one, a young woman laments having lost a promotion she was counting on. For each conversation, subjects were asked to choose the emotion which best characterized the conversation. Analysis of the results revealed that for all the learners, the task was relatively difficult. Beginners fared significantly poorer on the task than intermediate or advanced students, but even advanced students answered, on the average, only half of the questions correctly. Learners of different language groups also differed from each other on their scores, with speakers of Chinese answering differently than speakers of Arabic and Spanish. Details of this study are reported elsewhere (Rintell, 1984b).

This study strongly supported the notion that, for learners, discerning the emotion of a speaker in L2 is no easy task and that the native language and culture, as well as the learner's L2 proficiency, play a role. As Gumperz, Aulakh, and Kaltman (1982) point out,

> signalling at the level of discourse functions, that is, syntactic and lexical choices, and prosody, has direct consequences for interpreting what linguists refer to as indirectness, i.e. the implied, or to use Grice's term, the implicated meaning of utterances. (p. 29)

In other words, speakers are required to "read between the lines." Thus, when knowledge of sociolinguistic, culture-bound conventions for language use (as are apparently employed for communicating affect) are required for the interpretation of other speakers' intentions, second-language learners may be understanding the meaning of the words, but not the meaning (or force) of utterances or longer pieces of discourse.

A method of eliciting language expressing emotion was used previously by Collier, Kuiken, and Enzle (1982) and in a series of experiments by Davitz (1969). The method is, simply, to hand subjects a stack of index cards, each with the name of one of the emotions written on it. Then, the subject is asked to talk about what it feels like to experience that emotion or to tell about a time in his or her life when he or she felt that emotion. The subjects respond and the responses are tape-recorded and transcribed. For this study, data were collected in this way from native English-speaking and second–language-learning university students, six English speakers and eight learners. The learners were intermediate-level ESL students, with Michigan scores ranging from 41 to 83.

The main finding of Collier et al. (1982) was that sentences which describe a negative emotional experience are generally more grammatically complex. In a follow-up experiment, it was found that when a sentence could be rewritten in two ways—one simple and one complex, but both containing the same semantic information—the affect of the speaker of the simple sentence was judged as more positive, and that of the complex sentence more negative. This is consistent with the claim that we tend to use more complex sentences to describe negative emotion, and this complexity is used by the listener as a cue to the affect of the speaker.

This finding led me to ask the following questions about the way emotion is communicated: if the grammatical complexity of sentences is one cue to negative emotion, what are some of the other discourse features and patterns found in language in which emotion is conveyed or described? And how can the emotional expression of natives and learners be characterized and compared in a way that contributes to our knowledge about second-language acquisition?

In the Davitz and Collier studies cited above, the researchers were looking at the specific words employed by their subjects to label their experience and at the structure of the sentences in which these words appeared. In this study, it became apparent to me that taking a broader view of subjects' language would be fruitful. That is, by extracting specific words and even sentences from the discourse, the full meaning and force of spates of talk can be lost. Ignoring or discarding part of the data is, in effect, altering it. We thus lose the richness of the language of these speakers and what it can teach us about how the communication of emotion is achieved. When subjects were asked to talk about their own emotional experience, they sometimes attempted to describe in a general way what it usually feels like to be, say, anxious, giving some synonyms in a brief description. But most often, they told stories of emotional experiences in their lives. I believe that the best understanding of the linguistic expression of emotion comes from examining these personal narratives, although they are about the speakers' past experiences and not necessarily their expression of emotion felt at the time of talking (unless memories revive previous emotional experience). Then, within the narrative, one can see not only descriptive phrases but the discourse features which contribute to the emotional force of the language and the involvement of the listener.

4. THE ROLE OF EMOTION IN NARRATIVE

The narrative as a vehicle for expression of emotion has been discussed by others. As Gee (1985) states, the primary role of narrative in human life is to use it to make sense of one's experience. Certainly, to sort out one's emotional response to events by recounting the story of one's experience is to use narrative in this way. Conversely, Labov (1972) points out that the chief purpose of a narrative can be to provide a framework for evaluation—the description of one's emotional response to the events in the narrative. Telling such stories, and describing the emotion evoking events, gives the speaker repeated opportunities to deal with his or her own responses to the experience and to receive feedback, and possibly support, from others.

It is not our purpose here to either summarize or critique the growing body of literature on the structure of stories. (For discussions of the above, see, among others, Rumelhart, 1975; de Beaugrande & Colby, 1979; Wilensky, 1983, and the replies in the same volume.) Rather, we would like to choose one model, that of Labov (1972, following Labov & Waletsky, 1967), to which to refer as we consider the present data.

Labov's (1972) structure of narratives of personal experience consists of the following elements:

1. An abstract, providing a summary or encapsulation of the story.
2. An orientation, providing setting and background information.
3. Evaluations, which indicate the point of the story and the speaker's emotional responses to the events.
4. Narrative clauses, in temporal order and usually given in simple past tense.
5. The result, saying what finally happened.
6. A coda, which signals the end.

The minimum requirement for a narrative, however, is two clauses, temporally ordered.

The stories found in both native speaker and second-language learners' responses were easily recognizable as such when analyzed according to this model and according to one's commonsense recognition of a story. The following is an excerpt from the speech of an Arabic-speaking learner, who has been asked to describe the emotion guilt. (In the following examples, E. denotes experimenter, S., subject.)

(1)

    S. In my high school . . .
    E. In high school?
    S. Yeah, this is the first . . . this the only thing in my life . . . because when I took my mark, my grade . . .
    E. Uh huh?
    S. Really. I went with my friends. Uh, when I, uh, my friend . . . uh, he studied, y'know, all of and, uh, when we took the exam, I . . . made . . . sheated? . . . or sheated?
    E. Cheated.
    S. Yeah, this is the first . . . this the only thing in my life . . . because when I took my mark, my grade . . .
    E. Uh huh.
    S. I felt guilty because this my, not my grade or something.

In this response, "in my high school" serves as the orientation. The subject's account continues in the form of narrative clauses, using simple past tense in temporal order, until he states that he cheated. The evaluation comes when he seems to express that that was the one and only time he cheated, because he felt guilty. There is no abstract in the beginning or coda at the end.

Another example from a learner, talking about anger, is the following:

(2)

    S. Well, there was . . . I was younger and I was swimmin' in a pool, I don't remember exactly, and suddenly, an old man came over me and tried to touch me and, well, y'know . . . well, he was trying to make me think he was my friend, and I really got angry with him, and I told him "stop that I don't like it. If you want a bed mate . . . look for it in another place."

    E. Mmhmm

    S. And, well, he got angry with me, too.

    E. What did he do?

    S. Oh, he was really bewildered because he never thought a young child could react that way.

    E. How old were you?

    S. Oh . . . ten or twelve.

    E. Uhhuh.

    S. ummm, he didn't say anything so, I, I, I swam away from him.

Note that in this story, it could have been completed by its teller at "look for it in another place," except that the experimenter's "mmhmm" encouraged her to continue, and further details of the story were then related. This is a very good example of how a story in conversation is almost never solely told by its teller but interactionally built (Schegloff, 1981), and it suggests that the strategies chosen to perform these and other speech acts are also affected by the "hearer's" utterances.

This story illustrates also how a slightly more fluent speaker, and slightly more adept storyteller, highlights the most important event of the story by the word "suddenly." The story also has an orientation and narrative clauses. "I got angry" is evaluative, and "I told him 'stop that . . .' " is a possible result. As it happens, more details emerge as the conversation proceeds, and later, "I swam away" seems a better candidate for result status.

These stories are typical of responses in our data. The stories have the internal structure of narratives. Indeed, the fact that they are easily perceived as stories results from their having this structure. The telling of the story is a means of talking about emotion, and this is no coincidence, because, as previously noted, the emotional reaction to the events of a story is a crucial part of the structure of any story (Labov, 1972; Lehnert, 1983). Indeed, the more elaborate the units of the story are, the more emotional impact the story makes. Thus, the more fluent speaker of example (2) is likely to be judged as speaking better English, but this effect results not just from uttering more grammatical sentences but from telling a more coherent and elaborated story, that is, one in which the speaker employs various discourse features to elaborate the basic structural elements of a narrative. The result is that the story has greater emotional effect.

Compare the following story, about fear, to the previous ones:

(3)

> S. Mmm, sometimes I was driving a car on a freeway and a police car is following me.
>
> E. Oh.
>
> S. Yeah, but they don't want catch me, but y'know, always . . . slowly . . . don't go too fast, right, don't drive too fast, right, y'know.
>
> E. And then what happened? The policeman passed you by?
>
> S. I just wait until he passed, go away, then, y'know, everything will be fine.

The first line appears to be an orientation, marked by past progressive tense, "I was driving on a freeway." When the subject switches to present progressive, it can be interpreted as past progressive and a continuation of the orientation. The listener, a native speaker of the Labov and Waletsky (1967) narrative form as well as of English, waits to hear the events of the narrative. But the expected events are not given. That is, the policeman is said not to want to catch the speaker, and the phrases about driving slowly seem to simply describe the way the speaker was driving. So the listener tries to get the speaker back on the narrative track, the track she expects according to her narrative rules. She asks what happened, that is, what the point of the story is, and we find that essentially nothing happened, or, if something newsworthy did happen, the speaker is for some reason unable to say so or chooses not to. The story, which was told as an example of a time when the speaker felt anxious or fearful, seems to lack a point, and it clearly lacks an evaluative description of the speaker's response. So if the speaker was fearful, that point is apparently lost. The fact that the speaker never says directly or indirectly that he was afraid is not the only reason that the story apparently fails to convey emotion. As stated above, sometimes just stating the events of a narrative will indirectly convey the emotion of the speaker. But in this case, the "story" fails to hold up as a story and thus fails to communicate emotion.

There are many ways one might choose to interpret this apparent departure from familiar narrative structure in this speaker's story. One interpretation is that the speaker, a learner of English, was so involved in attempting to communicate in the target language that he became distracted from his own narrative, just as some learners seem to "forget" previously learned grammatical rules while attempting to communicate their ideas. Or perhaps he did not mean to describe a particular event but rather the general anxiety experienced when he would see a police car on the highway. Another possibility might be that the narrative structure we have been describing is not universal. This learner might be a native speaker of a different way of telling stories from the one we have been considering, and thus he is a learner not only of the English language but also of our narrative structure.

Difficulty in understanding the point of a story told by a native speaker of another language may in fact be due to interference stemming from differences in the narrative structures of the two languages in question. The work of Scollon and Scollon (1981) illuminates many aspects of cross-cultural differences in discourse, one of which is in narrative. They focus on the discourse rules of the Athabaskans, a native Alaskan people. One example is that Athabaskan stories, like those of some other native Americans, are organized around twos and fours, rather than the threes we are familiar with—our stories have a tripartite structure, with a recognizable beginning, middle, and end. Also, while English uses prosody to give important information about the speaker's attitude toward the information being expressed, Athabaskan does not. Instead, it uses morphemes as formal markers. Scollon and Scollon (1981) describe the misunderstandings that arise as English speakers try to use prosody to convey evaluative information when speaking Athabaskan, and when Athabaskans fail to use prosody but rely on lexical markers when speaking English. In the present study, the native narrative structure of the languages of the learner subjects has not been researched, so we are prevented from a complete understanding of how cross-cultural narrative differences might be causing interference in the learner data. Nonetheless, the work of Scollon and Scollon (1981) is very suggestive of the issues that must be taken into account when examining the narratives of nonnative speakers.

Now consider a story told by a native speaker:

(4)

    S. OK. Disgust. Mm. Well yes. Disgusted with life. It was a series of events that happened that, that made me feel like, um, like I hated the world and this wasn't fair. My, um, my mother and my father both had a heart attack within a six-week period. Or less than that. My father's in the hospital for three weeks and he's out of the hospital for four days and mother had a heart attack. I was going to school here at night until ten o'clock at night and working during the day and my boyfriend was in A_____. So. When all this happened I was pretty disgusted with everything. With school, with life, it wasn't fair. Um, my parents are quite poor and they certainly couldn't afford all of this, the problems they were having and I guess I was just disgusted with God, mainly, and I couldn't understand, and I couldn't understand why he was doing this to them and then I turned it on myself, that, why couldn't I do more? So maybe I was a little disgusted with myself because I couldn't go to B_____ and see how they were doing except on the weekend. But mainly it was that I was pretty fed up with the world, that everything bad had happened, everything within a four week period.

E. Hmm.

S. Yeah, it was four weeks. Two heart attacks, my boyfriend and I broke up, and and school and work and I already told you that my boss was a real jerk. So I was just disgusted with everything, my entire life, and I was contemplating quitting my job and getting a night job and going to school full time because I had had enough, where mentally it was driving me completely . . . So I guess that's all.

This story begins with an abstract, where a summary of what happened is given first. Then background orientation is given, then the events, and then the evaluation. These elements are recycled again, presumably for emotional effect; that is, after what happened is recounted, we hear more and again about why the speaker felt disgusted. At the end is another summary, in simple past clauses in temporal order, and an evaluation.

We see in this story how this speaker's elaboration of the basic narrative structure creates a vivid effect for the listener, a sense of not only what happened but how the speaker felt about what happened. Indeed, a story presented in such a way strives to involve the listener so that he or she, too, begins to empathically feel the speaker's emotion. The learner stories (1) and (2) are more elaborated and more effective than (3), but neither conveys emotion to the degree that the native speaker's story does.

In what follows, I attempt to look at the discourse features which achieve the elaboration seen above and which are characteristic of emotional expression. These features serve also as bases of comparison between the native speaker and learner stories, thus providing another means of viewing the process of acquisition.

The part of the narrative in which emotion is usually expressed as the teller explains his or her emotional reaction to the events has been called the evaluation. It can be internal to the telling of the events, and thus not temporally separated from the events themselves, or external comments about the events. It is here that much of the variation of the level of directness to which I referred earlier can be seen. This variation is accomplished in a variety of ways. On the very direct end of the continuum, speakers name the emotion and even find ways to emphasize the intensity of the emotion experienced by using emphatic modifiers or by adding details such as descriptions of their physical responses. Strategies to be indirect include, among others, using figurative language or language that mitigates or minimizes the emotional effect of the experience. In what follows, examples of such discourse features are given and discussed.

One strategy to be indirect is to use figurative rather than literal language to state one's emotional response. In our corpus, native speakers often use figurative language, as they express how they felt about the events of the narrative. Example (5) is a native speaker talking about being frightened:

(5)

It was that Camaro, *I died!* I couldn't believe it!

Another native speaker describes feeling guilty:

(6)

And we all denied it. And that, that's what made it so bad, 'cause none of us *had the guts* to say we did it.

It is notable that in no data collected from a nonnative speaker was any figurative language used.

In both of the above examples, the choice of metaphor was a physical one—in one case "death" for being afraid, in the other, "guts" for courage. This is not the only kind of figurative language used by native speakers, but it seems to be an especially appropriate type when one considers that many speakers describe physical sensations when they talk about their emotions, because these sensations are in fact physical components of the emotions. For learners and native speakers, physical descriptions paint a vivid picture and, normally, emphasize rather than minimize emotional intensity. Example (7) comes from the response of a learner:

(7)

There's a word that describes exactly how I felt: nauseated.

In Example (10), a native speaker describes feeling afraid: "My heart was pounding."

Another discourse feature which reduces directness is for the speaker to name the felt emotion but to minimize it with such phrases as "just a little," "a little bit," or by using a milder term (e.g., "annoyed" rather than "angry"). For example, the native English-speaking subject of example (8) is referring to an upcoming test on bible studies:

(8)

Well, here I am I profess myself to be a man of God, what'll it be like to have a low score on that? You know, because that's something that's really more important than what you study here, although most people don't think so. Your obedience to the word of God determines your possibilities here, and in heaven, forever. Well, what are people doing here that will provide them with things here? Well, probably a lot, but what about forever? What does this institution offer that will give you benefits forever? *So there is a little anxiety there.*

It is interesting to note that this particular speaker, who is talking about anxiety he feels as he is speaking (about how well he will do on an important examination), minimizes the intensity of his anxiety. This example supports the hypothesis that there is a greater need for indirectness when emotion is expressed as it is being experienced, as compared to emotion described as it was felt in the past.

A learner also used the phrase "a little bit" to minimize the emotion he names in the evaluation of his story about anger:

(9)

    S. Uh, I have my friend.

    E. Mmhmm?

    S. Uh, I studied with him in Lebanon for all in elementary school classes

    E. Mmuhuh?

    S. And, uh high school classes, uh, now we came to the United States, then, uh, there is a little . . . a little bit of discussion with him about different things in Lebanon, about the, for example, his parents.

    E. Uhhuh?

    S. Because he, a little bit, doesn't care about his family, or some uh, even though his family pay for him money for studying in the United States.

    E. Mmhmm.

    S. And now I am talking with him about the, the uh, specific things. He, he, he, told me that's that's not right, uh, everybody doesn't care about their, uh, his parents or, his family. *That's made me anger a little bit.*

By contrast, an example of more direct, unmitigated expression of emotion appearing as an evaluation of a series of events can be seen in the following example. Here, a native speaker tells her story about feeling anxious:

(10)

Anxiety. Fear. This is great because last night, I was coming home from school, and I stopped at a, uh, U-Totem, got out, went in, came back out, was driving down the street, and it's only three blocks from my house, and someone was flashing their lights at me and I ignored it and just kept going. I pulled into my apartment complex and parked and there was a man in a car that pulled up behind me. I left the car running and I opened the door and said, "I don't know who you are," and he said, uh, "just talk to me for a minute," and my heart was pounding *and I was really scared*—this is very new because it was just last night, and, um, so I shut the door and didn't know what to do, really. So I shut the door and waited a second and thought he would go away.

In this evaluation, the speaker not only states literally that she was scared but emphasizes this fact by using an emphatic: "I was *really scared.*"

Using direct descriptions of emotion is characteristic of the learner responses in our data. Some examples:

(11)

    E: How about pleasure? Pleasure is what you feel when you are happy.

    S: Very happy? When I receive my, um, when I received a letter from my girlfriend . . .

    E: Uh huh?

    S: *Is . . . Is very happy.*

    E: Yeah.

    S: Now that time, I read a letter so many times, y'know, forget everything.

    E: Uh huh.

    S: Just read letter.

    E: Uh huh, uh huh.

    S: And write letter to her.

In example (12) a learner talks about feeling depressed:

    S: Maybe when I first arrived into United States because I, I, have, I, I am alone in this country and at weekends Saturday and Sunday I feel more the solitude. I have some friends here, but, uh, it, it's not the same.

    E: No.

    S: If I, I . . . uh . . . I would be in my country . . .

    E: Do you have a family in your country?

    S: Yeah, I have a family in the country and, um . . . here I have some friends, some physicians, but, uh, we can, uh, *we can say I feel sad, depressed, sad, sad* and sometimes I wonder myself, why, why I, I came here?

This speaker not only explicitly names the emotion he feels but adds emphasis by repeating. Repetition, a discourse feature common to conversation, has a variety of functions. Tannen (1987) analyzes the phenomenon of repetition in conversation. She states that one function (among many) of repetition is that it enables a speaker to produce fluent speech while formulating what to say next. This is true for native speakers as well as learners, but it is an obviously practical way for a learner to convey his or her feelings through a still unfamiliar language.

Language can be used in a variety of ways to minimize or to intensify the speaker's apparent emotions throughout the telling of a story. It is often the way in which the basic structure of a narrative is elaborated that seems to convey its emotional effect. Some of the discourse features which vary the directness of expressed emotion are exemplified below. Again, we see that the stories elicited from learners in this study did not reveal the full range of features identifiable in those told by native English speakers.

The greater part of most stories is the recounting of the events rather than commentary on those events. The way in which those events are described can play a great role in conveying the speaker's emotion to the listener. One way to tell a story, which seems to aim at getting the listener to focus on exactly what transpired and to form a vivid image of what the speaker experienced, is to give a very detailed account of the events, even including what might appear to be insignificant details. Ironically, while a very detailed style of telling a story often succeeds in communicating emotion strongly, it is at the same time a way of being indirect. The more the listener empathically understands the speaker's experience, the more he or she can "read between the lines" and fill in unstated information. Under such circumstances, the speaker's subjective, emotional experience can be conveyed without the speaker having to literally "spell out" what he or she is or was feeling. The speaker in example (10) almost forces the listener to imagine the exact events leading up to her being frightened:

> . . . last night, I was coming home from school, and I stopped at a, uh, U-Totem, got out, went in, came back out, was driving down the street, and it's only three blocks from my house, and someone was flashing their lights at me and I ignored it and just kept going.

The speaker draws the listener into her normal, everyday life as she lists her very ordinary, everyday activities—a seemingly uninteresting list of facts sharply in contrast with the phrase "and someone was flashing their lights at me." Her statement that she ignored the lights and just keep going seems to say that the events were basically so ordinary that it hardly registered that anything unusual was occurring. At the same time, she is actually highlighting how unusual the flashing lights in fact were, and she cues the listener that something out of the ordinary and possibly disturbing is about to be told.

By contrast, in the following learner story about guilt, few details are given:

(13)

    S: Guilt.
    E: Mmhmm. Have you ever felt guilty?

S: Yes!

E: What made you feel guilty? Tell me about the time when you felt guilty.

S: Uh, once my mother . . . I . . . I came home late . . . and then my mother scold me. And then, um, it is Saturday night, so why my mother scold me just for that? And then, so I scold again to my mother.

E: Oh.

S: Right after that I think, I don't have to do that because maybe my mother have a reason why, mmm, why she do that, well, and so that I feel guilty that I scold my mother again.

In this story, the events are clear. The speaker was reprimanded for coming home late, felt the reprimand was unwarranted, and "scolded," that is, in some way spoke disrespectfully to her mother. As a result she felt guilty. However, the story is very different from the one told in example (10). Because the events are given in a somewhat sketchy way, without detail, the listener cannot predict what the point is or how the speaker feels. The listener is not given enough detail to form a mental image of what actually happened and therefore may not fully empathize with the speaker's emotional response. The storyteller's ability to paint a graphic image for the listener, so that the listener actively participates by placing himself or herself inside the events and imagining his or her own emotional reaction, is likely to be as important a factor in conveying emotion as is an explicit, literal evaluation. Linguistically, this strategy is an indirect expression of emotion, even while it serves to emphasize the emotion of the speaker.

Another way that a speaker can bring detail into a narrative, and thereby get the listener to focus closely on the speaker's experience, is to relate conversation as part of the story. While this strategy can effectively add to the emotion conveyed, it is also a way of using language indirectly to express emotion. Again, example (10) illustrates this point:

> . . . . so I opened the door up again and I said, "Look, I'm gonna back out of here. If you don't move I'm gonna hit your car," and he said, "Try it. You'll have to ram my car."

The reported speech is a kind of detail that conveys the speaker's affect by allowing her to incorporate her remembered affect as revealed by what she said and how she said it. Similarly, affect is revealed as she recounts what was said by the other character in her story. The reported speech is not language directed toward the listener. Rather, it is remembered language directed to a third party, in this case the man who had frightened the speaker. In her reported speech, the speaker threatens this man, and he replies by defiantly daring her to carry out her threat. The memory of such an interchange is clearly laden with emotion, in fact revealed by the illocutionary force of those utterances.

Describing this dialogue enhances the listener's image of the events and the emotional effect of the events.

While reported speech is a common aspect of stories told by native speakers, it is a rarer detail found in our corpus of learner stories. It was employed by only one of our learner subjects, the speaker who told the story given in example (2). Indeed, her inclusion of this detail functions to convey the sense that this story is more elaborate than stories told by other learners.

An additional discourse feature which can be employed to effectively convey emotion is the use of epithets or other figurative descriptions of characters in stories. For example, "she's an angel" conveys positive affect, while "he's a jerk" obviously conveys the speaker's negative attitude toward "him." This type of description never appears in our corpus of learner stories. In example (4), the native speaker states that her boss was "a real jerk." The fact that learners did not employ this discourse feature may result from a greater formality they possibly attributed to the data collection sessions, but I think it is more likely that this is a type of elaboration they had not yet acquired in their target-language discourse.

The last discourse feature I discuss is another nonevaluative example of indirectness employed in personal narratives. I interpret it as another means of minimizing emotion as directly stated by the speaker:

(14)

> *I* get real depressed on a beautiful Sunday or Saturday, you know, it's about 76 out there, it's real crisp, the sky is blue, the weather is like free air conditioning, it's not too cold it's just right, and there *you* are, studying, inside, the whole world is out playing, and there *you* are crunching numbers . . . and *you* want to run out and play . . . and the only thing *you* have time to do is sit and look at the books. And that's very depressing.

It is interesting that this native speaker begins by talking about when "I get real depressed" but as he continues switches from "I" to "you" in describing his emotions. This appears to be another variation of the strategy of being indirect. On one level, the speaker avoids talking directly about his own feelings. Instead, he switches to talking about a hypothetical, general "you" who might experience something like what he describes. On another level, the listener is in fact meant to understand that the speaker is describing his own experience. It is this subject's change from "I" to "you" while still referring to himself that I call depersonalization, a strategy to be indirect while expressing even strong emotion.

5. CONCLUSION

I have argued in this chapter that, for learners, to communicate emotion through language is a task which involves the acquisition of a complex set of sociolinguistic conventions about the distribution of talk in the target culture. Appropriate language for expressing emotion is sensitive to a number of contextual factors having to do with the interlocutor, the setting, and the type of emotion expressed. In order to adjust language so as to be appropriate, the language used to express emotion is varied along a continuum from very direct to very indirect. Many of the strategies speakers use to vary directness are seen most clearly in the discourse features of personal narratives.

From the data of this study, we see that a common way that people talk about their emotions is in the form of telling stories, and that a sense of whether emotion has been successfully communicated comes from how the story is told. While learners as well as native speakers tell stories, one example is given, (3), in which the learner's story lacks an essential aspect of structure, fails as a story, and the speaker's emotion is lost. On the other hand, most learner stories are seen as structurally similar but lacking the listener-involving detail and elaboration that are characteristic of the successful stories told by native speakers.

In general, native speakers were found to employ a wider variety of strategies to be indirect and to elaborate their stories. Many of the discourse features discussed above function to make the listener focus on the details of the story, allowing the listener to actively participate and thus be able to more accurately read between the lines and empathize with the speaker. In this way, emotion is successfully conveyed, even while the speaker is indirect, and avoids going ''bald on record'' as expressing emotion.

While learner stories are seen here as sharing some of the features of indirectness, elaboration, and detail with native speaker stories, certainly they lack others. Some features shared by learner and native speaker stories are direct, explicit statements of emotional response given as evaluations, minimized statements of emotional response, repetitions, and reference to physical sensations. On the other hand, in our corpus we find native speakers using figurative language, reported speech, epithets, and depersonalization, while no instances of those features are found in the responses of the learners in our study. Importantly, much greater detail is found in the recounting of events in the native speaker stories, a feature which, I believe, is extremely important to the expression of emotion because such detail serves to involve the listener's participation.

The difference in discourse features employed by natives and learners reflect not only a wider variety of strategies to express emotion on the part of native speakers but, clearly, in a more general way, their broader stylistic variation in discourse. As the second-language learner acquires a greater variety of the features of target-language discourse, he or she will control many other aspects of language function with greater ease as well. However, I do not mean to imply that the acquisition of linguistic strategies to express emotion is wholly a function of the acquisition of target-language discourse ability. Rather, it would seem that two processes occur simultaneously. The learner acquires a greater sense of the difference between his or her own culturally learned rules regarding the expression of emotion and those of the target culture and language. As more competence is acquired, the learner also gains facility with such discourse abilities as telling coherent, sufficiently elaborate stories and varying such features as indirectness.

I conclude this chapter with some questions raised by this kind of research which cannot be addressed within the framework of this kind of study. While research about the second-language learner's developing pragmatic competence and discourse competence is important for a broad understanding of the language learner, research is still needed which relates the acquisition of pragmatic and discourse ability to the acquisition of linguistic ability. We now know a little more about some of the differences between the narrative structures of different cultures (Scollon & Scollon, 1981). How did differences between native language and target-language narrative structures affect the narratives in these data? Does the prior knowledge of how to tell a story provide a familiar structure for the learner, motivating him or her to share a personal experience, while allowing him or her to concentrate on lexical and syntactic production? Or, on the other hand, is the ability to tell a story dependent on a high level of linguistic skill? How much interdependency exists, and how do we look at it?

REFERENCES

de Beaugrand, R., & Colby, B. N. (1979). Narrative models of action and interaction. *Cognitive Science, 3*, 43–66.

Collier, G., Kuiken, M., & Enzle, M. (1982). The role of grammatical qualification in the expression and perception of emotion. *Journal of Psycholinguistic Research, 11*(6), 631–650.

Davitz, J. R. (1969). *The language of emotions.* New York: McGraw Hill.

Ekman, P. (1984). Expression and the nature of emotion. In K. Scherer & P. Eckman (Eds.), *Approaches to emotion* (pp. 319–344). Hillsdale, NJ: Lawrence Erlbaum.

Eckman, P., & Friesen, W. V. (1969). The repertoire of nonverbal behavior: Categories, origins, usage, and coding. *Semiotica, 1*, 49–98.

Fraser, B. (1985). *Direct illocutionary force potential.* Unpublished manuscript. Boston University, Boston.

Gee, J. (1985). The narrativization of experience in the oral style. *Journal of Education, 167*(1), 9–35.

Gumperz, J., Aulakh, G., & Kaltman, H. (1982). Thematic structure and progression in discourse.

In J. Gumperz (Ed.), *Language and social identity* (pp. 22–56). Cambridge: Cambridge University Press.

Irvine, J. (1982). Language and affect: some cross-cultural issues. In H. Byrnes (Ed.), *Papers presented at the Georgetown University roundtable on language and linguistics* (pp. 31–47). Washington, DC: Georgetown University Press.

Knapp, P. (1980). *From force to meaning: Toward a psychoanalytic–psychosomatic theory of emotion.* Paper presented to the Meetings of the American Psychoanalytic Association, San Francisco.

Labov, W. (1972). *Language in the inner city.* Philadelphia: University of Pennsylvania Press.

Labov, W., & Waletzky, J. (1967). Narrative analysis. In J. Helm MacNeish (Ed.), *Essays on the verbal and visual arts* (pp. 12–44). Seattle: University of Washington Press.

Lakoff, R. (1976). Why you can't say what you mean [Review of E. Newman, *Strictly speaking*]. *Centrum, 4*(2), 151–170.

Lehnert, W. (1983). Moving toward a point of sure return. *Behavioral and Brain Science, 6*, 602–603.

Levy, R. (1984). The emotions in comparative perspective. In K. Scherer & P. Ekman (Eds.), *Approaches to emotion* (pp. 397–412). Hillsdale, NJ: Lawrence Erlbaum.

Ochs, E., & Schieffelin, B. (1985, July). *Language has a heart.* Paper presented to the Summer Institute of the Linguistic Society of America, Georgetown University, Washington, DC.

Plutchik, R. (1962). *The emotions: Facts, theories, and a new model.* New York: Random House.

Plutchik, R. (1980). *Emotions: A psychoevolutionary synthesis.* New York: Harper and Row.

Rintell, E. (1984a). But how did you *feel* about that?: The learner's perception of emotion in speech. *Applied Linguistics, 5*(3), 255–264.

Rintell, E. (1984b, March). *The pragmatics of expressing emotion in a second language.* Paper presented to the Eighteenth Annual TESOL Convention, Houston, TX.

Rumelhart, D. E. (1975). Notes on a schema for stories. In D. G. Bobrow & A. Collins (Eds.), *Representation and understanding* (pp. 211–236). New York: Academic Press.

Schegloff, E. (1981). Discourse as an interactional achievement. In D. Tannen (Ed.), *Analyzing discourse: Text and talk; The papers presented at the Georgetown University roundtable on language and linguistics* (pp. 71–93). Washington, DC: Georgetown University Press.

Scherer, K., & Ekman, P. (Eds.). (1984). *Approaches to emotion.* Hillsdale, NJ: Lawrence Erlbaum.

Scollon, R., & Scollon, S. B. K. (1981). *Narrative, literacy and face in interethnic communication.* Norwood, NJ: Ablex.

Tannen, D. (1984). *Conversation style: Analyzing talk among friends.* Norwood, NJ: Ablex.

Tannen, D. (1987). Repetition in conversation: Toward a poetics of talk. *Language, 63*(3), 574–605.

Wilensky, R. (1983). Story grammars and story points. *The Behavioral and Brain Sciences, 6*, 579–623.

PART V

Suggestions for Pedagogy

CHAPTER 16

Classroom Foreign Language Learning and Language Variation
The Notion of Pedagogical Norms

ALBERT VALDMAN

1. INTRODUCTION

There is a growing recognition among researchers and observers of second-language learning that the foreign language classroom constitutes a special environment for the learning and the communicative use of the target language. In a special issue of *Studies in Second Language Acquisition* devoted to that topic, several of the contributors underscore both the complexity and the specificity of the foreign language classroom (Edmonson, 1985; Faerch & Kasper, 1985; Kramsch, 1985). Edmonson neatly characterizes the special nature of the foreign language classroom environment by underscoring the paradoxical nature of the language behavior we wish to impart to learners: "we seek in the classroom to teach people how to talk when they are not being taught" (1985, p. 162).

To teach people how to talk when they are not being taught involves, in addition to simulated conversational interactions, metalinguistic, metadiscursive, and metacommunicative activity: focusing learners' attention on linguistic forms and functions and on the nature of discourse and communication. It also

This chapter is a modified version of a paper delivered at the 1987 University of Illinois Pragmatics Conference and scheduled to appear in a special issue of *World Englishes* (7(2), 1988). I am grateful to the conference organizers and to the editors of the issue for granting me the permission to include part of the paper in this volume.

ALBERT VALDMAN • CREDLI, Indiana University, Bloomington, Indiana 47405.

requires devising a special language-learning and language-using context in which the use of language will range from instructional to natural discourse, and establishing a set of social conventions that are as real and as valid as those that determine the natural use of the language in the target-language community. Part of these social conventions is the variety of the target language that is presented and imparted to the learners. In his seminal work, Harold Palmer (1917) observed that the majority of academicians and literary experts firmly believed the "popular superstition" that each language possesses an ideal "correct" form from which all divergencies constitute "impurities" or "mistakes." Indeed, this superstition, if we wish to call it such, is widely accepted by teachers and students alike. Yet, recent research has highlighted the ubiquity and centrality of variation in the development of the learners' interlanguage.

Traditionally, the monitored speech of educated native speakers (ENS) has been accepted as the appropriate target for classroom foreign language learning. But that target is too restrictive and reductionist. In their verbal interactions, native speakers, including ENSs, do not evidence an invariant form of the language but, instead, a *repertoire* of linguistic features and communicative strategies which they apply variably, depending on the numerous factors that determine the total communicative setting. Thus, the attainment of near-native proficiency entails the capacity to perceive and reproduce the total repertoire of target native speakers. To accomplish this, foreign language teachers and students must come to accept that all languages are heterogeneous entities encompassing constantly shifting varieties correlated with regional, sociological, stylistic, and situational factors. At the same time, however, we must not lose sight of the fact, mentioned in the foregoing discussion, that the foreign language classroom constitutes a special language-using environment. As Soulé-Susbielles (1984) insightfully observed: "the language that is produced [in the classroom] must be evaluated in terms of its own natural context and not according to external norms" (p. 183). The elaboration of special forms of the target language that takes into account both the inherent variability of language and the special social constraints imposed by the special nature of the classroom environment is precisely the issue I would like to address in this chapter.

My presentation comprises four parts. First, I develop a model of interlinguistic variation which, unlike those presented heretofore, attempts to take into account the inherent variation in the target language. Second, I present the results of a pilot study that suggests that advanced learners, including foreign language teachers, differ significantly from target-language speakers in the way they handle variation. Third, I argue for the establishment of special classroom replicas of the target language, which I label pedagogical norms. Fourth, I illustrate the notion of pedagogical norm with a variable feature of French, the phonological *è* variable.

2. A MULTINORM MODEL OF LANGUAGE VARIATION

The most notable attempts to account for interlanguage variability have adopted various aspects of William Labov's sociolinguistic model (1966, 1972). L. Dickerson (1975) and W. Dickerson (1976) have studied the development of phonological interlanguage features over time and in different speech situations. They show that in drawing closer to the target-language model, learners follow a course analogous to phonological change: they produce a variety of replicas of target-language features, each replica predominating in a particular environment. Over time, and differentially across speech styles, replicas closer to the target-language feature will spread progressively to new environments, just as in a natural language innovative variants of a phonological variable will spread differentially across various environments, word classes, social groups, and geographical areas.

On the basis of experimental studies focusing on morpho-syntactic as well as phonological features, E. Tarone (1979, 1983) hypothesized that learners' interlanguage constitutes a continuum analogous to the Labovian vernacular–standard one. The relative position of an interlinguistic variant on the continuum is a function of the attention paid to linguistic form (see Figure 1). The left-most pole of the interlanguage continuum corresponds to the vernacular on the natural language continuum. Vernacular interlinguistic features, which are produced when attention to linguistic form is lessened, exhibit greater regularity. In contrast, the right-most pole, corresponding to the standard end of the native vernacular–standard continuum, is likely to contain target-language and L1 features and shows the least internal consistency. Like Corder (1977) and Widdowson (1976), Tarone accounts for the internal consistency of the interlanguage "vernacular" in terms of universal language processing strategies and substantive universals appearing under conditions of reduced input, such as those that trigger pidginization.[1]

In complex societies one of the norms available in the overall speech community is endowed with prestige and/or political power. This norm undergoes a gradual progress of uniformization and gains the status of *standard*. It also becomes associated with the dominant social group (ENSs) whose vernacular will show less deviation from it than will those of the other social groups lumped together under the label *vernacular*. According to the early Labovian sociolinguistic model, all variation within a linguistic community can be lo-

---

[1] Elaine Tarone has since recognized some of the limitations of her model and is presenting a more elaborated version in this volume (Chapter 1). I have not had the opportunity to consult her chapter before drafting my contribution, and, regrettably, I have not been able to take the more recent model into account in this discussion.

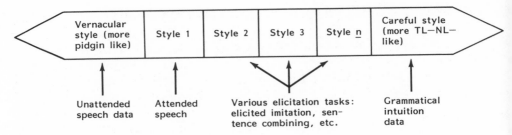

Figure 1. Interlanguage as chameleon. (From Tarone, 1979.)

cated on a vernacular–standard continuum. In other words, there are no variants that reflect orientation toward some norm other than that which characterizes the speech of ENSs. But in his study of urban Black English Labov (1972,
p. 249) accounts for the persistence of stigmatized forms in the vernacular
speech of black youths by invoking a set of covert norms that attribute positive
values to the vernacular. He also remarks that verbal behavior determined by
these norms is unlikely to appear in the formal situations that characterize sociolinguistic interviews. The following case also illustrates that nonstandard
speakers may be influenced by a variety of norms, including the prestigious
standard form.

In casual observations of linguistic variation in a small village in the Touraine region of France, Pierre Léon (1973) noticed that a group of male speakers
from farmer and worker backgrounds shifted away from local vernacular speech
in two directions. For example, they replaced the local apical tap *r* either by
the velar resonant of Standard French or by the pharyngeal resonant characteristic of lower- and working-class Parisians. The latter feature coincided with
macho behavior and was used typically at meetings in a café run by a retired
railway worker from Paris, a former militant Communist union organizer. This
social group's movement away from its vernacular proceeds in two different
directions, one oriented toward ENS speech (the standard norm) and the other
toward what may be termed Parisian proletarian speech.

The facts noted by Léon show that in complex linguistic communities not
all aspects of language variation can be accounted for only in terms of relative
attention to linguistic form. The factors that trigger native speakers' switching
among community norms are complex and must be sought in the nature of the
social relationships among participants in the speech event and in the situational
context. As an alternative to the unidirectional vernacular–standard continuum
model, I propose a multitarget model (see Figure 2). I posit that all social
groups in a speech community have available a range of speech styles and that
these reflect the influence of several norms. In Figure 2, the square boxes la-

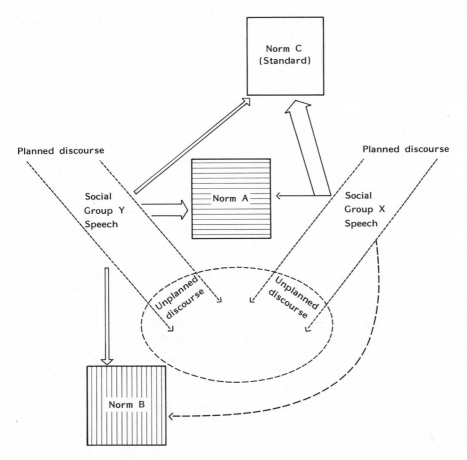

Figure 2. Multitarget model of language variation (see text for explanation of figure).

beled Norm A, Norm B, and Norm C, respectively, represent alternative norms available to the various social groups of a speech community. For the sake of simplicity, the model posits only two social groups, X and Y. The width of the arrows reflects the relative power of attraction exercised on a particular social group by a given norm. Shifts in norm orientation are determined by the social identity speakers wish to signify in the course of given speech events. In daily communicative interactions with members of their own social groups, speakers make use of their vernacular, which is targeted on the norm set by members of the in-group. In Figure 2, Group X represents the dominant group of the society whose speech networks are modeled. In the case cited by Pierre Léon (1973), the vernacular speech of local farmers is oriented toward the local rural Touraine norm, but it will shift toward the Parisian proletarian norm or Standard French, depending on the "acts of social identity" in which the farmers engage in a particular situation (Le Page & Tabouret-Keller, 1985).

In addition to reflecting orientation toward a variety of norms, a speaker's verbal production varies between planned and unplanned discourse. Unplanned discourse, which characterizes conversational interaction, shows the predominance of reliance on the situational context and on lexicon and, consequently, on syntactic reduction (Ochs, 1979). Planning involves attention to speech form, so that the distinction I am making between planned and unplanned discourse corresponds somewhat to that made between attended and nonattended speech in Tarone's model (1983) (see Figure 1). The chief difference between my model and hers lies in the independence as opposed to the convergence of two distinct continua: unplanned→planned discourse (nonattention→attention to speech form) on one axis and vernacular→external norm on another. As would be expected, because it relies on shared information and is linked to the *hic et nunc* of a specific communicative situation, the unplanned discourse of different social groups converges. Conversely, we would expect to find the greatest linguistic differentiation between two social groups to be located in their planned discourse.

Within the framework of the multitarget–norm model I am proposing for target-language variation, the interlanguage continuum may be viewed as a vector which is oriented toward a particular target-language norm by filtering input and controlling feedback (see Figure 3). In Figure 3, the largest square represents the totality of attested target-language variants. Following R. Chaudenson (1986), I call this system TL0. This system encompasses features shared by all target-language varieties as well as all variable features. The two smaller squares represent competing norms, one of which is the standard norm. In naturalistic second-language learning, the types of communicative situations encountered by the learner will determine in large part the orientation of the interlanguage continuum. In classroom interlanguage, the orientation may be controlled to a certain extent by the selection and sequencing of linguistic features, by classroom procedures, and more particularly by the elaboration of pedagogical norms.

3. LEARNERS' PERCEPTION OF APPROPRIATE TARGET NORMS

The varieties of the target language which are appropriate for classroom instructional and communicative activities are determined by the attitudes of the target-language community as well as those of the learners themselves. Miriam Eisenstein (1982, 1987) has shown that foreign learners rapidly acquire the ability to distinguish between standard and nonstandard varieties of the target language. She had a group of 74 learners of English in New York listen

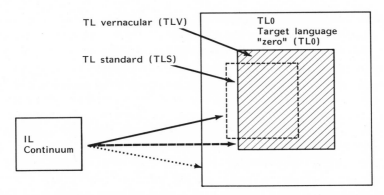

Figure 3. Possible orientations of interlanguage (IL) continuum toward various target-language (TL) norms (see text for explanation of figure).

to paired utterances, opposing standard American English and four types of nonstandard dialects (Black English, Irish-accented, working-class New York, and Hawaiian Creole). Learners at three different levels of proficiency demonstrated the ability to distinguish the standard from the divergent dialects. In fact, the advanced learners did not differ significantly from a control group of native speakers in their ability to detect socially based speech differences, and they evidenced negative attitudes toward certain dialects, notably Black English, paralleling those of the native speakers.

From casual observations and anecdotal reports it appears that target-language speakers expect those who have learned their language in a classroom environment to speak "better" than they do, that is to say, to evidence control of that range of the target-language community repertoire characteristic of formal usage and written texts. They generally ascribe low social status to foreigners who evidence what they consider to be grammatical errors or devalorized phonological features and lexical choices. Whereas there exists a considerable body of research on native speakers' reactions toward learners' interlinguistic features (see d'Anglejan, 1983, for a review of the literature), sociopsychologically oriented studies of native speaker attitudes have not yet been extended to the area of language variation and the definition of sociolinguistically acceptable learner norms for the target language. From the only available exploratory study (Swacker, 1976) it would appear that native speakers tend to downgrade foreigner speech that diverges markedly from the standard norm. Swacker observed that native speakers of East Texas English reacted negatively to a reading sample from an Arabic-accented speaker whose speech contained local pronunciation and grammatical features. A higher ranking was assigned to another Arabic-accented speaker whose English was free of local linguistic features.

Swacker concluded that certain regional markers may be acceptable when found in the speech of native speakers but are offensive in the mouths of foreigners. Swacker fails to specify, however, whether the local features noted also symbolize low social status within the target-language community.

In the absence of a substantial body of empirical research, we must resort to extrapolation from other areas of interlinguistic research to seek principles for the determination of target-language norms suitable for foreign learners. The reaction of Swacker's native judges may be accounted for in terms of a model of status and solidarity (Ryan, 1983). Foreign accents and other interlinguistic features are highly salient markers of membership in out-groups. Their presence in the speech of a foreigner would preclude features symbolizing ingroup membership, such as regionally or socially marked variants.

Appeal to the notion of linguistic capital (Bourdieu, 1977) converges with Swacker's and Eisenstein's observations to lend support to the choice of the standard target-language norm for foreign learners. The learning of a foreign language may be viewed as an economic investment whose value would be depreciated if the variety mastered contained stigmatized features. The higher the social status conferred by the learned speech forms and communicative strategies, the more remunerative the investment.

4. PILOT STUDY ON ADVANCED LEARNERS' PERCEPTION AND PRODUCTION OF TARGET-LANGUAGE NORM

That learners' overt production of the target language and perception of appropriate target norms may differ from those of native speakers of the target is suggested by a pilot study I conducted on the acquisition of a phonological variable of French on the part of advanced American learners. The subjects comprised two subgroups: (1) 28 advanced undergraduates enrolled in a course on remedial pronunciation, and (2) seven beginning graduate students who also served as instructors in the beginning French program at Indiana University.

The variable selected for the study was the *è* variable, a range of pronunciation varying between high-mid front unrounded [é] and its low-mid counterpart [è].[2] The contrast between these two phonemes, required in Standard or orthoepic French, is made variably, depending on geographical, social, situational, and other factors. The *è* variable is contained, for example, in the underscored items in Table 1. In all items, except *ferai* (#4), the orthoepic norm required the use of the phoneme /è/. The choice of the variable was determined by the fact that, as the best studied phonological variable in the language (e.g.,

[2]For the sake of convenience, I am using the symbols [é] and [è] for the standard IPA notations [e] and [ε], respectively.

Table 1. Forms Containing the French Variable
e ([é]—[è])

---

1. J'ai porté un *bérêt*.
2. Il est venu par les *marais*.
3. Elle se *dépêchait* pour aller à la banque.
4. Je *ferai* mes devoirs *après* lui avoir téléphoné.
5. S'ils le *voulaient*, tu *pourrais* partir avec eux.
6. En *effet*, on *voulait fêter* son anniversaire.
7. Tu vas *balayer* toute la *maison*.
8. Elle aime certains *aspects* de l'humour *français*.
9. Vous avez dessiné un mouton à la *craie*.
10. Ferme la porte *s'il te plaît*.
11. On a *fait* des *progrès* en histoire.
12. Cet enfant a *pleuré* toute la journée.

Gueunier, Genouvrier, & Khomsi, 1978, 1984; Léon, 1973), it offers a firm basis for comparing the behavior of advanced foreign learners with that of target native speakers.

The Gueunier *et al.* (1978) study stands as exemplary in its thorough application of the Labov variationist model. Gueunier and her collaborators studied the realization of the *è* variable among a representative group of 75 adult speakers in Tours, traditionally acclaimed as the region in France where the "best" French is spoken.[3] The distribution of the two canonical variants of the variable ([é] and [è]) was charted in various phonological environments and in two diametrically opposed styles: directed conversation, assumed to yield samples close to vernacular speech, and the reading of texts, sentences, and individual words. In addition, evaluative judgments were elicited from the subjects about paired variants. For example, they were asked to choose which of two renditions of the same utterance represented their habitual pronunciation (self-evaluation) and to indicate which of two renditions they preferred (normative judgment). The comparison of the scores in these two types of judgments yielded an index of *linguistic insecurity:* the more the second type of judgment differed in the direction of the orthoepic variant [è], the greater the linguistic insecurity inferred.

The results of the Tours study demonstrated that in that area of France the

---

[3] The result of the Gueunier *et al.* (1978, 1984) studies demonstrates how unfounded is that belief. A study of the same variable among working-class Parisian adolescents (Léon, 1972) revealed that even speakers of nonstandard varieties of Parisian French make a nearly categorical distinction between [é] and [è]. Or, to state it differently, among these speakers the *è* variable shows little variation; it is generally realized as [è]. Thus, since a firmly rooted contrast between [é] and [è] (invariable *è*) is a central feature of Standard French, Parisian pronunciation adheres more closely to the norm, at least insofar as this particular variable is concerned.

è variable functions as a *linguistic marker,* since the proportion of valorized judgments shifts in direct proportion to increased attention to speech. Although there were significant differences among the three social strata constituting the subject population, all speakers showed a marked difference in the proportion of valorized ([è]) variants in directed conversation, on the one hand, and reading tasks, on the other—about 5% and 55%, respectively, for the group as a whole. In addition, the linguistic insecurity index (the difference between auto-evaluation and normative judgment) was relatively low, 14%, compared to three other areas of France where regional varieties of French or other languages are still spoken (Lille, a Picard-speaking region; Limoges, an Occitan-speaking region; and Saint-Denis-de-la-Réunion, a Creole-speaking overseas department; see Table 2).

The application of Gueunier's methodology to the two groups of American learners produced markedly different results. The first group comprises seven graduate student instructors, most of whom had recently spent one year studying in France. The recordings of directed conversations designed to elicit verb forms containing the *è* variable (the imperfect, the future, and the conditional) were conducted by two native speakers and were transcribed by advanced graduate students in French linguistics; each recording was transcribed by two different judges. To obtain samples of more attended speech, the subjects were asked to read a set of sentences containing 18 instances of the variable under study representing the three morpheme classes and individual lexical items (see Table 1). The last sentence served as a control for the potential hypercorrect pronunciation of the invariable *é,* generally pronounced [é] in all parts of France. The subjects were asked to make auto-evaluative and normative judgments about paired renditions of the same utterance, one containing the high-mid variant [é] and the other the valorized low-mid variant [è]. In addition, they were asked to indicate whether items in a list were pronounced correctly or incorrectly. In all three tasks requiring a judgment, the subjects were provided the spelling of the variable words. Finally, the subjects' ability to distinguish between the two phonetic variants of the variable, namely, between [é] and [è], was ascertained by two different discrimination tasks (see Table 3).

Table 2. Linguistic Insecurity as a Function of Positive Answers to the Question: "Do You Have an Accent?"

Region	Percent insecurity
Tours	6.5
Lille (Picard regional variety)	57
Limoges (Occitan-speaking)	77
Saint-Denis-de-la-Réunion (Creole-speaking)	89

Table 3. Production and Evaluation of è Variable by American Graduate
French Instructors

Subject	Production tasks		Discrimination tasks		Perception tasks	
	Directed conversation (%)	Sentence reading (%)	Sound discrimination (%)	Sound–word correspondence (%)	Estimated use (%)	Preference (%)
2–7	54	24 (−30)	50	40	63	71 (+8)
2–8	46	56 (+10)	30	60	75	83 (+8)
2–9	44	71 (+27)	30	60	67	40 (−27)
2–10	44	47 (+3)	50	60	63	71 (+8)
2–6	39	72 (+33)	30	40	44	40 (−4)
1–1	23	44 (+19)	67	40	89	86 (−3)
1–3	12	24 (+12)	50	40	56	33 (−23)
Averages	37	48	45	49	65	64

As a group these advanced learners showed some sensitivity to the socio-linguistic value of the *è* variable: the proportion of their use of the valorized variant [è] rose from 37% to 48% with a shift to reading style. But the difference in the use of that variant in the two styles was much narrower than among the Tours speakers. Particularly noteworthy is the fact that, unlike the French speakers surveyed in the Gueunier *et al.* (1978) study, the American instructors of French showed no linguistic insecurity; the difference between their self-evaluation and their normative judgment (labeled *Preference* in Table 3) was −1%, with a range in individual indexes from +8 to −27. In addition, they overestimated their use of the [è] variant: 65% versus 48% in sentence reading and only 37% in directed conversation. The results of the data from the group of advanced undergraduate learners correspond closely to those of the graduate students, except that the former appear to evaluate more realistically their production of the variants of the variable feature (see Table 4). This may be interpreted as an effect of their training, which stressed the contrast between the two canonical values of the variable and included considerable discrimination training. To be sure, the results are not fully comparable between the two groups because of the difference in the size of the two populations and because the undergraduates' use of the two variants was not observed in guided conversation.

The results of these pilot studies support the claim that classroom foreign language learners speak "better" than even those native speakers whose behavior more closely approximates the highest-valued norm of their community. In the most formal style, reading of isolated words, middle-class Tours speakers produced only 47% of [è] variants. In reading of sentences they showed only

11% [è], as oppossed to 48% for the graduate students and 62% for the undergraduates. But precisely because they show a higher proportion of the more
highly valued [è] variant in the experimental mode that most closely approximates communicative use, the American learners distinguish themselves from
native speakers. To put it differently, they are still operating within an interlinguistic continuum. To pass as native speakers with respect to the è variable,
they must learn to introduce a larger proportion of the lesser-valued variant [é]
in communicative interactions.

It will be recalled that the graduate student subjects served as instructors
in beginning French classes. Their highly normative behavior with respect to
the variable studied supports the claim made earlier that the foreign language
classroom constitutes a special learning environment. Even though their production of the valorized variant falls quite short of their estimated use (37%
and 48% in directed conversation and sentence reading, respectively), the frequency of occurrence of that variant in their classroom speech would greatly
exceed that which learners would hear from native speakers in natural situations. From a sociolinguistic perspective one would say that the input they
provide to classroom learners is considerably impoverished, for it does not
contain the information on the basis of which the latter may derive appropriate
sociolinguistic rules.

5. PEDAGOGICAL NORMS

5.1. The Notion of Pedagogical Norm

In my introductory remarks I suggested that a surer road to the attainment
of the full range of native speakers' speech continua lies in the rejection of
traditional prescriptive norms in favor of more flexible continua. I would like
to apply the results of the study on the acquisition of the French è variable to
the issue of pedagogical norm, but before I do, I would like to define that
notion.

A pedagogical norm, like all norms, is an abstraction. Its distinguishing
feature resides in the fact that it is an artificial construct reflecting the special
conditions of classroom foreign language learning. Four principles guide the
elaboration of pedagogical norms. First, as suggested earlier, they should reflect the actual behavior of target-language speakers in authentic communicative situations. Second, they should conform to native speakers' idealized view
of their speech use. Third, they should conform to expectations of both native
speakers and foreign learners concerning the type of linguistic behavior appropriate for foreign learners. Fourth, they should take into account processing
and learning factors.

Table 4. Use and Production of e Variable by Advanced American Learners

	American graduate French instructors[a]	American undergraduate students[b]
Sentence reading (%)	48	62
Sound discrimination (%)	45	68
Sound–word correspondence (%)	49	54
Estimated use (%)	65	42
Preference (%)	64	47
Correct prescriptive judgments on deviant [é] (%)	33	43
Wrong prescriptive judgments on variable è (%)	32	32
Wrong prescriptive judgments on invariable [é] (%)	38	25

[a] $n = 7$.
[b] $n = 28$.

5.2. Pedagogical Implications of the è Variable Study

Although they evidence frequencies of use of the valorized [è] variant superior to those of a representative sample of ENSs (the Class 3 subjects of the Gueunier *et al.*, 1978, study), the advanced American learners of French deviated from them in several ways. For example, the graduate students discriminated inconsistently between the two canonical values of the variable. They scored only 45% and 49%, respectively, in two discrimination tasks, much lower than a group of southern French speakers (see Table 5). The southern speakers generally produced the è variable as [é], but they were better able to hear the difference between [é] and [è]. That the advanced learners were still operating within an interlinguistic system manifested itself also by inaccurate renditions of the two canonical variants, particularly gliding in final position. Their assignment of the variants to the various morphological and lexical classes was also erratic. In the sentence-reading task, they did not consistently differentiate potentially contrasting verb forms. In orthoepic French, the phonemic distinction [é] versus [è] potentially opposes the first-person singular future form to the corresponding conditional form, respectively, and the past participle to the singular and third-person plural form of the imperfect. These distinctions are not made consistently by the graduate student instructors (see Table 6).

To what degree advanced learners should adhere to the orthoepic norm is a decision that they and their instructors need to make for themselves. But the traditional approach which requires learners to differentiate between [é] and [è]

Table 5. Comparison of the Use of the é Variable

	Native speakers from Nice[a]	American graduate French instructors[b]	American undergraduate students[c]
Sentence reading (%)	—	48	62
Sound discrimination (%)	94	45	68
Sound–word correspondence (%)	63	49	54
Estimated use (%)	37	65	42
Preference (%)	30	64	47
Correct prescriptive judgments on deviant [é] (%)	38	33	43
Wrong prescriptive judgments on variable è (%)	50	32	32
Wrong prescriptive judgments on invariable [é] (%)	6	38	25

[a] $n = 15$.
[b] $n = 7$.
[c] $n = 28$.

Table 6. Performance on Prescriptive Judgment Task by American Graduate French Instructors

	Subjects							Average
	1-1	1-3	2-6	2-7	2-8	2-9	1-10	
Percent correct prescriptive judgments on use of deviant [é] in: *il dirait, elle dansait, je sortais, projets, suspect, laid, je vais*	0	29	14	14	71	57	43	33
Percent wrong prescriptive judgments on variable è in: *je serai* [è] (norm = [é]) *je prendrai* [é] (norm = [é]) *saison* [è] *tu dirais* [è]	0	25	50	75	50	0	25	32
Percent wrong prescriptive judgments on invariable [é] in: *ouvrez* [é] *poignée* [é] *boucher* [è]	33	33	67	33	33	67	0	38

from the very beginning and to distribute these two phonemes appropriately in morphemes and lexical items fails to take native speaker variability into account. It also assumes that target-language features are acquired linearly in a one-step operation, an assumption which in the area of phonology was falsified by the Dickersons' (1975, 1976) pioneering interlinguistic studies. On the contrary, learning proceeds by gradual approximation and involves the elaboration of highly variable autonomous interlinguistic systems (Corder, 1977; Nemser, 1971; Selinker, 1972). The following would be a dynamic pedagogical norm that would lead learners of French to gradually approximate the orthoepic norm for the *è* variable.

In their vernacular speech, Gueunier's Tours subjects, like the majority of French speakers, do not generally distinguish between the two front unrounded mid vowels [é] occurring in free syllables, and low-mid [è] occurring in checked syllables. This symmetrical distribution, which in some varieties of French extends to all mid vowels, is termed the *Loi de Position*. The distribution of the two vowels according to this rule does not lead to stigmatized pronunciation. Thus, it forms the basis for a pedagogical norm, that is, an interlinguistic system which (1) is simpler than the orthoepic norm, (2) conforms to the overt behavior of target native speakers, (3) is not viewed negatively by target native speakers, and (4) represents an intermediate step toward the orthoepic norm. Progression toward the latter would take the form of learning "exceptions" to the *Loi de Position,* that is, learners would gradually memorize morphemes and lexical items that contain [è] in their orthoepic variant. First, the exceptional low-mid vowel would be assigned to morphemes, such as first-person future, the plural, and third-person singular endings of the imperfect and the conditional, so that learners could distinguish such contrasts as *il a tiré* 'he shot' versus *il tirait* 'he was shooting' or *j'irai* 'I'll go' versus *j'irais* 'I would go.' Next, individual items would be added to the exceptional list as they were being introduced in the materials and classroom activities. Finally, wider generalizations would be made involving orthographic representations, for example, *-et, -ai, -ais,* and the like. In the proposed interlinguistic system, the *Loi de Position* would characterize the basilectal pole in the learners' interlinguistic system; the more complex behavior, approximating the orthoepic norm, would represent the mesolectal pole. Predictably, learners would revert to the *Loi de Position* in unattended speech, and, conversely, they would show greater conformity to the orthoepic norm in more formal situations. But this is precisely what is done by target speakers, who potentially contrast the two variants of the *è* variable. It is evident that, although their variable interlinguistic system departs from that of native speakers by its partial lack of coherence, the advanced American learners have drawn very close to the target.

6. CONCLUSION

I have attempted to show that one of the responsibilities of applied linguists is to formulate special norms suitable for learners who acquire a foreign language by means of formal instruction. Pedagogical norms should be dynamic. At the beginning level, learners should be exposed to models that involve the simplest syntactic machinery and offer the most regular target-language patterns. Where social and geographical diversity exists, sociolinguistic factors will be abandoned in favor of psycholinguistic ones: those variants will be selected that are most easily processible by second-language learners. It should be stressed that this approach does not involve the teaching of a pidginized form of the target language. The features that constitute the pedagogical norm do not have their origin in learners' interlinguistic approximations: they are drawn from variants occurring in a composite of actual native speech.[4] As instruction progresses, and as learners become more capable of processing the more complex syntactic features characteristic of planned formal discourse, the pedagogical norm must increasingly take into account sociolinguistic considerations. As I have shown, not only native speakers of the target-language community, but the learners themselves, set as suitable for formal foreign language instruction that variety of the target language which enjoys the greatest prestige and which, therefore, represents the most worthwhile investment.

REFERENCES

Bourdieu, P. (1977). L'économie des changements linguistiques. *Langue Française, 34*, 17–34.

Chaudenson, R. (1986). Norme, variation, créolisation. *AILA Review, 2*, 69–88.

Corder, S. P. (1977). Language continua and the Interlanguage Hypothesis. In S. P. Corder & E. Roulet (Eds.), *Actes du 5ème Colloque de Linguistique Appliquée de Neuchâfatel: The notions of simplification, interlanguages and pidgins and their relation to second language pedagogy* (pp. 11–17). Geneva: Librairie Droz.

d'Anglejan, A. (1983). Introduction to special issue, native speaker reactions to learner speech. *Studies in Second Language Acquisition, 5*(2), vii–ix.

Dickerson, L. (1975). The learner's interlanguage as a system of variable rules. *TESOL Quarterly, 9*, 401–407.

Dickerson, W. (1976). The psycholinguistic unity of language learning and language change. *Language Learning, 26*, 215–231.

Edmonson, W. J. (1985). Discourse worlds in the classroom and foreign language learning. *Studies in Second Language Acquisition, 7*, 159–168.

---

[4] Although a pedagogical norm should not include interlinguistic features that deviate from the target language, it may comprise features that are sociolinguistically stigmatized. In Valdman (1975, 1976, 1983), I show that American English appears to find most processible a variant interrogative structure of French that, though most frequent in the unplanned speech of native speakers, is highly stigmatized as non-standard.

Eisenstein, M. (1982). A study of social variation in adult second language acquisition. *Language Learning, 32*, 367–391.

Eisenstein, M. (1987). Target language variation and second-language acquisition: Learning English in New York City. *World Englishes, 5*, 31–46.

Faerch, C. & Kasper, G. (1985). Introduction to special issue, foreign language learning under classroom conditions. *Studies in Second Language Acquisition, 7*, 131–133.

Gueunier, N., Genouvrier, E., & Khomsi, A. (1978). *Les Français devant la norme: Contribution a une étude de la norme en français parlé.* Paris: Champion.

Gueunier, N., Genouvrier, E., & Khomsi, A. (1984). Les Français devant la norme. In E. Bédard & J. Maurais (Eds.), *La norme linguistique* (pp. 763–787). Québec: Conseil de la Langue Française; Paris: Le Robert.

Kramsch, C. J. (1985). Classroom interaction and discourse options. *Studies in Second Language Acquisition, 7*, 169–183.

Labov, W. (1966). *The social stratification of English in New York City.* Washington, DC: Center for Applied Linguistics.

Labov, W. (1972). *Sociolingistic patterns.* Philadelphia: University of Pennsylvania Press.

Le Page, R., & Tabouret-Keller, A. (1985). *Acts of identity: Creole-based approaches to language and ethnicity.* Cambridge: Cambridge University Press.

Léon, P. R. (1972). Etude de la prononciation de e accentué chez un groupe de jeunes Parisiens. In A. Valdman (Ed.), *Papers in linguistics and phonetics to the memory of Pierre Delattre* (pp. 317–328). The Hague: Mouton.

Léon, P. R. (1973). Reflexions idiomatologiques sur l'accent en tant que métaphore sociolinguistique. *French Review, 46,* 783–789.

Nemser, W. (1971). Approximative systems of foreign language learners. *International Review of Applied Linguistics, 9,* 115–123.

Ochs, E. (1979). Planned and unplanned discourse. In T. Givon (Ed.), *Syntax and semantics, Vol. 12: Discourse and semantics* (pp. 51–80). New York: Academic Press.

Palmer, H. (1917). *The scientific study and teaching of languages.* London: Harrap.

Ryan, E. B. (1983). Social psychological mechanisms underlying native speaker evaluations of non-native speech. *Studies in Second Language Acquisition, 5,* 148–159.

Selinker, L. (1972). Interlanguage. *International Review of Applied Linguistics, 10,* 209–231.

Soulé-Susbielles, N. (1984). La question, un outil pédagogique dépassé? *Le Français dans le Monde, 183,* 26–34.

Swacker, M. (1976). When (+native) is (−favourable). *Lektos, special issue,* 135–254. (ERIC ED 135 254)

Tarone, E. (1979). Interlanguage as chameleon. *Language Learning, 29,* 181–191.

Tarone, E. (1983). On the variability of interlanguage systems. *Applied Linguistics, 4,* 149–163.

Valdman, A. (1975). Error analysis and pedagogical ordering. In S. P. Corder & E. Roulet (Eds.), *Some implications of linguistic theory for applied linguistics* (pp. 105–126). Paris: Didier.

Valdman, A. (1976). Variation linguistique et norme pédagogique dans l'enseignement du français langue étrangère. *Bulletin de la Féderation Internationale des Professeurs de Français, 12–13,* 52–64.

Valdman, A. (1983). Language variation and foreign language teaching: Issues and orientations. In L. MacMathuna & D. M. Singleton (Eds.), *Language across cultures. Proceedings of a symposium held at St. Patrick's College, Drumcondra, Dublin, 8–9 July 1983* (pp. 171–184). Dublin: Irish Association for Applied Linguistics.

Widdowson, H. G. (1976). The significance of simplification. *Studies in Second Language Acquisition, 1,* 11–20.

CHAPTER 17

Discourse Conditioned Tense Variation
Teacher Implications

NATHALIE BAILEY

1. BACKGROUND

Grammar in its broadest definition is a form–meaning relationship, and there is almost nothing in language that is outside of that domain. Rutherford (1987a) speaks of language learning as the intersection of three systems: grammar, semantics, and discourse. He identifies semantics and discourse as the forces that shape language form and comprise the context within which the language learner becomes conscious of grammar. Rutherford's position tends to separate grammar from meaning by regarding grammar as form only. On the other hand, he recasts the relationship of form and meaning by triangulating it with discourse function. Larsen-Freeman (1987) also uses a three-part system to analyze the notion of learning difficulty in second-language learning. She claims that for any grammatical structure, either form, meaning, or pragmatics will be the key or essential learning difficulty. This position reflects growing awareness of the interconnectedness of all of the elements of language. This is a necessary stage of consciousness-raising on the part of both second-language acquirers and researchers and one to which this chapter contributes. It remains to be seen whether a three-part division of language is superior to a two-level analysis: form–meaning or form–function.

NATHALIE BAILEY • Puerto Rican Studies Department and ESL Program, Lehman College, Bronx, New York 10468, and Ph.D. Program in Linguistics, Graduate Center of CUNY, New York, New York 10036.

The study which I am reporting on in this chapter investigates the extent to which form, meaning, and function constrain the learning of the progressive in English. The answer that has most often been given in the second-language acquisition literature is that in the case of the present progressive, form is learned before function, especially in studies involving children (Hatch, 1984; Lightbown & Spada, 1979; Olshtain, 1979; Wagner-Gough, 1975). In studies involving adolescents and adults, a variety of explanations have been given for early progressive acquisition. Bailey, Madden, and Krashen (1974) reported that the progressive was the least difficult English morpheme for learners of diverse language backgrounds, but they did not explain why. Larsen-Freeman (1976) found the same result and attributed it to frequency of input. Pica (1983) concluded that much remains to be learned about the use of the progressive in discourse.

In a study of grammatical development in a 5-year-old child named Homer, Wagner-Gough and Hatch (1975) hypothesized that the simplicity of the form of the progressive may have accounted for its early acquisition. Referring to the *ing* suffix, they noted that the perceptual salience, regularity, and non-stem-changing nature of progressive morphology could account for its ease of acquisition. The form of the progressive was learned before the function, they felt, because Homer's progressive never distinguished semantic function (i.e., contrasted with the simple present). Frith (1977) also claimed that the progressive was used in free variation in its initial stages of learning by adolescents, who were inconsistent in their use of progressive forms and functions, many times failing to distinguish the past progressive from the present progressive. Similarly, Olshtain (1979) concluded that her 7-year-old subject was learning form before function because she sometimes used the progressive where the simple present was required, showing that its functional distribution had not been properly understood.

The object of this study is to investigate whether there is variable learning of the progressive in the present and in the past and whether this tense variation might be conditioned by discourse function. The common assumption in much second-language literature is that the past progressive is learned together with the present progressive because of its nearly identical form and apparent closeness of meaning. Frith presents this point of view when she says:

> The present progressive forms should not be explained in a completely different way from the past progressive forms. The present progressive form is a descriptive background to the actual moment of speaking, just as the past progressive is a descriptive background to another act in the past. (1979, p. 69)

While this position on the common background nature of the progressive has been maintained in linguistic literature in the past in connection with creole studies, current theory is more divided.

According to Woisetschlaeger (1980), the progressive is *phenomenal* or observable rather than *structural* or known (but not in the process of being observed). In the opinion of this researcher, this characterization of the progressive serves to distinguish very nicely the difference between the progressive and the simple in the present tense, but not in the past tense, even though Woisetschlaeger does not specify that his theory is limited to the present tense. By this analysis, the present progressive means *now,* and the simple present means *now* and *always.* The progressive is temporary, and the simple is habitual or universal or, generally speaking, a matter of knowledge. The meaning of the statement "She is living in Manhattan" as opposed to "She lives in Manhattan" conveys the difference between a temporary observation and a statement of fact.

Hopper and Thompson (1980) offer a slightly different interpretation of the meaning of the progressive. They claim that the progressive represents background information, and they cite its correlation with low transitivity (lack of clear results, lack of affected objects, and low number of participants). Unfortunately, they do not distinguish between the present progressive and the past progressive either, despite the fact that tne present progressive and the past progressive have different functions in discourse. The past progressive provides background information, and the present progressive presents foreground information. Background versus foreground, as in the sentence *He was talking on the telephone when I arrived,* distinguishes the progressive from the simple in the past. The simple past encodes completed past events, typically in a chronological, easy to understand order. The past progressive provides background information which is normally ordered before foreground information but can occur in flashback fashion embedded in the complication action section of a narrative (Labov, 1972).

Putting Hopper and Thompson's theory together with Woisetschlaeger's theory creates a more complete picture of the contrasting background and foreground functions of the progressive in the present tense and in the past tense. In the present, the simple present supplies background information, whereas the present progressive tells what is happening at the moment, for example, *Mary teaches at the Graduate Center. She's writing a book on markedness.* The simple past represents foreground events which are separate and completed, and the past progressive describes the setting in which the actions took place. An example is the sentence *Louie was reading when his wife came in. Reading* in this sentence describes the background activity to the punctual foreground event *came in.*

As the result of its background discourse function, the past progressive commonly occurs in subordinate clauses and, therefore, has a more complex syntactic usage than the simple past, in which a single event can be mentioned in isolation or two or more simple past events can be related without the aid of an adverbial clause, as in the sentence *We jumped in the car, turned on the motor, and took off.* A chronological order of occurrence is implicit in the order of mention of simple past events as opposed to past progressive events, which may overlap simple past events and even each other.

Foreground function in discourse and chronological order of mention both predict that the simple past will be acquired earlier than the past progressive. This variation from the present tense in which the progressive is acquired before the simple is conditioned by the greater importance of the foreground function over the background function in discourse.

In addition to discourse function, the semantic meaning of the progressive is more difficult in the past than in the present. The past progressive contains elements of both the present tense (ongoingness) and the past tense (completion). Comrie (1976) and Halliday (1976) call it a present in the past.

All of these meaning factors predict the late acquisition of the past progressive. How is it then that learners seem to use the progressive as the first marker of past meaning (Frith, 1977; Olshtain, 1979)? The reason for this could be that an early transfer stage exists wherein learners attempt to integrate their proficiency with the present progressive and their perception that the progressive is also used in the past by making a guess that the past progressive is the common and most useful past marker. Given the irregularity of the simple past, it would also be likely that learners would initially avoid using it. Hatori *et al.* (1987) found that the present progressive is heavily confused with the past progressive, indicating that transfer is probably going on.

2.   EXPERIMENT

A multiple measure experiment was designed to test the acquisition of the simple past and past progressive by measuring its accuracy and frequency of use by adults. About 1½ hours of oral and written production and imitation data was elicited from each of 26 ESL college students from four levels of proficiency (2–5) out of six in an intensive program at Queens College in New York. The resulting data were both cross-sectional and longitudinal, since each subject was tested twice over a 6-week interval.

At the initial testing (Time 1), subjects were first asked to write a story about a dangerous or embarrassing incident that had happened to them (following Labov, who originated danger of death narratives). A day or two later they were asked to retell the same story orally. At that time they were also given two cued picture tasks, one in which they told about and one in which they asked about a series of line drawings. Then they were given an imitation task based on four-frame Louie cartoons. Subjects were read two to four sentences about each of eight cartoons. They heard these sentences twice, once for understanding and once for repetition.

At Time 2, the storytelling task was adjusted to encourage more production. This time subjects were asked to tell their own stories about the Louie cartoons. The written production test was also revised at Time 2. This time they had to recreate in writing a modeled composition which was read aloud to them. This story was about a Middle Eastern folk hero, Nasreddin. This was a balanced task in which eight simple past verbs and the same number of past progressive verbs were used in the telling of the story. Both cued picture tasks were repeated at Time 2.

The design of the imitation task requires some explanation due to its complexity. Clause conditions were manipulated by making each sentence a combination of either a past progressive and a simple past or two of either one and varying the order of presentation of the simple past and the past progressive. Twenty-four sentences were given to the subjects for imitation, and because of the length of the task, one condition which remained constant was the order of clauses in each sentence, with the main clause preceding the subordinate clause. Each sentence for imitation comprised 15 syllables, which is a number thought to exceed short-term memory limitations.

3. RESULTS

The results of all of the tests taken together showed that the past progressive was learned later than the simple past. The simple past was used more accurately and more frequently than the past progressive on most tasks in this experiment (see Figures 1–10). The past progressive increased in frequency and accuracy later (at Level 5 in this experiment) than the simple past, which improved most dramatically on Levels 3 and 4. The dependent variables, accuracy and frequency, were measured by simple obligatory occasion methodology. Repeated measure ANOVAs were performed to confirm the statistical significance of the results. Significant independent variables included task, time, level, and grammatical structure. In addition to main effects, many interactions were found to be significant (see Bailey, 1987, for details on the statistical results).

3.1. Early Past Progressive Learning

One of the exceptions to the above generalization about the early superiority of the simple past occurred on Level 2 at Time 1 (see Figure 1) but was not evident by Time 2 (Figure 2). Past progressive frequency nearly equaled simple past frequency at Time 1 before changing dramatically at Time 2 to favor almost universal simple past use. This was interpreted as evidence that learners go through an early stage of progressive overuse in the past, due to transfer from the present tense.

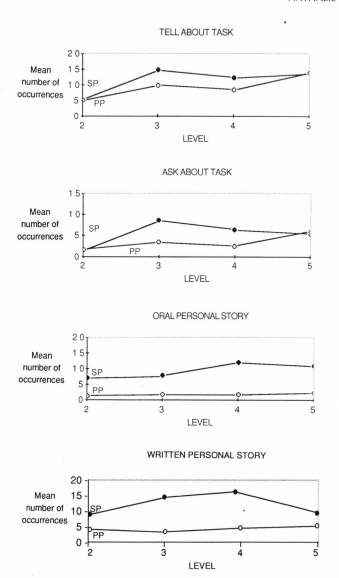

Figure 1. Production frequency (mean number of occurrences), Time 1; PP, past progressive; SP, simple past.

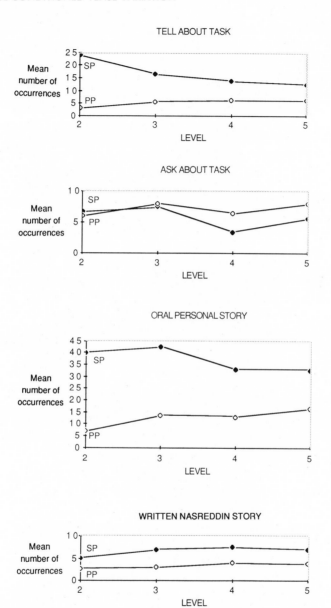

Figure 2. Production frequency (mean number of occurrences), Time 2; PP, past progressive; SP, simple past.

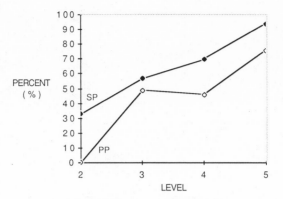

Figure 3. Accuracy on the tell-about task, Time 1.

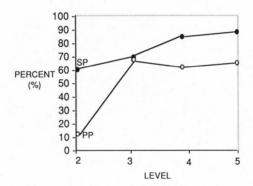

Figure 4. Accuracy on the tell-about task, Time 2.

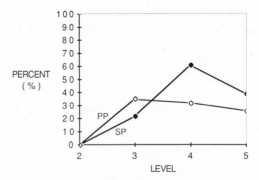

Figure 5. Accuracy on the ask-about task, Time 1.

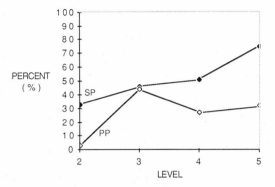

Figure 6. Accuracy on the ask-about task, Time 2.

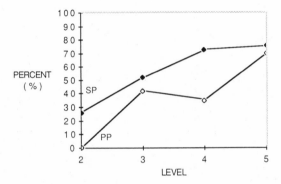

Figure 7. Accuracy on the oral personal story, Time 1.

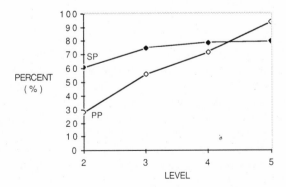

Figure 8. Accuracy on the oral cartoon story, Time 2.

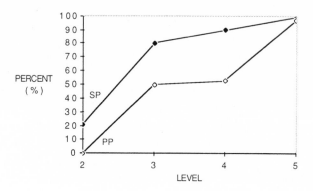

Figure 9. Accuracy on the written personal story, Time 1.

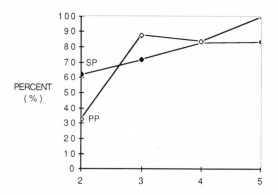

Figure 10. Accuracy on the written Nasreddin story, Time 2.

3.2. Question Asking

Another exception to the rule of early simple past acquisition occurred on the question-asking task. At Time 1, the past progressive exceeded the simple past in frequency on Level 2 (see Figure 1), but at Time 2, questions in the past progressive were more frequent on Levels 3, 4, and 5 (see Figure 2). This was interpreted to mean that the past progressive was easier for learners to use in question–answer sequences (all of the subjects' questions were answered by the examiners). The reason why it was considered easier for subjects to produce questions than statements in discourse was the isolated nature of question–answer sequences as compared to longer discourse units.

3.3. Writing

The personal story task given at Time 1 turned up some interesting variation in written versus oral production. The written personal story was longer and contained more past progressives than the same story told orally (see Figure 1), despite the fact that the written task preceded the oral task. It had been hoped that writing the story first would give subjects a chance to rehearse their story before what was expected to be a difficult oral task. However, the oral task was apparently even more difficult than was anticipated. It seems that the opportunity for subjects to monitor and edit what they produce in writing may be especially advantageous for such easily formed but complexly used grammar as the past progressive. Another possibility that must be considered is that past progressive distribution in relation to the simple past may be different in the written and the oral modes.

3.4. Regular versus Irregular Verbs

Learners' choice of tense was found to be influenced by complexity of form as well as by complexity of meaning, as seen in the distribution of regular and irregular verbs. Since irregularity is such an outstanding feature of simple past form, a special analysis was conducted of all of the verbs used on one task—the cartoon story retelling, Time 2. All verbs used in either the simple past or the past progressive on this task were categorized according to whether they had regular or irregular simple past forms. For example, verbs such as *come, go,* and *break* are irregular, and verbs such as *work, walk,* and *stay* are regular. The verbs that had been used in the simple past of this task were then sorted into regular and irregular categories, and the same was done for verbs that were used in the past progressive. It turned out that two-thirds of the verbs that subjects chose to use in the simple past were irregular. This in itself was not surprising. Kucera and Francis (1967) report that of the 30 most frequent past tense verbs, 22 are irregular. What was surprising, however, was that exactly the opposite ratio of irregular to regular verbs use was found for the past progressive. Two-thirds of all past progressive verbs were regular. An explanation for this systematic skewing of regular and irregular could be that it is a form effect. Learners may find it difficult to come up with the progressive form of an irregular verb because that involves using the regular stem. One learner, for instance, used the form *ranning* (for *running*) in the progressive, apparently unable to override the more frequently used simple past irregular. This close association of pastness and irregular form in the learners' minds may result in some avoidance of irregular verbs in the past progressive. Using a majority of regular verbs in the past progressive may be a formal means by which learners keep its meaning and use distinct from the simple past.

3.5.   Background before Foreground

Nothing in language learning is purely form related or meaning related, but, rather, it all seems to be a fascinating mixture of the two. The task of the researcher who tries to discover some pattern to the relationship of form and meaning is twofold: first, to tease form and meaning apart and second, to relate them. The following results have been defined as more meaning than form related. The first two come from the imitation task. When the sentences for imitation were presented in the order of past progressive clause before simple past, the accuracy of imitation was much greater than when the order was simple past before past progressive. The only explanation which seems reasonable is that the past progessive is understood better when it precedes the simple past in a sentence, because in that way background preceded foreground information in a given–new order (Givon, 1979). The order of mention is the order of occurrence. Examples of these two kinds of sentences are: *She was running away from the mouse when she heard the telephone ring,* and *She forgot about the mouse when she was talking.*

3.6.   Order of Mention

Another type of sentence that was tested had a combination of two past progressive clauses or two simple past clauses rather than one of each. This noncontrastive type of sentence produced unexpected evidence of the importance of order of mention. Sentences with two past progressives were imitated more accurately than sentences with two simple pasts. The reason seems to be that the overlapping action of the two past progressives meant that their order of occurrence was not a factor in their order of mention. For example, in the sentence *He was reading the newspaper while he was having breakfast,* the two events could be mentioned in either order and still have the same meaning with only a slight change of focus. On the other hand, a sentence with two simple past verbs, such as *She changed her dress when she read about the dress sale,* may not be presented in chronological order and, in fact, in this instance, is not; she actually read about the dress sale first. The difficulty the second-language learners in this study had imitating sentences which were unordered chronologically is reminiscent of the difficulty first-language learners have with *before* and *after* sentences (Clark, 1970).

3.7.   Subordinate before Main Clauses

An interesting finding on the cartoon-retelling task at Time 2 had to do with subordinate clause use. All of the two-clause utterances occurring on the cartoon storytelling task were categorized according to whether the subordinate clause or the main clause came first in the sentence and whether *while* or *when* was used. (See Figure 1; both Time-1 and Time-2 data appear for Level 5, since that group was asked to tell their own stories about the Louie cartoons at both testings.)

It was discovered that subjects preferred the order of subordinate clause before main clause. They also preferred to use sentences with two simple past verbs rather than sentences with one simple past and one past progressive. It is possible that learners begin to acquire subordination first by using the more familiar simple past and from there expand to producing the simple past and past progressive together in one sentence. These learners built slowly in their use of combined simple past tense and past progressive sentences, peaking at Level 4, Time 1, in their use of past progressive subordinate clauses ordered before the simple past main clause sentences. It was not until Levels 4 and 5 that main clause before subordinate clause sentences were produced.

In the case of two simple past clauses, the subordinate before main clause order is the one that preserves the actual order of occurrence of two events, for example, *When she came back, she brought his hat.* In the case of the past progressive before the simple past, the correct chronological order can be maintained with either the subordinate clause or the main clause coming first, as long as the past progressive precedes the simple past in background–foreground order. Examples of both types of chronologically correct orderings are as follows: *Louie was sitting on the chair when he heard the newspaper man,* and *When Louie was sleeping, his wife decided to take him inside to the kitchen.* It is very likely that this variation in form–meaning relationship contributes to the difficulty of learning the past progressive. In the case of the past progressive, chronological order is not rigidly signaled by clause type or order but rather by the meaning of the progressive itself. The progressive's difficult relational meaning is thus echoed in its variable clause use.

3.8.   First or Last Sentences

Another pattern which was observed on the Time-2 cartoon-retelling task was the occurrence of the past progressive in the first, second, or last sentences only (see Table 2). This finding is predicted in the literature on narrative structure (Labov, 1972), which points out that it is common to find many past progressives in the orientations section. Also, at the end of a narrative, a *coda* brings the listener back to the present, which could be why these second-language learners use the past progressive in that position.

4. IMPLICATIONS FOR TEACHERS

4.1. Summary

The most general implication of this study for teachers has to do with the most general finding that the past progressive is learned later than simple past, despite its easier morphological form, because it has a difficult semantic meaning, syntactic use, and discourse function. It functions as background to the simple past and has the marked past meaning of incomplete activity. Unlike the present progressive, which represents the most useful, core meaning of the present—ongoingness or incompletion—and therefore has a foreground discourse function, the past progressive does not mark the most common and useful meaning of the past but gives less essential background information.

4.2. Early Use and Late Learning

Teachers will find that the past progressive makes an early appearance in learner's interlanguage, possibly even before the simple past is marked in any way. Thus, it will appear that the past progressive is understood or, at least, that its form has been mastered. However, both meaning and form mastery are illusory at this early stage of past tense marking, because the progressive is functioning as an old form (common in the present) with a new meaning. It is a first guess for past tense marking.

Not until learners are very advanced do they start to overgeneralize the past progressive in the way they overgeneralize the present progressive and the simple past when they start to learn them, that is, by overusing them. Frequency of past progressive use goes up dramatically in advanced learners, showing that they are actively working on its distribution. A parallel situation in grammar learning exists with respect to present progressive and simple present learning (Eisenstein, Bailey, & Madden, 1982), where frequency of simple present use increases dramatically in advanced learners.

4.3. Question Asking

Due to the isolated nature of question–answer sequences, past progressive use in questions may be better understood than its use in assertions. Teachers might find that they can provide early comprehension practice on the past progressive with questions interjected during oral storytelling to amplify meaning (e.g., "What were you studying in Mexico?," "Were you working?," "Were you living with a family?"). Initially, learners may be more successful using the past progressive in interactive dialogues than in longer, more involved narratives.

4.4. Writing

The use of writing to encourage past progressive use is strongly indicated. Monitoring and planned discourse both seem to favor the past progressive. Writing could be started with presentation-of-self remarks and extended into narratives: journal entries, descriptions of events, and storytelling of all kinds. When learners are ready to learn the past progressive, writing may be the easiest way for them to make thoughtful selections of past progressive use.

4.5. Regular versus Irregular Verbs

The results of this experiment, although limited in scope, indicate that the majority of early simple past use is with irregular verbs, and the majority of past progressive use is with regular verbs. Learners identify the simple past with irregularly formed verbs apparently because the most frequently used simple past verbs are irregular. For that reason teachers might want to avoid irregular verb use in the past progressive or at least be aware of the learners' tendencies to do so. Where choice is available, regular verb use in the past progressive could be modeled or highlighted for clarity of formation purposes.

4.6. Clause Use

Another choice which teachers have in the presentation of models for understanding the past progressive is the matter of clauses. Clauses themselves may be a big problem for beginning learners. We have to question the customary method of introducing past progressive use by contrasting it with simple past use in the same sentence using a subordinate clause, for example, *I was eating breakfast when the doorbell rang.* This establishes the relational meaning of the past progressive, but that is a very difficult meaning for a learner to grasp. More helpful useage to model would be a more isolated single clause usage, such as *I was studying until midnight last night.* Bearing in mind the background nature of the past progressive and its correlation with low transitivity, teachers might present models for past progressive use which involve no result, no affected object, and a low number of participants. Any verb used nontransitively, such as *work*, which has no object following the verb, will satisfy these conditions. Instead, the verb will most helpfully be followed by adverbials such as *all day*, *yesterday*, *until noon yesterday*, and the like. This appears to be the earliest way in which learners use the past progressive.

4.7. Clause Order

Clause order has a lot to do with the clarity of meaning, as has been seen in the imitation results of this experiment. Mentioning past progressive activities before simple past events seems to facilitate listener understanding because of the resulting more natural background before foreground sentence order. Using *when* instead of *while* as a subordinating conjunction, as was favored by the subjects of this experiment, also seems to clarify the relationship of the past progressive to the simple past by providing an exact reference point in the past.

While use began much later than *when* use in subordinate clauses, even though *while* is heavily used with the past progressive in ESL texts. Overinsistence on *while* use may be counterproductive.

4.8. First Sentence

An ideal way for teachers to raise consciousness of past progressive use would be to begin stories with the past progressive and to use it initially only in that position. A bad way to introduce the past progressive would be to use it excessively in a given discourse unit, especially in complex sentences. ESL texts frequently overdo the density of past progressive to simple past use. They also try too hard to be clear about the meaning of the past progressive by using it in complex sentences.

4.9. Background versus Foreground

Bearing in mind the importance of the background function of past progressive use as opposed to the foreground function of the present progressive, the use of authentic or simulated authentic material in the classroom is strongly recommended. In this way learners will be exposed to actual distribution patterns in terms of both position in text and syntactic use. Whether a communicative competence model of classroom learning or a grammatical syllabus model is used, it will be advisable for teachers to forgo insistence upon past progressive use until learners are ready to acquire its difficult function. Even before students indicate their readiness to learn the past progressive by their attempts to use it, however, teachers can productively expose them to actual examples of past progressive use by native speakers (especially written uses, as in magazine articles).

5. CONCLUSION

Nothing in language learning is purely form related or purely meaning related. Language must have both, and this is what is meant when it is said that language is a form–meaning relationship. The importance of form and meaning may vary according to specific structures (Larsen-Freeman, 1987), with meaning sometimes representing the learning difficulty and form sometimes assuming greater importance. Language clearly is always a fascinating mixture of elements, with the task of the researcher being to find patterns in their relationships. At the present time a productive division of these elements seems to be into form and function. Ellis (1986), after surveying second-language acquisition research, calls for more attention to both of these aspects of language development.

REFERENCES

Bailey, N. (1987). The importance of meaning over form in second language system building: An unresolved issue. Ph.D. thesis. Graduate Center, City University of New York.

Bailey, N., Madden C., & Krashen, S. (1974). Is there a 'natural sequence' in second language acquisition? *Language Learning, 25,* 235–244.

Clark, E. (1970). How children describe events in time. In F. D'Arcais & W. Levelt (Eds.), *Advances in psycholinguistics* (pp. 275–284). New York: American Elsevier.

Comrie, B. (1976). *Aspect.* New York: Cambridge University Press.

Eisenstein, M., Bailey N., & Madden, C. (1982). It takes two: Contrasting tasks and contrasting structures. *TESOL Quarterly, 16,* 381–393.

Ellis, R. (1986). *Understanding second language acquisition.* Oxford: Oxford University Press.

Frith, M. B. (1977). *A study of form and function at two stages of developing interlanguages.* Bloomington: Indiana University Linguistics Club.

Givon, T. (1979). *On understanding grammar.* New York: Academic Press.

Halliday, M. (1976). The English verbal group. In G. Kress (Ed.), *Halliday: System and function in language.* London: Oxford University Press.

Hatch, E. (1974). Second language—universals? *Working Papers in Bilingualism, 3,* 1–17.

Hatori, H., Horiguchi, T., Itoh, K., Kanatani, K., Noda, T., Murai, M, & Yutaka, Y., (1987). *Acquisition of English tense and aspect: In the case of Japanese learners of English* (Interlanguage Development Research Project, Report No, 1). Tokyo: Tokyo Gakugei University.

Hopper, P., & Thompson, S. (1980). Transitivity in grammar and discourse. *Language, 56,* 251–299.

Huebner, T. (1985). *A longitudinal analysis of the acquisition of English.* Ann Arbor, MI: Karoma Press.

Kucera, H., & Francis, N. (1967). *Computational analysis of present-day American English.* Providence, RI: Brown University Press.

Labov, W. (1972). *Language in the inner city: Studies in the Black English vernacular.* Philadelphia: University of Pennsylvania Press.

Larsen-Freeman, D. (1976). *ESL teacher speech input to the ESL Learner.* Workpapers in TESL, UCLA.

Larsen-Freeman, D. (1987, December). *Developing strategies for teaching grammar.* Plenary address at Grammar Teaching and Grammar Learning conference, Atlanta, Georgia.

Lightbown, P., & Spada, N. (1979). *Can language acquisition be altered by instruction?* In K. Hyltenstam & M. Pienemann (Eds.), *Modelling and assessing second language acquisition* (pp. 101–112). San Diego, CA: College-Hill Press.

Olshtain, E. (1979). The acquisition of the English progressive: A case study of a seven-year-old Hebrew speaker. *Working Papers in Bilingualism, 18,* 81–102.

Pica, T. (1983). Adult acquisition of English as a second language under different conditions of exposure. *Language Learning, 33,* 465–497.

Rutherford, W. (1987a). *Second language grammar: Learning and teaching.* New York: Longman.

Wagner-Gough, J. (1975). *Comparative studies in second language learning.* Unpublished master's thesis, University of California, Los Angeles.

Wagner-Gough, J., & Hatch, E. (1975). The importance of input data in second language acquisition studies. *Language Learning, 25,* 277–308.

Woisetschlaeger, E. (1980). *A semantic theory of the English auxiliary system.* Bloomington: The Indiana University Linguistics Club.

CHAPTER 18

The Colloquial Preterit
Language Variation and the ESL Classroom

HELAINE W. MARSHALL

1. INTRODUCTION

A common cause of confusion for the learner of English as a second language (ESL) is the discrepancy between the rules learned in the classroom and the English used by native speakers outside the classroom. The mismatch is often the result of sociolinguistic factors that operate in spoken American English, causing native speakers to "break" the rules that ESL students have struggled to master. When language variation is not taken into consideration in ESL instruction and materials development, the students receive an inaccruate and confusing representation of current usage. This chapter focuses on syntactic variation, specifically in the present perfect, a notably problematic grammatical category in the ESL curriculum. Following a brief look at the most common approach to presenting the present perfect, the chapter describes a syntactic variation study, based on interviews with native speakers, and examines the findings of this study in light of the specific concerns of the ESL classroom. The final section proposes guidelines for a presentation of the present perfect that takes language variation into account and demonstrates how sociolinguistic analysis can have a direct bearing on ESL materials development.

An important part of most presentations of the present perfect in ESL classes is the differentiation between that form and the simple past, or the

---

HELAINE W. MARSHALL • Department of Communication Processes, University of Wisconsin–Green Bay, Green Bay, Wisconsin 54311.

preterit. Students are provided with sample sentences designed to illustrate how the two forms contrast, as in the following:

(1)

> Have you ever studied Spanish?
> Yes, I've taken two courses.
> *But:* I took two courses last year.

(2)

> Chuck has just returned from Seville.
> *But:* He returned three days ago.
> (Werner & Nelson, 1985, p. 15)

Commonly (Kapili & Kapili, 1985; Wishon & Burks, 1980; Wohl, 1978; and other ESL grammar texts), these examples are accompanied by a list of adverbs that co-occur with the present perfect, such as *ever, just,* and *already,* followed by exercises in which these adverbs contrast with adverbs of definite past time, such as *yesterday,* which require the use of the preterit form. However, the present researcher questioned whether contrasts between the perfect and the preterit accurately reflect current usage.

Thus, a tense variation study (Marshall, 1979) was designed to examine the use of the present perfect by native speakers of American English.[1] Results showed that the preterit is often used as an alternative to the perfect and can be found in sentences such as those in (1) and (2), where the perfect would traditionally be expected. Observe:

(3)

> Did you ever study Spanish?
> Yes, I already took two courses.

(4)

> Chuck just returned from Seville.

The use of the preterit as an alternative to the perfect will be referred to as the *colloquial preterit,* a term introduced by Vanneck (1958), who first investigated this phenomenon.

2.   BACKGROUND TO THE STUDY

The literature on the variation between the preterit and the present perfect is relatively sparse, the two major sources being Vanneck's, just cited, and

[1] The term *tense* is used here as it is used in most ESL texts such that the present perfect is refered to as a tense rather than an aspect. Because it is taught with this label and because we are here concerned solely with grammar as it is presented in ESL texts, the term *tense* has been chosen.

Defromont's (1973), an analysis of the present perfect in modern American plays. Vanneck (1958) obtained examples of the colloquial preterit in spontaneous speech. His data consisted of anonymous utterances, overheard and recorded by him in New York City. Observe:

(5)

    a. Did you have lunch (yet, already)?
    b. I live in New York but I never saw the St. Patrick's Day Parade.
    c. You missed him. He just went out. (pp. 238–239)

In such utterances, he believes, there is no longer an instinctive need by native speakers for the present perfect tense, and the traditional form is commonly replaced by the colloquial preterit. Vanneck claims that in informal conversation there are numerous instances in which British English would require the present perfect tense, while American English seems to allow the preterit.

Defromont (1973) conducted a more systematic analysis of the phenomenon. A representative sample of his examples from *Death of a Salesman* are given below:

(6)

    Willy: How much is he giving you?
    Biff: I don't know, I didn't even see him (Oliver) yet, but . . .

(7)

    Willy: They should've arrested the builder for cutting those trees down. They massacred the neighborhood. (pp. 101–103)

Defromont studies each example and shows it to be a predication that in British English would be expressed in the present perfect. He then shows how, for each example, the speaker relies on the context of the predication and any adverbs that may be present to convey the additional nuance normally expressed by the perfect marker. When no such aids are available, he claims, the speaker will use the perfect.

Although these are the two most extensive works on the colloquial preterit, other researchers have noted it as well (e.g., McCoard, 1978; Peterson, 1970; Traugott & Waterhouse, 1969).[2] All of these accounts characterize the colloquial preterit as distinctly American, restricted to certain linguistic environments, and found most commonly with adverbs such as those in the examples cited. Furthermore, it is suggested that sociolinguistic factors, such as degree of formality, may be relevant in determining its use.

The purpose of the study reported here was to determine the exact extent and nature of the colloquial preterit in an American speech community with a

[2]Comprehensive review of the relevant literature may be found in Marshall (1979).

view to revamping the presentation of the present perfect in ESL texts. Thus, in addition to documenting the colloquial preterit itself, it was necessary to develop a suitable theoretical framework for the perfect that would help to clarify those uses that are associated with the preterit alternative. Table 1, based on material from Leech (1971) and Dubois (1972), presents the present perfect as divided into six uses within three larger categories or, to use Dubois' term, overtones.

The single-action overtone characterizes an action which is viewed as occurring only once. Included in this category are: the recent past with *just, He's just sold his gas guzzler;* the recent indefinite past with *already* and *yet, Have they agreed on a fair price yet?*; and the present result with no adverb, *I'm afraid she's hurt herself.*

The second overtone, continuative, characterizes an action viewed as occurring over a period of time and includes: the general indefinite past with *always, never,* and *ever, Have you ever seen anything like it?*; and the period-up-to-the-present with durative expressions, *We've only lived here since last fall.*

The third and last overtone, iterative, characterizes an action viewed as occurring at least once and includes the meaning of more-than-once-before-now with frequency expressions, *I like that restaurant, I've eaten there several times.*

This framework provides the classification needed for relating the utterances produced by native speakers in the colloquial preterit study to uses of the present perfect.[3]

3. DESCRIPTION OF THE STUDY

The data for this study consisted of 30 interviews with native speakers of standard American English residing in Eastchester, New York. The sample population included informants from three age groups: 12-year-old children, their parents, and senior citizens. Within each age group, there were an equal number of informants from two socioeconomic levels, the lower middle class and the upper middle class.[4] The interview included role-playing as well as other speech situations designed to elicit spontaneous use of language.

---

[3] Following an examination of many perspectives on the present perfect, it was determined that a blend of these two perspectives provided the most promising framework for a classroom presentation in which the colloquial preterit could be properly identified. A complete discussion of the various analyses of the perfect, leading up to this choice of Leech and Dubois, may be found in Marshall (1979).

[4] Shuy, Wolfram, and Riley's *Field Techniques in an Urban Language Study* (1968) provided the basis for all sampling and interviewing procedures undertaken for the study. Class was calculated using a formula based on three factors: (1) education of head of household, (2) occupation of head of household, and (3) a rating for the place of residence.

Table 1. Classification of the Present Perfect

Single-action overtone	Characterizes an action which is viewed as occurring only once.	
Near past	*just*	He's just sold his gas guzzler.
Recent indefinite past	*already* *yet*	Have they agreed on a fair price yet?
Present result	(no adverb)	I'm afraid she's hurt herself.
Continuative overtone	Characterizes an action which is viewed as occurring over a period of time.	
General indefinite past	*always* *ever* *never*	Have you ever seen anything like it?
Period-up-to-the-present	*for* *since* (other durative expressions)	We've only lived here since fall.
Iterative overtone	Characterizes an action which is viewed as repeated at least once.	
More-than-once-before-now	(frequency expressions)	I like that restaurant. I've eaten there several times.

Note. Adapted from Leech (1971, pp. 35–41), and Dubois (1972, pp. 47–50).

Seven adverbs were selected for the study, and all of the tasks and exercises were designed to elicit one of these adverbs. The adverbs were: *already, yet, always, ever, never, just,* and *finally.* After several months of pilot work, these adverbs were chosen as those which seemed to be associated most often with the colloquial preterit. An example from the data of the preterit used with each of these adverbs is given below:

(8) Preterit with each adverb

    a. I *already* saw that movie.
    b. Did you stop the mail *yet?*
    c. Did you *ever* go skiing?
    d. I *never* heard of it.
    e. I *always* had good times here.
    f. They *just* got married.
    g. He *finally* sold the house.

In each case, the context required the perfect, and, in each case, many informants chose the perfect. For the same predications, then, both forms were elicited.

The percentage of preterits elicited for each adverb appears in Table 2. From these data, it is clear that the most commonly occurring preterits were with *finally* (83%) and *just* (80%). The perfect and preterit were used nearly equally for *always* (59%), *ever* (50%), and *never* (48%). The perfect was preferred, although by no means used exclusively, with *yet* (36%) and *already* (35%).

Details of the elicitation procedures are presented elsewhere (Marshall, 1979), but a sample task is given below to illustrate the manner in which a present perfect context was created during the interview:

(9)

Example of a task from the interview

Task name: Nagging Friend
Expected adverb: *already*
Stimulus: Why don't you . . .   You better . . .   Don't forget to . . .
Instructions: You are moving and you are ready to go.
　　　　　You want to get rid of me. Use *already*.
Informant: #80, an upper middle-class parent.

Form	Token #	Utterance
perfect	026	I've *already* taken care of that.
perfect	027	We've notified the post office that we are moving.
perfect	028	We've *never* had a newspaper delivered.
perfect	029	I've *already* notified the newspapers.
preterit	030	I *already* planned to have my mother-in-law come over to take the food away.
preterit	031	I *already* picked everything up at the cleaners. It's all packed.
preterit	032	I *already* did that. Yes. We use AMEX.
preterit	033	Helaine, I want to move. I *already* ate breakfast. I don't want any lunch.
preterit	034	I *already* saw that movie.
preterit	035	I *already* had my party, and I didn't invite you.

In this task, the interviewer played the role of a nagging friend who arrived on moving day with unsolicited advice for her neighbor. The informant was told to reject all suggestions and try to get rid of the nagging friend. The informant used both the preterit and the perfect here. A formal–informal distinction between the two forms appears to dominate, as the informant began with the present perfect (#026–29) and later, more annoyed and more involved in the role-play, switched to the colloquial preterit (#030–35). This pattern was typical.

Table 2. Percentage of Colloquial
Preterits in the 730 ITACs Broken
Down by Adverb

Adverb	%	n
Finally	83	83
Just	80	84
Always	59	117
Ever	50	89
Never	48	154
Yet	36	115
Already	35	88

Note. The unit of analysis was an ITAC, or
Informant Task Adverb Combination. An ITAC
consisted of all tokens elicited from one informant in one context with one adverb. A percentage of colloquial preterits for each combination was calculated, and the means of these
percentages per adverb resulted in the overall
figures presented here.[5]

Age and class patterns began to emerge in the data, revealing the preterit–
perfect variation as a sociolinguistic phenomenon. An analysis of the data broken down by adverb indicated age and class patterns that could be interpreted
to show how a different stage of development of the colloquial preterit is represented by each adverb. That is, each of the seven adverbs may be at a slightly
different point in the process of becoming widely used with the preterit, based
on the extent of its use by certain groups in the speech community.[5]

By way of example, the results for *never,* an adverb which appears to be
at an intermediate stage of change, are presented in Table 3. There was a
significant age difference: the children used the preterit 76% of the time; the
senior citizens, 42%; and the parents, 28%.

There was no significance for class overall, but there was instead a significant interaction effect between age and class. This interaction effect suggests
differences within age groups working in opposite directions, an interpretation
supported by the one-way analyses of variance. There was a significant class
difference for both adult age groups. The lower middle-class senior citizens
used the preterit significantly more than the upper middle-class senior citizens
(64% and 21%, respectively). The reverse was true, however, for the parents:
the lower middle class used the preterit only 18% of the time, and the upper
middle class used it 41% of the time. This pattern is consistent with Labov's

[5] A detailed analysis of each of the seven adverbs, with an interpretation of results as evidence of
change in progress, appears in Marshall (1981).

Table 3. Means and Standard Deviations of Percentages of Colloquial
Preterits Used with Never, Broken Down by Age and Class Groupings

	Class		
Age	Lower middle class	Upper middle class	Totals
Children	$n = 5$ $\bar{x} = 81$ $SD = 36$	$n = 5$ $\bar{x} = 70$ $SD = 40$	$n = 10$ $\bar{x} = 76$ $SD = 38$
Parents	$n = 5$ $\bar{x} = 18$ $SD = 36$	$n = 5$ $\bar{x} = 41$ $SD = 44$	$n = 10$ $\bar{x} = 28*$ $SD = 41$
Senior citizens	$n = 5$ $\bar{x} = 64$ $SD = 48$	$n = 5$ $\bar{x} = 21$ $SD = 34$	$n = 10$ $\bar{x} = 42**$ $SD = 41$
Totals	$n = 15$ $\bar{x} = 54*$ $SD = 48$	$n = 15$ $\bar{x} = 44*$ $SD = 44$	$n = 30$ $\bar{x} = 49**$ $SD = 46$

Note. An ANOVA was performed for significance of group differences.
*$p < .05$.
**$p < .001$.

(1972) model of language change in which the middle-aged, lower middle-class
speakers cling to the traditional form, here the present perfect, while the newer
form, the colloquial preterit, takes over the speech community.

This pattern for *never,* and that of the other six adverbs not presented here,
points toward the interpretation of the use of the colloquial preterit in place of
the present perfect as a sociolinguistically rooted syntactic change. A pilot study
of the colloquial preterit in another region, northeastern Wisconsin (Marshall,
1987), reveals similar patterns of colloquial preterit use among speakers in that
community. This investigation, essentially a replication of the original New
York study, was designed to determine whether or not the colloquial preterit
had spread to the North-Central states. In fact, the level of colloquial preterit
use is generally lower than in New York, but the distribution patterns among
speakers, according to the adverb used and their social class, support the analysis of the New York data. Thus, it may be claimed that the preterit is taking
over territory traditionally reserved for the perfect.

4. CATEGORIZATION OF STABLE AND VARIABLE USES

In this tense variation study, many types of utterances were found for
which both the perfect and the preterit were widely used by native speakers.

However, these utterances were not randomly distributed among all the uses of the present perfect. In fact, certain uses of the time relation were very susceptible to the variation, whereas others were highly resistant. For example, even with the presence of the adverbs that encourage the use of the preterit, that form appeared less often if a durative meaning was expressed in some way, as in

(10)
    a. We've already eaten all of it up.
    b. We've already eaten everything up that's in there.

Similarly, few preterits appeared when an iterative meaning was intended, as in

(11)
    a. I bet they've already visited the shore points.
    b. I bet they've already met the neighbors.

In fact, these informants switched from the colloquial preterit, which they had been using, to the present perfect for these utterances. Although some informants retained the preterit in examples such as these, the switching that did occur suggests that durative and iterative time expressions favor the present perfect.

The data on these two types were not extensive because the focus was on uses hypothesized as variable; however, the follow-up study in northeastern Wisconsin included tasks designed to test environments hypothesized as resistant to the variation. In these tasks, informants were asked to discuss recent accomplishments, given the cue *since 1980*, or to indicate how many times they had gone to a particular local attraction or restaurant. Informal analysis strongly suggests that the present perfect is the consistent choice in these contexts. There is also some corroborative evidence from other researchers suggesting that the durative type is beyond the scope of the variation. In their analyses of modern American plays, both Defromont (1973) and Peterson (1970) found that while the preterit was used for the types cited in the research here, the perfect was used almost exclusively when durative expressions, such as *for* or *since,* were present.

Returning to our original classification of present perfect uses, we can now identify the specific linguistic environments associated with the variation. Those uses corresponding to utterances in which colloquial preterits were commonly present in the data may be refereed to as *variable* uses of the perfect. Those uses corresponding to utterances in which the variation did not operate may be referred to as *stable* uses of the perfect. Table 4, an altered version of Table 1, indicates which of the six uses of the perfect were found to be variable and

Table 4. Classification of the Present Perfect with Stable and Variable Uses
Labeled

1.0 Single-action overtone	Characterizes an action which is viewed as occurring only once.		
1.1 Near past	*just*	He's just sold his gas guzzler. He just sold his gas guzzler.	Variable
1.2 Recent indefinite past	*already* *yet*	Have they agreed on a fair price yet? Did they agree on a fair price yet?	Variable
1.3 Present result	(no adverb)	I'm afraid she's hurt herself. I'm afraid she hurt herself.	Variable
2.0 Continuative overtone	Characterizes an action which viewed as occurring over a period of time.		
2.1 General indefinite past	*always* *ever* *never*	Have you ever seen anything like it? Did you ever see anything like it?	Variable
2.2 Period-up-to-the-present	*for* *since* (other durative expressions)	We've only lived here since last fall.	Stable
3.0 Iterative overtone	Characterizes an action which is viewed as repeated at least once.		
3.1 More-than-once-before-now	(frequency expressions)	I like that restaurant. I've eaten there several times.	Stable

Note. Adapted from Leech (1971, pp. 35–41), and Dubois (1972, pp. 47–50).

which, stable. Thus, all uses within the single-action overtone—1.1 near past, 1.2 recent indefinite past, and 1.3 present result—are labeled variable.[6] Within the continuative overtone, 2.1 general indefinite past is labeled variable, while 2.2 period-up-to-the-present is labeled stable. Finally, 3.1 more-than-once-before-now, representing the iterative overtone, is stable. For each of the four

---

[6] The resultative perfect with no adverb was not systematically studied as part of the colloquial preterit. However, numerous examples of tense switching appeared in the data, where the context for the present perfect was constant. Informants produced such pairs as *I skipped one/I've skipped one*, while responding to a list of items. This type also appears among the examples in other discussions of the colloquial preterit (Defromont, 1973, Vanneck, 1958).

variable perfects, a sentence using the colloquial preterit is given to demonstrate how the same use can be associated with either verb form, as, for example, 1.2 recent indefinite past:

(12)

    a. Have they agreed on a fair price yet?
    b. Did they agree on a fair price yet?

This classification accurately reflects current usage by dividing the perfect into practical categories which correspond to distinctions made by native speakers between environments in which only the perfect is used and environments in which the perfect and the colloquial preterit are alternatives. Thus, the categorization in Table 4 provides the necessary framework for a presentation of the present perfect that takes the colloquial preterit into account.

5.   THE COLLOQUIAL PRETERIT IN ESL TEXTS

We must now turn to the question of how to incorporate this information into the ESL syllabus. As mentioned earlier, the most common approach does not include material on language variaton and the present perfect. There are, however, a small number of texts in which some information is provided on the preterit as an alternative to the perfect (Danielson & Hayden, 1973; Dart, 1978; Frank, 1986; Leech & Svartvik, 1975). Frank (1986), for example, adds a footnote to the present perfect lesson, commenting that "informally, except for *since* and *for,* the past tense is often used with these time words that characterize past-to-present time" (p. 62). In completing the exercises, students are encouraged to "note where the past tense may be an informal alternative to the present perfect" (p. 64). A similar approach is taken in the teacher training materials provided by Celce-Murcia and Larsen-Freeman (1983). Teachers are informed about dialect differences between American and British English, which include the informal use by American speakers of the simple past with time adverbials traditionally reserved for the perfect, such as *just, already,* and *yet.*

A more extensive treatment of the variation appears in Martin, McChesney, Whalley, and Devlin (1977). In this text, students are provided with a list of adverbs under the heading "Past or Present Perfect." Included in this list are *just, already,* and *yet.* For each adverb, examples are given, one in the preterit and one in the present perfect, but there is no indication of why one tense is used instead of the other in these examples. In the following exercise, students are asked to indicate if sample sentences are correct or incorrect and to "discuss those cases in which either past or present perfect is acceptable" (Martin *et al.*, 1977, p. 40).

Undoubtedly, it is better to add a note or some examples of informal alternatives than to ignore the colloquial preterit totally; however, this could result in adding to the already confused picture students have of the present perfect. This is particularly true when the information is tied to lists of adverbs and sentences lacking context, emphasizing form rather than meaning. Not only does the student have the difficult task of differentiating the past from the perfect, but the variation is introduced as a further complication to the problem. Such an additive approach merely feeds the argument against the inclusion of language variation voiced by some, such as Greenbaum (1975), who contends that "until students reach an advanced level of proficiency, the deliberate introduction of variants can only serve to confuse them and to complicate unnecessarily the elementary stages of foreign language acquisition" (p. 172). Thus, we must seek to incorporate this information in a way that clarifies and does not confuse.

6. GUIDELINES FOR A CLEARER PRESENTATION OF THE PRESENT PERFECT

Several researchers, notably Moy (1977), Richards (1979), and Feigenbaum (1981), have directly addressed the confusion about perfect felt by ESL students and teachers alike. All have argued for more clarity and more carefully chosen language samples. Each has made a significant contribution to our understanding of how best to see the relevant issues. Any investigation of the perfect in ESL texts, particularly with a view to revamping the presentations entirely, can benefit from examining these researchers' perspectives on the problems and considering them in light of the colloquial preterit.

Moy (1977) rightly attacks presentations in which isolated sentences are given for which students are expected to fill in tenses. As he points out, and as the colloquial preterit study has shown, there must be a clear, unambiguous context for the perfect, and it may well be outside of the predication itself, such as time adverbials or tenses appearing in preceding utterances. Certainly, from a sociolinguistic viewpoint, manipulating language in a series of unrelated predications is virtually meaningless and unproductive. Moy suggests the use of the present tense as a key to showing the student how the perfect operates, for example, inserting present tense sentences before and after a section of a given passage in which the perfect would be appropriate.

Richards (1979), making a related point, has noted that many ESL texts begin the unit on the present perfect with the resultative perfect, as in

(13)

She has moved the chair.

She hasn't moved the desk.
Has she moved the chair? (p. 496)

Here, the perfect describes an event in the past with an emphasis in the present results (see Table 4, 1.3 present result). Richards asserts that "it would have been more natural perhaps to have used the past rather than the perfect throughout the lesson were it not for the fact that the lesson was supposed to be about the pefect" (p. 498). Essentially, he is claiming that this context does not provide a sufficient or significant contrast between the preterit and the perfect for use in an initial presentation. He goes on to suggest other uses that might better lend themselves to the first lesson, and he includes some, such as the general indefinite past with *never* and *ever,* which, in the study of American English reported here, were found to be environments in which the variation operates. Nevertheless, his proposal has merit and is consistent with the approach taken by the present researcher.

Finally, Feigenbaum (1981) focuses on isolating uses that will prove practical for the learner and points out that "since we are interested in teaching what native speakers do, we must determine what they do; there is no value in teaching semantic distinctions that they do not observe" (p. 404). He advocates data collection from native speakers with a view to determining the clearest, best defined uses of the perfect for the speech community. Thus, presumably he would be interested in finding the stable uses, where native speakers can be counted on to use the perfect, as starting points for the ESL learner. In Feigenbaum's study, the elicitation work resulted in finding two uses as most salient, which he refers to as "completed" (see Table 4, 1.0 single-action overtone) and "continuative" (see Table 4, 2.0 continuative overtone). As has been shown here, these uses must be divided into further categories to account for the variation. He also reinforces Moy's point about factors beyond the verb phrase itself, such as adverbials and accompanying noun phases, and beyond the predication itself, such as verb tenses previously used, as essential in determining the use of the perfect.

The guidelines provided by these researchers can aid in the development of ESL materials on the present perfect that include the colloquial preterit. Primary are the issues of clarity and appropriateness in the presentation. If it is possible to identify the environments in which the variation operates and those in which it does not, then should these evironments not be separated out and presented at different points in the syllabus? In fact, is was the failure to separate out the variable uses of the perfect that resulted in units on the present perfect in which sentences with *already* and *yet,* for example, were used to teach the perfect.

Although a majority of texts still present each tense in its entirety as a unit, there are increasingly more that present at least two units, dividing up the uses of the tense (Davis, 1977; Fingado, Freeman, Jerome, & Summers, 1981; O'Neill, Kingsbury, Yeadon, & Cornelius, 1978; and others). Rather than making this division arbitrary or based on a perception of which use is the simplest for the learner, would it not be preferable to base the division on the stable versus variable breakdown of uses? Thus, it is suggested that the perfect be introduced using either one of the two stable perfects: 2.2 period-up-to-the-present or 3.1 more-than-once-before-now (see Table 4). In presenting these stable perfect uses, it would be important to create proper contexts and to draw the learner's attention to the present tense use surrounding perfects. It would also be necessary to point out the determining factors within and beyond the verb phrase itself. An understanding of these factors for the stable perfect would provide a stronger base for an acceptance of the tense variation when it is later introduced, because tense itself would be seen as only one factor in the total process of indicating present perfect meaning. The emphasis in the introductory unit would be to establish a clear meaning for the perfect and one that could be counted on to appear where expected rather than be replaced by the colloquial preterit.

The syllabus might follow an outline similar to that proposed by Finocchiaro (1983), who advocates a spiral approach to the teaching of grammar as part of a notional–functional curriculum. She recommends presenting only one use of the perfect, the iterative (see Table 4, 3.1), suggesting that the instructor show a calendar along with the expression *many times*. In a later unit, the use already presented is reviewed and another use is added. Each use of the perfect is introduced separately, integrating them along the way.

One text that approximates this approach is Brockmann and Kagen's *Coping in English: Beyond the Basics* (1985). The present perfect is featured in at least four separate units, and in each case, separate uses are introduced (although there is some unfortunate mixing, due to a lack of information about the colloquial preterit). All presentations are contextualized, and the appearance of the perfect comes quite naturally. The first use is the durative expression *in ages,* as in

(14)

   Haven't seen you in ages. (p. 88)

This creates a context for the meaning of the present perfect for two friends catching up on their lives since they last met (see Table 4, 2.2). The second use, presented in a later unit, is the iterative (see Table 4, 3.1), as in

(15)

   This is the fourth time I have complained about my roof. (p. 99)

The context is a consumer problem—a repair that is awaiting attention. The durative is incorporated as well. Further along in the text, a job interview is presented, integrating the various uses. The colloquial preterit environments are, of course, not isolated but mixed throughout. Nevertheless, the basic approach to the stable uses is a starting point for materials development that would incorporate language variation. The specific content and style of the language samples presented in any such materials would, of course, be adapted to the particular backgrounds, needs, and interests of the ESL learners for whom they were designed.

The units on the variable perfects (Table 4: 1.1, 1.2, 1.3, and 2.1) would then be constructed so as to demonstrate the nature of the variation between the two tenses for the variable uses of the perfect. Because the distinction is largely one of informal versus formal, such factors as content, speaker relationships, and lexical choice would be signals to the learner. For example, in a job interview the present perfect would be used, whereas in a conversation among friends the same interchange would make use of the colloquial preterit. In an adaptation of the presentation cited earlier, example (1), two conversation samples could be given and subsequently examined for critical sociolinguistic features. Observe:

(16)

Interviewer:	Have you ever studied Spanish?
Applicant:	Yes, I've already completed two semesters.
Interviewer:	Have you visited Spain yet?
Applicant:	Yes, I've been there three times.

(17)

Bob:	Did you ever take Spanish?
Sue:	Yeah, I already took two semesters.
Bob:	Did you go to Spain yet?
Sue:	Yup, I've been there three times.

Contrasting dialogues is but one of the many techniques now being used in classes where language variation is under discussion. Most traditional ESL activities lend themselves very easily to language variation work, such as multiple-choice tasks, listening discrimination exercises, role-playing, and numerous others. An extensive array of classroom activities is available in Eisenstein's (1983) *Language Variation and the ESL Curriculum*.

Addressing language variation also provides an opportunity to point out how the spoken and written languages differ. In the case of the colloquial preterit, it would be important to note that the variation operates in spoken, and not written, English (with the exception of informal written communication, such as a letter to a friend), so that in their academic writing, students would retain use of the present perfect for all the uses presented.

7. RATIONALE FOR INCORPORATING LANGUAGE VARIATION IN ESL TEXTS

It now remains to address the question underlying the arguments presented here. This writer has examined how material on variation can be incorporated into the ESL syllabus and has offered concrete suggestions. However, one may well question the advisability of including such information in an ESL syllabus at all. It may be arugued that, although of great interest to a sociolinguist documenting changes in American English, the colloquial preterit is of little importance to a learner of English who primarily needs to master basic, functional patterns and get a point across to the listener. Such an argument may also hold that presenting alternative forms is potentially confusing to the learner, as mentioned earlier. It would seem, however, that to ignore the variation is infinitely more confusing. Current practice is to mix stable and variable forms in a single presentation. Variable uses of the present perfect are presented and are used to demonstrate how it distinguishes itself from the preterit. The result is an unreliable and unclear view of the perfect. The suggestions made here, then, are precisely designed to take the confusion out of the presentation. The intent is to clear out the variation so the learner can see something stable to work on in an early unit on the perfect.

With respect to the later unit, treating the variable perfects, Dickerson (1976), although speaking of phonology, makes a strong appeal for some attention to language variation in the ESL syllabus: "the language teacher cannot responsibly dodge variability but must arrive at a realistic strategy for coping with it" (p. 177). Other have come to share Dickerson's view in recent years. As Judd (1983) points out,

> it is now a widely accepted principle that language materials should be based on models that represent valid linguistic data. Artificial models, while perhaps useful to create linguistic security or to explain a specific grammatical point, fail to provide learners with the information needed to function successfully in an uncontrolled nonclassroom environment. (p. 234)

Eisenstein (1983) aptly states the "challenge" for those of us concerned with incorporating language variation into the curriculum:

> . . . to find a balance between the earlier approach, which was grammatically controlled but too limited, and the current view of language as a multidimensional communicative system. Our challenge is to analyze language so that it is understandable for the learner, yet provide a realistic picture of how language is really used. (p. 2)

The position taken here is that a realistic strategy is to create explicit units on variable forms designed to show the learner—once stable forms have been introduced—that language is variable, changing, has a range of styles, and interacts with social and other nonlinguistic factors. These principles of language variation belong in the ESL curriculum because the learner will hear constant evidence of formal–informal distinctions and other clues to variation in language. The teacher's role is to make explicit and clear what is lost in the stream of speech in the real world.

8. CONCLUSION

In this chapter, it has been argued that language variation can and should be a part of the ESL curriculum. The guidelines discussed here can lead us in the direction of incorporating variation in an effective and promising way. The variable perfects are but one example of language variation.[7] As more variation studies are conducted and the factors influencing the selection of each form are identified, materials developers will have a greater range of information available to them. It is hoped that they will make use of the new sociolinguistic information to clarify the presentations of the items introduced in their texts.

ACKNOWLEDGMENTS

I would like to thank the following colleagues for their helpful comments on an earlier version of this chapter: Theodora Bofman, Miriam R. Eisenstein, Michael Montgomery, Patrick S. J. Ruffin, and John J. Staczek.

REFERENCES

Brockmann, K., & Kagen, A. (1985). *Coping in English: Beyond the basics.* Englewood Cliffs, NJ: Prentice Hall.

Celce-Murcia, M., & Larsen-Freeman, D. (1983). *The grammar book: An ESL/EFL teacher's course.* Rowley, MA: Newbury House.

Danielson, D., & Hayden, R. (1973). *Using English: Your second language.* Englewood Cliffs, NJ: Prentice-Hall.

Dart, A. K. (1978). *ESL grammar workbook 1.* Englewood Cliffs, NJ: Prentice-Hall.

Davis, P. (1977). *English structure in focus.* Rowley, MA: Newbury House.

Defromont, H. J. (1973). *Les constructions perfectives du anglais contemporain* [Perfect constructions in contemporary English]. The Hague: Mouton.

Dickerson, H. J. (1976). Phonological variability in pronunciation instruction: A principled approach. *TESOL Quarterly, 10,* 177–191.

---

[7] Staczek (1985) has presented evidence of variation in the use of the reflecive, as in *I told Albert that physicists like himself (him) were a godsend* (p. 1). He raises issues similar to those discussed here, such as the likelihood of language change in this area, the lack of variation information for ESL students, and the potential confusion resulting from a mismatch of rules for reflexification and actual spoken usage.

Dubois, B. (1972). *The meanings and the distribution of the perfect in present-day American English writing.* Unpublished doctoral dissertation, University of New Mexico.

Eisenstein, M. R. (1983). *Language variation and the ESL curriculum,* No. 51 of *Language in education: Theory and practice.* Washington, DC: Center for Applied Linguistics.

Feigenbaum, I. (1981). The uses of the English perfect. *Language Learning, 31* (2), 393–407.

Fingado, G., Freeman, L. J., Jerome, M. R., & Summers, C. V. (1981). *The English connection: A text for speakers of English as a second language.* Cambridge, MA: Winthrop.

Finocchiaro, M., & Brumfit, C. (1983). *The functional–notional approach: From theory to practice.* New York: Oxford University Press.

Frank, M. (1986). *Modern English: Exercises for non-native speakers, Part I* (2nd ed.). Englewood Cliffs, NJ: Prentice Hall.

Greenbaum, S. (1975). Linguistic variation and acceptability. *TESOL Quarterly, 9,* 165–172.

Judd, E. (1983). The problem of applying sociolinguistic findings to TESOL: The case of male/female language. In N. Wolfson & E. Judd (Eds.), *Sociolinguistics and language acquisition* (p. 234–241). Rowley, MA: Newbury House.

Kapili, L. V., & Kapili, B. H. (1985). *Understanding American sentences.* New York: Harcourt Brace Jovanovich.

Labov, W. (1972). *Sociolinguistic patterns.* Philadelphia: University of Pennsylvania Press.

Leech, G. N. (1971). *Meaning and the English verb.* London: Longman.

Leech, G. N., & Svartvik, J. (1975). *A communicative grammar of English.* London: Longman.

Marshall, H. W. (1979). *The colloquial preterit versus the present perfect: A sociolinguistic analysis.* Unpublished doctorial dissertation, Teachers College, Columbia University,.

Marshall, H. W. (1981). Tracing a syntactic change using a closely related linguistic constraint. In D. Sankoff & H. Cedergren (Eds.), *Variation Omnibus* (pp. 387–392). Edmonton: Linguistic Research.

Marshall, H. W. (1987). *The preterit in place of the present perfect: A study of acceptability.* Paper presented at the Midwest Regional Meeting of the American Dialect Society, Cincinnati.

Martin, A. V., McChesney, B., Whalley, E., & Davlin, E. (1977). *Guide to language and study skills for college students of English as a second language.* Englewood Cliffs, NJ: Prentice Hall.

McCoard, R. W. (1978). *The English perfect: Tense choice and pragmatic inferences.* North Holland Linguistics Series, no. 38. New York: North Holland.

Moy, R. (1977). Contextual factors in the use of the present perfect. *TESOL Quarterly, 11,* 303–309.

O'Neil, R., Kingsbury, R., Yeadon, T., & Cornelius, E. T., Jr. (1978). *American kernel lessons: Intermediate.* New York: Longman.

Peterson, B. (1970). Toward understanding the 'perfect' construction in spoken English. *English Teaching Forum, 8,* 2–10.

Richards, J. C. (1979). Introducing the perfect: an exercise in pedagogic grammar. *TESOL Quarterly, 14,* 495–500.

Shuy, R. W., Wolfram, W. A., & Riley, W. K. (1968). *Field techniques in an urban language study.* Washington, DC: Center for Applied Linguistics.

Staczek, J. J. (1985) *Reflexive variation: L1/L2 speaker's acceptability and grammaticality judgments.* Paper presented at the 1985 TESOL Convention, New York, April.

Traugott, E., & Waterhouse, J. (1969). *Already* and *yet:* A suppletive set of aspect markers? *Journal of Linguistics, 5,* 287–301.

Vanneck, G. (1958). The colloquial preterite in modern American English. *Word, 14,* 237–242.

Werner, P. K., & Nelson, P. (1985). *Mosaic II: A content-based grammar.* New York: Random House.

Wishon, G. E., & Burks, J. M. (1980). *Let's write English, Book 2* (rev. ed.). New York: American Book Company.

Wohl, M. (1978). *Preparaton for writing: Grammar.* Rowley, MA: Newbury House.

Index